A Path Into

METAPHYSICS

SUNY Series in Philosophy

Robert Cummings Neville, Editor

A Path Into
Metaphysics

Phenomenological, Hermeneutical, and Dialogical Studies

ROBERT E. WOOD

STATE UNIVERSITY OF NEW YORK PRESS

Published by
State University of New York Press, Albany

Printed in the United States of America

For information, address State University of New York
Press, State University Plaza, Albany, N.Y., 12246.

Library of Congress Cataloging-in-Publication Data

Wood, Robert E., 1934-
    A path into metaphysics : phenomenological, hermeneutical, and
dialogical studies / by Robert E. Wood.
        p.   cm.—(SUNY series in philosophy)
    Includes bibliographical references.
    ISBN 0-7914-0305-X.—ISBN 0-7914-0306-8 (pbk.)
    1. Metaphysics. 2. Phenomenology. I. Title. II. Series.
BD111.W56   1990
110—dc20   89-38073
                                                               CIP

10 9 8 7 6 5 4 3 2

To Marjorie
and the Future . . .

To see a world in a grain of sand
And a heaven in a wild flower,
Hold infinity in the palm of your hand
And eternity in an hour.

William Blake
Auguries of Innocence

What sort of philosophy one chooses depends . . . on what sort
of man one is; for a philosophical system is not a dead piece
of furniture that we can reject or accept as we wish; it is rather
a thing animated by the soul of the person who holds it.

J. G. Fichte
The Science of Knowledge

For if that elusive concept "reality" has any meaning, it must be
that toward which the entire human being reaches out for satisfaction, and not simply some fact-and-theory mongering fraction of
the personality.

Theodore Roszak
The Making of a Counter Culture

Eyes and ears are poor witnesses
To men who have barbarian souls.

Heraclitus

If it is a remarkable thing when a nation finds that its Constitu-
tional Theory, its customary ways of thinking and feeling, its
ethical habits and traditional virtues, have become inapplicable,
it is certainly not less remarkable when a nation loses its
Metaphysic, when the intellect occupying itself with its own pure
essence, has no longer any real existence in the thought of
the nation.

G. W. F. Hegel
The Science of Logic

Not till we are lost, in other words, not till we have lost the world,
do we begin to find ourselves, and realize where we are and the
infinite extent of our relations.

Henry David Thoreau
Walden

Contents

PART ONE: HUMANNESS, METAPHYSICS, AND BEING

PART TWO: READING THE TRADITION

List of Figures

Preface

Metaphysics is a discipline that deals with the question, What is Being? Periodically it is pronounced dead, only to rise again.[1] We may or may not agree with Kant's judgment that it is impossible as an achievement,[2] but we do contend that his further judgment is quite correct: as an inquiry it is as inevitable as the tide. The latter is based, not simply on generalization from the history of the discipline, but upon the founding structures of humanness. That shall be our chief contention throughout this work, which struggles with the interplay between an analysis of the structures of human experience and a study of the masters.

The work is guided by a distinction the author explored in an early study, *Martin Buber's Ontology,*[3] namely, the distinction between the I-Thou and I-It relations. Properly understood, that distinction is not simply one between relations to persons and relations to things, but cuts across such a distinction. *Thou* is a term analogous to Tillich's Ultimate Concern:[4] that which involves the whole of ourselves, that which grips "the heart" and leads to a complete reorganization of our way of conducting ourselves. So understood, the distinction parallels closely Heidegger's distinction between two manifestations of truth involved in two Greek terms, *aletheia* and *orthotes.*[5] *Orthotes* is etymologically related to English terms such as "orthopedic shoes," which correct the feet, and "orthodoxy," which is right opinion. *Orthotes* is truth as *correctness of representation*, right formulation that corresponds to what is the case. On the other hand, *aletheia*, according to Heidegger's etymological suggestion, is truth as uncon-cealment (*a* being a privative prefix meaning "not" or "un-" and *letheia* derived from *lanthanomai*, "I conceal"). *Aletheia* stands for a more basic manifestation than *orthotes*, since there has to be a prior dis-closure of that about which we are able to form correct propositions and a prior space of meaning within which we are enabled to formu-late those propositions. Whereas the formulation of propositions is the work of what comes to be called intellect, detachedly surveying things, the prior disclosure has to do with another level of experience, which provides the hidden ground of metaphysics. At this level, Heidegger

claims, "*Denken ist Danken*," "thinking is thanking.[6] It is a matter of
what has laid hold of us at the level of "the heart," the old Anglo-
Saxon term for which is *thanc*. Being-claimed, being-apprehended,
and our appreciative response constitute the prior groundwork that
nudges us in the direction of corresponding modes of formulation,
development of argumentation, construction of worldviews. The shift
in this basic, orienting level of disclosure constitutes *Seinsgeschichte*,
"the history of Being."[7]

'Heart' as used here for the most basic level of experience, is a
symbol for the human totality, which parallels Buber's basic notion.[8]
Relation to 'Thou' is what touches the center, the core that gathers
one together as a whole. Great philosophy is rooted in a peculiar sort
of meeting with a peculiar Thou as one of the 'forms of the spirit' that
lay claim to the one called upon to respond in terms of creation of a
work. The work constructed is brought over to the impersonal It-world
and is thereby subjectible to the various modes of analysis and response
characteristic of that world. But that world in its inception and at
various phases of its development involves meeting with the Thou.[9]

Guided by that fundamental distinction, then, this work aims
at gaining some sense of the *Seinsgeschichte* of the West. It is divided
into two basic parts. In the first part we point to the aletheic aspect
by developing a set of secular meditations, (chapter 1), focused first
on the self: birth and death, consciousness and embodiment, self-
identity; then on the general context of human life: space, time, and
interconnectedness. We proceed, in the next and pivotal chapter (chapter 2), to locate the aletheic dimension within a general discussion of
the structures of human awareness based on phenomenological description, that is, a presentation of the essential features (*logoi*) of
appearances (*phainomena*) in the field of human awareness from which
we make our inferences and thereby build up our worlds of meaning.
As first enunciated by Edmund Husserl, phenomenology attempts
to put aside speculative constructions in order to attend to "the things
themselves" as they are available within the field of experience.[10]
Clarification of those structures will provide the basis for understanding the history of metaphysics as alternative construals of how to
position ontologically the phenomenologically given.

This and the next chapters are oriented toward coming to terms
with three difficulties encountered in dealing with metaphysics: (1)
the difficulty of adequate conceptualization, (2) the apparent impracticality of the venture, and (3) its alleged abstractness. In chapter 2
the model of multidimensional space provided by Edwin Abbott's
Flatland,[11] a fantasy about life in two-dimensional space, is developed
as an imaginative aid in overcoming the difficulty of thinking beyond

imagination that is involved in metaphysics. Chapter 3 then develops several interrelated definitions in humanness out of the relations between the dimensions of experience established in chapter 2, with a view toward coming to terms with the objection against the impracticality of the venture in chapter 4. Chapter 5 correspondingly deals with the question of abstractness and its correlative, concreteness.

Preliminary difficulties handled, we then proceed to part 2, a treatment of the masters. Here we lean particularly on the structures developed in chapter 2. Two major contentions that govern this part are (1) that the ontological construals of the masters are related to an extraordinary, but often only implicitly inferrable, attention to the phenomenologically given, and (2) that their constructions are articulations of a more fundamental *Gestalt*, a fundamental configuration of experience and reality as a whole out of which we will attempt to speak, perhaps not always with the same measure of success. We are in essential agreement with Henri Bergson here when he says that every great philosopher really only says one thing, speaking out of a central intuition that is more like a generative source, a great élan, than it is a static picture.[12]

A concluding chapter will attempt to draw some inferences, along Buberian lines, toward a philosophy of dialogue and encounter suggested by the studies developed.

In the contemporary context of growing global interdependency, an encounter with Eastern thought is an essential component of dialogical philosophy. I have attempted the beginning of such a dialogue from within Martin Buber's thought in an earlier essay[13] and have called attention to it in several places in this text. However, my own expertise is severely limited in this regard, approaching it as I do only in relation to the Western metaphysical tradition explored in this work. Much more needs to be done by Western thinkers to understand and assimilate Eastern thought. It is necessary for us devotees of the Western tradition to keep in mind our deficiency in this regard.[14]

I might call attention up front to another limitation: the lack of attention to contemporary deconstructive efforts as they bear on the metaphysical tradition. I have attended more to the "retrieval" rather than the "destructive" aspects of Heidegger's thought throughout, and am quite aware of (and to large extent sympathetic with) Nietzsche's critique as well as of Derrida's deconstruction (to which I am less sympathetic thus far). But one can only do so much, and I have already attempted much. This book is an opening to metaphysics for those who have not yet caught what to my mind is the deconstructivist fever. I hope the book is not a disease for which deconstruction will

furnish the cure. Be that as it may, my confrontation with deconstruction will have to await a future date.

Finally, I wish to thank several people who have been instrumental in the development of this book: first is my wife, Marjorie, to
whom the work is dedicated and who was intimately tied to its development. Then there are several who encouraged me and enlightened
me along the way: Kenneth Schmitz, my teacher; Paul Weiss, an
exemplar; and Jude Dougherty, whose confidence in me aroused me
from my nondogmatic slumber on several occasions. Then there are
my colleagues Abraham Anderson, Stephen Arndt, Donald Brinley,
William Frank, Joseph Lawrence, Mark Jordan, and John Nichols,
who read the manuscript at various stages and gave me several useful pieces of advice. I also wish to thank Muhammed-Ali Manoucheri-
pour for his work on the diagrams. I which to acknowledge those who
helped by typing the manuscript: Joanne Baird, Mary Jensen, and
Tina Lemmons worked on early drafts, while Edna Garcia labored
tirelessly on the final copy.

Institute of Philosophic Studies
University of Dallas
June 1989

Introduction

The kind of discipline to which this work is an introduction has been called by various names. Among the nonderogatory, Aristotle (fourth century B.C.)[1] and, following him, Descartes (seventeenth century)[2] termed it "First Philosophy," as a study of the principles which all other disciplines presuppose. It is a "science of first principles." In the school of Christian Wolff (eighteenth century) it was called "ontology," the attempt to get at the essential principles (*logoi*) of 'Being' (Greek *on*, genitive *ontos*). It was distinguished from and related to the earlier term *metaphysics*, which was originally a librarian's classification. When the various works of Aristotle were filed, the volume (up to that time having no name) that was positioned on the shelf after ₊the *Physics* was termed *meta* (meaning here 'after') *Physica*. It was a work which "raised the question, as of old, What is Being?"[3]

But *meta* also means 'beyond", and the way in which the discipline developed led to a treatment of those things that are considered to lie beyond the perceptible, changing realm of 'physics' or 'Nature': God, hypothetical angelic beings (pure intellects), and human intelligence considered as an entity separable from Matter. As having such objects, works on 'Metaphysics' are sometimes located in bookstores under the heading Metaphysics and the Occult; and Metaphysical Society is often the name given to a group that pursues "supernatural phenomena." The association is not one that most of those who teach metaphysics would welcome.

Nonetheless, metaphysics and ontology were considered in the Wolffian school as part of a division of labor within a single discipline. Ontology was viewed as that part of the discipline which dealt with the most general principles, while metaphysics was concerned with a special set of entities that were said to exist "beyond Matter." However, metaphysics as "beyond Nature" has also been considered to be a discipline that transcends or cuts across the division of being into various natures or kinds that are explored in the different sciences and deals with what they all have in common. Thus metaphysics itself is ontology.[4] In this sense, it is not contradictory to hold a

1

materialist metaphysics (though, of course, so much turns on what is meant by the enigmatic term *Matter*).

The notion of 'Being' with which Metaphysics is concerned has been conceived of in different ways. To begin with, one might think of it as the lowest common denominator of all things: Being is merely being-outside-of-nothing, blank existence, after which everything that is interesting about anything can be considered.[5] As such it is, as Nietzsche claimed, "the last trailing cloud of evaporating reality."[6] If we begin analysis with the fullness of concrete particularity met in experience and focus upon a given class of beings, we have already performed an abstraction in arriving at the class concept. The larger extension of the notion of 'human being' beyond this or that individual person is arrived at by leaving aside concrete differences between individuals. Sorting through universals of this type, one further leaves aside the concrete differences between species and arrives at the notion of 'animal', which includes the human being and all the other animal species as well. 'Organism' is a still more inclusive, but more empty concept, having left aside the concrete differences between animals and other living beings. 'Substance' as 'being-in-itself'—no matter of what kind or species—is the ultimate term of analysis in this line. One might understand this better by going back to immediate experience and contrasting nonsubstantial features such as color or height in order to arrive at the high-order genus parallel to substance, namely 'Attribute' or 'being-in-another'. A man or a tree or a dog or a rock is a Substance, i. e., a being-in-itself, understood as distinguished from, and correlative to, the being-in-another, i.e., the dependency upon another, of features such as color or height. There is, concretely, no color-in-itself, but only colored *things*, which things are not further features of something else, but exist 'in themselves'.[7]

One might attempt to make a final move from these (Aristotelian) categories to the highest-level notion, namely Being, which abstracts from the in-itself of Substance and the in-another of Attributes, in which case we would have a notion that applies to everything because it leaves aside every concrete feature. In that case, the only thing that can be said about the notion is mere contrast with nothing: Being is that which is outside of nothing, the lowest common denominator of the universe.

However, another look shows that Being cannot be a universal genus, the last and highest abstraction, for a universal genus is arrived at by leaving aside differences, yet all the differences *are*, just as well as a genus *is*. Substance and Attributes, universal and particular, actual and possible, finite and infinite—all are contained within Being. Being is thus the most concrete notion, including everything within it: Being is the plenitude, the totality. So Being seems to hover between the emptiest and the fullest notion.[8]

As a variation of the plenitude theme, the classical tradition, which we will examine in part 2 (from Parmenides through Plato, Aristotle, and Plotinus to Aquinas), will construe matters in such a way that Being as a Nature is located beyond the multiplicity of things that mirror in a scattered and inferior way the Plenitude that exceeds them. Pure Being is set off from beings who are more or less "mixed with nonbeing," coming into being, and passing out of being, limited in various ways. Being is thought of as an intensive notion capable of hierarchical gradation of greater or lesser intensity.

Spinoza (d. 1677) developed another variation on the theme of being as plenitude. For him, God could not be apart from His "creatures." Rather, Being-Itself, the fully concrete, is the system constituted by the interplay of an Infinite Ground and Its finite consequents. For granted one being other than God, there would be more to the fullness of Being than God alone.[9]

Hegel (d. 1831) will characteristically combine all these views. The empty generic notion of Being he takes as a first instance of the coincidence of opposites that expresses the very nature of Being. Being considered by itself passes over into pure emptiness, equivalent to Non-Being. But this identity-in-difference of Being and Non-Being is what is meant by Becoming: Being yoked to the Non-Being of no-longer-being what it was and not-yet-being what it is about to be. This gives a kind of logical "genetic pattern" for all reality. Being, considered by itself, empty generic Being, drives on to develop everything out of itself until it becomes the fully concrete totality, the interplay and identity of universal principles and particular instances, of subjective and objective, of Mind and Matter, of individual and society, of the present and tradition, of God (considered apart from other things, the equivalent of the empty generic notion of Being) and creation.[10]

More recently, Heidegger proposed yet another view. Past metaphysics has been "orthotic," intent upon forming correct propositions about beings (whether things, persons or principles). But it has forgotten about the "aletheic" space of more basic presencing which constitutes, for Heidegger, the meaning of Being. Being thus is not the highest and emptiest abstraction, nor is it the totality of beings, however conceived, nor the Highest Entity, the Plentitude apart from things. Being is other than all beings. It is the revealing-concealing process whereby beings are shown in various ways within the totality. The human being pried loose from biology and culture is referred to the totality and is thus essentially metaphysical animal. But the way of "showing" and of "reference" is what is crucial.[11]

We will explore the further context of these differing views in the course of this work. Our first step, however, is to evoke the aletheic basis for our orthotic investigation.

Kierkegaard has remarked that "most philosophers construct magnificent thought-castles but dwell in miserable shacks nearby."[12] Inspired by Kierkegaard, Heidegger pointed to a distinction in experience between abstract thinking and concrete "feel," our "sense of Being" whose grounds are never fully articulated, but are linked to the general process of culture. We are carried by such a sense, and it leads to the articulation of various ways of construing the totality that constitute the history of Being.

As we have already indicated, our text will take its general orientation from Heidegger's suggestions, beginning with an attempt to focus on the distinction between abstract thinking and concrete dwelling in the following chapter on secular Meditation. We will continue with analysis of the involvement of Being in human nature. Part 2 will trace some highlights of "the history of Being" from Parmenides to Heidegger, focusing on the central *Gestalt* from which all arguments proceed.

Part One

HUMANNESS, METAPHYSICS, AND BEING

1 *Secular Meditations*

Let not the mind therefore seek
itself as though it were absent, but
let it take care to discern itself
as present.

> Augustine, *De Trinitate*, X, 9 (12)

We shall not cease from exploration
And the end of all our exploring
Will be to arrive where we started
And know the place for the first
time.

> T.S. Eliot, *Four Quartets*

All this had always been and he had
never seen it, he was never present.
Now he was present and belonged to
it.

> Herman Hesse, *Siddhartha*

There are at least two forms of meditation that have entered into the West. A first form is exhibited in the title of one of the major works of the father of modern philosophy: *Meditations on First Philosophy* by René Descartes (d. 1650). The immediate aim of such meditation is the securing of "clear and distinct ideas" in metaphysics as the roots of the tree of knowledge. The ultimate aim is to pluck the fruits of the tree by securing power over nature in mechanics, medicine, and eventually morals.[1] Here thought detaches itself from the half-comprehended matrix of experience within which and out of which we perpetually think and act, and concentrates itself into a pure intellect for which everything becomes detached ob-ject or pro-blem, thrown (Latin *-jectum*, Greek *-blema*) over against (Latin *ob-* Greek *pro-*) the involuted self, which aims at the certitude of complete mastery. Such thought begins with distrust (methodic doubt) and fore-

7

shadows the "hermeneutics of suspicion" cultivated in a striking way
by Marx, Nietzsche, and Freud, but undercutting the lucidity of consciousness prized by Descartes.[2]

Such a pose was applied, after and following Descartes, in the
period called "the Enlightenment." It reached its first phase cf maturity around 1687 in Newton's *Principia*, the first systematic statement of modern mathematical physics. Of Newton Pope wrote: "The
world and its secrets lay hidden in night. God said, 'Let there be
Newton,' and all was light."[3] In 1690 Locke extended such enlightened
thought to psychology[4] and to government.[5] Power over nature in a
rationally organized society applied in industry and extended through
education would lead to indefinite progress. This was the program of
the Enlightenment, rooted in the pose of detached mastery exhibited
in Descartes's Meditations.

However, in that work such a pose and such a thrust is broken
in one place: at the end of Meditation III. Here, having, he thought,
proved the existence of God as Infinite Being, Descartes set aside
one short paragraph urging his readers to contemplate such a God.[6]
This solitary locus seems to display "the last trailing clouds" of an
evaporating tradition of medieval spirituality. For that tradition there
was another type of meditation: a movement of the mind from point
to connected point practiced specifically in order to arrive at the resting of the mind in the deepened presence of the contemplated object.[7]
Such meditation moves from detachment to a kind of inward participation, an interpenetration of subject and object. If Descartes's meditation cultivated the detached intellect and aimed at mastery, medieval
meditation cultivated the heart and aimed at participation in a Presence. Such presence is grounded subjectively in a detachment of
another sort: detachment from the grasping and split self. There are
thus two modes of detachment corresponding to the two types of
orientation: a detachment from the whole of experience leading to
the cultivation of intellect, and the detachment from the grasping
self within experience leading to a cultivation of "the heart." Descartes's brief paragraph on contemplation is but a momentary hearkening back to an earlier tradition. Its proportionate relation to the rest
of the book is analogous to the subsequent concern the West has
exhibited for such a participatory relation.

Interestingly, the state arrived at through meditation is called
satori in the Zen tradition, which translates as "enlightenment."[8] There
are then two modes of enlightenment, one represented by the modern
West whose mind-set now dominates the world, and the other by the
earlier traditions of spirituality in the East and in the West against
which — or against significant segments of which — the modern world

was launched. The two modes of enlightenment parallel Heidegger's distinction between *aletheia* and *orthotes*, which we mentioned briefly earlier. They are paralleled, in their turn, by the ambiguity of ordinary language terms connected with cognition.

Heidegger calls attention to the opposition in the use of the term *wonder* as awe on the one hand, and as curiosity on the other. 'Awe' involves being struck, being gripped, encompassed in the whole of our being by that which overwhelms us, whereas 'curiosity' involves a certain detachment, holding our own in relation to that which we can in principle master. Commentating on Plato's statement that "philosophy begins in wonder,"[9] Heidegger claims that 'beginning' here must be understood as a principle that pervades the whole enterprise rather than as a point of departure that we leave behind and that 'wonder' must be understood as awe. A better reading would be: "Philosophy is sustained by awe."[10] Aristotle, on the contrary, understands 'wonder' as curiosity that disappears once we come to know the fact or understand the cause about which we have 'wondered.'[11]

There are other parallel ambiguous terms relating to cognition: for example, at the origins of our culture, the Book of Genesis speaks of Adam's "knowing" Eve, and Homer's *Iliad* of Achilles "knowing" wrath. Here something different is obviously involved than the 'knowledge' that Eve's hypothetical gynecologist or Achilles' psychoanalyst might have. 'Knowing' in the former cases involves, again, a kind of total, encompassing state of mind, touching those involved "at the center," in the heart. It is a kind of *participatory* knowledge, whereas, in the latter cases, a certain detachment and thus partial involvement occurs.

Again, 'understanding' is different in the situation where, responding to one who turns to us in distress, we might be able to say and mean, "I understand," compared with the 'understanding' that occurs when I am able to explain the social, psychological, and physiological causes of the distressed state. "Under-standing" in the latter sense occurs when I can "stand under" the immediate presentation and grasp the intelligible patterns that "stand under" the appearances, after the manner of Plato who launched Western thought along the lines of rational science in his allegory of the Cave.[12] But in the former sense, 'understanding' involves empathy, participation, lived-through experience. Some schools of psychotherapy today are concerned with reestablishing the first way of understanding as part of their practice,[13] and certain approaches to the human sciences in general emphasize *Verstehen*, participatory 'understanding' in the manner of the German historian and philosopher, Wilhelm Dilthey.[14]

In the history of Western thought these two cognitive poles have continually jostled with one another. The distinction appearing in all these terms appears at the dawn of Western philosophy in the thought of Parmenides as the distinction between *nous* and *logos*.[15] The famous "Being is, non-being is not," surrounded by mystical-religious metaphors, follows from the aspirant's wandering "as far as my heart desires" and emerges as a gift from the goddess. *Nous*, activated in *noein*, is the capacity of being taken over by Being itself, "an event which has man,"[16] as distinguished from drawing out the implications or developing the presuppositions of our formulation of the experience by reasoning (*logos*). (Sophism followed as a playing of logical games in the service of a mode of life far removed from one oriented toward the full thrust of human desire.)[17]

In the High Middle Ages, with the rediscovery of Greek and especially Aristotelian rational science, a new kind of experiential pattern emerged. Thomas Aquinas speaks of '*wisdom*' (*sapientia*) in this line as "systematic knowledge of things in terms of ultimate principles" (*scientia rerum per causas ultimas et primas*),[18] whereas his contemporary and friend Bonaventure, dwelling on the etymological root of *sapientia* in *sapere*, "to taste" (from which we get "sap"), claimed that there was no wisdom without a "*gustus experimentalis*," an experiential tasting of "ultimate reality" by the "whole man."[19] In fairness to Aquinas, we might add that he distinguished at least three senses of wisdom: speculative, practical, and infused. His definition referred to above described speculative wisdom. Practical wisdom or "prudence" is a kind of "situation conscience" or ability to make wise practical judgments on the basis of a well-developed experiential background or "connaturality." Infused wisdom, however, is one of the "gifts of the Holy Spirit."[20] However we understand the latter, it involves an interpretation of the experiential dimension to which Bonaventure referred.

But the link between *nous* and *logos* was decisively strained with the emergence of modern thought in René Descartes, to whom we have already alluded. Descartes attempted a reconstruction of all thought from the point of view of an enclosed consciousness dealing only with its controlled representations or "clear and distinct ideas" patterned after the procedure that had had success for centuries in geometry and was enjoying new success in the analytical geometry introduced by Descartes himself. In this way he hoped to lay the philosophical basis for the newly emergent science of mathematical physics. This approach was immediately counteracted by the claim of Blaise Pascal (d. 1662), which became a kind of battle cry for the later Romantic period: "The heart has its reasons of which 'reason' knows nothing." Pascal sets *nous* in deliberate opposition to the self-contained *logos* of the "geometric spirit," bent on mastery of the whole, by reinvoking the "logic of the heart" that opened Western thought in the first line of Parmenides' poem.[21]

'Reason' changed its character in the work' of G. F. W. Hegel (d. 1831) by opening up a new kind of logic, a dialectical logic of patterned change that aimed at encompassing the whole panorama of experience in an immense system.[22] But immediately after, the Father of Existentialism, Sören Kierkegaard (d. 1848), protested against the presumptive adequacy of "The System," which treated the individual human being as the intersection of rationally discernible principles. According to Kierkegaard, in their preoccupation with all-encompassing objectivity, thinkers have forgotten what it means to be an existing individual, what it means to be a "subjective thinker," to exist with passion and "inwardness." They construct magnificent thought castles but "dwell" in miserable shacks nearby. Thinking as "dwelling," as "inwardness" has been forgotten in favor of thinking as "objective mastery." The accent has been on objectively discerning the "What," but men have lost sight of the "How" of subjective appropriation.[23]

The expanded development of science in the latter half of the nineteenth century led to the increasing dominance of the pattern of rationality called mechanistic materialism, having included the phenomena of life within the mechanical system through the success of Darwinian evolution. Henri Bergson (d. 1941) attempted to overcome such a form of Rationalism by a distinction between "intuition" and "analysis." 'Intuition' involves sympathetic identification with the flowing, cumulative "inside" of reality, first in one's own consciousness in which all the contents interpenetrate and affect each other, then in the moving interplay of the evolutionary universe, and ultimately in the mystical experience of union with the Creative Source Itself. Analysis, on the other hand, involves turning that flowing, interpenetrating inwardness into a set of timeless principles related to the temporally unfolding reality as a series of still photographs to the changing richness of the real. Mechanistic rationalism is an abstraction from the fullness of life.[24]

More recently, stirred by the impersonality of a technical system of applied science that involved, especially in the two great world wars, the increasing regimentation and depersonalization of human beings, French existentialist Gabriel Marcel (d. 1970) distinguished two modes of reflection that he called, rather unimaginatively, first and second reflection. *First reflection* involves a break with involvement in one's own life as rooted in the body and as sharing in the lives of other persons and things. First reflection, in its detachment, sets everything over against itself, including one's own life. Everything becomes *ob-jectum* or *pro-blema*. Everything "over against," everything "objective," is a problem, in principle capable of solution, whether it be a mechanical problem situated "over against" our look, or a mathematical problem situated "over against" our "mind's eye." But there is another mode of reflection and another kind of "object": a second reflection, thought trained on "mystery," on that "original participation," that basic presence involved in my being a body, sharing in the presence of persons and things.[25]

Other existentialists call attention to a similar distinction. Martin Buber early in his career distinguished between "orientation" and "realization." In orientation we have mastered our experience in such a way that we know our way about, whether practically or intellectually. Realization, on the other hand, involves a new mode of presence to what is already "known."[26] Later, as we have indicated in the Preface, Buber will distinguish, somewhat poetically, between two modes of relation: I-Thou and I-It. We will remark that distinction again, especially at the culmination of both parts of this work.

There has thus been an ongoing tension between the two modes of thought: one heads toward complexity, the other toward depth. One surges ahead, "makes progress"; the other returns to where we already are and recognizes it for the first time.[27] They have tended to be associated with objectivity and subjectivity respectively, though there are various complex relations between the subject- and object-poles of experience that led to a transposition of the two in certain cases. There are modes of 'objectivity' that could actually be considered as coconstituted by finite, cognitive subjectivity; and there are modes of 'subjectivity' that touch the heart of 'the objective' (i.e., the true, that which corresponds to Being). Whitehead, for example, contended that certain forms of poetry are, in a sense, "truer than science,"[28] and Heidegger held that often feeling is more carefully sensitive to the character of things than all logic.[29]

Reaching the depth-dimension occurs for the most part in accordance with what might be called "the law of opposites": opposites reveal in depth; negation reveals, in depth, affirmation. Heraclitus formulated this "law" very early in the development of Western philosophy: by sickness we know health; by hunger and thirst, satiety; by weariness, rest; and (as an interpretation of other texts) by death we know life.[30] Now, at this time more is "known" about health and pathology, nutritional problems, organic entropy and dissolution, and the like. But this kind of knowing is not what is at stake here: knowledge in depth, appreciative knowledge. Unfortunately, in the contemporary context 'to know' has been increasingly restricted to functions that could be described as carrying out appropriate verbal performances that can be linked to verbal systems on the one hand and to correspondent empirical observations and/or operations on the other, leaving any other mode of relation for the realm of emotional, merely 'subjective responses, responses that are either noncognitive or else revelatory of nothing but one's own internal states.[31] Contemporary knowledge is largely knowledge achieved within the horizon of the project of mastering the world, and therefore in terms of detached consciousness marshalling empirical objects over against itself. But the knowledge we here seek is appreciative knowledge attained by a reflective thinking that draws close to things, letting them be there in intimacy. To awaken such knowledge, I suggest that each of us pursue very quietly and alone a set of meditations on situations of opposites, which should gradually open up to us deeper levels of experience and thereby enrich the soil in which the seeds of metaphysical thought are to be planted. The direction in which I want to pursue these meditations initially is that of our own *self-experience*—and that by reason of the fact that it is only in our own cases individually for ourselves that we have knowledge of Being "from the inside." Of every being other than ourselves, our knowledge is external, knowledge "from the outside." Only if we deepen within our own self-experience can we begin to appreciate what it means for another to live his life "from the inside."[32] But then, following several suggestions offered by Teilhard de Chardin,[33] I want to turn attention to the context within which the human drama occurs.

And so, first of all, I want to offer meditations on five themes involving states of opposites within ourselves: on our own origination, on our own term, on our lived bodiliness and our own consciousness, and finally on self-identity.

Death

Turn to one end of our temporal span: consider death as a personal event.[34] Within the stream of ordinary consciousness (the *Lebenswelt* of the phenomenologist), our concern is usually, and perhaps exclusively, directed towards our projects, immediate or remote—death usually not entering in any direct sense into our consideration. But by extricating myself from this lived context, I can judge, on the basis of my experience of others, direct or indirect, that one day my projects will end, one day phenomenal nothingness will take hold of me and I shall no longer be as I now am. The judgment is objectively valid—true in my case because true for all. And on its basis I may even choose to reshape my projects, if not in themselves, by choosing an entirely different set of projects, at least in objective perspective.

But it is one thing so to view death objectively, i.e., in thought, detached from the stream of lived experience; it is quite another to lay hold of it *within* the stream itself. Proceeding only as far as the level of objective judgment, I have succeeded in effecting a dichotomy within my consciousness between the stream of lived experience and my objective thought. Proceeding to reshape my projects in the light of that judgment, I have allowed that objectivity to exercise causality upon the stream: it guides the direction of the stream, but without itself entering within it.

Now, however, on the basis of that judgment, we can go further, concentrating our attention not merely upon the direction of the stream, but upon its content. We are thus attempting to see the objective judgment become incarnate, so to speak, from its original detached position. And what emerges from this concentration is a new objective judgment: that the stream of lived experience occurs under an illusion, that of a kind of eternal present, i.e., that nonobjectively, unreflectively, immediately, I "live" as if I were eternally given, and given in the condition of experience in which I normally find myself. Notice, it is not a question of the way in which I *think about* myself; it is a question of my self-*experience*, that pervading sense of selfhood carried through all relationships. "Ordinary" philosophic thinking, engaged as it generally is with universal and hence transtemporal, impersonal truths, only serves to foster that experiential illusion of eternal presence.

The 'I' of the syllogism

All human beings are mortal.
I am a human being.
∴ I am mortal.

is the anonymous 'I', the universal concept into which any 'I' can "plug" himself. The dominance of such *logos* in the total system of which education is a part cuts the edges, so to speak, of uniqueness off the individual subject, shaping him into a conformist subject, an interchangeable cog in the economic-social machinery. Thought must become universal in a detached, impersonal sense. To think in this detachedly universal way is to create the subjective basis for the reification, the "thingification" of human subjects in an alienated productive society.[35]

The basis of the illusion of eternal presence lies in the fact that what each of us knows of the conditions that antedate, ground, or will follow his/her existence is anchored in his/her own temporality. My limited time-span is the basis of the appearance of the atemporal truths of, e.g., logic and mathematics and of the (in the order of appearance) potentially infinite span of time, past and future. The atemporal and omnitemporal character of certain objects of experience are spontaneously transferred from the object to the subject-pole of experience. We each "naturally" experience ourselves as always around, the permanent pivot of the universe.

But once convinced of the illusion of eternal presence, there is a deeper dimension to be secured, further progress to be made in the incarnation of objective thought. The task is now to attempt to dispel that illusion *within* the stream. And objective correction, though quite simple, is also by itself quite irrelevant to that end, for it corrects from an alien position outside the stream. The task is, then, to create conditions for entry into the stream itself—something not achievable as a general, objective truth-for-everyone, but something that each has to do for himself entirely alone. And in so doing, we enlarge and deepen that stream. Our lived-world is enriched. As we enter more deeply into such lived-reflection, death may emerge now and then in fleeting flashes, as a kind of a grace, "perceived," immediately seen as here and now taking hold of my existence, correcting for a brief instance the optics involved in the inner illusion that is constantly ours. However, objective alienation is a moment in the enriching of living experience itself, provided objectification can be brought back into living experience.[36]

To speak of the perception of death is *not* to say that of a sudden we experience an emotional reaction, a disturbance, a "fear and trembling"—though these factors may occur. But these are organically based reactions, not what, for want of a better word, we might call a spiritual perception. What characterizes the perception I am attempting to describe is, quite exactly, *sight*—or rather, sight become "vision" whereby we are "touched" by the reality of death—a situation of distance and participation at once. Whereas the purely emotional reaction is disturbing, unhinging, the perception is calm, serene, for it opens up to the reality-loving, illusion-hating consciousness the ultimate lived-perspective of one's own personal existence. Rather than an organ-based reaction, the experience is a perception rooted in the spiritual.

Of course, such perception has its preconditions. One who has never made the fundamental decision to accept reality on its own terms will probably flee from the thought of death. Or, if for some reason the thought of death pursues him, he may become morbidly preoccupied. In this case, he may lose the capacity for significant action by fascination with the morbid or he may become paralyzed in action by depression.

Now, the description of the "vision" of one's own being-toward-death is difficult, since description presents objectively what at this level is nonobjective; description presents impersonally, in common terms, what is deeply personal and highly unique within experience. All one can do, if one is not a poet, is to point to the fact: it is one thing to carry out the objective judgment; it is quite another to "see"—in the peculiar and totalistic sense in which we are using the term here—the objective truth incarnate within the stream of lived experience, to achieve personal, subjective transcendence of the everyday.[37] Such transcendence pries us loose from our factual involvements, places them all in brackets, provides a fundamental distance from which the whole of our individual existence is illumined. Standing at a distance from our culturally introjected self-image toward the ultimate aloneness of our own dying, we are radically individuated. But at the same time, we are most in communion with the whole of mankind, which stands condemned by nature to the same end.[38]

Birth

Turn attention now to the other end of the temporal span: consider birth. And focus first upon birth as discoverable in others—not just any others. Consider the birth of someone particularly close. Spend some time attempting to "get the feel" for what it means for that child to have been born, to have originated in such a way that, prior to conception, it absolutely was not itself in any way. The point of selecting someone close and recently born is to enhance the personal involvement, for what is crucial here is not the formulation of correct propositions, but the *realization* of what was already *known* in a detached sort of way. The task is to develop an insight into living experience—something that is a total-personal event and not simply the verbalization of a detached intelligence.

In the second place, give some attention to those immediately present. See them as having been born, as not having been. Grasp their present life-structure as the congealing of one line of possibilities out of the multiplicity opened up at the fresh moment of emergence into the world of humankind. In the light of the not-being of possibility, the being of present actuality is illuminated.

But the task is much broader: not simply to discover the inner meaning of origination in an Other, but rather to discover in a deeply personal manner what it means *for me* to have originated absolutely. Hence the third part of the meditation consists in returning, with our heightened grip on the origination of another, to the self. And what emerges from such a reflection is a new angle from which to assess our "usual" experience, for in a living way we grasp ourselves as if somehow we were always around, the permanent furniture of the universe—indeed, its very center. To think our way into an actual experience of the time when we were not opens up to us the strangeness (though indirect) of the fact that we are at all. Indeed, when we ponder the complexity that preceded our actual conception and the improbability, before the fact, of *this particular* human being that I call myself coming into being, a chasm of non-being opens up beneath us. If, in every act of coition, some 5,000,000 sperm are released, and only one of them penetrates the ovum, the chances of the individual who emerged as me coming to be were five million to one (even abstracting from the chance that my parents would not have had sexual relations while the particular ovum that developed into me was present). But the same chances were there for each of my parents; and the same was true for their parents before them, and so forth, down to the emergence of the first genetic code that led up to human life.

Were we to consider the history of life in terms of its prior possibility and its actual development, it would appear as a kind of infinite web of possibilities branching out from each intersection, like a vast switching mechanism. The course of actual life would be a luminous line or set of lines that, taking one turn at an intersection, closes off a whole set of possibilities that themselves branch off infinitely. In this view of things, the chances before the fact against this particular individual I call myself coming into being are well-nigh infinite. Each of us just made the train of life by one final desperate lunge as it left the station. I, the center of my world, might easily not have been! A different sperm, a different ovum, a slight modification of circumstances, and the world would have flowed on in its massive indifference, substantially unmodified, without me.

Nietzsche inquired: what is a human being? He replied: a question mark between two nothingnesses, an unknown, moving out of its own not-having-been into its own no-longer-being—but an unknown whose self-knowledge is of deepest concern.[39] And perhaps we might—less apodictic about our antecedents and consequents—reverse the aphorism: a human being is a nonentity strung between two question marks—or better yet: a question mark between two question marks.

Embodiment

We have thus far pondered two aspects of self-experience which, while obvious, are nonetheless temporally remote. We want now to consider something more obvious because more immediate—and yet it is something that we scarcely ponder with sufficient depth: our own embodiment.

Consider first of all body-in-general as a perceptual object. Simple reflection upon the microscopic discoveries in biology and physics shows that the situation of relatively smooth and solid bodies standing over against us and separated by empty space is only apparent, at least insofar as the use of refined instrumentation reveals greater roughness and less solidity in the bodies and much less emptiness in the space that separates us. The world of everyday experience does not coincide with the world of full reality. The marvelous strangeness of the body-object lays hold of the scientific investigator and draws him on towards an ideal term of full being, the path toward which reveals wonders that, for the everyday focus of awareness, are bizarre. Ponder that sufficiently and the underlying strangeness of the everyday world of familiar bodies will slowly enter into the depth of consciousness.

Consider then the human body in particular as revealed through biological investigation: what emerges is the fantastic complexity and unbelievable interrelation of the elements within our organic being. Consider that within each of our heads there are some one hundred billion connections, each one of which is, in turn, related to all the chemical-physical factors that go into a single nerve cell. Consider the constant anabolism and catabolism, the buildup and breakdown that occurs each second within a system that looks to the external observer—and even to the one who *lives* that body—as if it were very quiet and rather grossly articulated morphologically.

For example, one cubic millimeter of human blood contains some five million red blood cells.[40] The cells contain hemoglobin molecules that are combinations of four heme groups and four polypeptide chains that form the globin, each chain being a sequence of over one hundred forty amino acids. One of the amino acids—for example, histidine—is a six-carbon molecule. The carbon atom itself exhibits two electron shells with four electrons in the outer orbit and two in the inner. When we are at the electron level, the size is in the neighborhood of one trillionth of an inch. And besides the electrons orbiting a proton-neutron nucleus, work with high-speed accelerators has yielded at least eighty other manifestations of energy at the subatomic level.

The complexity of a single cell is indeed staggering. But when one considers that there are some sixty trillion cells in the human body, each dynamically engaged in maintaining the balance of that staggering complexity of its own components, and each functioning in perfect conjunction with all the rest, and that fifty million of these cells are perishing and as many coming into being each second, we are faced with a truly incredible situation.

What we are trying to do is to exploit the contemplative possibilities opened up by scientific discoveries, to use them not just to gain practical control or to satisfy intellectual curiosity (or to show off how smart we are or to get good grades!), but to deepen our sense of the strangeness of our own being, to render more profound our mode of dwelling in our life-world. Part of the problem is that what is discovered under the microscope, e.g., always appears in the plane of our ordinary visual experience on a scale proportionate to the scale of what appears in that plane. For practical and theoretical purposes, the objective inference that arrives at the scale is sufficient. For contemplative purposes, one has to work at reforming one's *Gestalt* on the basis of the observations and inferences that we make within science until the firm surfaces that appear in ordinary experience are, as it were, dissolved by the power of imagination to conform more to the fullness of what is actually there but does not directly appear. Seeing might then on occasion and for an instant be transformed into vision. (In this direction one might reflect with profit on the role of the arts.)

But perhaps the most astonishing aspect in these considerations is that all the staggering complexity of the physical-physiological mechanisms is just what is involved in the apparently simple acts of writing and reading this page. Consider, then, the self as the one who does live that body: consider the body-subject.[41] To me in my everyday consciousness, these factors mentioned above occur beneath the level of my conscious life, supporting it as an ocean supports a cork floating upon its surface. Kierkegaard reminds us: we are floating over waters seventy thousand fathoms deep.[42] That ocean is me—and yet I am scarcely aware of it.

Ponder then what is involved in the astonishment of the young man, who, having experimented with mind-expanding drugs, asked in astonishment: "Did you ever hear your body move?" The body, after all, does make sounds constantly: the flow of the bodily fluids, the movement of the electro-chemical impulses, the creaking of the joints, the beating of the heart. Gurgling, thumping, humming, wheezing, creaking, cracking: the dance of life goes on, for the most part beneath the level of consciousness which springs from and floats upon it. In suddenly hearing such things as within *himself* and *as* himself — things of which he was not usually aware, except occasionally in a detached sort of way in books and in lectures, or perhaps even in scientific experiments—he suddenly grasped the strangeness of his being.

There is a peculiar sort of identity/nonidentity relationship operative here. It was not simply a matter of hearing some new audile datum—that need not provoke astonishment. It was a matter of hearing *himself* internally moving (identity-factor). But still, the astonishment emerged from the simultaneous nonidentity: such sounds and therefore such movements are not usually lived through *as me*, do not enter into the sphere of awareness which is the self-familiar side of myself, the side with which I am most intimately identified. The strangeness of bodiliness and consciousness coemerge out of their unquestioned unity in the region of the familiar. We live our lives within the daylight of consciousness, which is a small circle of light partially structured by our intentions, fringed by preconscious directedness, and surrounded by the darkness of our physiological processes. What is this strange substratum that supports us, which is ourselves, and yet of which we are rarely aware in any fully living way? What is our bodiliness?

Consciousness

Already in our consideration of our own bodiliness we have been led (again by "the law of opposites") to grasp something of what it is. Let us now consider it more explicitly.

Awareness is something rather illusive—so illusive in fact that many people (even those of good intellectual capacity) are led to deny its existence by reducing it to factors that can be publicly verified through the senses. More than one thinker (and many more nonthinkers) has considered consciousness to be nothing but a matter of electrochemical factors. But what is peculiar about the situation is that, though the electrochemical factors appear to a public sensory inspection (they can "lop off" the top of my head and peer inside), my awareness does not so appear. Neurosurgeons are able to stimulate certain areas of the brain in order to produce recall of certain types of experience or to induce fantasies; but the way in which they verify the experiences is not by looking at the electrochemical events in the brain: it is rather by asking the patient what he is aware of when such and such an area of the cortex is stimulated. And even if scientists might develop laws of correlation so exact that they might no longer need to ask the patient but only study the electrical pattern, consciousness remains a strange Other.[43] Consciousness itself slips out of every attempt to trap it within the net of our sensory observations, for it is the condition that makes possible the sensory observations. It is the frame within which everything appears, but it itself does not appear. And even though we may deny it or not even bother to consider its existence, it is the region within which we dwell and which is negatively illuminated by meditation upon the factors of bodiliness which are not immediately explicit in experience but which factually support experience. All of our meaningfulness stems from this region of our being, for it is in terms of our mode of awareness that we judge ourselves fulfilled or unfulfilled, happy or unhappy, in the truth or deluded or confused.

Awareness is set in motion by the presence of a perceptual object. Reflection on the status of the perceptual object in the field of everyday attention moves us back to consider the coconstitutive character of that attention in relation to its objects. Bodies appear only in terms of thresholds set up by *our* organic situation. The perceptual *Umwelt* is our world. Nonetheless, the object is given for us as existing in itself, as *other* than our awareness of it.[44] The otherness is more fully uncovered in a controlled way by scientific investigation drawn on by the dim recognition of a term which would be full manifestation of the full being of the object. Human consciousness is an anticipation of the full being of any other.[45]

But when we consider the distinction between body-subject and body-object, we see that that full term is more than object of scientific investigation, and we are then turned in the direction of intersubjectivity. The eye of the other is not the same object for the oculist and for the lover. The oculist's "concrete" focus on the eyeball mechanism abstracts from the essential expressivity of the look of the other person.[46]

In both cases, that of body as object-for-consciousness and that of the lived body-subject, we are thrown back upon a nonobjectified conscious-subject whose self-identified self-presence is the condition for the progressive revelation of otherness, and which comes to its own self-possession in that revelation, dimly but more deeply in interpersonal relations, clearly but more superficially in scientific investigation—and somewhere in between in phenomenological reflection.

Reflection upon the anticipation of the full being of any other, in conjunction with the ideal of full theoretical comprehension of a total domain of objects in science, could open up an even deeper thrust toward the fullness of being that is the deepest ground of consciousness, drawing the lover and the knower on toward the term to which authentic religious consciousness aspires. Again, mind emerges into the field of our attentiveness as anticipation of the total-real.[47]

Self-Identity

The consideration of bodiliness and consciousness will have, I hope, led us to see what earlier people had seen: that there is an "inner" dimension to our being that is the source of all personal meaning, without which being in the mode of bodily existence means nothing: "What does it profit a man if he gain the whole world but suffer the loss of his soul?" ("Soul" here is another one of those overworked terms which, like an old coin that has passed from hand to hand—to borrow an expression from Heidegger—soon loses all trace of its real meaning. But the meaning here should be sufficiently clear for our purposes at this point.) But once having discovered the interiority of the human being as an other in relation to the object-body, in spite of those massive efforts of the modern world to eliminate that interiority, the problem has always been to put the human being back together again: Am I simply an angel (or devil) driving a machine? a spirit fallen into a heavy, distracting matter—so distracting that I am often led to consider my spirit as an explanatory fiction? Or am I essentially bodily? And if so, what is this interior dimension I have uncovered? How is it related to the bodily dimensions that I and all others can observe about me?

The practice of becoming aware of one's own breathing is a significant method for returning from *logos* to *nous*, for *logos* involves a detachment of thought from its object. Standing at an inward distance, thought gains mastery. But the price it often pays is the loss of unity, the introduction of an existential split within the self. Thought desires completeness, independence, self-transparency. But try as it might to achieve this, it is always compelled to face up to the partiality, dependency, and unclarity rooted in the existential situation of its own essential embodiment.

Identification with the breathing process is a *conscious* letting-be of that without which we are not humanly conscious. It is a bringing to participatory (and not detached) awareness of that which goes on even without our awareness. Such a practice is a return from the pretension of a de facto "idealism" to existential (as distinguished from theoretical) realism. It is, in the words of Paul Ricoeur, an inward movement "from refusal to consent," a reintegration at the level of reflective consciousness, of that unity with the rhythms of the cosmos enjoyed unreflectively in more primitive states.[48]

In our usual states of awareness, we are involved in the thinking of objects—usually objects distinct from ourselves. Occasionally—as we are attempting here—we might give some attention to the process of thinking itself: we think about it. But even here, the subject who is doing the thinking—the center and ground of thought—is involved in a duality with that which is being thought. Thinking about thought is still thinking about an object—even though this object is discovered to be of a radically different structure than the usual objects that people our consciousness, namely, the world of bodies. What about the subject itself? What is the subject? Consciousness alone? Then what is it when I am in dreamless sleep? What about consciousness and its somatic ground considered together? We can never fully objectify that, never fully get it in front of ourselves, for it is the condition that makes objectification possible. It is that in front of which we get everything else—like a hand that is there for grasping all sorts of objects, but that cannot grasp itself. How do we grasp selfhood itself, which is that whereby everything else is conceived, grasped? Through the attempt at the complete emptying of the mind of all images, all concepts, all contents in general. This annihilation of all objects leads to the experience of that nothingness which is the subject, the self itself. Here the self spontaneously grows in its own power; here it removes all the arbitrary personal and social elements that have accumulated through personal and social history; here it readies itself for the reception of the authentic objects, linking itself to the ground that supports it to achieve psycho-somatic integration.

It is the self that has possession of itself that is capable of being really there for others, really there for the task at hand. The self is cleared of all the accidental accretions it has accumulated throughout its history: a clearing is made within which things and persons can appear in their real worth; a "cushion of silence" is established in which things can be "heard";[49] a new "light" is enkindled within the self that intensifies the revelation of the Other. No new items of information are added, but everything is given a new mode of *presence*.[50] The self establishes in itself an inward purification, an openness, a self-emptying (or rather an ego-emptying, since the self is openness by its very nature).

It is from out of the achievement of this sort of meditative self-identified self-emptying that we will be enabled to extend our meditation to other areas and to circle back upon the objects of the four previous meditations—birth, death, bodiliness, consciousness—in order to let them be more deeply present before us. No new contents are added to consciousness, but there is a new mode of *being present*, a new inner light is enkindled in terms of which we are more fully there, really with whatever manifests itself, and not daydreaming in that mode of self-absence that characterizes our usual mode of awareness.

* * *

In two short pages at the beginning of his *Phenomenon of Man*, Teilhard de Chardin has laid out several parameters of the general context of our existence.[51] He entitles the section "On Seeing" and calls for the development of several new "senses" based upon the extension of knowledge achieved in the natural sciences: a sense of spatial immensity, of temporal depth, of complexity, of levels of scale, of long-term movement, and of organic, environmental connectedness. Such new "senses" would be matters of "vision," of a "seeing" that "touches." They would serve to dispel the short-sighted illusions of human scale that center on size, disconnectedness, and immobility.

We have already alluded to the levels of scale of complexity in our reflections on embodiment. Following this lead, then, we continue our meditations, focusing now on the "outer world," its space, time, and interconnectedness.

Space

Consider first of all the sky on a clear night. From the perspective of "eye-ball" seeing, the sky always looks to us as it looked to the primitive (abstracting from the problem of mythical configuration which most probably altered his perception of things qualitatively): we see, as it were, the inside of a kind of half-egg beginning at the horizon and vaulting over our heads to a height of . . . ? fifty miles? a hundred miles? maybe even a *thousand* miles? But of course we *know* that the stars are millions upon millions of light-years away, that the known universe is over ten billion light-years across, and that a lightyear is something on the order of seven quadrillion miles. And so there we have again our by now familiar split between what we know orthotically and what we know by way of our lived perception. Meditation in the actual presence of the stars on the known distances can on occasion enter into the "aesthetics" of our greater lived perception. We learn to "see" the stars from time to time more in accord with their true distances.

We have already pushed into the other direction of space in meditation upon bodiliness-in-general as a prelude to meditation upon our own embodiment. What is important to recognize, once more, is the immense gap there is between propositional correctness—truth in the orthotic mode—and presence. But it is also important to recognize the great labor involved in arriving at the scientific revelations at the micro- and macrolevels extending beyond the scale of our immediate perception. Meditation here, recalling scientific truth from its alien position in relation to "life," can significantly deepen our sense of presence and, to some extent, recall commonsense experience as well from its surface relation to things. We learn thereby to dwell in a deepened sense of space—or at least to become aware that the commonsense world where we all dwell is for the most part girt about by spatial depths that we may, in privileged moments, "see."

Time

We dwell in the present in virtue of anticipation of the future and recall of the past, whether deliberately going in search of the past and the future or spontaneously being carried by immediate anticipations and recollective associations. Both directions open out to an indeterminate past and future incapable of being completely filled. And within those empty references to the indeterminate past and the indeterminate future, a more or less concrete filling goes on, involving a more or less profound concreteness in the present. Typically the past trailed off into "once upon a time" until people took it into their heads to fix genealogies and eventually keep records.[52] The best that men of the West could do until the eighteenth century was develop a sense of the extension of the past that went no further than 4004 B.C.[53] But men eventually set to work to develop the tools of criticism, working simultaneously from assessment of historical sources, from archaeology, paleontology, and biology, until the past concretely stretched into increasing depth, the past of the human race extending to some two million years, of life to four billion, and of the cosmic system as we know it to over ten billion years, corresponding to the over ten billion light-years across the known universe.

But again, the point for our purposes is to bring this orthotic yield into relation with our lived experience in order to gain a "sense" of what underlies our everyday world *temporally*, as we attempted above to gain a similar sense spatially.

The "reality" of the present moment and the presence of things to us is as thick and as deep as we are capable of bringing to bear upon it a recollective sense of their being the cutting edge of a growing past that bites progressively into the future. In an ancient Greek ruin twenty-five hundred years of history are sedimented. The pillars of the temple of Apollo at Delphi still gather the world of the ancient Greeks, though we may be no more present than to the sensuous immediacy of erect, fluted, weathered piles of ivory-colored drums among the dark, waving columns of cypress outlined against the sky beneath Parnassus. Around the winding path up to the temple, on to the theater, and up further to the stadium there still seems to float, for one properly alert, the sound of the footsteps and the hymns of the worshippers of old, some doubtless going through a relatively mindless social routine, others coming into contact with the holy that even today engulfs the sacred place. When thoughts such as these gradually or suddenly rise to the level of vision a genuine historian is born, the "dry as dust" comes to life, and the present moment deepens.

But twenty-five hundred years only defines the entry into the human world of marble that had been billions of years in the making. The "stability," the "durability" of the artistic medium wavers and dissolves before the physicist's vision of long-term development linked to the underlying rhythmic expenditures of energy that constitute the deep-structure of the hoary pillars. And the surrounding vegetation—indeed, we ourselves—are eddies in the great, almost undetectable upward surge of life that has moved from level to level in the journey toward humanness. Carried by that surge, we lived our lives almost oblivious of it. But if and when it becomes focal, we awaken.

Interconnectedness

Atomism, whether in the physical, the psychological or the social sense, is the result of a peculiar abstractive methodology that has led to significant discoveries, but also to significant omissions that now have to be underscored. Field theory in physics, reaching toward the conception of the unity of the space-time matrix in which all events are embedded,[54] reestablished connectedness as a fundamental feature of things. In biology, the organism has increasingly been thought of, not in terms of relatively separable stimulus-response mechanisms, but in terms of wholistic functioning.[55] And one can scarcely do justice to organisms apart from considering their inseparable relations to their environments. Today, by reason of the systematic impact of the consequences of industrial development, we have become more sensitive than ever before to "the web of life" as a single system of which we are only relatively independent parts.[56] In psychology, there has been emphasis upon the significance of the *Gestalt*, the configurated whole, not only in single perceptions, but also in the overall style of behavior and fundamental "feel" for things characteristic of the person.[57] Finally, the rise of sociology since Comte and Marx—by characteristic overreaction— reemphasized what the ancients clearly understood, that the human being is a "political animal," rooted in a tradition of sedimented "words and deeds," outside of which there is no true humanness.[58]

More concretely, the very process of writing and reading this page rests upon the structures of the English language tradition into which we enter and whose virtualities we are unable to survey with any adequacy. Linked to language, our whole sense of things is a product of the entry of the Western heritage into the present.[59] It is the metaphysical aspect of that heritage that we will explore throughout the work, but especially in part 2.

Our self-determination is always determination within, resting upon, the complex webs—physical, biological, psychological, and social—that enter into the very fabric of our subjectivity. When that orthotic knowledge rises to the level of vision, our sense of Being is altered and the subjective ground for creative science—in physics, in biology, in psychology and sociology—is established. And when we ponder the sense of Being that plays in all these fields of awareness, the question of Being emerges with greater depth and we are launched upon a more than abstract and merely academic metaphysical quest. For in each field, vision leads to the wresting of Being, the More, the Not in relation to ordinary awareness, from the immediate Appearance. What is Being? And who are we that are constantly nudged in the direction of Being?

* * *

Meditation, persistently practiced along these lines, moving within everyday awareness toward openness to those intuitive flashes that momentarily heal the rift that exists between the orthotic and the aletheic, between thinking and dwelling, between knowledge and presence, sensitive to the undisclosed wholeness of our own existence within reality as a whole—such meditation may occasionally be graced with a glimpse of the presence of those truths that we may know in the alienative mode of detached thinking, but which, until then, did not fully involve us. Such intuitive moments are not simple additions to our repertoire of experiences strung out along the ongoing course of our lives. They gather our life together as a whole and throw light upon what we have been, what we are, and what we will be. The clarity that fills us and the awe that accompanies such moments hint at an openness and a filling beyond the closure and emptiness that afflict us on the well-trodden paths of our everyday dealings. Touched at the level of our heart—that center where thought, will, and feeling are at one—we might glimpse a transcendent fullness, promise of a completed relation of our underlying desire for fullness in reference to the fullness of reality.[60]

2 The Many Dimensions of Humanness

If we find a thought content
difficult to understand, the
difficulty lies in this: that we
possess no pictorial idea of it; it
is by means of an example that it
becomes clear to us and that the
mind first feels at home with itself
in this content.

G. W. F. Hegel, *On Religion*

He who does not know may still
have true notions of that which he
does not know.

Socrates, *Meno*

We are led to believe a lie when we
see with, not through the eye.

William Blake, *Auguries of Innocence*

Both thought and the senses were
fine things, behind both of them
lay hidden the last meaning.

H. Hesse, *Siddhartha*

Experience and Conceptualization

Philosophy grows in the dialectical interchange between the deepening of the experience of presence and the cultivation of objective reflection stemming out of experience. Experience is the soil within which the objectification of philosophy is rooted. And as the soil enriches the trees, so the trees enrich the soil.[1] The simple presence to a heightened consciousness of birth and death, consciousness and

bodiliness, space, time and interconnectedness stimulates the basic
philosophic questions and leads on to questions about the totality
and the ultimate. Once the grip of the apparent, of the familiar world
is broken by the revelation of the strangeness underlying the everyday, awe provokes and sustains the metaphysical quest.

But one of the major problems we meet in undertaking that
quest is that a great part of what has migrated into the common
consciousness today has been patterned after what appears to sense
experience, generally reduced to the status of object of visual observation and from thence to quantification. The tendency is to conceive
of all reality after the mode of being of such an object. Thus heat,
e.g., is reduced to the status of being object of visual observation
by correlating it with a column of mercury whose rise and fall
through the application and withdrawal of heat can be calibrated;
sound is reduced to oscilloscope readings. Visual terminology dominates our vocabulary: "Let's see how this record sounds, or how
this fruit tastes or how this perfume smells or how this velvet feels."
We would never say, "Let's taste how this sounds."[2] And yet, taste
metaphors have at times challenged visual dominance, as when we
speak of musical taste, or when, in contrast to the metaphor of
the beatific vision, Bonaventure speaks of an experiential tasting
of God.[3]

Contrasted with touch, vision involves distance from the object
and the experiential elimination of the organic self (you don't see or
feel your eye when you look at a tree), whereas touch involves proximity and the mutual experience of the organic self and the other.
Contrasted with hearing in the interpersonal situation, vision involves
the immediate availability of the total field and consequent master-
ability of the field *qua* visible, whereas hearing another speak involves
a dependency upon the other, both for speaking and for revealing
himself through his speaking (unless, obviously, one is eavesdropping).
Distance, elimination of the organic self, and dominance are three
basic characteristics of visual culture.[4] Marshall McLuhan suggests
that the visual imbalance in the interplay of the senses may be correlated with the dominance of the notion of rugged individualism in
recent centuries.[5] In the previous chapter we have attempted to
reawaken a sense of interconnectedness and, simultaneously, a "seeing"
that "touched" the center of ourselves.

Hypnotized by the senses, and especially by visual metaphors,
we fail to develop adequate concepts for dealing with that which does
not (indeed, we will argue, *cannot*) appear as sense-object. Such is
the metaphysical object of our quest in this work. And without concepts adequate to relate fundamental awe, the lived source of meta-

physics, to the total fabric of life, awe itself tends to perish, swallowed up by the commonplace.

Because of our situation, we are (obviously) closely tied to our sensory observations and the imaginative constructions bound up with them—so that if we attempt to transcend this situation in the direction of something metaphysical, we can do so (if at all) only in terms analogous to our sensory situation. When imagination fails us, our alternatives are usually to opt for a radically sensory empiricism as alone revealing of the real or, acknowledging the import of the metaphysical, simply to rest content with silence in the fact of that of which one cannot speak (in sensorily empirical terms).[6]

However, the failure of imagination is something more than a speculative hampering. If a man's thought is to be not merely the region where he speculates, but also the house wherein he dwells, imagination plays a key role in the incarnation of thought within the stream of life as lived. We have, then, our abstract thought about the metaphysical and our concrete set of life relations. What binds them together is analogy.

In the situation of analogy, what we are involved in is a shift in levels of discourse, so that, even were we to admit of metaphysical levels, there is always the danger of carrying over to one level of discourse without modification relations which belong to another level of experience. However, if we have an imaginative model constructed in such a way as to call attention to the possibilities and pitfalls of thinking in metaphysical dimensions, discourse may be helped along. We might then be able to "see" more clearly what has "touched" us.

Flatland: An Imaginative Model

Such a model appeared in the novel *Flatland*, a geometrical fantasy written in 1884 by Edwin Abbott and revived in recent years as a model for aiding our understanding in two seemingly new dimensions: relativity physics[7] and the I-Thou relation. In the latter function, it was employed by Lutheran theologian Karl Heim.[8] It was also used by philosopher C. D. B. Broad[9] and picked up by psychiatrist John Smythies[10] for integrating the notion of consciousness into a broadened scientific view. More recently it has led to an extensive elaboration of two-dimensional operations that have run-off effects in engineering.[11]

The novel describes the experiences of an individual within two-dimensional space or Flatland. The character is A. Square, so-called by reason of his shape. Bound by perception and operation within his planar world, when Mr. Square encounters an obstacle within the plane, his only options (besides remaining where he is) are to retreat or move *around* the obstacle. But one who perceives and operates in three-dimensional space has the additional options of going *under* or *over* the obstacle—operations which, from the viewpoint of A. Square, are strictly inconceivable, i.e., unimaginable. From his position within the plane, our Flatlandian would observe only the starting position of the three-dimensional agent on one side of the obstacle and his resting place on the other side, with no detectable passage through the intervening two-dimensional medium. Miracle!

A. Square is primed for an encounter with such a three-dimensional creature by his prior meeting with the King of Lineland. The boundaries of a Linelandian body are the two sides it presents to those on either side; but for an observer from two-dimensional space, the Linelander's insides are likewise exposed. One-dimensional sound propagation can only enter from the outside that a Linelander's one-dimensional body presents to other Linelanders. But when A. Square speaks in two-dimensional sounds to the King, A. Square's voice seems to the king to come from within the king himself. When A. Square tries to show himself to the king as proof of a second dimension by contacting the linear space and moving through it, all the king observes is a point appearing, persisting for the duration it takes Mr. Square to move through the position, and then disappearing. All this appearing and disappearing seems indeed odd, but the king can accept no explanation that transcends the boundaries of his one-dimensional imagination; hence communication breaks down.

Primed in this way, our Flatland hero is then visited by a three-dimensional creature who, for the purposes of some of the incidents, is of spherical shape. Initially, the voice of the sphere sounds from within A. Square—who is, obviously, amazed. The sphere attempts to manifest himself by passing into the planar space: but all A. Square visually perceives is a point which grows into a progressively longer line until it reaches the length of the diameter of the sphere and then recedes back to a point before disappearing. And from the perspective of tactile sensation, he perceives a progressively augmenting and diminishing circle.

After a series of incidents with the sphere, the analogy binding together A. Square's various encounters suddenly dawns upon him. He confronts Mr. Sphere with the possibility of a fourth and fifth dimension, and beyond to n-dimensional space. "Impossible!" is the sphere's initial reaction—but then he recalls the report of certain events where, with all entrances barred, a man suddenly appeared in a room and then just as suddenly disappeared; of other cases where voices allegedly came from within, and so forth. A. Square and the sphere then ponder the possibility of a multidimensional universe and the problems of communication that arise at the junctures of the various dimensions, The novel develops within this setting.

But so much for the model. Combining imagination and judgment, Edwin Abbott has brought us above the limitations of an imagination tied too tightly to three-dimensional possibilities and opened up the possibility of dimensions beyond. Our task is to offer suggestions concerning the reality of such "metaphysical" dimensions.

Among other things, Abbott was a Christian apologist. The value of his model in this respect is significant. Jesus Christ's alleged appearance and disappearance after the Resurrection seem 'miraculous' and thus impossible only within the context of an empiricism which has (by a fiat) limited the scope of its interpretative apparatus to the condition of objects appearing in three-dimensional space. There is really nothing to preclude the possibility of Christ's (or the Buddha's or Sam Smith's) contemporaneous existence in another dimension—and the witnesses testify to events seemingly explainable only through this hypothesis. Positing another physical dimension would likewise serve to explain the periodically reoccurring phenomena of "inner voices," and may aid in beginning to understand many peculiarities of parapsychological phenomena. From the viewpoint of contemporary physics, it would likewise serve to explain why certain particles appear to leap orbits angelically without passing through the intervening (three-dimensional) space.

But apart from the interesting applications to these rather specialized and highly debatable examples, I prefer to focus attention upon another set of dimensions within which, I am prepared to argue, we already exist, of which we already possess implicit experience, and which we will be able to employ as the door to the metaphysical: I am referring to the whole domain of consciousness. Because our consciousness is generally caught up in the revelation of three-dimensional entities moving in time—indeed, we might say it is usually hypnotized by the appearances of these entities—what is required in attempting to unlock these other dimensions is, in Henri Bergson's description, a movement against the outer-directed mental current back toward the source. We attempt to turn "within."[12]

Imagination and Judgment

Begin by considering a body existent as a three-dimensional being, moving in various ways. Body, extended in space and moving in time, making its appearance to a sense-percipient, is the object of the physical sciences. However, in order that physical science be able to deal with bodies the way that it does, there is implied the scientist's own awareness, which makes it possible for bodies in motion to show themselves. Thus bodies in motion not only *are*, but are *manifest*, and manifest in the peculiar way that the scientist can move from his particular observations to statements about the structures and laws of all similar bodies. Dwelling in the dimensions of consciousness is implicit in the very activity of doing physical science.[13]

Give some attention to the way we can deal with the dimensions of bodily being: let us proceed to construct the objects of geometry. Begin with a three-dimensional solid—a cube. By bisecting the cube and bisecting that bisection and so forth, at the end—at the ideal limit of this operation carried out to infinity—we arrive at a pure two-dimensional object, the region of plane geometry. Proceeding with the same operation upon the resultant plane, we approach practically and reach theoretically a pure one-dimensional structure, the line, which has no thickness or depth but only length. And once more, by bisecting the line ad infinitum we reach the ultimate limit, namely the point as pure dimensionless location.

Now reverse the process: move the point and you generate a line; move the line perpendicular to itself and you generate a plane; move the plane perpendicular to itself and you generate a solid; move the solid and you generate time (a dimension presupposed but not focused on in the Flatland story); move the four-dimensional space-time continuum and you generate . . . ? Image making ceases at this point. But it is possible to proceed with the geometry of five-, six-, seven- . . . *n*-dimensional space, for whose generation and development there are rigid rules that are discoverable. Note how we arrive at these notions: strictly speaking, pure bidimensionality, unidimensionality and extensionless location are not picturable, nor, in the other direction, are the fifth, sixth . . . *n*th dimensions of multidimensional geometry, since picturing involves the tridimensionality of the observable world (or quadridimensionality, if we consider time a fourth dimension, for *moving* bodies are picturable). Though we can *draw* lines, planes and points, we draw them as *three*-dimensional suggestions of one and two dimensions and of the simple location of a geometric point. But the dimensions above and below the experienced four-dimensional space-time continuum are evidently judgeable as the basis for geometry. Such judgment is made possible by a kind of leap that we perform from finite operations to the ideal term of an infinite number of such operations; as in our example, a theoretically infinite number of bisections of a cube yields a geometrical plane. Note two things here: 1) there is a distinction between image making and judgment; and 2) the basis for constructing such objects is the idea of infinity as employed in thinking an infinite set of operations. Using first of all the distinction between judgment and imagination, we can begin to explore the internal dimensions where being not only is but is manifest. We will make more of the notion of infinity as we proceed.

Intentionality

What seems to be characteristic of this whole region is a self-gathered subject standing at a certain "distance" from an object that is thereby opened up to the subject. Every act of awareness is *of* or *about* something, is (technically expressed) *intentional*, in such a way that the subject, in at least an implicit way, takes possession of itself in the very act wherein the Other is revealed.[14] But from the pose of empirical objectification (e.g., the looking characteristic of the optometrist as he adjusts the eyeball mechanism), such a dimension in no wise appears.

Spontaneously, the famous man-on-the-street accepts immediate experience as empirically objective. Objects are "out there," other than myself, and are just what they appear to be. But when asked to account for the way in which he comes to know things "out there" and the nature of his awareness, led by the popularity of the natural sciences, he tends to look for explanations along the lines of empirically objective factors. Of course, conscious others—animals or persons— are also given "out there." But in their case the sensory data are immediately "read" not as self-contained *sensa*, but as expressive of the presence of a conscious being, recognized through its overall behavioral style. But in the past few centuries, a scientific mode of explanation modeled on physics has come to be identified with explanation as such, and people have come to ignore the expressivity of behavior in giving a theoretical account of humanness.[15] Thus the common tendency to seek the explanation of consciousness wholly along the lines of the sensorily observable.

Proceeding further along the same lines, the scientist shows the basis for such knowledge in the registration of wave impulses upon receptor organs that electronically transmit these messages to the brain where, at "point x" in the back of the brain they are interpreted and awareness occurs, But up to this point nothing whatsoever is said of awareness: what *is* this awareness that allegedly occurs "at point x" in the back of the brain? Some have concluded that awareness is nothing but an electronic activity internal to the nervous system.

Such an attempt, I submit, involves itself in a contradiction. To claim that there *really are* such things as waves coming from light sources and being reflected from visual objects, that there *really are* optic and cerebral structures, and simultaneously to claim that awareness is exclusively an intracerebral event, leaves us with no basis for knowing whether there is even such a thing as a brain or visual objects or light waves, for the ground upon which we could know the reality-status of such things is their givenness *as other than* the awareness that observes them. The knower must be endowed with a structure of transcendence, a leaping beyond that in himself which is accessible to the pose of empirical objectivity, beyond what we are wont to call "the body." To attempt to conceive of all things in the form (*morphe*) of what appears to the senses (as empirical object) is thus to fall into what I call *the empiriomorphic* fallacy constituting the positivism that has dominated Western thinking for centuries. It involves a basic and uncritically accepted metaphysics for which to-be is to be object of observation, and the theory of knowledge for which to know is to look.

Such a metaphysics has served well to widen the sphere of phenomena and to enhance our ability to predict and control—even, indirectly, to deepen our sense of awe, as we have indicated in the previous chapter. Beginning with those regions most removed from immediate human concern, empiriomorphism has progressively driven out the anthropomorphic elements—will, feeling, purpose, consciousness—from all the objects of experience: the stars, the elements, the plants, the animals, and now, in behavioral psychology and neurophysiology, the human being. One would have thought that the one thing that should properly be conceived anthropomorphically was surely *anthropos*, the human being![16] This present work aims at the restoration of a purified "anthropomorphism" at the core of a theory of Being, which would thereby aid in overcoming, not by eliminating, but by resituating the dominant empiriomorphism.

Ordinary language usage suggests that we know better than to fall for the empiriomorphic theory of Being—though strangely, we do not seem to know that we know better, else we wouldn't so facilely accept the empiriomorphic fallacy. Consider a common linguistic situation: If one were to burst into the room crying, "I'm aware" and then, to the excited query "Of what? Tell us!" he were to reply, "Oh, of nothing: I'm just aware"—that would make little sense and we would be left floundering. Similarly, to claim to see but to see nothing, to have an idea but not an idea about anything, makes no linguistic sense. But likewise, if one were to ask what an empirically given object, such as a stone is *of* or *about*, the would-be answerer is left suspended.

Things appearing in the mode of empirical objectivity are, as such, just what they are and are not *of* or *about* something; whereas consciousness is not what it is unless it is *of* or *about* something. Consciousness always intends another to which it is intrinsically and necessarily related. This is the basic structure of consciousness: its transcendence towards another, its intending another—in short, its *intentionality*. Note the extension of the term 'intentional' from ordinary usage, where it qualifies acts of willing, to the whole range of conscious acts. Thus, e.g., acts of sensing, imagining, and remembering are intentional in the sense of object-directed and object-revealing, but may or may not be intentional in the sense of deliberate. An acquaintance to whom I owe fifty dollars that is several months overdue might appear in my visual field. He is an intentional object but certainly not an intended object. Again, a tempting but immoral prospect might appear as an object in the field of my imagination, but I need not have intentionally conjured it up nor intentionally entertain it nor intend its actualization. Willful intending does not exhaust intentionality; it is merely one of the subspecies of the generic character of intentionality that distinguishes consciousness.

Intentional transcendence toward another is in the mode of making possible the appearance of that other. And that the other be manifest as other, there is implicitly involved the self-manifestation of the knower as that other than which the other is manifest.[17] (This principle is basic to our whole approach in this book.) However, ordinary consciousness easily misses this because it tends to think in terms of empirical objects.

One way of defocusing that tendency is the employment of Descartes's methodic doubt, which is aimed at focusing attention upon a different type of evidentiality than that characteristic of the way such objects are present to us.[18] For practical purposes one cannot doubt the ordinary deliverances of experience, but one might put into question the whole framework within which the experience occurs. Perhaps I am dreaming, systematically deluded by an "evil genius" who, to employ Emerson's colorful expression, paints the world on the dome of my intelligence. More plausibly the world of ordinary experience may be a series of appearances linked to the needs of the organism (Descartes)[19] or to the finite (Kant)[20] or to the historical (Hegel and Heidegger) character of thought.[21] But even so, what cannot be doubted is the self-presence of consciousness in the very act of being deceived, either about a particular experience or about the framework within which it occurs. The massive certitude of the world over against me is suspended in order to allow the peculiarity of consciousness to show itself as the most certain of all apprehended existents.

The self-manifestation of consciousness is in a mode completely different than that of the manifestation of the empirical object upon which attention is fixed. One is not aware of the other and, in the same mode, aware of the self, like a computer scanning its internal states as well as what is presented through a photoelectric cell in its milieu. What would be the "awareness" in such a scanning?[22] The registration of impulses is not the awareness thereof, else hearing, e.g., would occur when we are asleep. The world of natural processes goes blindly on in accordance with the regularities that obtain within it. The self of consciousness is a unique clearing in the dark field of material processes, a gap, a light that allows some of the processes not to be, but to be *manifest*, to appear. That clearing, that gap, that light is the ground of self-presence, self-consciousness.[23]

One must distinguish here several modes of self-consciousness. First of all, there are two negative modes: (1) *timidity*, or a shrinking of the self before the look of the human Other, and (2) *egoism*, or an attempt to turn the attention of the Other to the self as dominant Other. If we call such states of mind "reflective," they are, none the less, immediate, within lived experience, focused upon one's own individuality. By contrast, in our attempt to begin the task of fixing attention upon and describing such states of mind, we are engaged in an act of deliberately detached reflection that we might call (3) *objective self-consciousness*, wherein the self appears as an instance of a universal meaning. This is orthotic self-awareness, fruit of "first reflection." However, within everday experience—indeed, within all experience—there is what we are basically interested in at this point: what phenomenologists call in contrast to the thematic awareness of an explicit object, (4) *prethematic self-consciousness*.[24] I always "know," and can always within wakeful experience reflectively, thematically remind myself that what I am aware of is part of *my* experience, that *I* am aware of it, the perpetual subject-pole as a necessary condition for the manifestation of any object. There is still another form. This we might call (5) *subjective self-consciousness*, or self-consciousness in the aletheic mode, toward which we directed our attention in the previous chapter. Its ground may or may not be reflection, since occasional flashes of "seeing" the self can occur without deliberately seeking them. But they may also be a result of deliberate "second reflection" recovering from the abstractness of first reflection, synthesizing the "lived" with the apprehension of the universal arrived at in objective self-consciousness.[25] Thus we arrive at a kind of synthesis of the third and fourth modes of self-consciousness: the lived prethematic self, objective instance of the universal, open to the universal, now as a realized, lived instance of the universal.

Because of the merely implicit, pre-reflective character of consciousness's presence to itself as it focuses on empirical objects, because of our natural tendency, by reason of practical adjustment, to think in the mode of empirical objectivity, and (finally) because of the cultural habits contracted along the lines of this tendency, especially as we have become so adept at scientific exploration, we have to undertake constantly a reflective autotherapy in our usage of terms. In the Aristotelian tradition, for example, the usage of such terms as 'reception' and 'possession' of form 'in' the mind to describe cognitive situations has to be understood in terms of the basic structure of the mind as transcendence. Consciousness stands out, is ec-static (Greek *ek*, "out of," and *stasis*, "standing") with respect to our empirically given structure; it is "out there," "in the world," so that something exists "in" the mind insofar as the mind ex-sists (Latin *ex*, "out of," and *sistere*, "to stand"), stands out of the empirical phase of the self and stands toward something other.²⁶

We seem, then, to have a radical cut in our experience from a phenomenological point of view, that is from the way things make their appearance (from the Greek *phainomai*, "I appear"): the structure of objects in three-dimensional space moving in the fourth dimension of time is radically different from the structure of consciousness to which the objects are revealed. Empirical objects *in their object-structure* are not "of" or "about" something, whereas consciousness is not consciousness unless it is "of" or "about" something. Consciousness has a basic "of and to" structure, involves the appearance of an object to a subject that is prethematically present to itself. If this be so, we have uncovered a whole new region within which we may perhaps uncover progressively deeper dimensions.

The discovery of a new set of dimensions, not seeable, touchable tastable, smellable or hearable, but *knowable*—and indeed, ever, in a very real sense, *known*—leads to the creation of a new aspect of language by taking relations found within our sense-experience as its objects and applying them analogously to this new set. Sense language thus becomes *metaphorical* (from the Greek *meta*, meaning in this context "over," and *phorein* meaning "to carry"): meanings are carried over and applied in a way partly the same as, partly different from the way they apply literally in sensory language. Hence we speak of the new dimensions as regions of "interiority" (indeed, also as "dimensions" and "regions") to suggest something "closer" to the "core" of our being than sense-perceptible regions that are *objects* of sense-experience—to suggest the nature of experience itself. Consider some of the terms we use for mental states: (1) *mental* comes from *mens* (Latin), which is related to *mensura*, "measure," an empirically discernible activity; (2) *concept* comes from *concipere* (Latin), which means "to grasp" (*capere*), "together" (*cum*) and from which we also get our notion of the *conception* of a child; spirit comes from *spiritus* (Latin), which means "breath"; *psychic* comes from *psyche* (Greek), which likewise means "breath"; *comprehend* comes from *prehendere* (Latin) meaning "to grasp with the hand." We have also our own English metaphors: "to grasp" a "point" in an argument; to be "enlightened" or to "see the light," and so forth.

So we get this kind of proportion:

$$\frac{\text{spatial outside}}{\text{spatial inside}} \;\; .. \;\; \frac{\text{the whole region of space (inside and out)}}{\text{the region of consciousness ('interiority')}}$$

This is to say, then, that consciousness is not "inside my skull"; it would be *closer* to the truth to say that my skull is inside consciousness; but *closest* to the truth, insofar as it can be adequately expressed, is the fact that consciousness is the "inside" whose outside is the region of space-time in relation to which consciousness is brought through the skull and what it houses.[27]

If empiriomorphism is a first temptation, the discovery of "inwardness" has its own temptation, namely, to conceive of consciousness too much in terms of the literalness of the metaphor, as an "interior chamber" into which contents are poured,[28] rather than as ecstatic manifestation of what is "outside." To say 'that consciousness is "outside itself," "in the world," is to correct the misleading (as well as illuminating) metaphor of "interiority" and to claim a certain priority of our knowledge of the sensorily given other. Even "within" the "container" of our minds (in memory or imagination) where the other is not "outside," there is yet a directedness to the other, a split between the act (prethematically self-manifest) and the object and a derivation of these secondary objects from being-in-the-world. Further, as we shall explore below, in the apprehension of intelligible necessities, awareness is directed to an otherness, an objectivity that is not simply a matter of my private "inside," but of a kind of publicity, in principle available to others and holding for all instances "in the world." The "inside" of consciousness is the capacity for being "outside" the self-contained boundaries of the sensorily observable body, and even outside the privacy of one's own inner feelings.

In terms of our usual modes of explanation, based as they are on the metaphysics of observability, we are, relative to forming adequate concepts of consciousness, in a position parallel to A. Square in his relation to the third dimension. It is essential that we constantly attend to that fact.

Our next step will be to proceed in a way analogous to the geometric procedure alluded to above, considering abstractly the various dimensions of consciousness. Just as, in actual experience, length does not exist apart from depth and breadth, so also, in actual experience, each of the dimensions of consciousness does not exist apart from the others or apart from the body with all of which it continually interplays.

Sensing

At a first level, we tend immediately to identify the reality of things with their status as objects of perception. Hence Berkeley's claim that his much-maligned principle—for such objects, their *Esse est percipi*, their being consists in their being-perceived—accords with common sense.[29] Without entering into the problems this generates, note again that scientific investigation has shown that the *full* being of things is not identical with the being-perceived that they have in ordinary awareness. As we have already called attention to in the previous chapter, our senses operate within thresholds set up by our organic needs. Initially, we perceive the way we perceive because of the survival value of *this* mode of perception for *this* kind of organism that we are. The thresholds and modes of perception are products of the millennia during which the dialectic between organism and environment came to terminate—at least for this world-epoch—in the organic entities that we are. *Sensation is thus the manifestation of limited aspects of the bodies in the environment corresponding to the thresholds set up by our organic situation.* The dimension of sensation is, as it were, a luminous bubble blown by the nervous system, beyond which, for sensation as such, there is only darkness.

The problems in any further interpretation of this ground level of our experience are multiplied by the fact that, as we become reflectively aware of it, it has already been configured by a second level of dialectic: the dialectic between individual and society that has distinctive structures of its own.[30] Granted our initial observations on intentionality (the "of and to" structure of awareness that involves the simultaneous but differentiated manifestation of the other and the self), sensory awareness would involve a kind of fifth dimension, an incipient in-growth of the organism based upon its complexity and centralization. But the mode of *self*-manifestation at this level remains problematic. Reading backwards from our immediate situation, from awareness as we have it in this moment, the self-manifestation that is involved in a reciprocal founding and being-founded in relation to the sensory manifestation of otherness would seem to be a prereflective self-presence incapable of becoming in any way reflectively thematic.[31] And, because it is bound within the ambit of our organic need, such manifestation is limited to the surface of the other as other-for-self and not as other-in-itself (of which more later).

But once more, as ecstatic manifestation of what is other, "out-there" and not "in-here," sensory awareness is not available to an inspection that looks in-here, into the empirically objective structures of the organism. Sensing is directly available only to the one sensing, who *is*, in a way, this sensing.[32]

The confrontation of this mode of analysis with the ordinary meaning of 'dimension' may be useful at this point. Originally, *dimension* signified the measurable aspect of things; it implies a certain side-by-sideness of things, along with a sequentiality itself subjectible to measurement as time. The "what" of the measurable, however, is not the spread-outness and consequent side-by-sideness and sequentiality of things, but the qualitative properties given in the sensory field: the colors, the sounds, the texture, and so forth. The perception of these properties involves a radical transformation of spatiality and temporality, in terms, first of all, of perception's transcendence of the mode of being in space and time that the objects of perception exhibit. Perceiving involves not simply being caught up in the regular movement from the no-longer of the past to the not-yet of the future, but a retension and protension that opens up a space of proximity and distance in terms of a relationship to the needs of the organic percipient.[33] Even what is measurably "close" to the percipient may be, relative to the field of its consciousness, "distant" from its lived perception. In this sense, my neurons and my DNA are further from me than my family, students, colleagues, and friends.

Perception further involves not being confined within the limits of my objectively circumscribable organism. Even at the level of my perception of the qualitative sensory features of the bodies in my environment, perception is ecstatic with respect to its own organism. Though "in" the spread-outness of three-dimensional space, perception is not circumscribable by an outside empirical inspection. Hence the suggested fifth dimension.

Visually we may represent the relation between sensing and the observable as analogous to the relation between the line and the point, reducing four-dimensional space-time objects to a point and considering the succession of sensory experiences (fifth dimension) as a one-dimensional life-line. (See figure 2.1.)

Conceptualization

The attempt to determine the essential features of consciousness in general (intentionality) and of sensory awareness in particular intro-

Figure 2.1   SENSING

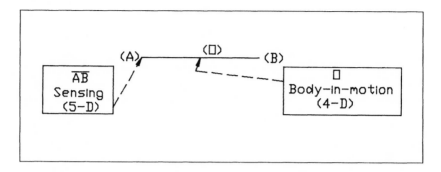

duces us to another dimension of consciousness not tied to the particular object the way the dimension of sensing is. For the mere determination of the differentness of sensing-as-such implies a capacity on our part to transcend the here-and-now sensed object in relation to the 'as such,' the realm of universality. The 'as such' involves an anticipatory reference to all actual or possible instances of the notion in question, and therefore to the whole of space and time, wherever and whenever the essence in question happens to be realized.[34]

Edmund Husserl, the father of phenomenology, termed the apprehension of such universality "eidetic intuition"[35] or immediate insight into an *eidos*, Plato's term for universal Forms or Ideas that are, like a geometric theorem, "seen" by the "mind's eye." Such insights are not merely private episodes within one's own individual circle of experience—as one's toothache would be (though in knowing it "as" a toothache we know it in terms of the universal). Rather such insights involve in-principle objective, public claims. The capacity to apprehend principles is thus radically different in structure than either the sensory object or the sensory act correlated with it.

The denial of the eidetic continually occus in the history of philosophy. If we understand, by reason of insight into both the expressivity of behavior and the intentionality of consciousness linked thereto, that being cannot be restricted to being object of sensing—and thus surmount the empiriomorphic fallacy—there is a more general "empiricistic fallacy" that has yet to be surmounted. 'Empiricist' is linked to the Greek term *empeiria*, which simply referred to "experience," but was later limited to sensory experience, whether conceived externally (seeing, hearing, etc.) or internally (kinesthesia, sense of health or sickness, etc.) or both. In a broader employment, it tends to be associated with a nominalism that allows no reality to the *eidos*, though it may admit (with Locke and against Hobbes) to perception of one's own interiority, (with James and against Locke) to "ec-static" presence to what lies outside the self, and (with James and Bergson) to mystical experience.[36] The empiricist fallacy holds that all reality is composed of particulars in the here-and-now and that there are no real universals.

But the position refutes itself both in terms of its content and in terms of the act of holding it. The claim is a claim to the reality of the universal truth, namely, that being as such is the sum of all individuals—whether the universal exists "in itself," "apart from things," or "in the mind." And the claim bears witness to a mind that thinks—and must think—in terms of universal meanings transcending the here-and-now, and thus as itself *in some way* so transcendent. If we transcend empiriomorphism by recognizing the "interiority of consciousness" and transcend Locke by recognizing consciousness's transcendence of its alleged character as an inner chamber, we must also transcend Bergson's "integral empiricism" which also recognized mystical experience, and follow William James from such empiricism to the even more "radical empiricism" that includes (following Husserl) the experience of the eidetic.

Another way to get at this region of universality is to deal with an element of a proposition: take, for example, the concept 'pen' in "This is a pen." Ask: To what does the concept apply? The question is ambiguous because it refers to at least three related referents: (1) obviously, to the individual thing observed (*"this"* pen); but also (2) to the *meaning* (sometimes called the "comprehension" expressed in the "definition") of the concept; and (3) to the *extension* of the concept. In the case of the third referent (we will examine some features of the *meaning* of a concept below), we are asking: to how many particulars does the concept apply? And upon reflection we see that it applies to all actual instances of the kind in question, past, present and future—indeed, also to all *possible* instances.

Thus the notion 'pen' is not restricted to the one I am using now to insert remarks into my typescript nor to those that stand ready to be of service in the box on my desk, nor to those now running off the assembly line at the Papermate company, nor to all those now existent nor to those that will exist in the future; but it extends even to those that could have existed but did not, could now exist but do not, could exist in the future but will not. 'Pen' holds for all actual or possible particulars because it is a human construct, *made* to so hold. But what is not a human construct is the essential reference to all possible particulars, and thus the prior eidetic recognition of particularity, possibility, and the whole of space and time as the field within which the instances have occurred, are occurring, or will occur.

The introduction of the *possible* here introduces a negation into the fullness of immediate presence, for the possible is the *not*-realized, the *non*-actual. Thus Sartre: consciousness is essentially negation of the fullness of material being, a Nothingness in the polarity of *Being and Nothingness*. It is on the basis of the not-immediately-present that the immediately present is revealed as what it is: this here-and-now *as* a pen, which is what it really is.

The number of particulars that are the *possible* subjects of the concept are virtually unlimited, are infinite. (Again we meet the notion of infinity.) To be a meaning applicable to an unlimited number of individuals-of-a-kind is to be *universal* (from the Latin, *unum-versus-alia*, "one-turned-towards-[as-pointing-to]-others"). We may or may not be mistaken in what we understand by the notion; but there is no mistake, it seems to me, that the employment of the notion intends, by its very nature, all actual or even possible realization throughout the whole range of space-time. This immediacy-transcending intentionality points to a distinction from our immediate sensory involvement with the bodies about us. Wrenched thus out of the empirical present, we can reflect upon and thereby interpret it. We thereby have a basis for the revelation of the not-sensorily-revealable region of intentionality. This is the basis traditionally called "intellect" as the capacity to "read interiorly" (Latin *intus* and *legere*), a capacity of re-flection, "bending back" upon oneself and thereby objectifying one's experience.[37]

It is important to distinguish the universal orientation of any capacity—for example, of seeing to any seeable whenever and wherever it might be met—from the universal orientation of the concept. Any capacity or power is a universal orientation activated by its object. But whereas other powers are activated by particular objects, and sensory powers by manifest aspects of particular things, the universal orientation involved in the concept is that of manifest universality in which the power of manifestation is activated by the universal as such. And just as the revelation of the intentional character of sensation led us to posit a fifth dimension to experience, standing as inside to outside in relation to the four-dimensional continuum of space-time within which the objects of sensation appear, so our discovery of the immediacy-transcending intentionality of the concept open to an infinite number of possible instantiations throughout the space-time continuum brings into the picture a sixth dimension related to the five-dimensional space-time-sensation continuum as inside to outside. Relating this to the image of the life-line of ungoing sensory experiences which, as "interior," transcend the "point" of space-time objects, we could say that eidetic intuition and its universal objects

Figure 2.2   INTERPRETING

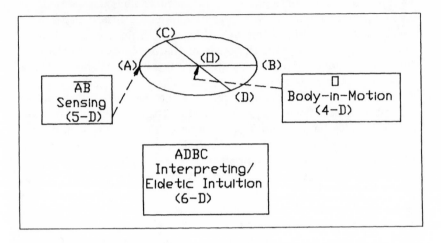

(sixth dimension) constitute a two dimensional circle that surrounds our sensory life-line. (See figure 2.2.)

Reference to Being

Finally, however, the sum total of experience developed in relation to the universal is linked to the radical intentionality of the mind expressed in the most prosaic of judgments such as we have been examining. Pay attention now to the 'is' in "This *is* a pen." It performs, first of all, a copulative function, joining the universal pen" to the particular "this" to form the propositional synthesis. But as employed by a consciousness whose character is to transcend itself in the direction of its objects, the 'is' functions as the vehicle of reference to the in-itself-ness of the thing encountered. We use the propositional synthesis to make a truth-claim: that our proposition corresponds to the thing. The evidence verifies the proposition. The thing presents itself as a realized synthesis of meaning and datum.[38] Orthotic truth is achieved.

But the radical intention of Being expressed in the 'is' goes further. Just as we asked, in effect, of the notion 'pen,' "Of what can we say 'It is a pen'?" and replied, "Of all actual or possible individuals that answer to the description," so also we might ask, "Of what can we say "It is'?" And the answer is, "Of everything actual or possible." The notion of Being involved in the 'is' refers to that outside of which there is nothing at all. It is all-englobing. Such reference includes within it reference to the total being of any encounterable other, only aspects of which are met in ordinary awareness. The 'is' thus refers us even beyond the thing as realized synthesis of meaning and datum, for our ordinary propositions are focally modes of "dashboard knowledge." The sensory surface is itself a kind of dashboard whereby things present themselves for our operation upon them. We learn in-put and out-put, but not necessarily what lies on the other side of the dashboard. However, we are by nature referred to the ultimate depths of things which indeterminately exceed the character of our experience and modes of conceiving. Of course, where we stand in making such a reflective judgment involves a mode of conceiving that does include them, but only by an empty rather than by a filled intention.[39] We are conceptually articulating our reference to the things rather than the inner fullness of the things themselves. Perhaps Buber put it best: things themselves are *met* but not *comprehended* in all of our wakeful dealings.[40]

Whereas concepts such as 'pen' are unlimited in extension to their particulars, they are yet limited in applying only to those particulars that answer to their definition. Thus 'pen' obviously only applies to pens and not also to people and puppets and penguins. Such concepts are limitedly unlimited. However, the notion of being, including as it does *all* that is or can be, not only individuals of a kind but all kinds as well, is an infinitely infinite notion, absolutely and not simply relatively unrestricted.[41] And it is this notion that comes into play in all our judgments, in most of which the notion of "all that is or can be" is contracted to "all that is or can be of the kind in question" (in our example, pens).

This opens up then, a seventh dimension, distinguished from the first four by being, along with sensation and conception, *intentional*; differing from sensation, along with conception, by being *universal*, but set off likewise from conception by being *unrestrictedly universal*. (See Figure 2.3.)

With the opening up of the sixth and seventh dimensions, we can then extend the application of the original metaphor of "interiority". Recall:

$$\frac{\text{space (outside)}}{\text{space (inside)}} \quad \cdot\cdot \quad \frac{\text{space (as a whole, inside and out)}}{\text{consciousness}}$$

Continuing now, we get:

$$\frac{\text{space-time-sensing}}{\text{eidetic intuition}} \quad \cdot\cdot \quad \frac{\text{space-time-sensing-eidetic intuition}}{\text{reference to Being}}$$

Openness to the Whole, and thus openness to the wholeness of individuals within the wholeness of reality as such is the basic dimen-

Figure 2.3   THE RELATION BETWEEN THE DIMENSIONS

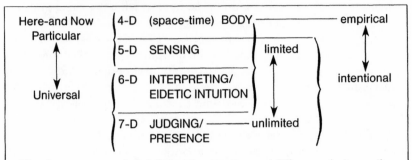

The diagram suggests relations of sameness and difference between the various dimensions—the braces indicating sameness, the arrows difference. Thus *sensing* is the same as a body in being a here-and-now present particular, but differs in being intentional; as intentional, it agrees with judgment and interpretation, but differs from them in being a here-and-now particular; and it agrees with both body and interpretation in being limited, thus differing from judgment which opens to the unlimited. And so with the other dimensions.

In this scheme, *body* is thus a limited here-and-now particular empirical structure; *sensing* is a limited here-and-now particular intentional structure; *interpreting/eidetic intuition* involves a limited universal intentional structure; and *judging/presence* involves an unlimited universal intentional structure.

sion of interiority before which all else is exterior. In terms of our continuing geometric diagram, reference to Being is the depth-dimension). But that mere reference is capable of being filled in as the fully vibrant, possibly deepening sphere of human life in relation to the encompassing Whole. (See figure 2.4.)

Beginning with the ordinary sensory objects and reflecting upon how they can be known, we discover the non-sensorily-perceptible character of our sensing that supplies the framework within which sensory objects appear. Reflecting upon the *essential* distinction between the framework and the objects that appear within the framework and how an essential distinction can come to be known, we discern another stratum to the field of consciousness. Both the sensory object and the sensory act are particular entities within the here-and-now of our bodily presence. But the object of our reflection upon that situation extends beyond the here-and-now, for the essential distinction is universal, applying to all sensory objects and acts, wherever and whenever they might exist. And reflecting, finally, upon the reference to all times and all places involved in the universal inten-

Figure 2.4 THE SEVEN DIMENSIONS OF HUMANNESS

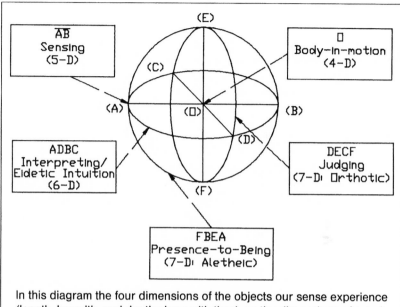

In this diagram the four dimensions of the objects our sense experience (length, breadth, and depth along with time), as the dimensions of exteriority, are contracted to point (O) encompassed by the three dimensions of interiority. *Sensing* (line AB) is the "length" of our particular experience of exteriority; *Interpreting/Eidetic Intuition* (plane ADBC) is the "breadth" of our universal frameworks; *Judging* (plane DECF), relating our sensations and interpretations to reality, opens out to the fullness of *Presence* represented by the completed sphere.

tion, we discern a reference to the totality lying at the base of the ability to apprehend universals.

Thus we have a seven-dimensional continuum covering the whole of human experience. The explicit focus of attention of our day-to-day living is upon sensorily appearing individuals; but implicit in the way in which we have that experience is this seven-dimensional structure.

Implicit Features of Inwardness

Now that we have laid out the distinctions between the dimensions in a general way, let us give further attention to making explicit some of the particular features of the inner dimensions.

First of all, at the level of bodies in motion, our body is not only the body of science, that is the body as observed; it is also, and much more fundamentally, the body as I live it, not fully capable of becoming an object of observation since the lived body, the body-subject, is necessarily tied up with the subjectivity of awareness.[41] The lived body is that from which I pay attention to anything else. But I pay attention by indwelling in my body at the prereflective level. I have a pervading kinesthetic sense that allows me to retain my balance and overall behavioral style through differing situations, to focus my eyes, to speak. I "know" how to maintain my balance and my gestural style, how to focus, how to fix tongue and teeth and lips and palate in order to speak. But the "knowledge" here is prearticulate. I really know explicitly very little of how I know how to do these things. I dwell in a language, drawing upon it and being carried by it. I generate relatively clear English sentences without knowing much at all of how I am able to do so. The prereflective self-consciousness that the Cartesian argument brings into focus in such a way as to make it seem wholly other than the body, is in fact continuous with the body. The body "knows" how to do things without my consciously knowing them at all; and I as a conscious agent know how to do whatever I do without knowing fully how it is I know how to do it. Consciousness and unconsciousness interpenetrate in a prereflective lived body.

This helps us with a very important problem in the history of thought. If we were able to pry loose the inwardness of awareness from our hypnotic identification of it with an in-principle observable object, noting the essential intentionality or self-transcendence of awareness, the first question that might emerge is: "What is a nice inwardness like that doing in a place like this, in an organic body with its creeks, gurgles, groans, hums, and thumps?" (Recall our meditation in chapter 1.) But reflection on prereflective knowing suggests an answer: continuous stimulation of the organism by the physical environment provides clues that are continuously processed to achieve the adjustment necessary for focusing attention. Though attention is fixed upon a focally given object, and consciousness is directly preoccupied with the object, the act of adjusting and readjusting the eyeballs to suit the movement of the object and/or of oneself as a perceiver involves a wholly unconscious level of information processing that supports the focal acts of attending.[43]

Again, notice that at the level of sensation the theme of any given sensory act is a figure, but a figure that always appears against a ground. So in the visual act, as I open my eyes the whole field of vision is available: the book shelf, the wall, the curtains, the desk, the typewriter, the picture, objets d'art, the clock, chairs, ceiling, and so forth. All are there within my visual field. And as I zero in on any one of the factors to avail myself actually of it in consciousness—a particular red book that stands out next to an orange one—the whole field still remains as ground and the figure appears only against that ground. So here attention is a kind of congealing, a centering upon single objects within the field of vision, The ground remains prethematic but it is capable of being made the theme of attention. I can focus upon each item in the field, but only one by one, not all at once.[44]

Within the figure itself we have further to distinguish subsidiary and focal features:[45] a face appears in an overall focal *Gestalt*, a configurated whole; but the elements which comprise it, though implicit in the field of focus, are subsidiary aids and clues gathered prereflectively into the total focal *Gestalt*. In this example, the face is normally the object of another kind of Gestalting process insofar as the face is itself an expressive datum. In this case, the whole sensorily verifiable *Gestalt*, with all its subsidiary elements, is itself subsidiary to the "reading" of the conscious person present in, and revealed and concealed by, the expressive surface.

Actually, attention can and does shift between these various aspects: from the presence of the person to the sensorily observable character of the face as a whole ("Well, he's not exactly Robert Redford"), and to various aspects of the sensorily observable whole ("Redford does have moles on his cheek, but his eyes are so blue!"). In the context of a conversation with two long-time colleagues, after a half hour I noticed for the first time that one of them had shaved the moustache he had sported for nearly a decade. The other colleague, who would regularly look straight into your eyes from two feet away, intensely intent on the person, remarked, "Did he have a moustache?" A trained observer would pick out details of a situation, but for a participant in the interpersonal situation, the details would be only implicit. (By the way, that does not make the observer superior. One might argue that observation is actually a mode inferior to participation, and that observation is a peculiarly abstract stance made for a limited purpose and subserving participation. Reflect once more on the relation of the oculist to his patient's eyes, shifting from their expressivity in the look of the patient to their sensorily verifiable presence as eyeball mechanisms.)[46]

Our focusing of attention stands in immediate relation to the upsurge of desire around whose ends the sensory field tends to arrange itself—though desire itself has been prearticulated and directed in terms of the mediations of the culture within which we have been raised and within which, and on the basis of which, we continue to exist. These cultural mediations immediately bring into the picture the level of the concept.

As medium of interpretation, the concept functions in a twofold way: as embedded in the structuring of experience and as detached therefrom (corresponding to *aletheia* and *orthotes* respectively). As embedded it spontaneously guides the shaping of the experiential *Gestalt*. In the field of immediate experience I can so pay attention to a given sensory constellation—for example, three parallel lines arranged as follows:

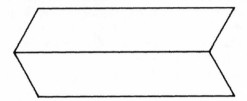

that the whole can present itself to vision in three ways: as three lines in a plane, or with center line jutting out toward our eye or receding from it, while the flanking lines occupy the same plane. This would supply the basis for a distinction between the *sensa*, or the qualitative features that seem to remain unaltered, and the *percepta*, or the wholes that admit of differing modes of configuration. Much recent discussion in philosophy of science and philosophy of mind deals with an attack on "the myth of the given"[47] (as if something could be presented to us apart from our active—though not usually deliberate—shaping) and with an emphasis on "the theory-ladenness of perception."[48]

The concept can also function in a detached way, as when I "orthotically" entertain the options just indicated. Though in both conditions it is not just a matter of applying a concept to a situation. The concept itself makes sense only within the structures of a conceptual field within which we present its "comprehension" or define its meaning. So that to understand, for example, what a pen is, we have to understand *this* pen as an instance of pen universally and communication universally, in relation to writing universally, ideas universally, persons universally, and communication universally. Only against the prethematic background of the whole world (as distinguished from the environment) of communication can the single concept 'pen' be understood.[49] Indeed, the reality of a concept consists in its being a node of relations to the totality. In our usual immediate experience, the concept itself remains prethematic in a way, that is, we are not usually aware of our concepts; but rather we attend to the things that come into focus through our concepts, in much the same way as we are not normally aware of our glasses when we wear them and when they are performing their function of clarifying the things we look at.[50] And just as we can make an object out of our glasses, attending to the structure of the lenses, so also can we make an object of our concepts and of the interpretative or thematic field within which these concepts have their reality. And this tends to occur again by the law of opposites: absence reveals presence. Consider a primitive with mastery of the bare rudiments of English looking at our pen and asking a bystander, "What is that?" "That's a pen," would come the reply (and those who think naming is simply a matter of associating a sense experience with a single sound or visual pointer would expect no more). But the primitive who doesn't share our world of meaning would not be satisfied—for the next question would be, "What's a pen?" It would be cruel and viciously circular—not to say misleading—to reply, "It's what you see." One would have to explain the concept to him by revealing the world of interrelated universals within which it fits.

But to point to the world of communication within which 'pen' has its meaning is to point to a set of interpersonal meanings developed by a community in the course of its history as the "house" within which that community "dwells." Within the latter world we have the distillates of human freedom, which is the realm of history: freedom made and in the making, freedom interlaced with the realm of natural necessity and both sustaining and blocking future freedom.

This communal housing of meaning is a multileveled affair. The first world within which we house the data immediately available to the senses when we call it 'pen' is a *world of instrumentality*.[51] 'Pen' is the shape given to the data as useful to man in a specifically defined sense. We might say that what is "really" there is metal, plastic and ink, which we might then begin to define in terms of molecular, atomic and subatomic properties discernible, directly or indirectly, through observation. The instrumental world of meaning is laid over this scientific world of meaning[52] in such a way that the former can function well enough for the most part without any but a very gross knowledge of the latter (although, the more sophisticated the technology, the more it is dependent upon knowledge of the scientifically discernible structures underlying our gross sense envelopes).

But we might question the ultimate meaning of the scientific by inquiring into the conditions in the knower and in the known that make a scientifically observable object possible. Is the thing as observable object identical with the thing in its own reality? Are appearance and reality identical? If we grant that the senses are basically instruments for adjustment and thus always yielding appearance-relative-to-perceiving-organism, then the answer would be no. This introduces us to the level of philosophic meaning discernible basically not by observation but by reflection: it deals, not with objects detached from knowing subjects, but with the subject-object relation and its ground.

Subtending these instrumental, scientific, and philosophic levels is what we might call the symbolic level of meaning. "The pen is mightier than the sword, laying waste the deadly foes of ignorance and prejudice; subduing, not only the body, but even the mind; powerful not only in destroying but also in raising up." The pen would then carry collective emotional overtones, not simply purveying value-neutral information but evoking profound personal resonances.

By "symbolic" here we thus intend something richer than the univocal single-meaning context of symbolic logic. We refer rather to the dimension articulated in poetry and myth, which work out of analogical, plural-meaning contexts. Myths operate first in the direction of suggesting multiple linkages among the objects of our experience, and second, in the direction of the deep-structures of the human psyche explored by the psychologist Carl Jung.[53] Myths and symbols are not what we employ in lieu of adequate objective explanation, as scientism and rationalism would have it. As Plato and the ancients before him recognized, myths and symbols are richer than any objective explanation,[54] bringing us into the sphere of mystery, of the nonobjectifiable mutuality of subject and object that underlies and makes possible objective explanation.

The fields within which particular concepts occur, though prethematic or implicit in our usual modes of attending, are nonetheless capable of being rendered progressively more explicit as we attempt the reflective clarification of conceptual meanings. Just as all the items in the field of vision, present implicitly as we attend explicitly to any one of them, are capable of being made explicit objects of our attention—though only one by one as visual objects (they may be thematized as a whole field by thought, as we are now doing)—so also it would seem that, at least in principle, all the conceptual linkages within our interpretative fields could be made explicit. It is the task of the various sciences to further that explication, though the question of developing adequate interpretation of the symbolic field poses special problems for which the discipline of hermeneutics has been developed.

However, when we pay attention to the structure of the seventh dimension, that from which stem judgments rooted in the notion of Being, notice that the prethematic can never be adequately thematized. It would seem at first blush that this is not the case: do we not, after all, form the concept of Being, which is all-encompassing?

Is it not an explicit conceptual object? It is indeed all-encompassing, englobing all particulars as well as all universals. And yet the notion is an absolutely *infinite* one, built into the structure of which is negativity, for the concept of the infinite is, notice, *negation* of finitude, *not*-finite. Those who ridicule metaphysics frequently point to the utter emptiness of the notion of Being—and well they might. But its emptiness is that of Platonic Eros, born, Plato says, of Poverty and Plenty, on account of which it is wholly lacking but nonetheless has designs upon plentitude.[55] The notion of Being standing over against the mind's eye as a conceptual object is a kind of mirror of the soul. It expresses objectively what the mind is subjectively: Eros for the Absolute, hunger for the Totality. It is, we suggest, by reason of this reference to the Totality, outside of which we cannot be, that human subjectivity is and remains essentially a mystery, never fully capable of being objectified. Subjectivity, as the inner condition of objectivity, as that over against which something is object, cannot be objectified and thus cannot be mastered.[56] It always stands at an infinite distance from all objectification and as such is fundamental freedom. It can only be let be, thankfully, reverently, before its unfathomable sense is unveiled, at least in part.

And since subjectivity is reference to the all-encompassing Totality, growth in the sense of subjectivity as such involves growth in the awareness of the not-positively-revealed reality of things appearing positively in our sensory and interpretative fields. It involves a fundamental "feel" for things, a mode of presence which is a sensitizing to mystery such as we have attempted to evoke in our secular meditations. Hence it exceeds the merely conceptual and objective determinations of detached intellect, while preserving the space within which conceptualization can go on in a manner meaningful to the wholeness of the person. Subjectivity so understood is "the single root of the soul's powers,"[57] the *apex mentis*[58] in which the wholeness of the self can be gathered up. Relation to the Whole of Being means openness to the whole of *each* being and thus also to the whole of oneself—on account of which one's being is an issue[59] because the whole of oneself includes the open field of possibilities from which one is called upon to choose.

As openness to the encompassing Whole, this primordial presence to Being is the ground for the distinction between Reality (as the whole of any given being) and Appearance (as the partial manifestation made within our biological-sensory sociocultural envelopes); it is the prethematic basis for forming the concept of Being as unlimited; it is the basis for generating the geometric objects mentioned earlier by bringing into play a theoretically infinite set of operations:

it lies at the ground of any interpretation of individuals as instances of meanings with relatively unlimited applicability; and it is itself capable of deepening through a meditative dwelling that involves our total subjectivity. Note further that reflection upon this relation to individuals against the horizon of the Whole may serve to ground poetic claims, such as that of Blake, "to see the Infinite in a grain of sand," "to dwell in Eternity's sunrise" in the presence of a butterfly,[60] or Buber's glimpse of the Eternal Thou through the sunlight shining on a maple twig[61] or the mystic's claim of a simultaneous revelation of God and the self or of the world as theophany.[62] The depth of the "interior" life lies in the development of such presence.

But the visual metaphor tends to mislead us here into thinking that the "interior life" consists in a retreat from the "outside world" as revealed, through our lived bodiliness. Rather, by reason of the fact that consciousness is intentional, is manifestation of 'otherness,' the interior life is matter of establishing a certain "distance" which allows the deepest meaning of the sensorily appearing Other to manifest itself, and which therefore allows us really to get close to individuals. Those who are closest to things (see Assisi's expressions, "Brother Worm," "Brother Wolf," "Brother Sun," etc.)[63] are those who know most how to dwell in infinite distance, in relation to the Infinite Itself. Conversely, those who dwell purely in terms of their sense-life are more superficial and glide over the surface of the Other (persons and/or things): they lead an exterior, an extrovert life. Thus Augustine speaks paradoxically if we stick to the literal meaning, perfectly clear and perfectly true if we consider the metaphorical meaning) of living "outside oneself," "locked up within oneself."[64']

* * *

The most significant distinctions to apprehend in this work are the distinctions that obtain at the level of "the seventh dimension." I call it the dimension of "judging/presence." But the analysis of the structure of the judgment is only, for our purposes, a way of entering into what is implied in the notion of 'presence'.

The explicit focus of the pedestrian judgment-type we have been attending to ("This is a pen") is upon the sensorily given individual ("This" here-and-now present). We are employing other judgment-types in our analysis of that judgment, judgments upon the not-sensorily-given structures of intentionality involved in the initial judgment, judgments whose focus is likewise only mediately concerned with the immediate structures of *my* consciousness here and now, but more basically zeroed in on the *eidetic* features of consciousness-as-such, and so forth. But we are claiming that the meaning-field involved in the notion of 'pen' is synthesized "in reality" "through evidence" in the here-and-now present, existent thing. We "look" *through* the meaning-field *at* the individual, focused in a particular way. But—and this is crucial here—we also "look" at the individual (and in reflection also at the meaning-field) *from* a peculiar presence to the totality of Being.[65] "Being" is the encompassing matrix containing everything: sense-datum, meaning-field, thing sensorily displayed, consciousness sensorily and intellectually attentive, and everything else besides, the most abstract and the most concrete at once.

Meaning-fields grow up over the time of a culture and of an individual assimilated to the culture. They expand to fill the space between sensory presence to the here-and-now given environment and inward presence to the encompassing Whole. 'Pen' means something insofar as it is understood as related to the world of communication between persons who, in turn, are understood as inserted into the material and the spiritual worlds. The mysterious Whole is interpreted in the worldviews operative within the culture and between cultures.

Meanings mean something in terms of (1) their reference to their instances, (2) their significant linkage with a meaning-field, and (3) their ultimate connection with the Whole. The latter can be developed as a completely articulated worldview, but it may not "mean" anything to a given individual. In this case, meaning has to do with (4) the mode of presence, the meaning that "draws close" and touches oneself. Meaning in this latter sense, affecting our basic "feel" for things, is significantly linked to our motor habits, behavior patterns, routines—the aesthetics of the worldview is linked to the pragmatics of the worldview. But 'aesthetics' here is not a matter of a subjective effect of objective reality, but of a deeper reference than can be formulated in propositions. One can elaborate the meaning and check its correspondence, but one can also dwell more deeply in the reference and thus touch the fuller reality of the Other in another and closer manner than through such objective judgment alone.[66]

All the explicated and explicatable elements contained within these structures are finally rafted upon a not-fully-explicatable presence, a felt *Gestalt*, a "sense of Being." *Orthotes* is both distinguished from and related to *aletheia*. Our relation to the Totality is, at base, a total relation. And that total relation is understood in the long line of thinkers we have referred to in chapter 1 as a matter of "the heart,"[67] the core (Latin *cor* means "heart") of our Being, "the single root of the soul's powers," "the divine spark" (Eckhart's *Funklein*),[68] the "I" of Buber's I-Thou relation, wholeness related to wholeness.[69]

If the sensory features of things constitute one level of appearance relative to our organic needs, the result of organic preselection from the totality of stimuli bombarding us from the environment, the meaning-fields are culturally induced by means of selective focus and constitute another level of appearance. There is an inertial tendency to settle down within the comfort of this culturally mediated appearance. But there is also the deeper thrust of our nature toward Being which makes imperative a continual struggle against appearance, within appearance, for Being, the hidden wholeness, partially revealed, partially concealed in any appearance. It is the struggle that is both orthotic and aletheic, where the orthotic formulates the aletheic against less adequate or erroneous formulations, but where the aletheic struggles likewise against the limited and limiting modality of the orthotic itself for the sake of the undisclosed depth of Being.

The aletheic "feel" for things that tends to spell itself out in terms of certain worldviews and to generate certain lines of action finds its more immediate full expression in poetry, where the sensuous music of the words themselves incarnates in the very rhythms of our bodily feelings that presence that the poem mediates, where the metaphorical meanings cut across the analytical divisions and bind together in a new way wholly different areas of thought and experience. Poetry is the language of *aletheia*. Philosophy's task in this regard is to comprehend that by carefully distinguishing the boundaries between the different areas of thought and experience, by analyzing the movement of the mind that cuts across these boundaries, and by attempting to tie the whole together in the wholly different register of the conceptual medium.

But to carry out this sort of reflection is to carry out a type of alienation from the original presence to reality given in our childhood. It is to introduce more sharpness into the experienced duality of mind and body and to create a whole set of dualities in our experience: intellect and sense, universal and particular, world and environment, the self and the Other, finite and infinite. But again, by the law of opposites, these dualities are the basis for revelation-in-depth. The task is to attempt to reachieve in a heightened awareness at an adult, conscious level the psychophysical unity of the self from which we began as infants. The task is to weld these reflections back into presence through our body whereby bodily being itself participates in the depth of meaning secured by our own reflection meditation that reaches its high point in the deepening of presence. It is out of that deepening that significant activity occurs. But that activity, which attains vital expression in our various forms of behavior and in our various institutions, becomes ambiguous in the degeneration whereby our habits and customs become expressions of a mere routine from which the spirit has long been absent, a facade behind which we hide our reality in hiding from reality. But the forms that we use can also become expressions of a spirit that is entering into self-possession. And that is the aim of these reflections. (Figure 2.5 presents an overview of the material we have been discussing.)

Figure 2.5 THE MANY DIMENSIONS OF HUMANNESS

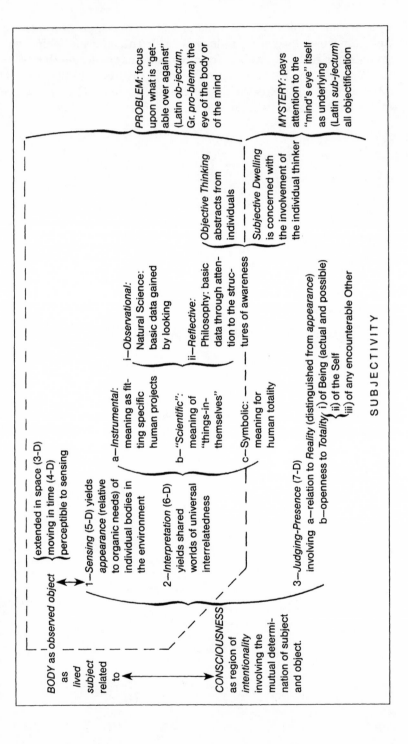

3 *Toward a Definition of Humanness*

We are men and have reason; what
is human or, above all, what is
rational echoes within us, both in
our feelings, mind and heart and in
our subjective nature generally.

If we say . . . that man is by
nature rational, we would mean
that he has reason only inherently
or in embryo.

> G. W. F. Hegel, *On Philosophy*

In order truly to understand one
single word, not as a merely
physical stimulant but as an
articulated sound describing a
concept, language must reside in
man as a whole.

> W. von Humboldt

The spiritual . . . only constitutes
itself effectively as spirit on
condition of becoming flesh.

> G.Marcel, *The Mystery of Being*

The distinctive faculty of the active
and intelligent being is that he can
attach a meaning to the word 'is'.

> J. J. Rousseau

Our theme is Being and humanness. We have therefore attempted to
lay the basis for metaphysics by broadening the experiential and con-

ceptual aspects of humanness in their interrelatedness. Now we wish to give some attention to the reflectively available features of humanness. Beginning with the observationally available surface, we will attempt to integrate into our seven-dimensional scheme a number of definitions presented by various thinkers.

If we persist in the practice of the meditations suggested above, the notion of a 'definition of humanness' will begin to lose its abstract academic character and will begin to blend with the question of deepest existential importance: Who am I? The procedure need lose none of its rigor, but it remains bathed in the solution of deepest concern.

Now, definitions do not necessarily express insight into the heart and core of things. Definitions need be no more than convenient sorting devices arrived at by comparing our various experiences, finding what the thing to be defined has in common with other things and what is different in it. So we search for samenesses and differences: the common features are located in what is called in logic the *genus*; what a species has proper to itself is termed the *difference*.

In the case of the definition of humanness, it becomes evident that we share corporeal, organic and sentient characteristics with other things—which characteristics, compressing in themselves a whole host of general features, are in turn compressed into the generic notion 'animal'. The surface meanings of all these terms are initially reducible to what presents itself to observation. Their depth-meaning will have to be considered in terms of integrating the observational surface with the structures we have already uncovered by reflection upon ourselves as self-conscious.

Examining the overt behavior of other entities, reflectively explicating the structures determining our own individual awareness, and tacking back and forth from one approach to the other allows us to deepen our appreciation of these regions of being. The reading of animal behavior involves an attempt to disengage levels in the concrete field of our own awareness and to speculate on that basis regarding the subject side of animal behavior. Studies in the genesis of adult consciousness from the infantile stage would also be helpful (and here the same tacking manuever is required). But the process is obviously frought with great difficulties, since infant awareness is oriented toward adult human awareness, and sensory awareness at the adult human level is already shot through with intellectual operation.

Observational Differences

But remaining for the moment at the observational level, two characteristics peculiar to humanness are typically noted: a human being is a *tool-making animal*,[1] and a human being is a *symbol-making animal*.[2] Obvious qualifications have to be made.

In a certain extended sense, beavers, for example, make "tools"— dams and huts; bees make hives; birds build nests, and so forth, One obvious difference is that technology has a history; animal technology has remained the same from time immemorial. In a sense, though, this only puts off the problem: granted evolution, the technological feats of a given species had to have been created over a period of time. Higher animals do exhibit some creativity: Köhler's apes, for example, discovered that by piling boxes and assembling a collapsible cane-pole they could reach an otherwise inaccessible supply of bananas.[3] However, the tools thus created seem to have an ad hoc status: they are not set aside for future employment, nor are they creatively reproduced. In the history of human technology both of these characteristics are outstanding: creativity and futurity. Among the animals, these features do not seem to occur together: either the tool-making involved is for the future, and then non-creative or it is creative, but not for the future.

A distinction might help here. An animal may hit upon an ad hoc solution to a problem posed by a situation. By association he might recall it in similar circumstances. He might even teach it in those circumstances to his offspring who would learn it by mimesis and thus a species-habit might be inculcated. But the origination, recall, and mimesis all occur in a here-and-now context. It is quite another matter to recall or create merely "in the mind," outside of any similarity in environmental contexts, a tool that one would then make for future use in a context other than the one in which the tool is conceived or produced. This would involve a process of disengagement, abstracting a universal principle from a particular context, and explicitly relating it to all similar contexts. Once that is possible, not only is creative technology possible but pure theory as well.

Human symbol making and symbol employment also stand in contrast to their analogues in the animal kingdom. Parrots can "parrot" human sounds, but sounding is not equivalent to speaking, except by extension. Bees and porpoises have elaborate systems of communication. Chimpanzees and apes have been taught rudimentary sign language and some of them are teaching it to their offspring. The study of bees has yielded some interesting results. Observers discerned that a bee would fly into a hive and go through a kind of dance, after which the other bees would fly directly to some supply of nectar. Careful study showed that each movement was coordinated with a set of directions, so that the bee was actually telling his fellows where to locate the supply.[4] Now, in the human situation, what appears to be a striking difference is the creativity in the formation of symbols by reason of the dissociability of the sensory patterns from the meaning-fields. Any visual pattern can come to stand for any meaning: *man, homo, anthropos, Mensch, hombre, l'homme* stand for the same meaning; but we could let $xy2$ serve the same function—or even $]'\&^®$ or just x. Furthermore, there is no necessary correlation between the sounds I make and the meaning, nor between the sounds and their current visual correlates listed above. The sound correlated with the visual pattern 'man' might be conventionally agreed upon to be that correlated presently with the visual pattern 'zyfl.' Only by convention, growing up out of a long tradition, are sounds and visual patterns correlated with meanings and with each other. There is thus a freedom from the empirically discernible features in human language, hence the possibility for creative symbol formation.

Moreover, communication between bees or apes or chimpanzees or porpoises seems restricted to biological purpose—perhaps at times spilling over into a kind of playfulness in the immediately present context—a kind of anticipation of the theoretical attitude as detachment from biological purpose. But as far as anyone knows, no animal disengages meanings from immediate contexts and/or biological purposes in order to develop a theory of biological purposes or of communication within biological contexts. Apes do not discuss or write treatises on *The Mentality of Apes* or bees on *The Communication of Bees*. The attempt to do theory in this way is the attempt to disengage the universal, as the focus of attention, from particular contexts.

A biologist who, like Darwin, claims that the whole phenomenon of humanness is simply another part of a mechanized system geared toward adjustment to the environment, is involved in that curious contradiction between form and content that is one of the profesional hazards into which scientists are prone to fall. For the content of the claim that all is simply relative to environmental adjustment involves a form of consciousness, which stands beyond adjustment to view it for what it is. It involves precisely a detachment from the vast struggle of life in order to make it an object of speculative vision.

A similar difficulty we have indicated above (chapter 2) in the claim to reduce consciousness to a set of complex observables: observables are all individuals in the environment; the claim involves standing beyond the environment to consider all such environments. And the same type of problem is present in the situation of the biologist who writes a lengthy treatise for the purpose of showing that there is no purpose in nature fully convinced that he is part of nature! Detachment from the observable environment and from the struggle for existence purposely aimed at theoretical comprehension of the universal principles of what is the case—such is the peculiar cosmic position of *Homo sapiens*.

The Proximate Inner Ground: Rationality

This brings us to a third definition of humanness—one that is not a matter of observationally discernible properties, but which grasps by reflection the inward ground of both tool making and symbol making: *A human being is a rational animal.*[5] This is a traditional definition in the Aristotelian line, often made fun of by those who don't know any better but think they do. It really means three things: (1) a human being is a *reasonable* animal; (2) a human being is a *reasoning* animal; (3) a human being is a *reason-grasping* animal.

It is the first meaning that critics latch onto: "Look around you: all the people most of the time, most of the people all of the time are unreasonable animals. How incredibly unperceptive those speculative daydreamers of the Aristotelian tradition! " But 'reasonable' describes a possibility, not something accessible simply by counting noses. Furthermore, reasonable and unreasonable are opposed characteristics of human conduct alone: they are the essential possibilities of an animal who has reason. Reasonable *activity* may or may not follow after a man has carried out a reasoning process; but if reasonable activity occurs, it follows from a reasoning process, working with principles and making inferences.

Reasoning is the activity of a rational animal and is usually associated with the explanation of the definition. It is correct, but not fundamental enough, for one can be a reasoning animal only if one has grasped the universal notions that form the premises of a reasoning process. Thus the reasoning process involved in the syllogism

All humans are mortal.
I am a human being.
Hence I am mortal.

is only possible after one has grasped the universal meanings 'human' and 'mortality'. In the Greek tradition, a human being is the animal that has the *logos*, the universal; and from this characteristic flows the capacity that we call logic—the ability to weave universals into reasoning processes.

The Greek *logos* is related to *legein*, which means "to gather." *Ratio*, its Latin translation, means "proportion" or "relation." Grasping the universal means seeing a relation to all actual or possible instances of a given meaning (the property of 'extension') and seeing that universal in relation to the world of meaning that defines it (the property of 'comprehension'). Man is the kind of animal who always distinguishes himself by grasping meanings, even though he may not always be very adept at reasoning or very reasonable in his actions.

It is this grasp of meaning that is brought into the space-time world in our written and spoken language, in our technology, and indeed in the totality of our institutions. Human language is only intelligible when the visual and audile patterns immanent in the immediate space-time context are attended to in their relation to the interrelated sets of universals that constitute our worlds of meaning. A graphic illustration of this may be seen were we to bring a physicist and a physiologist into a lecture to determine the sum total of immediate space-time events occurring there. The physicist sets up his oscilloscope and various other sensing devices; the physiologist wires the lecturer with electrodes. Everything is carefully charted. At the end of the lecture, someone asks the two scientists: "How did you like the lecture?" The reply: "We don't know—we weren't paying attention. But here are all the graphs and charts recording the physical and physiological features." It requires a special effort for the scientists to tear themselves out of the full concrete situation—the multi-dimensional world of interpersonal communication—and focus attention upon the abstracted portion that constitutes the region of empirical science.

Actually, though, the scientists are dwelling in that world in a different way, for performing scientific experiments takes place in terms of interpersonally developed categories of interpretation. Further, looking at and adjusting the machinery is analogous to the optometrist measuring the eyes. But when the scientists address one another about the apparatus, the glances they exchanged are not matters of checking apparatus, but of encountering persons, present in and exceeding the biological mechanisms of the eyeball.[6] The scientists are functioning as members of the scientific community. But the fact is that their *focus of attention* is not upon the interpersonal character of that world.

Actually, the physiologist is not really dealing with the full phenomena of human life, since the meaning-fields constitute the distinctive way in which the human body is alive. The object of biology, insofar as biology restricts itself to the observational surface and is not concerned with the act of sensing as well as the presence of meaning-fields, is only an abstracted portion of life. Human behavior as an empirical fact is the incarnation of the life of human consciousness.

Plato presents an example similar to that of the scientists at the lecture in the *Phaedo* where he speaks of the ridiculousness of explaining Socrates' sitting in prison by the position of his bones, joints, and so forth. The real explanation lies in the clash of human purposes borne by, and expressed in the embodied situation, subsuming under itself the laws of mechanics and organics: Socrates' purposes were opposed to the general purposes of the people of Athens.[7]

There is a similar truth in the field of technology. Individual tools are embodiments of the mental apprehension of general laws, creatively interrelated in view of general ends, a kind of mirror of the powers of the human mind. An adequate analysis of technology thus involves reflection upon the structures of human interiority, which grasps the laws disengaged from particular contexts and projects the general ends.[8]

And we could apply the same reasoning to the objects of sociological analysis: institutions. They are not identical with the space-time structures that incarnate them. Institutions are what Hegel calls Objective Mind, having space-time appearances intelligible only in relation to the universal meaning-fields that they embody.[9] Thus a college is not the buildings alone nor the sum of space-time events that occur in the buildings: it is rather these things as incarnating a set of goals and meanings[10]—though quite often, through stress on rote memorization, there is the tendency to reduce the institution to a set of space-time events.

Consider finally the difficulty of interpreting any of the expressions of the deeper realms of human experience: the printed page of poetry or prose or sacred writ have the same chemical content and sensory value as the sports page, a political propaganda sheet, or a business letter. Only he who has an inner eye with which to see and an inner ear with which to hear—an interiority developed to an underlying attunement to the depth behind the outward manifestation—can begin to "see" and to "hear." "Abyss cries out to abyss!" But surface can only be attuned to surface. "Eyes and ears are poor witnesses to men with barbarian souls.[11]

The Ultimate Ground: Metaphysicality

There is a more fundamental analysis to be made, yielding the fourth and ultimate definition: *A human being is a metaphysical animal.* The animal who grasps reasons, i.e., universals, is the animal who projects possibilities beyond immediate contexts: he is thus the animal who must choose. Hence the rational animal is traditionally considered to have *intellect* as the capacity to grasp the universal and *will* as the capacity to choose. Both aspects proceed out of a deeper ground.

Reason grasping, Aristotle claimed, takes place through the "illumination" of sense experience by the active intellect.[12] And we might illuminate that obscure statement by referring back to our analysis of the sixth and seventh dimensions. The sixth dimension deals with interrelated sets of restricted universals; the seventh deals with the unrestricted universality of the notion of Being as reference to the whole of what is or can be. Whence derives this notion of all that is or can be, of the absolute Whole? Could it come from the restricted objects of experience? How derive the unrestricted from the restricted, the totality from the part? The notion of Being, we suggest, is not derivative: it is the root from which all other notions are derived— though not without relation to experience. To be a mind is to be a (relatively) self-illumined relation to the totality of the actual or possible. (And the notion of Being expresses objectively what the mind is subjectively.) Coming into this field of reference to all actual or possible instances, particular objects are seen "in the light of" this reference: the notion of "all actual or possible instances" is contracted to the limits specified by the particular objects while the particular object is extended to all of its kind. A particular pen is thus seen as an instance of a meaning extending to all actual or possible pens. The restricted concept 'pen' is abstracted from sense-experience through the illuminative action of the mind moving in the direction of the whole of Being. Thus 'rationality' is founded upon the reference to Being, upon 'metaphysicality'.

Figure 3.1 illustrates this analysis of the two sources of concept formation. The process involved in concept formation is thus dual-directional: *illumination* by the notion of Being, of all actuality and possibility—a movement from mind to things; *abstraction* of the form of the individual as sense object from its individual context—a movement from things to mind. The resultant of the process is a *contraction* of the notion of all actuality and possibility to all actual or possible instances of the form in question, and an *extension* of the form to its universal applicability.[13]

This implies no intuition into the inner essence of a being. What is universalized in the first place is the sensory surface. Through the slow but developing interplay of sensory surface and the inner reflectedness of living experience, the "inner meaning" of that surface is interpreted in various ways. When the depth of inwardness is flattened out—as it is in our cult of outwardness, of "images" and "looks"—some form of positivism or empiriomorphism is the result. The sensory surface becomes self-referential: all meaning is derived from *its* structures. Consciousness, inwardness, is explained away as being simply a matter of complex exteriority.

Figure 3.1   THE RELATION BETWEEN MIND AND THING

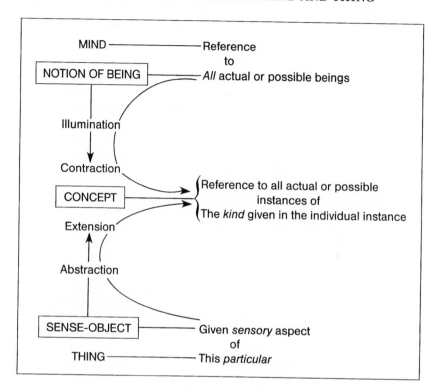

But the form of the claim refutes the content: all the content of exteriority is content *for* consciousness and thus involves the forms of consciousness in its explanation. However, this is not to say that the human being remains locked up in his own subjectivity and that the thing-in-itself remains unknowable. For subjectivity is, at base, reference to Being as the mysterious Totality and is thus self-present as part of being. The human being is an instance of being in the state of self-illumination, of being revealed from the inside. It is this self-presence that is the primary referent in terms of which the sensory surface is to be interpreted.

Take another route. Reasoning is made possible not only by the ability to grasp the universal concepts (and judgments) that form the premises of the reasoning process. There is also required insight into the fundamental principles that govern the process itself: identity, noncontradiction, and excluded middle.[14] Being as the encompassing Totality, both collectively and distributively, i.e., with every form and instance of being considered together or in each individual case, is such that each item remains itself throughout its span—even such that, after it passes, it remains "forever after" with a kind of "objective immortality," always true, unalterable in its facticity.[15] Each being, being itself, can be identified or separated from a basis of comparison, and therefore identified or separated from other self-identified beings. And each being is such that it either has or has not a given property, does or does not exist outside being merely thought about. "The light of Being," shining throughout the whole, makes possible all predication and all inference made by the rational animal.

Self-presence in relation to the disclosure of the mysterious Whole is likewise *the ground of human freedom.* For to be referred in this way to the whole is to be inwardly pried loose by nature from closure within particular contexts, physical and cultural: it is to be inwardly free in the most fundamental dimension of our being. Because of this freedom we are "condemned to choose" and thus to be responsible for our situation. But such freedom is *incarnate* freedom, dialectically tied to the physical situation, dependently independent of it.[16]

Contents constantly flit in and out of our field of attention, arising from without but also from within, floating up from the unconsciousness substratum of our lives. However, we might or might not pay attention to them, work with them, develop them and act in terms of them—indeed, *humanly* working, developing, and acting takes place within the field of "paying attention." which is the focusing of our center of freedom. The mode of attending is, of course, a function of our basic projects, which are largely functions of our interaction with the culture; but the *fact* of attending stems from our radical freedom, in terms of which we can always say no and thus also yes. The human person's being a "Yea-sayer" to beings is dependent upon being, at base, *negation* of finitude through infinite, metaphysical distance. The human being is a "Yea-sayer" to Being and thus a potential "Nay-sayer" to beings by his nature.

There are several important distinctions that have to be made when speaking of freedom. At a first level there is the notion of the free, i.e., unimpeded, functioning of a nature: the free fall of a stone, the free flight of a bird. Freedom of such functioning implies freedom from whatever restrains it. Such freedom is obviously not at all incompatible with a completely deterministic view of things. Political freedom as not being determined from without by authority is itself compatible with such a view. And what is often meant by such freedom is removal of the political-legal-social blocks that stand in the way of letting ourselves be determined by our urges.

Within the complex field of consciousness, restraint of urges is the premise for the freeing of a rational pattern of experience that sets limits to urges and to envisioned possibilities in view of some end to be achieved.[17] One significant such end is coming to understand the character of the urges that well up within us. The rational pattern of experience is freed through the chaining of the urge-dominated pattern. So we exchange one kind of freedom for another. But the ground of the possibility for making the choice is our primordially being-pried-loose from determination by biology and culture—even the culture that teaches us restraint of urges—and our being referred to Being, referred to the Whole. Metaphysical distance grants us a kind of free-floating freedom, a capacity of radical self-unchaining, irrespective of the grounds for the chaining. But it also means that we are "condemned to freedom," "without excuse," i.e., that we cannot simply drift with our biology or our culture without taking responsibility for that drift.[18]

It is important to point out, however, that the premise for that freedom is the capacity of self-possession sufficient to make a responsible judgment. In sleep, in states of drunkenness, when overcome by passion, when suffering severe disturbances based upon chemical imbalance, or in psychotic states, we are not self-determining. In approaching these states of consciousness, the self-determining self tends in the direction of a passive center, being carried by the interplay of stimuli arising from without and "from below," i.e., from the physical-physiological mechanisms, until the conscious self fades out entirely and the organic center resumes control—at times, in semifunctional interplay with the environment. Think of the case of the drunkard who, oblivious of what he is doing and of his surroundings, yet finds his way home. But in the normal mode of human wakefulness we are able to "back off" from the semiautomatism of the biological-sensory situation, "return to ourselves," reflect and bring to bear upon the situation various frameworks of meaning for which we then take responsibility in applying them to the situation. I make the claim to tell the truth, the claim that the framework of interpretation I bring to bear upon the data really fits in such a way that all observers would, if properly instructed and willing, be able to make the same claim. Making a judgment and taking responsibility are equivalent acts. Judgment is a mode of responsible self-possession, of free employment to commit ourselves to that to which, at the seventh dimension of our being, we are directed: the real-being-in-itself of what is.

The free-flowing movements of biological urges, of habit-structures, feelings and desires built up over a lifetime of interplay between the self and the social environment, and within the self between biological-social rootage and deliberate choice—the swirling mass that constitutes the "me" of the moment—is the artist's material given over to the self to fashion within the limits of possibility here and now afforded by the way the past enters into my present. Oddly enough, though, the "material" is not other than I myself, for I myself am this very totality in tension with the capacity for relative self-determination. The Whole is determinate-indeterminate. And depending upon what one chooses to do at any given time, the total mass of the self entering into the present may be experienced as supportive or obstructive—or, more likely, a mixture of the two. One might freely, happily choose to consume alcohol to excess, enjoying the exhilaration, the freedom from inhibitions that it affords. But if one becomes an alcoholic, one may reach the point where he no longer chooses this state because of the attendant lack of ability that alcoholism brings in its train to engage in more controlled activity. But he is now captive to the sedimentation of the results of past choices, split in two by habitual desire on the one hand and current choice on the other. His free choice to engage in a rational pattern of experience is rendered ineffective by the nonfreedom of the result of past free choices. In moments of lucidity he has free choice: minimally the choice of the attitude he takes toward his addiction; further, the possible choice to develop a rational pattern of experience; but his effective freedom is greatly inhibited if not obliterated by the prior institution of habit-structures that preclude effective freedom.[19] However, the development of the rational pattern of experience as a matter of habit opens up the possibility of ever more effective freedom. Freedom of choice means very little if it is not significantly linked to freedom to carry out that choice. And that involves not only the negative freedom from outside restrictions but, more deeply, inner freedom developed by rational habits. How free am I to play the piano? I am free to *choose* to play the piano; but I am not effectively free because I have not narrowed down my past possibilities, submitted myself to grueling discipline, attended a conservatory, and annexed myself to a master in order to free that potentiality I might have for playing the piano.

There are at least two different sorts of habits. There are those like speaking or walking and the whole range of skills that we may or may not wish to employ at any given time. And there are those that are compelling or repelling, whose objects we cannot do without or do with. The latter set ranges from habits like compulsive eating and drinking, alcoholism and drug addiction, to "doing your duty," responding to those in need, and being unable to perform deliberate acts of murder, rape, theft, and the like. In the latter cases, one has become so connatural with the good and so instinctively set against evil that one feels empty in not performing the good and anguished at the very thought of performing the evil.[20] One is then "more free" to avoid the evil and pursue the good insofar as one prereflectively, instinctively moves away from the former and toward the latter.

But there are difficulties in the situation. Such connaturality is deeply tied to socially conditioned reflexes that are based upon differing values. The same compulsiveness that might draw us to the genuine good and repel us from the genuine evil might also function in the "duty" to eat one's captured enemy and to avoid various "taboos." The superego as the introjection of the norms of the community can be as irrationally compulsive as the id, the impersonal insistence of our bodily desires.[21] And even our connaturality with the genuine good may be such as to operate independently of developed prudential judgment which alerts us to the ever-changing character of circumstances that require modification in our application of fundamentally good orientations. Basically good people can be afflicted with a blind and unintelligent stubbornness, especially among those who are religiously committed. Perhaps nowhere else does the blind adhesion to tradition without the intervention of intelligent assessment appear as genuine nobility more than in religion. Hence the tendency to closure and fanaticism that crops up continually among religious people.

Effective freedom is tied to "institutionalization" in the broadest sense of the term, understanding by 'institution' here a mode of routinization.[22] First there is the prepersonal institution of biological routines that is the indispensible foundation for everything else. Then there is the institution of habit-structures in ourselves. That is significantly related to the prior institution of 'institutions' in the narrower sense, of social structures, beginning with language. Institutions at the distinctively human level (beyond the necessities of biological nature) are the sedimented result of past choices of those long dead, of those now surrounding me, and of me myself. Decisions are literally "cuttings-off," the killing of possibilities—though we like to think of them more positively as actuating possibilities. But the killing or chaining of possibilities—their nonfreedom—is the condition for the emergence of other possibilities for individuals and for groups. Social institutions make sense insofar a they effectively bring about the freeing of the potentialities they are meant to free.

There are several factors that have to be considered when it comes to applying these considerations to social institutions. One has to do with the overall set of possibilities whose freeing is institutionalized in a given society, since choosing some leads to blockage of or to lesser support for others. Another factor is the effective organization of the institution for the achievement of its ends. Different societies choose to organize themselves in different ways. The development of one way leads to the inhibition of another. Consideration finally turns upon the question of the possible hierarchical structure to human potentialities, which we will treat in our next chapter.

The emergence of a rational pattern of experience is fundamental to the freeing of our possibilities to shape our institutions in more efficient ways toward the ends we project. The establishment of institutions as cultural habits is reciprocally tied to the formation of habits in the individual. Insofar as such habits allow people to function freely within a horizon of possibilities, they extend to the culture and the person the free functioning of a nature. Culture, social and individual, becomes second nature. Culture then establishes what we might call "freed freedom": institution frees potentialities for free (i.e., unimpeded) functioning. But the freedom that sets up such institutions is a "freeing freedom," a movement beyond current possibilities. But this itself is significant only insofar as a rational pattern of experience is instituted (i.e., freed to function) within society and within individuals. A rational pattern involves the pattern of assessment and consequent action based upon full alertness to all the significant parameters of a given situation. This moves beyond a rationalism that applies rules to situations by deduction to a rationality that attends to the *ratio*, the immanent *logos* of a situation that demands the modification, suspension, elimination, and generation of rules.

But even such a pattern has its own dangers, insofar as it may lose sight of the fundamental potentiality of humanness and the fundamental freedom: the freeing of our thrust toward the Whole, developing at its most inward level our presence-to-Being. It is this primordial dimension of presence-to-Being as fundamental freedom that bathes the whole of our situation in its light. This fundamental open attunement to the manifestations of Being subtends all other forms of human meaningfulness. In attending to that dimension of our being, each of us begins to answer the basic question, Who am I? I am basically a metaphysical animal—but that is to say, an existent emptiness hungering for the Absolute, fundamental negation of the immediate, absence from the flowing present—away in the direction of the Whole, incarnated in the look, in the gesture, in the word, in the total comportment of my here-and-now-present bodily reality. (See Figure 3.2 for a diagrammatic summary of the basic distinctions we have been considering.)

And yet the direction of the dominant culture, whose metaphysics of observedness finds philosophic expression in positivism, is to conceal the negativity by focusing upon the actually posited data and interpretations, patterns of behavior and institutions forming

Figure 3.2 FREEDOM AND NATURE

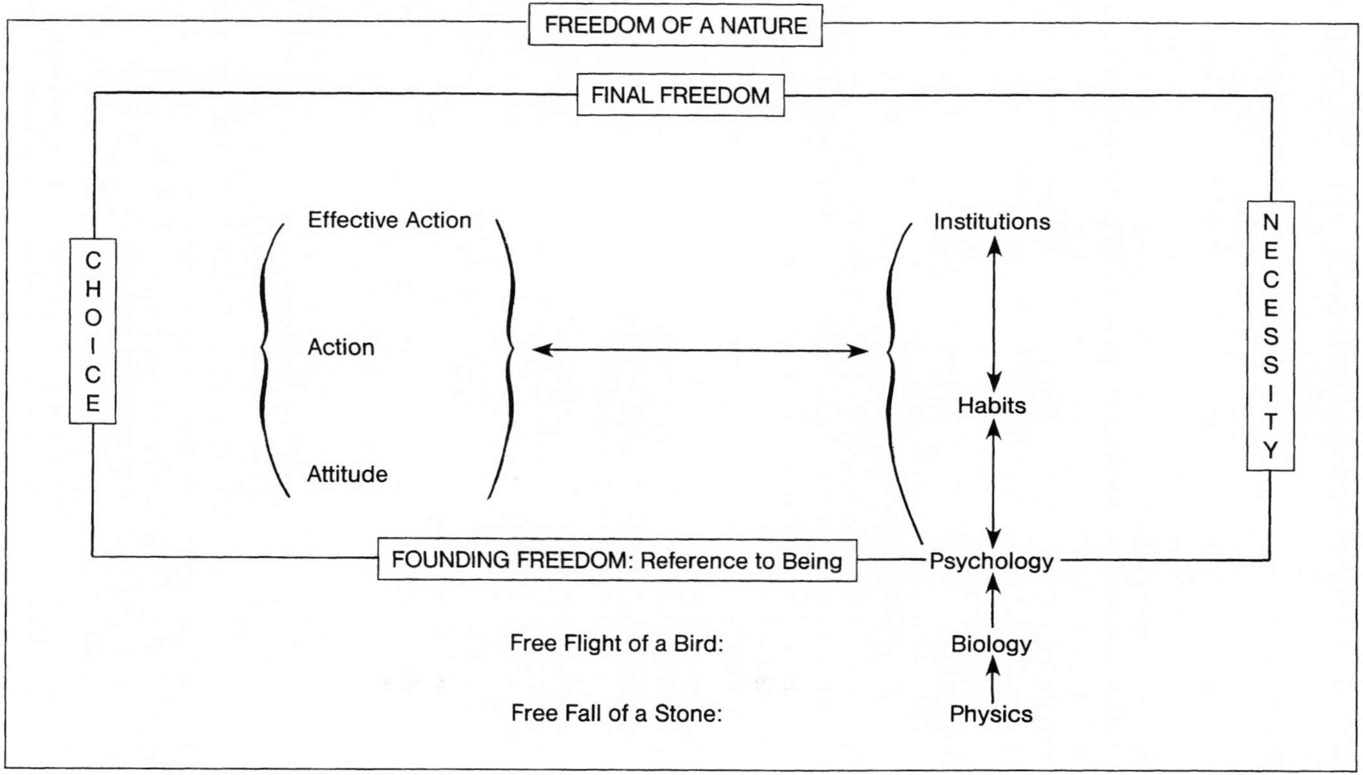

the current system.[23] The fullness and comfort of this womb of actuality is broken and the transcendental freedom of man developed by critical questioning, by the development of new possibilities not determined by the current social and cultural parameters, and by the cultivization of a sensitivity to mystery. Questioning calls attention to a negation, a hole in the fullness of positive presence, a discomforting Not.[24] Concern with the opening of possibilities again disturbs the Here in terms of the Not-Here. Sensitizing to mystery involves a projection into the Not and the More in the things that already stand in the field of positive sense-presence and interpretative focus.[25] A priori relation to, in the mode of prethematic manifestation of, the mysterious Totality of Being includes prethematic manifestation of the whole of any given being—both the self and any Other. We know that there is the More, the Beyond, the not-manifest Whole—which is manifest therefore as not-manifest. It is the function of one form of poetizing to attend to the Not and the More by means of the here-and-now manifest.

Insofar as the current educational system emphasizes mastery of techniques and accumulation of information, it tends to discourage questioning, stifle creativity, and close off mystery. Insofar as the now quiescent counter culture promoted critical questioning, explored alternative possibilities of life-style, and promoted the sense of mystery, it reached toward the metaphysical center of man whose essence is freedom. But insofar as asceticism and meditation gave place to a kind of formless indulgence in the gratification of urges, the metaphysical dimension was swamped and freedom in its full dimensionality progressively lost.

"Soul" as Center of Meaning

One might ponder with profit the wisdom of the Aristotelian notion of 'soul' implicit here. 'Soul' for Aristotle is the life of a body; and soul can be vegetative in a growing, nourishing, reproducing organism; it is sentient in the sensing animal. (Seeing is the 'soul' of the eyeball.)[26] In the case of the human being, 'soul' is the meaning-bearing, meaning-grasping, meaning-expressing life of the body.

Attend once more to our seven-dimensional model presented in chapter 2. Notice that two-dimensional space (the plane) is contiguous to, though distinct from and irreducible to, one-dimensional space (the line); three-dimensional space (the solid), in turn, similarly follows inseparably upon two-dimensional space and is related inseparably to time—all without destroying the unity of the space-time body. The plane is not separable physically from the solid, from the line, from the point, nor also from time; nonetheless it is necessarily distinct from (not identical with) them. In other words, in our model we have a case of *distinction without separation or separability*. This is not the case when we consider the actual parts of a four-dimensional body: my hand is not only distinct from my head, it is physically separable from it.

Applying this consideration to the inner dimensions indicated by the ancient notion of 'soul', we have the possibility of conceiving of a radical distinctness of dimensions without having to yield to a sort of dualism which views 'soul' as one thing complete in itself related to a body as another complete thing — the old "ghost in the machine" doctrine.[27] Sensory consciousness, though factually dependent upon a four-dimensional nervous system, is, by reason of its intentionality, structurally distinct from that system. Intellectual interpretation, though dependent upon the sensory-nervous system for its activation, yet transcends, in its intention of universality, that five-dimensional continuum and is transcended in its turn by the basic structure of mind as infinite openness. Using the analogy of dimensions and their relatedness, we can thus conceive of the possibility of a unitary entity simultaneously existent in seven dimensions. 'Soul' is the innerness of that multidimensional entity.

'Soul' and 'inwardness', however, have to be broadened beyond their manifestation in consciousness, for the wholeness of ourselves is not our consciousness, especially not our focal consciousness. As we have seen, the focal is always linked to prior, implicit, nonfocal features: to the lived body and its motor habits as they are available to and supportive of the focal region of conscious life, to the conceptual field, to our primordial presence to Being.[28] The clear zone of focal awareness is girt about by a zone of lesser clarity as material open to conscious shaping (within significant limits). But the lived body in its broadest sense is expression within the region of prereflective awareness of the nonconscious dimension of biological process, the darkness of preconscious nature. 'Soul' comprises all that as well, being *the life* — biological, appetitive, intellectual and spiritual — of this sensorily present body-object.

The focus of conscious life is thus supported by three great unconscious spheres which, together with consciousness, comprise our being. One is the underlying thrust of our biological nature. We experience it as hunger, as thirst, and as sexual desire. Conscious life acts out of the experience of desire and turns it to whatever purposes it will. But the underlying biological nature moves in a determinate direction, prepersonally pushing toward the maturation and sustenance of the organism and toward the perpetuation of the species.[29]

The second great unconscious sphere is that of culture-impregnated habit-structure, learned in great part prepersonally, structuring the field of attention, acting as a selective filter in relation to what is sensorily presented.[30] But this second sphere is made possible by interplay with the first, the biological sphere, and the third sphere, the underlying, prepersonal but personality-grounding movement of our nature toward Being, toward the Totality.

The task of becoming human is the task of gathering the multiple and conflicting drives that come out of the lived body as mediated by the culture into a unity more and more deeply penetrated by the transcendental thrust. Learning to quiet the clamorings of all these drives in order to make room for the calm insistence of the metaphysical dimension is the indispensable condition for penetrating our own lived embodiment with ultimate meaning and thus raising the body itself to a higher mode of being. Detachment from the body through meditative and ascetical practice is the condition for immersion in the body through meaningful speech, gesture, and action. The inward dimensions of 'Soul' thus penetrate the outward dimensions of 'body' to tighten the bonds of our seven-dimensional unity.

The Human Being as the Sick Animal

Peter Weiss has one of the drooling inmates of the asylum in his play *Marat/Sade* proclaim that "man is a mad animal."[31] Ludwig Klages viewed "the spirit as contradictory to the soul."[32] Freud saw the inevitability of discontent as resultant from the necessary suppression of instinctual desires that civilization requires.[33] The mythology of the centaur expresses the odd duality of humanness. Sartre speaks of consciousness as a disease that Being has contracted, a worm gnawing at its heart, a source of perpetual, irremovable lack of self-coincidence.[34] Traditional Hebrew-Christian religion divines an original Fall and consequent present split in human experience.[35] Platonism views the soul as entombed in the body.[36]

The basic tension of humanness is set up by the interplay, on the one hand, of an animal-based immediacy that is a dialectical circle of sensory surface and animal desire locked within the flowing Now and, on the other hand, a reference to Being that requires situating the sensory circle within the anticipated but not properly known totality of Being encompassing and transcending time as a whole. The reference to Being unsettles the tendency to settle down in animal immediacy;[37] and animal immediacy disallows the flight into an initially vacuous Beyond.[38]

The difficulty involved in that basic tension is compounded by the fact that the space between the animal Now and the empty reference to the Whole is always partially filled with the residue of culture as a created/discovered mode (or actually overlapping, conflicting, and corroborating modes) of concrete relationship to the Whole. The necessary partiality of culture sets up a conflict between itself and the Whole to which it refers, revealing and concealing that Whole. This leads to an intrinsic conflict between the culture and those individuals particularly sensitive to the More, as well as between the culture and those individuals (of much greater numbers) immersed in their animal immediacy. Culture is both cure and disease for the sick animal who seemingly can never be fully healed. Otherworldly religion and Kantian moralism are admissions that healing lies only on "the other side" of temporal existence.[39]

The Human Being as Religious Animal

'Soul' and 'religion' are notions that typically go together, not so much insofar as 'soul' is conceived of as the animating principle that brings unity to the organism, but insofar as it is conceived of as the locus of reference to Being, reference to the totality. The religious animal is not simply preoccupied with how to get his food, to mate, and to care for his offspring while avoiding or overcoming his natural enemies. Nor is he simply concerned with how to adjust to the culture. Beyond all this, he is concerned with his place in the whole scheme of things and how he might come into proper relation with that Whole. However, the scheme presented varies significantly and often contradictorily from culture to culture and even within a given culture. And the methods for coming into proper relation to the Whole so conceived a fortiori differ—even within the same overarching scheme. Dogma, liturgy, and morality (creed, cult, and code) differ widely, but their presence bears witness to the underlying structure of humanness we have been at pains to elaborate thus far. As Schopenhauer claimed (and Aristotle before him), metaphysics as putative vision of the whole, or at least as a concern for the totality, is a necessity of human nature. He went on to point out that religion itself is actually metaphysics for the many.[40]

It is within the context of the religious orientation in particular that the aletheic dimension is a special matter of concern. Always it stands in some tension with the orthotic. The Buddha, e.g., renounced dogma entirely in favor of the practice of the eightfold path to enlightenment and liberation.[41] St. Francis held in great suspicion the scholastic theology that developed during his time, viewing it as a threat to the spiritual life.[42] "Living in the presence of God" is the core of religious life, with creed, cult, and code dialectically related to that center, both being fashioned by the modality of that presence and fashioning its character.

Though the just man may live by faith, faith itself must be distinguished from a mere social reflex and a way of feeling comfortable and superior. Living faith is more like the belief involved in our earlier meditation where everyone *knows* he is to die but no one *believes* it. Belief involves "a real presence." More than the thoughtless claim to be a believer, faith is "being gripped by ultimate concern."[43] The religious animal lives aletheicly in the seventh dimension.[44]

The Human Being as Historical

Man's being metaphysical means that there is a fundamental dimension transcending both biological immediacy and cultural mediation in the direction of the whole of reality. That transcendence is a transcendent emptiness hungering for the Whole, not a revelation of the positive features of the Whole. Such transcendence is dialectically tied to our biological insertion in the immediate spatioltemporal environment that situates us bodily. Consequently the data gained through our biological senses has to be interpreted in terms of the transcendental thrust: sensing has to be mediated by meanings that specify and concretize for us the way in which we are related to the whole. Cultural systems emerge as differing ways of concretizing that relatedness. Philosophical systems develop as later stages of a culture, attempting to make explicit, critical, and integral the cultural system. But all stand relative to the material available at a given time and in a given place. All bear the stamp of their spatiotemporal origins, and yet all rise above their origins as designs upon the whole.

Our being a metaphysical animal therefore involves our being an historical animal, i.e., one who defines and redefines from differing perspectives the way he is inserted into the Whole. But this need not involve a purely relativistic view. The conditions for historical existence and the concept of historical existence itself fix the transhistorical conditions of historical existence. And should these transhistorical conditions not be recognized, we would then be caught in the paradox of relativism—the occupational hazard of the social-behavioral scientist—claiming that the absolute truth about the human situation is that all is relative, The structure of the claim again refutes the content, for the claim is absolute and is an instance of the content that relativizes all claims. The human being is an historical animal because he is a metaphysical animal; because he is a metaphysical animal, he must be an historical animal, one engaged in a never-ending search for fuller relations to the Whole.

4 *Metaphysics and Practicality*

The practical thing for a traveler
who is uncertain of his path is not
to proceed with the utmost rapidity
in the wrong direction: it is to
consider how to find the right one.

> R. H. Tawney,
> *The Acquisitive Society*

The inaptitude of the run of men
for metaphysics, particularly in our
period, is certainly bound up with
the fact that they find it impossible
to conceive of a purpose which lies
outside the order of the practical,
which cannot be translated into the
language of action.

> Gabriel Marcel, *The Mystery of Being*

Are we so much fools of organization, bustle, and speed that we are
no longer able to be friends of the
essential, the simple, and the
stable?

> Martin Heidegger,
> *Kant and the Problem of Metaphysics*

Nor are those ideas only to be
regarded as practical which are
pursued for the sake of practical
results, but much more the
thoughts and contemplations
which are independent and
complete in themselves.

> Aristotle, *Nicomachean Ethics*

81

At this point we should be in position to deal with some of the standard blocks that prevent serious consideration of metaphysics. Invariably people complain that metaphysics is too abstract and too impractical and what they need, obviously, is what is concrete and practical. Such statements do not stand isolated, but grow out of a context afforded by the interaction of the individual and his total cultural milieu: they incarnate a communal *Weltanschauung*, a vision of the Whole. Our task is to uncover that vision reflectively and subject it to critique so that the relevance of metaphysics may be demonstrated. The vision incarnates the fundamental thrust of the human being for what is real and what is good: in the antimetaphysics of the dominant culture, these are the concrete and the practical specifically defined. In this chapter we will complete the exploration of the question of humanness that has been our major concern thus far by a consideration of the question of value in relation to the notion of practicality. In the following chapter we will effect the transition to the question of Being, of reality, via consideration of the question of abstract and concrete.

The Meaning of Practicality

Note first of all that there is a latent tendency in approaching the question before us, namely the question of the practicality of metaphysics, to identify the practical and the good. To ask, "Is it practical?" is often equivalent to asking, "Is it good?"

It takes little reflection to see that this will not do: it is the good that makes something practical, not vice versa. Business courses are practical because they enable us to get a job; the job is practical because it enables us to make money; money is practical because it enables us to purchase maximum gratification in the areas of food, drink, sex, sight, and sound. Business courses, jobs, money—all are practical. But what is practical about pleasure? Nothing, really. Pleasure is just good; and anyone not spoilt by prejudgments knows that to be the case in the experience of it. And it is the good of pleasure in this case that makes the other things to be good in the sense of practical. But whether such hedonism is the basic good for human beings depends upon a view of humanness as a kind of pleasure-machine, a mechanism to whose correct manipulation states of satisfaction correspond.

But there are other ends and other concepts of humanness possible, even in the sequence of business courses-job-money. One obvious and widespread alternative is to conceive of the sequence as income for the support of a family, where the closeness of family ties is the true center. Further, one might stop at the job as an end and conceive of money only as a by-product: to be active and creative is the good. Again, one might consider service toward others exercised through the job as the good. Or one might view the exercise of power that both job and money bring as the good and spurn the softness involved in hedonism. In any case, it is the end that confers the character of good upon the "practical" tasks that lead to the end—and it is a view of the nature of humanness that underpins that.

There would be some sense, then, considering an expansion of the notion of practicality in keeping with its correlation with the good by reflecting upon the origin of the Greek word *praxis*, making. We might "make" means—money, tools—and we might "make" ends, e.g., health, pleasure; but the fundamental making involved in all human activity is the self-making of the human being. The ultimate form of practicality, that which makes all practicalities practical, is the making of humanness.

Since, as we have been at some pains to show thus far, a human being is a seven-dimensional entity, there are various levels of self-making. And these levels are hierarchically arranged. If it is the case that hyperconcern with achieving levels of self-making that will turn out to be hierarchically lower tends to block off development of what would be higher levels, we would have a highly impractical situation developing. A business, e.g., whose marketing research grew to such proportions that it left no capital adequate for the production and distribution process would be a highly impractical enterprise. So also with the building of humanness.

A distinction at this point may help us to see, hopefully in a more than verbal way, what self-making might mean at the higher levels. Here we turn to a consideration of value. But instead of approaching it solely from the viewpoint of what might be called objective value, i.e., value that allegedly can be seen by the unprejudiced, I suggest we place objective consideration within the wider horizon of the life-world. By that I mean we ought to take into consideration the lived involvement of the person in disclosing values. And here the fundamental distinction would be between what I call *values of immanence* and *values of transcendence*. The ground of the distinction lies in the essential structure of the valuing subject. Although all values, I claim, are linked to the actuation of levels within the human subject, some values tend toward closure, and others open us up. And the distinction between closed and open, immanent and transcendent, depends not only upon the structure of the value but also upon the mode of appropriation by the valuing subject.

In our seven-dimensional approach, we have distinguished three dimensions of interiority: sensory, rational, and metaphysical. They are distinguishable but not dissociable: they ever impinge upon one another, each level modifying the others (cf. our reflections in the second chapter upon the formation of an inner *Gestalt*). The higher are informing of and informed by the lower: sense experience modifies both our interpretative frame and our fundamental mode of presence, and is, in turn, modified by the latter. But one or the other level can and does constitute the center of focus both in the case of individual situations and in the case of one's overall life thrust. To the actualization of each level there correspond distinctive values. (See the chart in figure 4.1, which links this chapter to chapters 2 and 3.)

Immanence

Corresponding to the achievement of the sense level there are first of all values and disvalues of sense: pleasure and pain.[1] Anyone who experiences them knows that they are—at least apart from the way in which they are integrated into the fuller human context—good and bad respectively. It is a rather sophisticated mode of self-deception that can find no good in pleasure, and it is a perversion to find satisfaction in pain for its own sake. But as Plato pointed out long ago, pleasure tends to generate its own antinomy, not only in the obvious sense of the hangover after the party, but also in the sense of the deeper possibility of debilitating or even destroying its organic base. Though animals generally are governed by restraints built up in terms of a desire-tension-pursuit-acquisition-release-rest cycle, the presence of openness to the infinite in our case pushes us to exceed the bounds of such cycles and exposes us to the temptation of "infinitizing" all our desires. Reflection has to come to the aid of pleasure to rescue it from itself, at least aiding us in "tuning up" the machine for maximum performance and thus maximum gratification within reasonable limits defined by organic well-being (Epicurean wisdom).[2] Relative to our metaphysical thrust for the fullness of being, the sensations of pleasure and pain, remaining at a level of response to appearance-relative-to-organic-need are values of immanence. But they can also be assimilated into our metaphysical thrust and thereby sublimated into Eros for the highest, as Plato described in his *Symposium*.[3]

As a sensing body, i.e., an animal, we are born into a herd with its peculiar living habits: in the human group, by reason of the presence of the metaphysical dimension, the dimension of creative freedom, such life habits exhibit an immense creative variation from group to group. But insofar as the mode of appropriation rests entirely upon the acceptance of the herd mores without reference to the broader reaches of the universal, corresponding to the rational-metaphysical

Figure 4.1 METAPHYSICS AND HUMANNESS (A Tabular Summary)

JUDGMENTAL MODEL	STRUCTURES OF INTENTIONALITY	DEFINITIONS OF HUMANNESS	VALUES
This	*Sensing:* yields the appearance of individual bodies in the environment relative to organic needs.	From an observational viewpoint, compared with others a human is: *same* as body, organism, animal; *different* as tool maker and symbol-maker. The basis of the differences: →	*Sense:* as individual organism *Life:* as herd-member: courage, family-feeling, patriotism
a pen	*Interpreting:* in terms of shared universal meanings in worlds of meaning. INTELLECTION	A human is a *rational* (i.e. a universal-conscious) animal, having intellectual and violational functions, grounded in: →	*Spirit:* {Moral, Aesthetic, Intellectual} Objective
is	*Judging-Presence:* unlimited openness to the whole range of what is or can be.	A human is a *metaphysical* animal.	*Sacred* ———— Subjective
Chapter II. "The Many Dimensions of Humanness"		Ch. III. "Toward a Definition of Humanness"	Ch. IV. "Metaphysics and Practicality"

structure of humanness, even objectively higher order values, assented to, can become immanent values and not transcendent values.

Transcendence

The distinction between immanent and transcendent values emerges clearly when we focus attention upon the rational and metaphysical levels, for in their basic intentionality they relate to that which transcends all particular contexts. It has been argued by some that the formal property that makes a position truly ethical is its universalizability. That means that, regardless of the *content* of a particular position, the *structure* or *form* it must take in order to have its enunciator accounted moral is that he sincerely consider it to be universalizable: i.e., that any person situated the way the individual in question happens to be, with certain habit structures and a specific limited fund of insight would have to take the same position. So a sincere Nazi (presuming that to be possible) holding as ethical the position that all Jews must be eliminated and discovering that he is really the bastard son of his mother's Jewish paramour, would have to turn himself in for slaughter. He would be ethically sincere inside the area of ethics but by no means at its center.[4] Kant saw this clearly: the basic formal property of the ethical disposition is the disposition to "act only according to that maxim by which you can at the same time will that it should become a universal law."[5]

However, ethics (even Kantian ethics) is not, as many claim, merely formal. One might (as Kant did) come to some insight into a particular *objective content* founding ethics by focusing upon the same tendency toward the manifestness of the universal in the human subject:the objective truth about human subjectivity is that it is a relation of manifestness to the universal, ultimately to the Whole. It is this transcendence of all systems of closure in the direction of the Whole that confers dignity upon the human subject. More than a piece of complex matter within the here-and-now, more than a particular subject in a particular historic community, the human subject has, by reason of its metaphysical thrust, something of the character of the Absolute. Hence at this level the first principle of content in an objective value scheme is the inviolability of the human subject. Thus in one of Kant's formulations of the unconditional, "categorical" imperative at the basis of ethics: "Act so that you treat humanity, whether in your own person or in that of another, always as an end and never as a means only."[6]

"Humanity" here does not mean the collected whole of mankind, but a peculiar feature of the human species distinguishing it from all others. According to Kant, things of nature (and we ourselves insofar as we are things of nature, i.e., in the nondistinctively human aspect of ourselves) act in accordance with the laws of nature, doing what they do necessarily. But humans, in their distinctive humanness, act in accordance with a *conception* of law.[7] That involves an awareness of the universal and, by reason of the freedom—linked to such awareness—from being wholly determined by the laws of nature, the capacity to give ourselves our own laws, i.e., to determine the principles for shaping our actions. Things of nature are thus heteronomous (from the Greek *heteros*, "other," and *nomos*, "law"), determined by law; humans are autonomous, self-legislating. The mutually implicated capacity of the apprehension of universal law and of free self-legislation is what Kant means by the quality of "humanity." And that, whether in ourselves or in others, as an essential possibility of humanness, ought to be treated as an end in itself and not merely as a means to something else. It deserves fundamental respect. So the cultivation of the intellect and the development of creativity constitute ends in themselves and ought not simply be treated as instruments in the service of bodily based desires. But one respects humanity also in seeing to the sustenance of the biological prerequisites, in ourselves and in others, for the functioning of those higher levels.

The prereflective, grounding openness to the whole makes possible our choice either to follow out that openness in an explicit, deliberate way, or to remain locked within certain aspects of biology and culture. But following out that openness means relation to the wholeness—beyond and through appearance—of each being (and not simply each human being). Respect for the integrity of all things is thus essential to cultivating our own center, attaining to our own self-realization as metaphysical animals.

Integral to our respect for our fellow humans as transcending relations to the whole is concern for their (and our own) respect for the integrity of things. Hence we can move beyond the enlightened species-egoism of many contemporary ecologists who are challenging the unenlightened individual egoism of the industrial exploiters of nature, claiming that, for the sake of our own survival, we ought better to calculate our treatment of nature. The principle we are proposing is that respect for natural things as values in themselves progressively establishes, in that very act of respecting, fuller humanness, without which survival itself would only have minimal meaning.

There is also a reciprocity here between individual ethics and social ethics. Respect for one's own dignity as a person involves the obligation of developing fundamental openness and removing the blocks that stand in the way of such openness. It also means that one places no blocks in the way of another's openness and thus does nothing to fortify him within the closed circle of the values of immanence. Indeed, respect for the other implies a self-purification just in order that one does not, by lack of witness or in some positive ways, fortify him in his closure.

It is the structure of humanness that gives human beings an inalienable dignity, and from which eventually follows the principle that a person is always an end and never solely a means. It seems to me that from this principle certain consequences could be deduced: respect for the dignity of a person as an end implies that one does not simply use him the way one uses tools or animals or any other creatures of the subhuman environment (though these too should be treated with respect); that one respects a person as an end means that one does not arbitrarily exterminate him (although in the tragedy of war or in his attack on the innocent, one may be required to do so), does not arbitrarily remove his possessions from him; does not deceive him, but always has respect for the fundamental truth of his transcending relationship towards the Whole. And this I would claim can found an ethic.

Relativity of Norms

Our approach is based on a transcendence of the relativity of norms proclaimed so loudly in contemporary culture, but also held so anxiously against the background of Dachau and Buchenwald. One of the major bases for ethical relativism has been the acute awareness of the great diversity of ethical norms in differing cultural groups. Valuable as cross-cultural and historical studies are in many ways, they are inconclusive in ethics. Apart from the implicit norm that the publicists of such views exhibit, namely, that the poor, deluded ethical absolutists *should* really be disillusioned, there are other problems. A priori it is true that a multiplicity of views does not necessarily involve a multiplicity of truths—or rather falsehoods. If twenty people, without calculating, hold twenty different views of the answer to the problem, $13,276 \times 14,278 = ?$ (or if the mathematical example poses problems, the answer to the question, "Whatever happened to Amelia Earhart?"), none of them need be true, but one of them *may* be true; and one answer *is* true, whether anybody has an opinion on it or not. Multiplicity of views by itself proves nothing at all as far as the basic truth in question is concerned. And in such a complicated field as ethics, it might be the case that there is a hierarchy of approximations to the pure norm, that there are also many false modes, and that there may be different ways of realizing a basic norm. Furthermore, it might just be the case, as I argue here, that cross-cultural relativism at one level involves cross-cultural absolutism at another. All cultures have languages, all languages involve judgments, all judgments have the structure of a background reference to the whole, and thus every culture involves a worldview. Thus the *form* in which the relative contents appear remains constant. And from this a basic ethic may be derived.

In all the attempts at refounding ethics in the contemporary world, is there not always implicitly and as the ground of the attempt itself, even an attempt which claims the absolute relativity of all norms — is there not by that very claim an appeal to a transcending ground, an appeal to the truth of what is there? Emotivism, for example, claims that value judgments are statements of emotional preference and therefore not at all objective. To say "One ought to do X" is merely to state that "there is or can be x; I approve of it (for whatever reason); do so as well." Sartrean existentialism claims that all values are the creation of human freedom.[8] But the very performance of these modes of theorizing involves an implicit recognition that the truth about the situation *ought* to be unveiled. One *should* know the truth about the situation, even if the truth be that illusion is necessary for life.[9] But that is self-refuting in the very act of affirming it.

The 'ought' of natural moral law theory has its root in the tendencies of living beings — indeed, in the regularity of nature as a whole. For example, on June 21, the sun *ought* to be in position X in the sky, passing through an arc at that definite position; if we perform x, y, and z operations, the result *ought* to be R; the fertilized ovum *ought* to develop into the fully mature organism; and so forth. In the human case, many of the natural and vital 'oughts' are capable of being modified by reason of the human's being relatively given over to itself, "condemned to choose" how to fashion the law-governed mass of physical, biological, and psychosocial conditions entering into the Now of choice. But that also introduces a new level of 'oughts': one ought to take responsibility for shaping his own life and not merely let it be molded by others; one ought to free himself from illusion — and not only those induced by others, but especially those elaborate webs of self-deception woven, consciously or unconsciously, by oneself; one ought to seek the truth. But if, qua human — that is, as a matter of principle — each person ought to take responsibility and to seek the truth, we ought also to foster the conditions for doing so in society, each considering his/her subjectivity as an instance of a principle. This is involved in following out the pre-personal, natural, founding tendency of distinctively human consciousness as reference to Being.

The status of the ethical norm is that of an end to be realized. And that realization need not be universally realized, but may—and the history of humankind man suggests does—have to be progressively discovered. In each set of institutional arrangements, i.e., in each culture and in each epoch, we have to determine both how to achieve maximum humanness, given the factual arrangements thrust upon us by the past as both legacy and chain, and how to shift the given arrangements progressively toward a set of arrangements into which the ideal would wholly penetrate.[10] Indeed, the achievement of the ideal would, because human creativity produces differing cultural contexts, admit of plural forms. There may be many shifting ways in which the ideal can be realized, part of which depends upon the present stage of inquiry, part upon the choices built up in a community. These same principles would apply to the ethical development of the individual.

But all of this is rooted in the possibility of the transcending inquiry, i.e., upon the metaphysical structure of humanness.[11] If humans are to realize their humanness fully, they must maintain openness to the disclosures of Being, evoked ever anew in differing contexts, appeal to which furnishes the ground for judging the given order—else the given order becomes a matter of values of immanence.

Levels of Transcendence

Values of transcendence divide into values of objective transcendence and of subjective transcendence, corresponding to the rational and the metaphysical dimensions respectively. The rational level involves intellectual, moral and aesthetic values corresponding to the achievements of intellect, will, and feeling.

Intellectual values, values of objective insight, range from the value-neutral insight of disciplines like mathematics to the highest levels of insight in metaphysics, which have a certain dependency upon one's own metaphysical subjectivity. The Platonic dialogues are structured around this hierarchy. Mathematical insight furnishes the initial entrance into the transcendent realm, for mathematical relations are eternally valid, governing the relation between temporal things. In the *Meno* Plato employs a mathematical example to move Meno beyond the blocks that Meno's orientation in life puts in the way of insight into moral matters. As in every person's case, Meno's life orientation involved the center of what he was as an individual man. Socrates' questioning threatens that center. But mathematical considerations pose no apparent threat, so one might move more easily in employing them. But the aim is to evoke ultimately a "reminiscence," and a release from bondage, of our total thrust for the Good as source of all reality. It is this commitment of our total self to the total Good that generates the insight into the Good.[12]

Ethical values begin with something approaching pragmatic conditions for the functioning of society and range all the way to the achievements of love and mysticism, which again involve the whole of one's metaphysical center. At their highest reaches, intellectual and moral considerations become more and more intimately related to the depth of subjectivity.

Aesthetic values seem to have the widest reach, stretching from self-turning sensibility all the way to the perception of Beauty itself. Beauty is initially confused with appetitive gratification, then manifest to detached appreciation as a property of things; it is transferred further to the innerness of human character and to the customs that form character, to the elegance of intellectual constructions, and to the grounding cosmic order they reveal; and finally it is seen as a Real Presence showing itself in, but transcending everything else,[13] as in Augustine's "Beauty ever-ancient, ever-new, too late have I loved Thee!"[14] I would even suggest that the aesthetic constitutes the heart of the deeper reaches of the moral and the intellectual. Creativity in the intellectual realm involves the sense of overall *Gestalten*, a certain "feel," a "sense of direction," an "impulsion" out of which concepts are generated as groping attempts to clarify the initial "feel."[15] And morality, in terms of subjective appropriation, extends from external observance, to rule apprehension, to a full sense of situation and value, a connaturality out of which moral judgments and moral behavior flow, and which, indeed, is the source for generating rules that fit deepening insights and the fluctuation of overall contexts.[16]

Subjectivity and the Sacred

Return again in this connection to Marcel's notion of problem and mystery in human embodiment.[17] The Greek term *pro-blema*, as we observed above, has an etymology parallel with the Latin *ob-jectum*: problems are capable of being brought out in front of us—either before our physical eye (as, e.g. a mechanical problem with a car) or before the mind's eye (as a mathematical problem). But there is also the subject paying attention to the problems. And in the famous Zen simile, the subject is like a hand that is there for grasping all objects, but which cannot grasp itself. The mind's eye cannot focus upon itself: it can only be itself and grow in its sense of itself. For Marcel this subjectivity—not only in the self, but also in things—is the mystery of being. It is not that which is not yet known but will eventually be

Figure 4.2   THE HIERARCHY OF VALUES

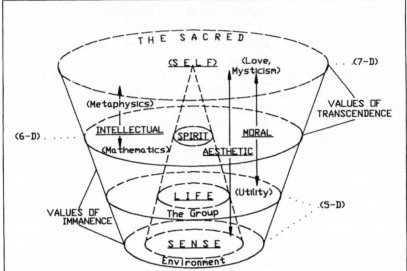

The central cone suggests a progressive concentration within the person as he develops progressively higher-level values: from the scattered multiplicity of the values of sense, upward to the higher levels of self-integration. The inverted truncated cone suggests a parallel broadening of relations to what is outside the self as it moves to more interior and higher values. At the level of "spirit," *intellectual values* begin with mathematics which requires the least subjective committment, and extend to metaphysics which involves the whole of the person and opens beyond itself to the Sacred. *Moral values* begin with something like utility for the organism and the group and extend all the way to love and mysticism, which are related to the Sacred. *Aesthetic values* stretch from the sensorily present, through the fundamental "feel" for any area of human endeavor, to the possible perception of Beauty itself. The broken circle at the top suggests the infinite openness that the Sacred requires, and the infinite value that the Sacred is. The two cones taken together suggest that the self gains its own unity to the extent that it is capable of rising to progressively broader and deeper relations to what lies outside itself. Interiorization is exteriorization.

revealed; it is that which in principle is unknowable in the sense of not being objectifiable, overtakable, masterable.

We dislike dealing with mysteries because we like to feel ourselves absolute masters of things. It is significant to consider in this respect those thinkers who laid the basis for the *Weltanschauung* of modern science: Francis Bacon and Thomas Hobbes. For both, the kind of knowing that is sought is not the kind that sinks into the mystery of things, but the kind that overpowers things. Relation to mystery requires the full subjectivity of the knower for whom no one else may substitute. Since there are deeper subjectivities in some cases than in others, there is a hierarchy of "sinking into the mystery of things" as exhibited in the history of the humanities: in literature, art, philosophy, and religion. But Bacon had no use for these "Idols of the Theater," as he contemptuously termed them. He wanted rather a "democratic" type of knowing where one observer could substitute easily for another—e.g., any man of average intelligence can clock rats running through mazes, and any other man could take his place. Many such observers could build up huge mountains of information and thus, Bacon thought, progress in science would go on—though these laborers would need the direction of those Bacon called "lights."[18]

Hobbes recommended not worrying about the things we cannot master: let us deal only with the world as it appears and expand our conquest of the *Scheinwelt*.[19] And it has been along these lines that the modern world has gone. We dislike considering mysteries, things independent of our own will. We feel ill at ease talking about something like "grace" as a pure gift of God to us. We like to feel ourselves complete masters of our own destinies. But what we can in no wise master is our own fundamental givenness, the givenness of the kind of subjectivity capable of mastery: our own being—and with that, the manifestness of things, the openness of the Whole.

Reflection upon ordinary usage of the term 'grace' here is illuminating. In a theological context, it means 'gift'. As an adjective—'graceful'—it applies to aesthetically satisfying performance. The two are not unrelated. Consider an ordinary activity like bowling or indeed any performance that involves smooth coordination. First of all, there are no great athletes without certain athletic talents—i.e., 'gifts.' But the gift cannot be received at any given moment if one considers it rationalistically determinable by a perfectly self-lucid mind/will standing outside the instinctual sphere of the basic gift. To think "at a distance," so to speak, of each movement one has to make—in bowling, e.g., how the hand should be at each moment in retaining and releasing the ball, and what its relation should be to the stride, and so forth—and thereby to attempt wholly to dominate the gift, is to put oneself in the position of extremely ungraceful performance. One is most free and thus most himself in this context when he aligns himself wholly with his gift—neither dominating it nor being dominated by it.

One could see the same structure involved in ordinary speaking and writing: one does not normally know beforehand how he will end any given sentence when he begins it, nor how the whole will unfold and cohere point by point. Gracefulness occurs again by the lived synthesis of the gift of spontaneity with free control. Here, in the controlled spontaneity of speech, we have the lived achievement of our multidimensional unity as ensouled body.[20] Contrariwise, in the lived pose of detached mastery "from the outside" of our instinctual sphere, we have the lived basis for dualistic notions of soul *and* body.

In this context consider Socrates' identification of knowledge and virtue.[21] At first blush it seems easy to dismiss it by pointing to the everyday situation where one *knows* what he ought to do, *feels* like doing something else and thus *chooses* one way or another. The problem here turns upon what one means by 'knows.' Is it not the case that often when we say, "I know what I ought to do," we should perhaps be more exact were we to say, "I remember what I have been told I ought to do"? What would really constitute ethical insight? At least ultimately, it involves a situation of the fusion of faculties from which emerges a knowing-willing-feeling act, an "affective intuition" in the line of Bonaventure,[22] which is achieved only occasionally as a 'gift', an inspiration, for which we must be prepared. At this level virtue and knowledge are identified in the identity of freedom and dependency. Might this be what lies at the ground of Socratic virtue, so deeply sustained by and interpenetrated with Eros?

Such Eros draws one from surface attractions to the depths of the other and ultimately to the depths that sustain the self and all others.[23] Eros breaks the crust of everyday relatedness in the common, routinized world where others appear as pragmatic objects, functions of a social system held in place by formal rules. It terminates in a response to the full reality of the other, dynamically revealed — indeed, dynamically sustained by our responsiveness. Ingredient in the fullness of any human is its being opened to its own depths, and this opening is closely tied to the mediations of others. The self as metaphysical animal is itself dynamically revealed to itself and dynamically formed by this manifestation of the being of the other (as distinguished from its appearance biologically and culturally filtered). Such responsive manifestation breaks through all systems of closure: (1) the unauthentic systems of isolated biological drive, unintegrated within the full life system of the metaphysical animal, (2) prejudicial or intellectually anachronistic cultural systems, and (3) authentic systems developed in keeping with the fullest range of systematically assimilable material available in the cultural milieu. All of this belongs to the immanent world, what Buber calls the world of It. The Thou, the intimate, inner reality of any Other stands beyond all this, met but not comprehended, affirmed in its unrevealed wholeness.[24] Subjective transcendence, i.e., transcendence that draws upon the whole of what we are as individual persons—thinking, feeling, willing, sensing, acting—relates to the Thou, to the sacredness, the "poetry" of persons and things, to their basic reality. Dwelling thus in the ever-dawning, ever-setting realization of beings, the meaning of Being itself as the sought-after Fullness, the mysterious Totality, the Absolute, ever distant, enters the circle of human meanings, shaking them up, breaking them apart, opening them to new perspectives. This response to the Sacred through the sacredness of beings, this "sacramental sensibility" is the core of authentic religiousness: the world is a word spoken by God and addressed to human beings. All the technically objectifiable elements involved in the communication may be isolated and considered by themselves in the various sciences—as the physicist and physiologist might treat an interhuman verbal communication; but if one is to attend to the communication, the technical aspects must be bathed in the solution of the relation of person to person.

Immanence and Transcendence

But there is a tendency to exalt the lower-level values at the expense of the higher, a most impractical situation when we consider the multi-dimensional character of the enterprise of building humanness. Indeed, one of the factors in this situation is the ambiguous status of the higher-level values in the community. Intellectual, moral, aesthetic, and religious values are assimilated into the mores of the herd, where they become a matter of the "cultured," the "decent folk." and the members of "Christendom" who look down upon the great unwashed others, thinking that, because they themselves conform to certain formulae and modes of behavior, they have reached an authentic relationship to intrinsic value. One belongs to the caste and performs its actions and repeats its words ("One mustn't do this," "One must speak thus," etc.) and thinks that thereby one is related personally to value. Actually, in this situation the person has scarcely begun to exist as a person: he is still largely the resultant of biology and culture. The objectifiable features, both at the empirical level (what we can observe) and at the level of reflection, constitute the outer shell of value achievement; the inner kernel lies in relation to the Thou of all beings.

If we press more deeply our analysis of the relation between the individual and his culture, we might gain some insight into the possibility of understanding another ancient notion totally foreign to modern notions of individualism: original sin. Typically, people take the notion of inherited guilt (though not inherited wealth, if one happens to be the recipient) as an affront to the notion of individual autonomy and responsibility. But consider that by the time the individual reaches

a stage where autonomy and responsibility become crucially significant issues—namely, during adolescence, when most people begin to
realize they must carve out their own niche, take their own stand in
life—they are already shaped and moving in terms of their patterns
of thought, feeling, choice and action, or their basic "sense" of values,
along lines largely given by their upbringing, in dialectic with their
genetic endowment. Contemporary writers at times protest: "We didn't
ask to be born!" I would also add, "We didn't ask for the cultural
shaping we've received." As Plato observed, we are chained in a cave,
capable of seeing only the shifting, shadowy images of reality
projected by our social (as well as cosmic) position. Orientation toward
what is deepest in us is realized only in rare individuals, it would
seem almost by way of some intrusion from outside our world, forc-
ing the one unchained out of the cave, against the social preset in
which he had originally found himself enmeshed.[25]

Notice, however, that because of the peculiar structure of the
human person as an *incarnate* spirit, higher-order values do not negate,
but rather build upon lower values, so that the order of the group and
of external action are necessary to the achievement of personal value.
Spirit becomes itself only on the basis of group values, residue of the
work of the interplay between the living network tying generations
and the creative geniuses which has formed the value-tradition within
which we find ourselves. The very language structure within which
we might be able to think beyond certain elements in our tradition is
itself a creation by tradition and contains in itself a given philosophical interpretation of reality. Social order, likewise, though external,
forms the necessary structure within which the free individual can
develop. In a situation of primitive struggle for existence, little time
and energy are left for the release of spirit from mere biology.

Yet conformity to a well-structured social order is not sufficient;
a person must become *himself* within that order through his personal, subjective response to the valuable. And at the highest level,
this value-response, as Kierkegaard noted in his own situation, is not
something achieved once and for all, so that one can say, e.g., that he
is a Christian because he happens to have been born into a Christian
society and conforms to its external practices. Rather, having taken
the necessary steps of baptism and external works (necessary in the
context in which Kierkegaard spoke), a man *learns* to become a Christian, i.e., to deepen his response and thereby to become really identified with Christ.[26] Transferring the principle involved outside
Kierkegaard's context: each value situation demands a new and total
response, since lower demands are always threatening to close us to
transcendence, and most especially to subjective transcendence.

Immanent values, then, can be either good or bad, depending upon several factors. Taken in abstraction from every other consideration, pleasure and group spirit are goods. However (still abstractly considered) they are immanent relative to the transcendental thrust toward the development of rational and metaphysical goods insofar as, *by themselves*, they are closed up within the organism or the group. But concretely considered, they do not exist "by themselves." Taken into the dynamic of a life opening toward transcendent values, they are capable of sublimation. In the *Symposium*, Plato describes the dynamic movement of this sublimation: Eros being aroused by the sensuous presence of another qua bodily, but through discipline, leading inward and upward toward the highest Good.[27]

Sex is extremely illuminating in this respect. Sexual relations can be entered into purely for the sake of pleasurable gratification. They can also become a medium for the establishment of a mutual egoism in the partners and/or in the offspring which might follow. They can likewise function in the development and expression of an interpersonal relatedness of broadening scope built upon the mutual stimulation of openness toward truth and goodness and beauty wherever they are to be found. Taken into the dynamic of the human spirit, sense pleasure and group spirit become ultimately instruments of theophany. Eyes and ears are good witnesses to men whose souls are attuned. Or, as Blake would have it, "If the doors of perception are cleansed, everything would be seen as it is, infinite."[28]

Immanent values become immanent in the negative sense, become "bad," first when they are pursued in such a way that they block transcendence—to take an extreme case, when sensual overindulgence leads to alcoholism; or when considerations of a patriotic nature lead to the support of injustice, as in Nazi Germany, or elsewhere. They also become "bad" when values that objectively are transcendent become subordinated to the organism or the group, e.g., when intellect is cultivated solely to serve one's own bodily pleasures; when honesty is considered "the best policy" because it leads to social success; when "culture" is sought as a status symbol; or God is treated simply as a hidden ally in one's struggle for socially defined success—to mention some of the more obvious examples.

But the demon of immanentization is much more subtle. What is better may become the greater enemy of what is best. Apart from the obvious considerations of intellectual values as functioning within the context of all kinds of academic games set up by "ego-tripping," defense mechanisms, sheer pedantry, and the like, openness to the objective truth in a given discipline or further openness to the location of objective truth from various areas of the life-world into a consistent intellectual scheme may themselves be occasions for closing off openness to the highest value of the Sacred which asks from us our total subjecthood. As Kierkegaard observed, philosophers tend to construct magnificent thought-castles and dwell in miserable shacks closeby. (Lest I seem overly prone to call attention to "occupational hazards" in the practioners of the other disciplines, here's one for philosophers too—among others.)

Objectively ethical values too are subjected to a similar immanentization. It is not too subtle a matter to detect a sort of hyper-rigid "propriety," a set of behavior routines mimicking the outer forms of ethical conduct. But immanentization becomes more difficult to detect when ethics, authentically considered, takes the place of religion. This is what is at stake in Kierkegaard's famous disagreement with Kant in his discussion of the case of Abraham. Child of the Enlightenment—perhaps one of its noblest, and clearly one of its most competent products—Kant considered Abraham mistaken. When God supposedly told Abraham to sacrifice his son Isaac, instead of blindly following the order, said Kant, Abraham should have said (in effect), "If you tell me to break one of the basic principles of the moral law and kill my son, you cannot be an angel of God. It must be some devil who tempts me."[29] But Kierkegaard protests: ethical good is not the same as relationship to God; a good man is not the same as a religious man. The religious man is ethical because of something more than ethics: he is open to the divine.[30]

Obviously, that does not settle all the problems with the Abraham story. Though for an ethics, common at an earlier stage of culture, that sees evil only in overt actions, Abraham was still prevented from the ultimate unethical act, still, for an ethics of intention ("He who lusts for a woman in his thoughts has already committed adultery with her in his heart"),[31] the evil deed is already in the intention. Kierkegaard agonizes over this. But at a less complex level (which may be the level intended by the scriptural writer anyway) the point is clear: ethics is not the same as religion. Ethics involves following our nature; religion involves attention to the ground of that nature. Whatever one may think of the ultimate claim of the Judaeo-Christian tradition reflected here, the basic point is that the metaphysical thrust in us, open to the Totality, requires an attentiveness deeper than our most cherished norms. Far from involving a kind of irresponsible anarchism, such a thrust involves a more demanding sense of obligation.

So we see a stratification of values. At a first level, there is an *essential* stratification answering to the stratified essential structure of humanness. But at the *existential* level, as lived by the individual person, the essentially higher values play over the whole register of essential levels. At the highest essential level we have religion as the relation of the whole of ourselves to the fullness of reality. Existentially it may be entered into because of an emotional charge, because it helps one become a good man, or because it aims to bring one face to face with the living God, or perhaps to the "God beyond God."[32] And so with all values: existentially all are ambiguous. Sense values and group spirit are ambiguous in a reverse manner: essentially lower values may become vehicles of transcendence.

As Martin Buber put it: every Thou is fated to become an It. Every ecstatic relation to the full being of any being—a person, a natural object, a work of high culture, a sacred text—falls back into "our side" as object-for-man. However, everything depends upon whether the forms on "our side" remain flexible, opening out to the manifestations of Being, or whether they harden into fixed objects, all the worse the higher the order of values they are constructed to mediate and house within our world.[33]

Metaphysics and Practicality

Viewing practicality in terms of various levels of self-making, metaphysics as a conceptual enterprise would be at least as practical as the pursuit of the means for pleasurable gratification at the level of our biological being, in that it involves a higher level of self-making. It thus needs no more apology than sensory satisfactions involve. The latter do not seem to involve apology because, being most readily accessible, requiring least preparation for achievement, they are lowest-common-denominator goods, whereas the cultivation of the intellect in metaphysics requires both peculiar capacity and (prior and present) peculiar effort. Thus there is a certain intrinsically elitist character to such cultivation, as there is a certain democratic character to sensory gratifications. The latter are likewise the more easily producible by technical efforts. By reason then of democratic prejudices, hedonistic preferences, and technical capacity, we tend to accept intellectual cultivation only insofar as it can be tied to the production of such gratification and the conditions, biological and political, that make them possible. Hence we readily accept medicine, engineering, and (perhaps) political science (tied in with social and psychological engineering) as proper objects of intellectual cultivation. But intellectual cultivation is not seen as valuable in itself.

However, metaphysics as an elitist conceptual enterprise is practical in the more ordinary sense as instrumental to the aletheic (and more democratic) cultivation of our metaphysical center—and that in a two-fold sense. First, in a time where the conception of the human being as a pleasure-machine is reinforced from so many angles, metaphysics holds open the space for, and points to the possibility of the cultivation of one's metaphysical center, which is available to any person. This is a kind of external function in relation to the spiritual life: *orthotes* opens out to *aletheia*. But secondly, there is also a more internal function, in that metaphysics promotes the intrinsic quality of that life, aiding in its clarification to itself by relating it to the whole context of human existence. The orthotic and the aletheic thus develop hand in hand, stimulating our deeper presence to Being and providing the ultimate visionary context for all our action.[34]

5   *Abstract and Concrete*

The concrete is the abstract
rendered familiar through usage.

Langevin

Healthy human reason goes out
towards what is concrete; the
reflection of the understanding
comes first as abstract and
untrue, correct in theory only, and
amongst other things unpractical.
Philosophy is what is most
antagonist to abstraction, and it
leads back to the concrete.

G. W. F Hegel, "Introduction,"
History of Philosophy

Perhaps . . . what we call feeling
or mood here and in similar
instances is more rational, that
is, more intelligently perceptive,
because more open to being than
all reason . . .

Martin Heidegger,
The Origin of the Work of Art

Identifying the Context of the Terms

At this point we have to overcome one more block in the way of
metaphysics. The end of the last chapter suggested the relation
between experience and metaphysics; chapter 1 offered suggestions
for enriching and deepening the experiential ground through secular
meditations. We have also suggested a number of times that the character of contemporary experience, along with the metaphysics of
observedness that heavily conditions it, makes metaphysical conceptualization increasingly difficult. But once the experiential ground is

tilled, conceptualization can be helped along by the visual model provided in chapter 2. With the levels of this model linked to the definitions of humanness (chapter 3), we were then in a position to deal with the motivational block afforded by the contemporary prejudice in favor of practicality (chapter 4).)

Now, we can go on to deal with one last block: the objection that metaphysics is too abstract, and what is, after all, real is the concrete. What I want to emphasize is that just as metaphysical considerations are not only not impractical but are indeed ultimately more practical than our immediate practicality, so also are they not only not abstract but are more concrete than our usual concreteness. This may seem like the employment of Orwellian "Newspeak," but its roots lie not in motives of manipulation and control of others, but rather in attention to that which discloses itself in experience.

Initially most people identify the concrete with the sense-perceptible. If you press that further, you will find the somewhat wider notion of "the easy of access," i.e., the concrete is something we are used to. And behind that lies something of a value judgment that it is the concrete, after all, wherein we find what is of basic value: it is the concrete that is "real." Contrasted with this is the abstract, which is not sense-perceptible, which is difficult of access, which is associated with the unreal and thereby with the valueless.

If we begin to examine the terms themselves, we find that the 'abstract' is that which is "drawn away from" something (from the Latin *abs*, "away from," and *trahere*, "to draw," past participle, *tractum*, "drawn"). The question here, in relation to the overriding metaphysical question of the nature of reality, is: *From what* is it drawn away? From "the real," of course, which is "the concrete." Again etymologically, 'concrete' derives from *cum* ("together with") and *crescere* ("to grow"; past participle, *cretum*): the concrete is that which has grown together.

It is then a question of relativity: relative to what is something abstract—and impractical? I want to argue that relative to the full thrust of man's nature as a metaphysical animal, metaphysical considerations are eminently concrete and practical. But relative to our biological and most of our inner-cultural needs, they are not very concrete or practical—indeed, they are, just as most people think, abstract and impractical.

Bodiliness and Concreteness

Begin now with the "concrete" objects of our sense experience. And consider the possibility of a distinction between concreteness as the full reality of a thing—the growing together of all components into its full selfhood—and our concrete perception of things, "drawn away" from the full reality of things. I would argue eventually that the whole realm of perception concretized as far as possible would not replicate the full concreteness of things. How would one go about demonstrating these (at first blush absurd) claims?

Any of the sense powers *considered by itself* presents an abstraction from all the objects of the other sense powers: the approach through vision abstracts from that through hearing and touch, and so on. And within the field of functioning of each sense power, each act of that power is an abstraction from all the possible perceptions available within the field of that power.

The scientist gets more concrete about things by extending his observations, putting together all the perspectives available from the outside and the inside of the bodies with which he deals—indeed, adding new perspectives through the expansion of the thresholds of his unaided senses by means of refined instrumentation. However, this extended concretization takes place primarily in terms of a reduction of each aspect to some visually discernible effect, and thus the relation to perceived being is still abstract.

But the man of common sense, though generally prone to identify the concrete explicitly through a single sense, as a matter of fact has in mind the cold, juicy, smooth, red apple when he speaks of a concrete experience. That is, he transfers the notion of concreteness (which, as over against abstractness, has been identified with reality) from the objectpole, constituted out of the habitual association of many senses, to the subjectpole, where the abstractness of vision may be the only operating sense.

But even if we extend all the thresholds to their ultimate limits and gather together all the perspectives within these thresholds, the fully concreted perceptual experience would not be a complete replication of the concrete reality of things. Why not?

Consider the distinction made by Sartre and others (to which we already called attention in chapters 1 and 2) between the body-subject and body-object, between the body as I live it and *am* it, and the body as observed. Sartre, in his usual jarring way, suggests that the latter body, which is the body of science, is really the equivalent of a corpse, since scientific observation abstracts systematically from what it is like for that bodily being to know its life.[1]

Note the ambiguity between these two concepts in the curious expression people use: "I know that like I know the palm of my hand." This is supposed to indicate thorough knowledge of a situation. But tests have shown that it is a rare individual who "knows" the palm of his hand. Pictures of the palms of each member of a group of people were taken and then distributed to the group, each member being asked to identify his own. And, apart from those who had obviously eccentric features — scars, warts or particularly crooked fingers — none were able to identify their own. Such identification calls for viewing the hands as objects, open to public inspection; and from that point of view, my hand is — even for me — no different than the hand of any other. However, the body as object is not the body as subject, is not the body as I live it, "from the inside." From the latter point of view there is a "knowing" of my hand (by being it) such that no one else can quite know it in the same way. But that lived relation is something that cannot be subjected to a public inspection. The body as object of science is the body considered in abstraction from that lived relation which constitutes the body as me. The concrete apprehension of bodiliness would have to bring together the growing concreteness of science with a mode of self-reflection.[2]

The notion of body-subject introduces us to the notion of the *expressivity* of what appear as living beings, especially as consciously living, and most especially as living in a humanly conscious manner. Positivism or empiriomorphism takes the sense-datum as self-contained, nonreferential, or at least only referring to other like data. Primitive anthropomorphism, by contrast, sees all *sensa* as expressive.[3] The latter view would seem to have its origin in the fact that as children we come to understand anything only within the circle of the expressivity of the behavior of our parents, encountering their love or hostility or indifference. It seems natural then to transfer the expressivity of such phenomena to the whole of our encounters. As Thales, the first philosopher (fl. 587 B.C.), saw it: "Everything is full of gods."[4] The primal ground of things tends to be seen as "Father" or "Mother," whose desires all things express. Positivism reverses the tendency completely, scrubbing the sense-data clean of all expressive references, abstractly looking away from what is said in the encounters with other humans and a fortiori from the possibility that all things "say" something of primal but hidden reality.

Attend to an ordinary experience, e.g., going to an optometrist. Consider "the look of the Other."[5] As you enter the room, eye meets eye in the context of encounter with a total *Gestalt*, gathered around the eyes, but not usually fixed thereon. Conventional greetings follow, chatting about the weather or recent sports events. But then he sets to work. Your eyes become the center of his attention, but purely as mechanisms that he is attempting to adjust. He abstracts completely from whatever the eyes might express, from the way you *live* in those eyes. This is a perfect example of what happens when natural science sets to work upon human beings: a complete abstraction from all expressivity and thus from the core of humanness initiates the scientific quest.

Contrast the relation on the other end of the scale: consider the looks exchanged between people who love one another deeply. The eyes of the other in this case are not simply expressive media of a conventionally judging consciousness. They are windows of the depths of "the soul," of a center attracted, accepting, confirming, longing for the mutuality of presence, even in the context of conventional relatedness, beneath the surface of ordinary conversation. Of course, such expressivity can range from beast longing for beast, through person longing for person, to mutual longing for relationship, to the Primal Mystery that surrounds every encounter and to which we are essentially related, whatever that Primal Mystery might be conceived to be.

Encounter with the human other is concrete meeting, indeed meeting capable of a growing concrescence as the sensory surface more deeply "says" and the one encountering more deeply "reads" what is said. The fully concreted scientific object never touches such concreteness.

Here we would then have to reconsider the metaphysical status of four-dimensional empirical objects considered in their phenomenal aspects in chapter 2 and develop the basis for a depth interpretation of the surface definitions of the elements that entered into the genus of humanness in chapter 3.

Consider another less immediate but most consequential approach: the notion of evolution. Leaving aside the peculiar problems involved in the case of the emergence of human beings, consider three premises: 1) Animals who exhibit every behavioral characteristic of being aware have sprung from the centralization and complexification of material elements. Such an assertion is not immediately evident, but requires the accumulation of vast quantities of information secured by taking a careful look: evolutionary theory in its modern form is a little over two hundred years old,[6] and men have been observing and thinking for many, many centuries. (2) Consciousness is not a residual but a central function of an organic entity (something that our own situation suggests, but that has to be bracketed out by a strictly observational approach in biology): consciousness is self-presence and self-directedness of which fact scientific activity is an exemplary instance. (3) Consciousness is known, but not by sensory observation, since awareness provides the framework within which things appear and the framework itself does not appear within the framework. It then follows that a nonobservable has sprung from what is observed; that what is observed at the "lower" end of the evolutionary chain has about it an intrinsic relation to the nonobservable as being able to produce it; and that there is thus a nonobservable component to "mere matter.

The second premise is added to distinguish the case of flying, e.g., from the case of consciousness. A flying creature could still be itself without being able to fly; but awareness is central to the being of things that are aware. There is a dimensional and not simply a functional shift in the emergence of awareness. Matter is not then preflying the way it is preconscious.

The conclusion is scarcely orthodox vis-a-vis the common opinion—and that includes the common scientific opinion—in our culture. What it means is that physics is not really asking the question What is matter? but rather the more limited question, What is matter as it appears to observation and quantification? Teilhard de Chardin has seen this.[7] He distinguishes between what he calls the "Without" of things with which the tradition of Western sciences has thus far been preoccupied, and the "Within" of things, which is the domain of their inner reference to consciousness. The tradition de Chardin represents is that of emergent evolutionism which stands in opposition to mechanistic evolutionism. For the latter taking a careful look reveals particles that combine in certain ways to produce the complex beings of immediate experience. In the laboratory, conditions are replicated wherein certain organic compounds were formed in the sea by mixtures of various chemical compounds. The possibilities of combination led to the formation of the proto-organisms which gradually worked their way up through genetic mutation and natural selection to the point of complex and centralized organisms that began to perceive and eventually also to think. The material elements that lie at the base of the process are simply what appear to a look; the consciousness that emerges from the process is simply a matter of complex observables or an embarrassing epiphenomenon.[8]

But one could not have found out about the particles at the base of the evolutionary scheme nor about the scheme itself if it were not given "out there" to awareness as other than the organism of the scientist-observer. Consciousness is a hidden premise in mechanistic evolutionism.

Emergent evolutionism is less philosophically naive. It does not assume that things are just the way they appear to observation, even to very careful observation. Things are more than they can in principle yield to a look. Since consciousness comes out of matter, matter is not "mere matter," i.e., having only an extrinsic relation to consciousness as object of observation; rather matter is preconscious. We only know what matter is when we know what comes out of it.

And since we have no means of knowing whether evolution is at an end, we have no way of knowing the full reality of matter. We are always in the middle.[9] But once again, not to come to the end of our penetration into the full concreteness of matter is not necessarily to get nowhere.

If what we have said holds, then there is a distinction between what can be gained through the senses about matter and the reality of matter. These two aspects are obviously not unrelated: matter is the kind of thing that can be perceived by the senses and understood in terms of its law-governed functions. But it is more than that: it not only bears an extrinsic relation to consciousness as object, but an intrinsic relation to consciousness as producer of consciousness!

What concretely—and that means, considered in terms of the fullness of its reality—what is a body? Something more than the summary of data we casually identify when, with a smug wave of our finger, we point to the things we touch, taste, see, and feel, the things with which we have achieved an adjustment, but which we scarcely know. And that "more" is only accessible when we bring the conscious structure of the self as well as the data of observation into the picture.

That is not to say that in this way we now know the inner essence of matter. It is rather to situate the explanatory framework of mechanistic evolutionism within a broader but complementary framework that would have to be included in any further explanation that claims adequacy. What the explanation would be has to be determined by particular investigations within each framework. What we are attempting here is a horizon analysis, a form analysis, not a content analysis.

Concreteness and Universality

But even if we integrated these two explanatory frameworks, there is still another framework to be considered in getting at the concreteness of things: an explanation of the relation between the universal structures constituting the frameworks and the things to be explained. What is the status of the universal? Is it merely a form of the mind, whereas things are merely particulars? But if mind emerges from matter, how can we account for the universality in mind unless it is already in some way prefigured in matter? How is it that things exhibit generalizable aspects? Are our concepts a means for groping toward another dimension of the universe itself, a dimension of laws, principles, essences, eternally existent, separable from things, but governing things and being mirrored by things?[10] Or are universal essences and particular things dialectically related, the particulars being a kind of outgrowth of the essences the way particular acts are an outgrowth of the individual's own essence? (Roughly the position of Hegel.)[11] Here the universal would be Real Presence in particulars, containing the essential potentialities of a given class to which each actual individual only approximates— wholly in each individual of a class as a potency, but only partially realized in each; beyond each individual as universal, but dependent upon particulars for instantiation.

Whatever be the case, we get to the fuller concreteness of material things through the universal explanatory framework of physics, which moves from the surface of instruments observable within the thin band of visible light as a segment of the electromagnetic spectrum to the fullness of the spectrum; and through the universal explanatory framework of biology, which operates in terms of mechanistic and emergent evolutionism. Hence, the universal plays an indispensable role in coming at the fuller concreteness of things. The particular sensed object and the universal framework are each abstracted in their own ways from the full concreteness of things. We begin with our attention focused upon the sensed individual and then proceed to consider the universal components involved in that individual and in our sensing of it. At this stage we have isolated two abstract moments: the abstractness of the universal thought apart from the sensed particular. The dialectical circle is completed when we learn to see the particular in the universal and the universal in the particular. It is thus not enough to synthesize perceptions: one must grasp the concepts immanent in things. Theory is thus not an escape from the concrete reality of things, but a detachment from the abstractness of sense perception.

In lieu of the impossibility of the possession of a fully fleshed out theoretical framework (by reason of lack of omniscience), the fully human mode is and has to include a mythico-poetic mode that deals with the basic symbols that suggest, without being able to explain fully, our a priori presence to the Whole.[12] Science itself—as well as philosophy—depends upon such a prior sense of the Whole whose fullness has yet to be revealed. Great advances that lead to technical dominance have followed from the scientific pose, but often this has been at the expense of philosophical consciousness, and most especially at the expense of mythico-poetic consciousness. As Comte put it, the scientific age has superseded the metaphysical age, just as the metaphysical age superseded the theological age.[13] I would suggest a dialectical relation rather than a relation of linear succession between the three, each having priority in a different way. Neither philosophic nor mythico-poetic consciousness are simply anticipations in an inferior mode of what science eventually discovers in the only adequate mode. Mythico-poetic symbols are the base of our mode of dwelling as humans. They appear in severely atrophied form in many philosophic accounts; they operate in their most abstract form in scientific theory. But philosophic reflection upon the foundation of science can open up the founding priority of symbolic consciousness. Theory as relation to Being must return from orthotic abstraction to the fuller concreteness of aletheic manifestation within immediate presence to beings. In that context, relation to persons has a certain priority.

Theory is doubly embedded in the context of relation to persons. At one level, by reason of the fact that we are referred to the never fully disclosable mystery within which everything is rooted, all theory falls short of comprehensiveness and thus requires supplementation by alternative approaches provided by partners in the dialogue aimed at the final truth of Being.[14] But second, by reason of the fact that the deeper reaches of Being are available only in the human person, at least in human experience, theory must be returned to the situation of encounter with other persons.[15] Our own inwardness is discovered only on a rebound off of the Other, more deeply off of the human other, and most deeply off of the significant human others, those whom we most deeply love.

Return to the key notion of intentionality here: All consciousness is consciousness *of* something on the basis of being consciousness (of) itself. Thematic, focal awareness of objects is linked to prethematic, nonfocal, self-presence. Awareness is manifestation of otherness, presupposing a manifest self-identity, other than which the other is manifest—problematic though this "self" may be. But otherness is capable of differing—more profound or more superficial— levels of manifestness, linked to the establishment of deeper or more superficial levels in the self. To manifest otherness in an increasingly deeper mode is to enter into selfhood in an increasingly deeper way.

We have observed three levels in the field of consciousness: sensing, interpreting, and judging/presence-to-Being. At the sensory level, abstractly considered—i.e., apart from its concrete interplay with the other levels—the other is revealed only in terms of an aspect filtered off relative to the needs of the perceiving organism. What is manifest is the other as other-for-me-as-needy-organism, not other in its own selfhood. At the level of interpreting there are two aspects: one is the constructed aspect, the other is the eidetic. 'Pen' for example, is a constructed notion; but sense-object, color, seeing, extensity, space, and so on are eidetic aspects, given as the frame within which our constructions go on. In terms of construction, then, the other is manifest, again, not fully in its otherness, but as other-relative-to-a-framework, usually constructed to serve certain needs. At the eidetic level, we lay hold of an objective universal meaning; and yet the basic question, which we have already raised in this regard, is whether 'reality' is the universal or the individual. What is the true correlate to our reference to Being? Does intellect considered as the faculty of the universal lay hold of Being-Itself, or is such universality only Being-relative-to-intellect? Is the being-in-itself of individual existents, most specifically of human persons, more or less than the eidetic? Does the eidetic only relate to the matrix within which the excess, the creativity of the person operates? When we reach the level opened up by the judgment, this problem emerges. Judgment *refers us* to the full in-itself-ness of existents, but by itself leaves open a decision as to where that being-in-itself lies. And this touches directly on the question of abstract and concrete relative to Being.

But even if one takes the (Platonic) position that Being-in-itself— understanding by that: Being in its pure nature—is the universal (as we will explore shortly in part 2), or if one takes the Parmenidean position (conventionally interpreted) that Being-in-itself is a One beyond all multiplicity, it is still the case that there is a surplus "beyond Being" (so conceived), for all-that-is is included in Being, outside of which there is nothing at all, and all that is included within Being is not universal. Reference to Being, given initially in the judgment, moves beyond intellect conceived of as faculty of the universal. My being is more than my intellect as the being of any existent is more than what can be apprehended in terms of the universal. The existent Other as instance of the universal is Other-as-related-to-intellect, not fully Other-in-itself, and thus incapable of grounding fully the self-as-itself. There would thus seem to be a level beyond intellect so conceived, a level of relation to wholeness. And that relation, I would claim, is a relation of our wholeness to that wholeness in others that appears at the aletheic level. In deepening presence to another as fully being-in-itself—not being as related to organic need, nor being as fitted within a cultural framework of interpretation, nor being as object of eidetic intuition—we meet, without fully comprehending, the Not, the More than what fits within our capacity to comprehend within a universal framework. Such a relation is a relation of love fully conceived, and it fully grounds the self in itself, for it manifests the Other wholly as other and fulfills the whole intentional structure of consciousness as relation to Being. Better: by reason of the reference-to-Being as the basis of our existence as human, relation to another wholly as Other not only reciprocally founds the full self-gathering of the self as self, it also opens up to the ultimate context, the mysterious Totality of Being. Each being encountered founds our relation to the Ultimate.

We should underscore here the polar character of the relation: *relation* to *otherness*. Otherness may be misconceived as the alien, the hostile (Sartre).[16] Such otherness is not the otherness of being, but only other-for-me. The manifestation of the otherness of being involves a simultaneous but paradoxical *identification* with otherness, an acceptance of otherness—ultimately of the incomprehensible mystery at the heart of each being. It is a mystery that draws near, that discloses itself as such while remaining mystery, other-in-itself.

The only one that would have a fully concrete understanding of things would be a hypothetical, Unlimited Being in the seventh-dimension whose awareness is not a matter of perspectives and envelopes and limited theories, but one whose awareness of things is wholly coincident with their being. Such a being would be God.

And if it turns out that the concrete being of things is their constant rootedness in the unlimited Being, we would have the ultimate framework including all the others. Then the most concrete relationship to things would be a relationship to the world as theophany, the manifestation of God, as in William Blake, Francis of Assisi, or Martin Buber. Our first reaction to such claims is usually something on the order of, "What's he been smoking?" But in this case our criterion of judgment is our comfortable world of collective abstractions, which seal us off even from the sensory data immediately available to us, not to mention their sealing off of the detailed explorations in experimentation and theorizing and the depth experiences of poetry and mysticism.

Most of our perceptions and understandings of things is, relative to *their* concreteness, abstract. Racist consciousness furnishes a paradigm case of an abstract relation. The racist is convinced that he is the supreme realist, "telling it like it is." But no one is more fixed on abstractions than he. The racist dwells in the stereotypical concept that has been reinforced in him by the cultural process. Such a concept involves a value-judgment linked to a mode of behavior. It determines only a very selective attention to the actual facts of the matter in the case of a given individual member of a minority group. Only so much is allowed within the field of attention as fits within the stereotype.

What is important to notice is that such a stereotyping process, with its social origin and reinforcement, is the paradigm for all our relations to Being—to ourselves, to others (whether persons or things, natural or cultural) and to the Totality. The social process is a stereotyping process, a restriction and chaining of the possibility for fuller concrete awareness that is attentive to the deeper disclosures of Being. But it is at the same time a kind of protective womb—this is its positive significance—that provides the narrow circle required in order to learn initially to cope with situations. At a certain stage, a man has to be "born again," moving out of this second womb—though formed within it. This second birth is an opening to Being itself, the Primal Mystery. But for the most part we dwell collectively in abstract worlds. What makes us think that they correspond to the concrete reality of persons and things is not only that they enable us to adjust to persons and things functionally, but that we inhabit these worlds *together*: together we dwell in worlds which alienate us from our deepest substance, our transcendental nature, our metaphysical thrust toward the Whole of what is or can be. There is then the smaller circle of our ordinary but abstract relation to things, and there is the wider circle of the concrete reality of things. We canonize the smaller circle and call it concrete and real and valuable. But our nature moves beyond this small circle and it bursts through in many individual cases.

There are ancient witnesses to this situation: in the Hebrew scriptures it says that God made the world and all that is in it and saw that it was very good. Then he made man in His own image, mirror of the Infinite among the finite. And man spoke to Him and He spoke to man in the garden of nature.[17] But man sought his own knowledge and his own mastery: he made his own world, the collective world of his own small circle of light. And then the ancient witness tells us, "Love not the world or the things that are in the world."[18] There are two worlds: the fully concrete world that manifests the Infinite, and the abstract world of man's own self-enclosure.

Is this then "new-speak"? The "concreteness" of our common world is "abstract." The real world is already subverted. This is also the message of Plato's Cave. (See Figure 5.1 for a schematic summary of our considerations thus far.)

Object, Subject, Praxis

But there are three further ramifications to the problem of abstractness and concreteness that will bring our exposition closer to the concreteness of real beings by rendering the view dynamic and concretely applying it. One aspect has to do with the concreteness of the things to which we attend, a second with our attention to these things, and a third with the interrelation of persons and things through contemplative praxis.

First of all, since the beings of experience are beings in process, things developing both individually and in terms of the species, beings within the context of a developing, interacting, evolving universe, one can never have a fully concrete relation to their reality because

Figure 5.1   FRAMEWORKS OF EXPLANATION

Corresponding to the four outward and three inner dimensions of human experience, four basic explanatory frameworks would have to be taken into consideration in any view of being that would claim adequacy in principle. The elimination of any of the frameworks would lead to a truncated view.

The first framework is that which works in terms of observable correlations between observable four-dimensional objects. The second integrates the situation of the sensorily conscious subject. The third opens up to consideration of the status of the universal, while the fourth attends to the openness of the Totality.

that reality itself is always on the way, always open to new development. Furthermore, their reality is, in a real sense, the totality of their life span, past, present, and future. But that totality is never capable of being laid hold of properly, for it is available as a completed whole only after the future of a given individual is sealed off through destruction; and the mode that the thing then takes on is the mode of having been, which is not identical with the mode of being—processive, emergent—that it had while it existed. And yet, while it exists as processive, as emergent, it is never fully concreted! Hence its status as being-in-itself remains problematic, for it is never fully itself.[19]

Secondly, in terms of our relationship to such beings, because we are finite beings limited by our biological and cultural-historical situation, we can relate to others only in terms of a certain focus of attention that is necessarily abstracted from their full concreteness. We pay attention to things, gather up, concretize our past experience in relation to things in terms of the way in which we project our fundamental meaning-structure, which determines what we consider to be the good and determines the hierarchy of goods in terms of our primary, secondary, and tertiary (etc.) values. By reason of these finite projects, we focus upon some things as more fundamental than others, upon some aspects of persons and things more than upon others. The crucial thing is to realize that our modes of projection are limited modes, that they create perspectives within the system of biological and cultural needs. And yet by nature we are pried loose from all these forms of closure and are referred to the full being of things. What therefore is essential is that in and through all our finite perspectives we remain open to the deeper manifestations of being, that our systems do not harden into absolutely closed and rigid sets that make it impossible for things and persons really to speak to us in ways that are not already anticipated by our current projects.

However, we should realize that part of the concreteness of the human situation is the discovered and/or created character of the frameworks of interpretation and behavior, individual and social, within which we operate. These various levels of "institutionalization" are the expression of the creative possibilities of human choice, a new level of being beyond that dictated strictly by 'nature' understood as prepersonal necessitation—though in necessary dialectic with that nature.

The play between discovery and creation of frameworks of interpretation requires a dialogical approach to the significant positions operative throughout the history of thought. To this we will turn in the second major portion of this work.

Furthermore, with reference to the things whose concreteness our frames of interpretation partly reveal, partly conceal, it is not simply a matter of our becoming a kind of perspectival mirror which our finite and historical and their processive character keep from becoming fully concrete. Part of *their* concreteness is their capacity of being subsumed into and fashioned by human projects, some of which are based upon the necessities of survival, others of which are rooted in pure human creativity. Human creativeness is that which can bring out of things potentialities that they could not otherwise realize. But things are not simply there for man as Homo faber, as the maker; they are also there as beings in their own right. And so we have a kind of dual relationship to them, fashioning them and contemplating them. Both can likewise coalesce. Some great artists speak of their work as a matter of assisting nature to give birth to something with which nature herself is pregnant, but which she cannot deliver by herself. Michelangelo once spoke of the statue as being in the block of marble prior to his work: his task appeared to him as one of liberating the form from its hiddenness in the material.[20] And the great Zen painters take an essentially contemplative approach to their work, where it is a matter of becoming so totally immersed in the situation that it is not so much they who do the painting but, so to speak, the brush and the paper that in some sense paint through the artist.

There is a profound complementarity that nature and culture can have, where nature speaks of its deepest potentialities when man works to tend it, fashion it, and cultivate it. One might see this more clearly by contrasting it with a situation of suburban real estate development that I once had occasion to observe. The terrain was a slightly rolling, wooded area. Two developers each bought tracts of land of some two hundred acres side by side. One moved in with his bulldozers and removed all of the trees, scraped off and flattened all of the surface, and divided the denuded area into geometric squares— blocks and lots—upon which he placed a series of boxlike houses differing only in superficial arrangements. The second developer surveyed every major tree in the area, determined to preserve whatever natural beauty there was and to add trees and shrubs in order to enhance the total effect. He developed winding thoroughfares so as to slow down traffic and located the houses along cul-de-sacs so children could play in the street without danger of through traffic. He then oriented the houses for maximum view and laid out the lot lines after the human visual relationship to the environment had been established. He proceeded to locate and form a small lake in an esthetically proper spot in the village and to establish footpaths and recreational areas as well as areas for thought, quietude, meditation. For him, as he said, architecture is essentially an affair of the spirit. It is a matter of fashioning nature so that she complements humankind, stimulating us so that we complement nature in the type of activity—building, landscaping—that cooperates with nature to bring out those features that speak profoundly to the spirit attuned to the possibilities in nature for her own enhancement and the enhancement of the human spirit. The first developer took nature merely as an object, destroying it, creating the slums of the future, demeaning and degrading the human beings who moved into the dehumanized environment. Nature here was not lovingly tended, not fructified so that it could bring forth its most beautiful offspring, but raped and deprived of its own children. In the second architect we have the paradigm of the concrete, concrescing relationship with things, responsive to what nature is attempting to say to us, to tell us of ourselves, to tell us of itself, and to tell us perhaps of what lies beyond itself, of which we and it are simply the expressions. The concrete reality of things is progressively achieved by the loving care and attention we give to them, contemplative and active at once.

What holds for relation to prepersonal nature holds all the more for our relation to human others. A fully concrete relationship is one that becomes increasingly sensitive to the depth of the other, "letting the other be," but not in a wholly passive way. What the other says (what indeed I myself say) is always more than what is expressly intended, for our prepersonal nature—at the level of biology, at the level of the cultural pre-conscious, and at the level of spirit aimed at the Totality—always speaks of its ends, with significant variations in differing individuals. "Letting the other be" involves a deeper listening, a detection and evocation of deeper possibilities in the other, so that one becomes the occasion for the fuller concrescence of that other. But of course that might become simply a pretentious bypass of what that other is explicitly and personally saying. The prepersonal depths can only be most concretely present when one allows the depth of the personally understood, controlled, and articulated features of the other to be displayed in interplay with the prepersonal More.

But here we rejoin our analysis of practicality: in the contemplative-active attention to the other a man is gathered into his own full concreteness, formed in his fundamental selfhood in relation to the full being of the other. The words and deeds that follow from this relation are the fundamental metaphors of our human dwelling: that which appears to exterior observation is expressive of the fullness of the person, present in, but not wholly encompassed by its manifestations. And the shapes given to the manifestation of the other likewise stand for the wholeness of that other gathered in the creative moment.

However, any person, whether self or other, only exists in dialectical relation to the historical shapes of the manifestness of the whole operative in the effective history of the culture, rendered dynamic by reason of each person's founding and initially empty reference to the totality. Such reference makes necessary a mode of disclosure of the Whole and taking responsibility for appropriating and modifying the modalities handed down. Dialogical relation to other persons takes on the character of dialogical relation to the mode of manifestness of the Whole that constitutes our history.[21] To that task we will turn in part 2.

Part Two

READING THE
TRADITION

Section A

THE ANCIENT-MEDIEVAL TRADITION

If we have failed to understand,
it is that we have thought of
knowledge as a mass of theorems
and an accumulation of
propositions.

Plotinus, *Enneads* V, 8, 4.

Our chief intention in this work is to open up reflection on the question of Being. Following the clue offered by Heidegger's distinction between *aletheia* and *orthotes*, we attempted first to awaken the reader (and ourselves) to the aletheic dimension via several deliberately secular meditations. This put us in a position to begin to comprehend conceptually what we might have experienced through meditation — fundamental presence — by devising a seven-dimensional model of human experience. The deepening of presence, we suggested, is a development of the seventh dimension, the reference to Being that stands beyond (though not without) sensing and conceptual understanding as well as judgment — though the latter introduces us only to the outer rim of the seventh dimension. The seven-dimensional model, in turn, made possible relating and grounding several definitions of the human being, culminating in the open definition of metaphysical animal, referred to the Whole and thereby required to choose, indeed, to a large extent to create, his own way among beings.

All of the above, if understood, should aid in removing two of the common blocks in the way of even attempting metaphysical reflection: its apparent impracticality and its apparent abstractness. Ordinarily understood, practicality is a preoccupation with means, and raises the question of ends. But the question of ends is linked to the question of the nature of humanness. We have suggested that ends can be arranged in a hierarchical order based upon the hierarchical relations between the dimensions of humanness. The most practical of all pursuits would be that which leads to the cultivation of our metaphysical center. Orthotic reflection opens but that center in an age when so many factors coverage to close it, points to an aletheic cultivation as the final depth-dimension, and clarifies such a relation to itself by relating it to all the other factors of humanness.

The objection as to the abstractness of metaphysics is removed by rethinking the questions of abstract and concrete, distinguishing between the abstract and the concrete relative to full being and the abstract and the concrete relative to our experience. What we ordinarily call "concrete," i.e., the sense-perceptible as so perceptible, is an abstraction from the fullness of the being in question. The latter we meet only through the mediation of the "abstractness" of universal reflection. The interplay between the universal and the sensed particular within the field of deepening presence moves us from the first, but spurious, concrete toward the ultimate concreteness of the whole of any being within the Whole of Being. In addition, the use of the *Flatland* model was intended to bring out more clearly the abstractness of our initial approach to things. Its imaginative character should afford a crutch to aid in getting a sense of metaphysical reflection, which otherwise seems too "abstract."

The entire work pivots upon the seven-dimensional model. For we will use it in this second part to approach the great texts of the classical tradition in metaphysics, the second major intention of this book. First and foremost, of course, without which the reading of the tradition could become sheer pedantry, our aim is to get to "the things themselves," to the displays of Being in our experience. We have attempted that in part 1 as well—though in fact that attempt was only made possible through a reading of the sources that we will now approach directly. Our penetration in part 1 was just a beginning. For the development of metaphysics we must turn to the masters, for they are the ones who have penetrated "the things themselves" to such a profound extent that reflective persons have been perpetually instructed by them ever since. So, part 1 has been preparation for part 2. Not that phenomenological reflection on "the things themselves" is a means for historical knowledge of past philosophers. Rather, our initial experiential analysis opened the field, the deeper comprehension of which is made possible by the mediation of the classical masters.

The founding reference to the whole of Being grounds the factual plurality of metaphysical views in the history of thought. In retrospect, they make their appearance as a series of perspectives on a Whole that no one has been able to encompass. One might emphasize diversity and disagreement; one might also stress continuity. I have chosen the latter, displaying the history of certain high points in the history of metaphysics as the unfolding of a single tradition from Parmenides through Plato and Aristotle to Aquinas. A second selection from modern philosophy will attempt to show variations and new emphases and developments in addition to divergences from the continental rationalists through Kant to Hegel and Whitehead. Heidegger will afford us a different look that has been especially influential in developing this entire study.

The text at this point is not to be taken as self-sufficient. Rather, it is employed as a preliminary guide to the indispensable, but difficult reading of the primary sources, which should be studied as coordinate with this text. It is a major contention of this work that it is through such wrestling with the classics that the mind stretches and grows in a significant way by establishing a set of epicenters that inhibit premature claims for finality and drive us toward a rich set of perspectives on the Whole.

6 Parmenides

"Heart" as Starting Point

Parmenides is traditionally approached in terms of his basic distinction between the "Way of Truth" and the "Way of Seeming." We prefer to begin with a distinction implicated in the very first line, a distinction little attended to by interpreters of Parmenides, but a distinction of pivotal importance both for the understanding of our relation to Being and for a rapprochement between Eastern and Western thought: "The steeds that carry me took me as far as my heart could desire."[1] Heart, the *thumos*, and the limits of its desire initiate Western metaphysics. Not thought, not logic or reason, but "the heart" and its desire is first. And not the heart's desire in any one of its moments, but the heart at its outermost limits is what opens that metaphysics. We are thus installed from the very onset in the seventh dimension of aletheic relation to Being as the Plenitude.

The correlation between the deep center of the self and its total object pushes us to the limits within and without. What a contrast to the "Here, now, red spot" of those who would construct all from bare *sensa* without consideration of what animates such desire. What a contrast even to the ordinary language of "The cat is on the mat" of contemporary language analysis or the early phenomenologists' attempts at such things as the phenomenology of a mailbox. But sooner or later sensist language reconstruction gives way to attention to ordinary language, and phenomenology to the life-world. And sooner or later our ordinary language runs up against religious language and phenomenology against religious phenomena.[2] Then a re-visioning is called for, a reconfiguration of the ordinary world in terms of those extraordinary experiences that situate the immediate in relation to what it ultimately reveals and conceals.

We have attempted to anticipate that by beginning with an equally prosaic "This is a pen" and, through an orthotic examination of what is implicit in its employment, opening toward the possibility that the ultimate horizon of reference to Being might become aletheically focal. Parmenides thus begins with "the heart" as center of aletheic focus.

'Heart' is a cross-cultural constant expressed in the ordinary language of many different peoples. It has four basic levels of meaning:

1) the literal meaning, the organic pump in the center of the chest, which is an abstraction from 2) the metaphorical meaning of a psychological center between *Bios* and *Logos*, center of vitality, will, memory, and thought; (3) an extension from the subject to the object, indicating the binding tie of the heart's desire, used primarily in song, e.g., "dear heart" or "heart of my heart," but also commonly, though a bit mawkishly, as in "sweetheart" ; and (4) a "transcendental" level, extending to all things the notion of center and functioning as equivalent to 'essence' in expressions like "the heart of the matter."[3]

The proem to Parmenides' solitary extant work, the exceedingly short On Nature, expresses in terms appropriate to the heart, that is, in metaphorical terms, the movement of the heart. Metaphors function appropriately here since heart is the medium between the too-often dichotomized literalism of a mechanized body and a logicized reason.[4] Drawn in a singing chariot, led by the daughters of the Sun past the gates of the ways of Night and Day opened by avenging Justice, the aspirant is greeted by "the goddess" who teaches him the momentous truth.[5] Corresponding to the heart, which one does not give oneself (whence the liturgical prayer, "Create in us a new heart, O Lord"), the truth is not wrested from things as a conquest but is given as a gift, a grace from the goddess, hence the contention of many commentators that Parmenidean metaphysics is rooted in a kind of mystical experience, a revelation.[6] Hence Heidegger in commenting speaks of Parmenides' use here of *noein* (Greek 'to know" from which the English "noetic" is derived), the activity of *nous* (the "faculty" of "knowing"), as "an event which has man," to be distinguished from a mode of apprehension that is something man has.[7] *Nous* is the capacity of being apprehended by things, a being-taken that is the condition for "letting them be," i.e., be manifest to us. The "whole person" is involved, "grasped," "touched" to his very heart.

The Logic of Being

But what is this astonishing revelation? "It is and It-is-not is not." More precisely: " 'Is' [*estin*] and not 'is not.' " Or: There is Being, but no nonbeing.[8] A revelation? What could be more obvious? In order to get some insight into the content of the revelation aspect, Parmenides asks us, in effect, to work out the logical consequences of this compound proposition. He asks us to "test by *logos* the truth of what I say."[9] (*Logos*, basically "word," is used here for the first time in history as "logical deduction.")[10]

Try to think of change in terms of 'Being.' In order to change, a thing must *be*, alright; but it must also *not be* what it will be. In other words, to think change, we must think that *not being in some way is*. But to think Being by itself, i.e., apart from all non-being, we must think changeless Being.

Or come at it another way, lest the above appear a mere verbal trick. Consider that which is most deeply implicated in the changing world, either as its measure or in some way as its inner reality: consider time. Time must be thought in terms of its three dimensions:past, present, and future. But what is the ontological mode or mode of being of each of these dimensions? The past is not: it is what is no longer; the future is not either: it is what is not yet. But what of the present, that which is between the no-longer and the not-yet, which are themselves distinguishable both from each other, from absolute non-being, and from the present. Just what further is the present or the Now? Can we be more precise as to its function between the no-longer and the not-yet? We tend to use it with more or less stringency: e.g., *now*, in the era since man appeared on the planet; or *now*, since the appearance of Christ; or *now*, in the twentieth century; or *now*, in 1990; or *now*, in March; or *now*, Friday; or *now*, at the tenth hour; or *now*, at 10:08. . . . For everyday purposes, that is usually as far as we precise the Now. But in the case of an Olympic swimmer, we go to the hundredth of a second to determine the Now of his or her finish; and in the case of the measurement of subatomic events, to micromilliseconds, etc. As we attempt in this way to make the Now precise, it tends to disappear, or rather to be viewed in its "reality" as a non-temporally-extended divider moving from the no-longer to the not-yet: a not-being between two not-beings! Well then, ordinary experience and its objects have to be thought of as in some way both being and non-being. But then we have to think the seemingly impossible: that non-being *is*!

Parmenides attempts to "think" Being itself, apart from all non-being. Being itself thus shows itself to "logic" as changeless, though things in experience and our experience of them do indeed change. But "logic" for Parmenides is only a kind of exterior test for what is essentially a matter of direct revelation: an experience that fills the heart, an experience out of the ordinary "flowing Now" (*nunc fluens*), an experience of the "standing Now" (*nunc stans*, as the medievals, who knew these things so much better than we, expressed it).[11] So we must distinguish between the Now as one moment, the pivotal moment, of temporality and the Eternal Now standing beyond time-burdened-with-non-being.

Consider a second approach Parmenides used. Think, in terms of Being, the multiplicity of and in the things of experience and in our experience of them. For each member of this multiplicity to *be*, it

must *not be* the other things that are. And each of the things that are
is itself an internal multiplicity, composed of parts, each one of which
is not the others, and each one of which is, in its turn, composed of an
internal multiplicity: from organism to organs, to cells, to molecules
to atoms, to subatomic particles, to . . . ? Press that to its logical
limit, and you see that any item of spatial extensity even of a supposedly homogeneous, i.e., finally noncomposed body (in Greek noncomp-
osition was expressed in the term *atomos* which meant uncuttable"),[12]
is such that its center is not its periphery and any point on its surface
is not any other point either on the surface or between the surface
and the center.[13] Theoretically, there can be no *atomos*, because one
can always think its in-principle divisibility ad infinitum. The concept of the *atomos* is rooted in a decision to stop analysis and to flee
(as later Leibniz and Kant were not to flee) from the paradox of infinity involved in the notion of spatial extensity. Parmenides' conclusion
is that Being itself must be absolutely One: not a one-of-many. It is
Absolute Plenitude, full, with no cracks of division or negation.
Parmenides' follower Melissus concluded, following these lines, that
it could not be material because it could not be spatial.[14]

One obvious problem is that an absolute unity considered apart
from the multiple also has to be thought of as *not being* among the
multiple— and thus, paradoxically, as included in the multiple, being
part of the total system comprised of itself and the others. As we
indicated in our Introduction and will consider again later, this is a
move Spinoza and Hegel make. Parmenides would undoubtedly seek
for a distinction, since "logic" is only an outside test for the "noetic"
(aletheic) experience of Absolute Plenitude apart from things. The
One is "wholly other," with no internal multiplicity, and including in
itself in absolute simplicity what the many contain in scattered fashion. This is essentially the classical position taken up by Plato, Aristotle, Plotinus,and the Judaeo-Christian tradition.

And Parmenides' immediate follower, Melissus, likewise concluded—in a peculiarly un-Greek fashion—that it must be infinite,
for what is there to limit it?[15] I say "un-Greek" because the Greeks
tended to view the infinite (Greek *a-peiron*) as indeterminate: as
lacking *fines*, or boundaries, and thus lacking de-finition, having no
termination and thus being indeterminate. Hence the infinite was
conceived of as chaotic, imperfect.[16] In spite of this, Parmenides' logic
led Melissus to conceive of that which filled the heart's desire as
beyond finitude, thus introducing the notion of the finite (and therefore also of de-finition) as itself a limitation, the negation of the plenitude of the infinite which we now express negatively as a negation of
negation (of which Hegel makes much).

Logic thus tests the truth of the heart: the experience in question is not only an experience of the *nunc stans*, but an experience of perfect plenitude, absolute fulfillment. Parmenides says in the poem, through the mouth of the goddess (or, Parmenides would probably say, the goddess says through the mouth—or stylus—of Parmenides) that "thought and Being are one."[17] This could be read in several different ways, conceiving it first of all in terms of ourselves as subjects thinking, then in terms of Being as object of such thought. Our thinking at this level could be related to pure Being either by way of identity or by way of union. The former is the tendency in the Hindu tradition: Atman is Brahman, the Self is the All. The "I" for which everything, even its own structures, is an object, is not simply the I viewing itself as correlated with empirical objects or with intelligible relations, for all this is maya, the web of illusion wherein we misconstrue both Being and ourselves. Beyond all the distinctions provided at the empirical and rational levels, the I and the All are nondistinct, are identical.[18]

On the other hand, the way of union is the dominant tradition of the West, rooted in the doctrine of God as Absolute Other.[19] But on Parmenidean grounds, the union could be conceived as linked either to a nonconscious *principle* or with Thought that is itself pure Being. In the latter case, Being as a nature would thus not only be the unchanging One, a pure principle, dead, dull, unaware. It would be self-presence, without the distinction of subject and object, pure *noein*. This is a reading that developed, through Plato and Aristotle, into the Hebrew-Christian tradition as classical monotheism.

But with the Parmenidean thrust immediately locating itself in the seventh dimension, at the outermost limit of the heart's desire, experience is cleft in two: our experience of the ordinary world of "unthinkable" (but experienceable and imaginable) multiplicity and change, and the extraordinary experience of Eternal Fullness. The hard headed, tough-minded, no-nonsense, red-blooded objector will ask: "But what of the 'real world' in front of us now?" One who has experienced Eternal Fullness might reply, "What of it? It's not a world that can fill the outermost limits of the heart's desire. And there is Something that can." But Parmenides insists that one who would walk The Way of Truth (*aletheia*) must also know "the wandering opinion of mortals" on The Way of Seeming (*doxa*).[20] And on this Way of Seeming, Parmenides himself positions Eros in the center, "first of all the gods."[21] One who walks The Way of Truth must come to see "how the things that seem, as they pass through everything, must gain the semblance of Being."[22] The semblance of Being shows by virtue of Eros as desire for the Fullness. Such Eros is symbolized by the moon, wandering about the earth with borrowed light, looking always to the Sun.[23] The plurality of changing things, "unthinkable" (i.e., nonidentical, in their plurality and change, with the changeless One with which thought is identified) nonetheless shows the Absolute Fullness to the Eros, which is man who reflects "the light of Being" upon things.

Historical Aftermath

The function of *nous* in the ecstatic experience of identity with the Absolute Fullness is corroborated by the deductive power of the *logos,* both operating within the single experience of Parmenides. But in Parmenides' followers, Zeno and Melissus, *logos* takes on a certain independence, controlled, it is true, by the contents of Parmenidean *nous*, which are then taken as postulates for which, and against the opponents of which, logical dexterity is exercised.[24] This ushers in the severance of *logos* (understood as logic) from *nous*, serving the victory of one's own petty subjective preferences and desires for socially defined success, which ushered in the seemier side of Sophism.[25] The *sophos*, or wise man, attuned to the whole, became the "wise guy," clever at achieving his own aims through the use of "logic."

Unable to countenance relation to the Absolute Fullness, necessarily grasped by the multiplicity and change of the apparent world, but impressed as well by the logic of Parmenides, the atomists presented their doctrine. What we ought to call Being Itself is, as Parmenides claimed, internally changeless and unitary. It resides, however—so the atomists claimed—in a plurality, the members of which are separated from each other by an existent nonbeing: spatiality as the Void. Apparent reality is composed of indivisible, homogenous bodies, the Atoms or uncuttables that change only externally, by shifting relative positions within the Void, to produce the changes in the things that appear to ordinary awareness.[26]

The mind/heart which thinks/desires the Fullness is forgotten, though it remains the foundation of thinking the whole-as-atoms-in-the-void. For an atom, confined within its own boundaries, would scarcely raise the question of the nature of *the Whole*. Relation to the Whole remains at the foundation for the peculiar way in which the Whole is thought: as atoms in the void, as involving possible divinities capable of operating through the whole of our lives and a possible existence after the whole of our life span. Fear of such divinities and of the afterlife furnished one of the classical props to atomism as expressed in Epicurus.[27] If we and our loved ones are really not the wholes we appear to be, but are actually conglomerations of atoms that never change, then there is no self to fear the gods and thus no afterlife—and there is just as much being around before as after our dissolution. But the very thought of the whole of one's life implicated in the fear of death and the thought of the nature of the Whole whose proper conception can remove that fear presuppose a peculiarity in the atomic configuration here and now present that we call a human being: sprung out of the here-and-now, referred to the whole as a matter of deepest concern—the Ultimate Concern of the human heart.[28]

The Epicurean direction likewise has significant parallels with the thought of the Buddha in India for whom the self is a heap, that is in reality reducible to the plurality of its parts. The realization of this situation aids in achieving nirvana or the blowing out of desire, which is the source of suffering in life. However, there are significant differences, for the Buddha is also the compassionate Buddha concerned with the sufferings of others and aimed at an unsayable relation to Absolute Mystery.[29] But the typical Epicurean atomist is one concerned with his own pleasure, who leaves the gods to their own separate realm, limits his association with others to a few like-minded intimates, and, like Voltaire's Candide, "cultivates his own garden."[30] Epicurean atomism remains an insufficiently thought-out vision of man's place in the Totality. The Parmenidean background from which it comes makes explicit both the relation to the whole and the character of Absolute Fullness as transcendent of the multiplicity of changing things given in experience. Parmenides thus provides a first, powerful answer to the question implicit in the fundamental structure of our humanness: What is Being, this Totality to which we are referred at the center of our being?

Heidegger's Approach

What I have presented is a variation on what might be called the standard interpretation of Parmenides, a variation, however, inspired by Heidegger's distinction between *aletheia* and *orthotes*, carried over into the *nous-logos* distinction. Heidegger's fuller interpretation moves away entirely from the standard interpretation. Being, in this view, is indeed other than the multiplicity of beings. It abides, one and permanent, the imperishable, but not apart from things. Being is the light that gathers beings together and allows them to make their appearance to us. Being provides the meaning-field within which we dwell and within which our relation to other beings (and to ourselves) is realized.[31] The way of *doxa* is simultaneously appearance and opinion: the way beings show themselves is a function of the modes of meaning through which we take them. Acquaintance with the realm of seeming is thus "needful," as Parmenides says. But so is the unthinkable way of non-being, struggle with which provides the contrast in terms of which Being itself grips us. As with Heraclitus, through death we "know" life, so here, through nonbeing we know Being. Beings manifest themselves in deepening presence as we are drawn away from them through the realization of the otherness of Being itself and impelled more deeply to them in a way analogous to the way we are impelled more deeply to the realization of life through the realization of death.[32]

As richly suggestive as that analysis is, it does not necessarily have to be (as Heidegger thinks) incompatible with the standard interpretation of Parmenides' Being as transcendent, existing eternally in itself apart from the multiplicity of changing beings. Heidegger's understanding highlights the aletheic aspect of our relation to Being and draws a tighter link between the realm of seeming and the realm of Being. But there is room for an otherness of Being as a nature linked to beings through the light of the human being's openness to the Transcendent.

7 _Plato_

In Parmenides we observed a split between pure Being as the fulfillment of the seventh dimension and the realm of shifting particulars
correlated with changing _doxa_ and constituting the first six dimensions. In Plato we find, in effect, the interposition of an elaborate
network of principles that connect the final reality with the changing
scene. The sixth dimension—at least the eidetic aspect of that
dimension—is fitted securely into the intervening space between pure
Being and the realm of change. Plato calls this novel space the place
of the Forms or Ideas or _Eidoi_, linked downward to the changing
realm through participation, and linked upward to the One through a
deductive process (at least in one approach—we will see later that
Plato may be guided by another sort of aspiration.)[1] The One remains
the ultimate and Eros the subjective correlate to it,[2] the interplay
between which establishes a center at rest in the dance of individual
beings and opinions, "the still point of the changing world" that makes
the shifting, scattered plurality into a uni-verse.

Metaphor and Allegory

Though Eros in all things seeks the One, the human being, caught in
the tension between such Eros and the pull of plurality and surface,
loses sight of where he belongs and flees from the One. Plato describes
the situation of conscious or unconscious flight from the One in his
famous Allegory of the Cave, perhaps the most extended and complicated allegory ever constructed. It differs, however, from allegory in
the conventional sense in that, though there is a rational translation
of the elements, it rests upon what I will call "primary metaphors"
that are richer than any literal translation: basically the metaphors
of light and darkness and of ascent and descent, coupled with the
central metaphor of the dream.[3]

Like Abbott's _Flatland_, the cave allows us a certain imaginary
distance from ourselves in order to allow that which we take for
granted, i.e., our ordinary mode of presence to the world around us
and to our very selves, to come into focus in a new and revealing way.
Plato's basic structural metaphor here is the dream as a state of mind

133

lived in relation to images of reality rather than to reality itself: a dream consists in taking an image for reality.[4] In what does such "taking" consist? In the mode in which the dream is *present*. In imaginary projection, whether deliberately guided or free-floating day-dreaming, the image is not "taken" for, and is thus not present as, reality. But in the actual dream, what is later discovered as only an image is present *as real*. And it is the sense of "as real" that is of special interest to us. Plato is asking us to consider our ordinary mode of awareness as a dream—which is more difficult to do insofar as this mode of dreaming is collectively corroborated, intersubjectively verifiable.

Plato overlays this metaphor of the dream with the metaphoric contrast of light and darkness. The situation in which we find ourselves, to which we are "chained," is one of darkness lit by a dim and flickering light. And this, in turn, is correlated with the image-contrast of ascent and descent. Thought is capable of grasping the situation of darkness as darkness, and thus of descending as thought into the darkness, only insofar as it can at the same time ascend to the light, see the reality of which the originally present is only an image. In fact, light itself only appears *as* light in contrast with the darkness because contrast affects the modality of presence. Seeing our situation as a whole by reason of its insertion into the interplay of light and darkness and of ascent and descent within the framework of the dream metaphor allows us to view the familiar as indeed astonishing. All our ordinary points of reference are reversed. And this new point of view allows the ordinary to be seen, as it were, for the first time. It ascends from ordinary unquestioned presence—even the presence of critical questioning of it—to the extraordinary presence of aletheic "vision." By vision here I understand a peculiar fusion between a new framework—or perhaps even an old framework (cf. our meditations in ch. 1)— and a new mode of presence (wonder, astonishment) that can easily slip into simply a new intellectual, orthotic framework for "taking" or construing the data of experience, seeing them *as* something, but which does not necessarily affect our ordinary full sense of presence (cf. the transition from Parmenides to Zeno). "Awe (*thaumazein*)," says Plato, "is the sustaining ground (*arche*) of philosophy."[5] But what is it that allows this "seeing-as" to be verified as anything but a fiction? Plato approaches it on several levels; indeed, the dream-reality relation, and hence the ascending process of "waking up," has six levels in Plato's view, underpinned by a basic, but only inferentially available level. The underlying level is the unconscious body, rooted in what Plato calls "the Receptacle." The levels of awareness that rest upon this are (1) the dream; (2) ordinary wakefulness; (3) awareness of the empirical causes of the everyday world; (4) grasp of mathematical principles; (5) grasp of the structures, goals, and ultimate context of awareness and its objects; and (6) awareness of "the Good," which I will claim is identical with Parmenides' One/Being.

Dreaming in the Cave

We have already begun with (1), the dream, as furnishing us with the basic metaphor for the relation between the lower and higher levels. Each higher level is a mode of "waking up" from the next lower level and is itself, relative to the next higher level, a dream, leading us to take images of reality for reality itself.

(2) The world of ordinary wakefulness is itself a dream. Plato claims it takes place, metaphorically, in a deep, dimly lit cave wherein we are all chained so that we can see only shadows on the cave wall, the shadows being images of reality. The chaining process and the images have a twofold character. In the first place, we are cognitively chained by our biological nature, which allows sensory disclosure to take place only within very limited thresholds relative to what is fully there.[6] We have made similar observations in the first two chapters. Nature provides us with highly selected images of physical reality. But underlying the images is the hidden *phusis* which brings forth not only our perceptions, but also the things perceived. Release from the circle of perception and the view of it as appearance or image of physical reality demands a reflective disengagement from the immediately given, already spontaneously accomplished to a certain extent by reason of memory and the process of association that enters into the configuration of the immediate.

The world of ordinary wakefulness is not only filtered biologically, it is also overlaid by a second filter derived from the socialization process. Consider racist consciousness. The racist derives his images of the members of a minority group primarily from significant others—parents, associates, family members—always in some interplay with what sensorily presents itself. However, only so much of what presents itself is allowed to show itself, namely, that which reinforces the stereotypes and provokes the typical negative response in behavior. What the racist is indeed fixated upon is not the reality of what appears within the circle of the sensory filter, but the socially constructed and socially sustained image. Plato, in effect, asks us to generalize that observation. We are dominated in every area of experience by socially constructed images that determine the degree to which, and the manner in which we focus our attention in everyday life. We are indeed chained from birth, biologically and culturally fixed on images of reality, doubly removed from things and persons, living a collective dream. This second level of dreaming Plato calls *eikasia* or image fixation.[7]

Sensing is itself a function of biological need and thus correlated with the upsurge of biological desire. Human transcendence of biology makes possible a deliberate reshaping of the environment. Cultural shaping of the environment through art is exposed thereby to the permanent possibility of producing images that evoke bodily resonances. A culture of luxury emerges, fixing us in the cave of sensuous indulgence. And while desire in the brute animal is tied directly to the wholistic functioning of the organism so that the animal may safely follow its instincts, human transcendence of biology makes possible the infinitizing of desire and thus the loss af all measure. Plato calls such a culture "swollen, feverish, bloated."[8]

(3) At a further level, which Plato calls *pistis* (usually translated, rather unhelpfully, as "faith", but signifying rather something like "educated opinion"), waking up involves, in one of its moments, a turning around of the soul from socially predefined "reality" to the actual facts of the case, the sensory data: a breaking through customary perceptions to a new and fresh encounter which allows hidden or previously distorted or unnoticed aspects to emerge. The things themselves are allowed to speak again. We pay attention to the facts and form our opinions accordingly. Clever people are especially adept at grasping the situation and learning how to manipulate the opinions of the less attentive many.[9] In the cave imagery, the shadows on the wall are projected by puppeteers carrying images of natural and manufactured things. I suggest the puppeteers are the lesser divinities of the *Timaeus* who project the images of natural things into the cave of our sensibility[10], and the clever people who project public opinion, "images of justice in the lawcourts."[11]

In another moment, aesthetic cultivation involves a conversion from luxurious self-indulgence to an attitudinal fixation, not upon our feelings, but upon the fine qualities of things. Hence a distantiation from biological appetite and a kind of aesthetic objectivity. Indeed, for Plato an education that purges us from the culture of luxurious self-indulgence culminates in the appreciation of beautiful things.[12]

The two levels of *eikasia* and *pistis* Plato calls, following Parmenides, the realm of *doxa*, which term carries several meanings.[13] Usually in this context it is taken to mean "opinion," as in 'orthodoxy,' or "right opinion." It is also used to mean "glory" as a kind of external aura provided by one who honors another, as in the liturgical 'doxology,' or "Glory be to the Father." It is thus linked to *dokeo*, "I seem" or "I appear" as the way things/persons show themselves.

Doxa could then be seen as a phenomenon of the interplay between awareness and things: it is a dialectical phenomenon of "showing" and "taking," an interplay between the way we construe things ("form our opinions of them") and the way they present themselves. Neither pole is completely independent of the other: though things do limit and tend to coerce our opinions, it is also our opinions that limit how things can show themselves. *Doxa* is thus the realm of appearing/ opining.[14] We construct our interpretations in the sixth dimension, based either upon relatively uninformed popular stereotypes, often deliberately manipulated by the clever, or upon a greater or lesser measure of attention to empirical fact. And we live with primary attention directed either to our appetitive gratification or to the fine qualities of empirically present things.

In the Light

Not everything is a matter of opinion, educated or not; and the possibilities of attention are not confined to the empirically given. There is a further region of what Plato calls *episteme*, a firm stand (from *histemi*, I stand) taken upon (*epi*) firm-standing, changeless reality.[15] There are certain eidetic necessities which govern the whole realm of *doxa*, both on the subjective side of opinion formation and the objective side of sensory, changing reality. There are changeless objective principles governing objective but changing things. The awakening to objective principle beyond social or individual construction appears most clearly in geometry, to which we will shortly return. That which allows the underlying *phusis* to come to our awareness, however, is not merely means to redescribing the individual reality announcing itself in the sense-appearance. It is itself a level of reality that, for Plato, is deeper than the individual realm itself. It is, indeed, akin to Parmenides' other realm of pure Being, for it is the changeless and universal realm of principle. Plato calls it *ousia*, a noun possibly derived from *ousa*, the participal form of *einai*, "to be."[16] The changing realm he calls *genesis*, or "becoming."

In preoccupying itself with that other realm, other than that given in sensory immediacy, Platonism post-Plato tends to focus our sense of presence "elsewhere" and to deny our at-homeness "here".[17] At the same time, however, it mitigates the severity of the Parmenidean separation of pure Being from the immediate by the doctrine of participation. The immediately given participates in and thereby mirrors the realm of Being.[18]

What moves us out of the cavelike situation of collusion between biological proclivity and cultural shaping is an awakening to the ground of *that* dialectic. Culture provides us with "images of justice": that means that one might begin with the images and discover, especially in the interplay between alternative, conflicting images, the original of which they are the copies.[19] For Plato, this clash opens us to an awareness of an ineradicable desire: a desire for the Good, such that, though one might be contented with appearance elsewhere in life—for example, the appearance of justice to others— no one is contented in himself with a merely apparent good.[20] Such desire is for the real, which would satisfy really and not only apparently. But what are the criteria for "real" satisfaction? The Parmenidean background appears: that which would be an absolute and eternal Plenitude. One approach to it is through reflection on what is involved in mathematical understanding, both on the part of the knower and on the part of the known. Mathematical insight would characterize level (4), the first stage of emergence from the cave of *doxa* to the sunlight of *episteme.*

The apparently value-neutral region of mathematics stands over against both personal and collective preference and imposes itself upon us as possessing its own intrinsic logic. But the conditions for the possibility of our recognition of that involve our own not being wholly absorbed in the realm of personal and collective preference, the cavelike collusion/conflict between biology and culture. When Plato speaks of mathematics, he thinks paradigmatically of geometry.

Geometry as Paradigm

Geometry had its origin (as its name *geo-metria,* "earth-measurement," indicates) in empirically derived metric rules geared toward laying out fields, building canals and roads, erecting buildings, and so on. But among the Greeks, a different kind of interest arose apart from the pragmatic and empirical.[21] It was an interest continuous with our ordinary need to make sense of things. 'Making sense' consists in discovering and/or creating a coherence in what would otherwise be a scattered plurality of experiences. 'Understanding' in general consists in grasping a coherence—even in the most prosaic examples, such as our by now tedious 'pen,' understood only when we grasp its coherent connection with paper, writing, ideas, persons, communication.

Geometry moves from its empirical-pragmatic phase under the guidance of a desire, detached from pragmatic considerations, to grasp unity in the multiplicity of metric rules: a purely theoretical interest. And that takes shape not simply as a one-leveled apprehension of relations, but as a grasp of a hierarchy of relations stemming from a few axioms from which the theorems flow. The unification of the empirical-pragmatic realm is established from another level of relative unity guided by interest in unity as such. But the empirical-pragmatic consequences themselves are immense: a quantum leap occurs. For not only are the known metric rules unified, but a powerful instrument is formed for generating an indefinite number of new rules that run ahead of the slower process of empirical acquisition through trial and error. The desire for unity and the discovery of a hierarchy of simpler but broader principles sets the mind on another course.

But the achievement of theoretical unity within a given region of experience—geometry—does not fill the total thrust of the mind for greater unity. So Plato projects, in addition to "the downward way" from axioms to theorems, and from theory to application, an "upward way" from the multiple axioms in different regions toward (6) "the One" that would unify them all.[22] Here he projects the ideal of rational science, as Einstein for one reexpressed it in more recent times: to find the single equation from which all known and future empirical regularities can be deduced.[23]

The state of mind that apprehends mathematical objects Plato terms *dianoia*, usually translated (again unhelpfully) as "understanding."[24] Since we begin geometry by drawing or looking at empirically observable figures, what is at stake here is a knowledge embedded in images. It would be more helpful to translate the term as "knowledge (*noia*) through (*dia*) images." (And this has further ramifications in Plato's thought, which, unfortunately, we cannot explore here. But it involves the whole "poetic," mythical metaphorical, image-based thinking that we find throughout the dialogues.) And just as our everyday awareness is "dreaming" by being fixed on "images" or shadows of real things, so our awareness of mathematics is a fixation on "images" or shadows of something higher. Plato indicates this by using the same expression for the objects of the mind on both levels: shadows or images reflected in shiny surfaces such as pools of water and the like—"if you know what I mean."[25]

It is extremely instructive for philosophic procedure to attend carefully to what Plato does here. Instead of simply "doing" mathematics, he is engaged in a metareflection or second-order reflection upon mathematics, reflecting simultaneously upon the character of the strategy of proof (deduction of theorems from axioms and postulates), the status of the objects known (universal, changeless principles reflected in particular changing images), and the nature of the knowing subject (sensory and intellectual). This reflective procedure specifies one kind of eidetic object found at the next highest level of insight, (5), called *noesis*.[26]

The sensorily given triangle drawn on a blackboard, like all things encounterable in sensory experience, has to be considered in terms of a time-coefficient. The truth of its sensory existence expressed in the proposition "There is a triangle" assumes the addition of some qualifying phrase like "as long as it's there." And it is there, perhaps, from 10:05 to 10:50 during the geometry class when we were demonstrating the Pythagorean theorem, before which it did not exist, and after which it was erased forever.

But the Pythagorean theorem itself does not have a time-coefficient fixed to it. Though it comes into human consciousness at a specific moment and under specifically favorable cultural conditions — the provision of a measure of leisure, the emergence of a theoretical interest within the leisure tradition, and the development of both pragmatic-empirical and theoretical geometry — and though it might pass out of human consciousness if the earth is destroyed or if civilization crumbles, yet the theorem seen is seen to have held before it was discovered and to hold still even though it should be forgotten. The theorem thus exists in a kind of eternity over against the flow of time, shifting at the level of nature and at the level of culture.

So we indeed have two realms of objects: the temporal realm of mutable individual bodies perceptible through the senses, and the atemporal realm of changeless universal principles apprehensible by the mind. And this simultaneously tells us something about ourselves. We are bodies on the one hand, limited to our own boundaries, but we also exceed them through our sensory awareness of the environment. Both bodiliness and sensory awareness are immanent in the flow of the space-time world. But beyond this, through eidetic insight we exceed the boundaries of our own temporal span guided by a desire for unity.

The character of material things is such that a given theorem can be realized in an indefinite number of particulars throughout space and time. Space and time, in turn, are factors of negativity ingredient in changing things (cf. our discussion on Parmenides). And the possiblity of theorems extends beyond mathematical principles to the archetypes of living things and to other Ideas as well. Theorems and archetypes are "mirrored" in different times, in different places and in different degrees of exactitude because they are embedded in a matrix of essential restlessness and negativity that Plato calls "the Receptacle."[27] There seems to be a sort of mutual immanence here. The Receptacle enters into the constitution of material beings as an element of non-being, involving a need to develop through struggle and a requirement of dissolution; but it is also a matrix in which such things are embedded. It is a kind of mirror, but it is a shattered mirror that multiplies the forms (principles, theorems, patterns) in many times and places. It is likewise a restless mirror that does not mirror in a static Now, but mirrors in temporal sequence the atemporal intelligible sequence of coherent unfolding applicable to Ideas. And the restlessness of the mirror disallows the fully matured form to remain forever. Dissolution inevitably follows emergence. "The Receptacle" of space-time is thus like a stream whose wavelets mirror in a shifting and multiple manner the static context through which it moves.

It is of extremely important consequence for the history of thought to attend to the distinction between two sorts of causality that emerges from reflection upon the different ontological levels of mathematical principles and observable instances of those principles. The observable instances are linked together in a temporal sequence of causes and effects that might be called a "horizontal series" of causes. A particular right-angled triangle comes into being and passes out of being through the action of some agent who temporally antecedes the given triangle. The agent himself was generated by another agent, and so on. But this horizontal series of causes in temporal sequence is perpetually intersected by a vertical series that transcends time, namely the series of deductions by which the theorem exhibited in the example of the right-angled triangle flows from the axioms and the postulates of the geometric system. And though in terms of cognition we have to go through a temporal process in the horizontal series to move from the axioms to the theorems, nonetheless, the character of the deductive "flow" is such as to exhibit a nontemporal relation of principle and conclusion, of ground and consequent that perpetually intersects the horiontal series. The geometric theorems are understood at this instant within time as eternally following from the axioms. This relation will furnish the pattern for the understanding of the most basic level of causality in Aristotle and Aquinas: the causality of the divine in relation to the nondivine.

Eros and the Good

The ascent to the One/Good through reflection on mathematics and the eidetic features of Being, of Becoming, and of the soul implicated in mathematical apprehension is only one approach. The superrationalism of that approach has to be supplemented by the "irrational," inspired approach through Eros awakened by the perception of beauty as described in the *Symposium* and the *Phaedrus*. Apollonian light, clarity, and sobriety has to be supplemented by Dionysian madness, the mysterious emergence of inspiration. In the former dialogue, Eros is presented as the bond between the mortal and the immortal. Operating in all living things, it is the desire of the mortal, in the mode appropriate to it, for immortality. In prehuman forms and in the prepersonal thrust of biological desire in us, Eros is desire for the mirroring of the eternal in time through the perpetuation of the species. At the distinctively human level, it further expresses itself, by reason of our ability to think beyond the immediacy of our urges and beyond our own limited life span, in the creation of "immortal works," in great words and deeds that will live on in the memory of, or in their enduring effects upon, posterity. But the same Eros, sublimated in these works of culture, can be further sublimated into a direct relation with the eternal realm that governs the temporal flow: the realm of Forms which exhibit the deeper beauty of their harmonic integration into the system of nature. But surmounting even the Forms is eternal Beauty Itself, a "Real Presence" that shines forth in a privileged way in all beautiful things and evokes our most passionate desire.[28]

The *Phaedrus* links this sublimated passion to the interpersonal realm of Eros for a single beloved in which "the image of god" is seen. Such Eros, properly channeled, and not exploding into a riot of possessiveness and sexual abandon, causes the soul to "grow wings" and gives it the power to ascend, with the beloved, to the region of the god they mutually follow. Desirous of perpetually being in the presence of each other and threatened by the dissoluteness of "the dark horse" of possessive, selfish sexuality, if they endure in harmonious pursuit of the god, they will have received the greatest blessing the gods can give and will grow their wings together.[29]

Eros is one of the four forms of "divine madness"—the highest form in Plato's estimation—that brings us from the cave of conventional relations and sets us on the path to the highest. The other forms are prophecy, religious purgation, and inspired art. Philosophy, as Plato envisions it, encompasses all four.[30] Eros is thus the hidden ground of the rational ascent to the convergence of the Good, the One, and the Beautiful, which illuminates the intelligible realm of the True.

Plato's universe, then, is like Parmenides' in that there is Being as the Eternal Fullness, as the One, as the limit of the heart's desire. There is also the realm of the mixture of being and non-being. But Plato's genius interposed between them the intelligible realm of *ousia*, mirroring the One in its coherence and being mirrored by the realm of Becoming in the intelligibility that Becoming exhibits. Plato also inserted "beneath" the things composed of being and non-being a negative matrix of space and time, "the Receptacle." The realm of *ousia*, nonetheless, is not the realm of the Fullness because it too is riddled with non-being, the non-being of multiplicity. In Plato's terms, this realm participates in the negative Form of Otherness.[31] But the One/Good is "beyond *ousia*," although not "beyond Being," (*to on*) as the highest, most manifest level of Being.[32]

In the *Republic*, Plato has Socrates describe the sighting of the Good Itself as "his dream," that is an image of reality, suggesting there is really perhaps no sighting of the Good.[33] The image of the Sun implies as much, for we cannot look into the Sun without being blinded. As Aristotle will later express it: our eyes are to Being Itself (Pure Form) as the eyes of the owl to the light of day.[34] "The dream" is that *philo-sophia*, or love of final wisdom which is not now possessed, would terminate in the possession of *sophia*. But both before and after the *Republic*, Plato claims that wisdom consists in knowing that one does not know, that is, in awareness that human knowing is not God's knowing, that human knowing, like Eros, is a phenomenon of the in-between, moving from the changing matrix of Becoming and the partialities of limited regions of intelligibility toward the as-yet-unpossessed whole and/or its Source.[35] The human being is poised in the in-between, inclined to take the apparent for the real, both in the realm of Being and in the realm of value (though the two are not ultimately separable).

The Cave, that is, our ordinary situation, "the human condition," is a dream, governed by the tendency to take an image of reality for reality itself. That means to rest content—insofar as we are able—with the appearance *as* reality. The Cave is lit by a fire which Plato identifies with the Sun. But the Sun, in its turn, is to be understood as the principle of sense-perceptibility. The source of light governs the realm of the seen and the seeing.[36] And our 'seeing' vocabulary structures our talk about all our senses (and indeed all our cognitive states, as we have already indicated in chapter 2): "*See* how this food tastes, this perfume smells, this velvet feels, this record sounds," and not "Smell how this looks" or "Hear how this feels" or "Feel how this tastes." The Cave is the situation in which the proximate criterion of reality and value is sense-perceptibility. What is real? What I can touch, taste, see, and feel (though interestingly, not what I can hear, ordinarily). What is good? Food, drink, sex, sights, and sounds.

But in neither case will the proximate criterion do as ultimate criterion. It is not a criterion of reality, because the senses yield appearances within thresholds that have to be read as indicative of the reality of what appears within the thresholds. At the level of everyday experience, perceptual illusions and dreams are incorrect readings insofar as they are taken for reality; they have to be corrected by

establishing their coherence or incoherence with the regular connections of wakeful life. But beyond this, the awareness of the envelope
character of the perceptual field requires a level of reflection that lays
hold of the eidetic. And the appeal to theory in the sciences allows for
a further extension of our understanding of what underlies the sensory appearance in our everyday experience. But if theory is anything, it is an appeal to the coherent, that is, to the mirroring of
the One in the intelligible.

The senses as criteria for ultimate value likewise fail. Minimally,
one has to establish a certain limit to the mad pursuit of pleasure so
as not to destroy the organic basis for pleasurable gratification. The
good of that base is coherent functioning, the harmonious interrelation of the parts, with a *nisus* toward fuller actuation. But what allows
both the breaking of natural bounds within which animal organisms
are held and the intelligent establishment of limits is a relation not to
appearance but to what is absolute and real. For the intelligent establishment of limits looks beyond the immediate to our life as a whole:
Epicurean wisdom consists in determining how one might limit one's
current pleasures for the sake of future prospects throughout one's
life.[37] And prereflective grounding relation to the Whole tempts one
to take the immediately present for that Whole.[38] Value, then, the
Good-for-oneself, appears in a standing beyond the apparent toward
the real judged in the light of the whole of one's life and established in
terms of criteria of coherence. But the conditions that make that
possible point beyond the senses to a deeper region to which we are
essentially related, a realm that is eternal and complete, a realm
governed by the One for which our hearts are made. "The Good" is
thus not simply "my good," nor simply the good for all mankind, but
the irradiating Source of all reality. The good-for-me involves a movement from the privacy of my biological gratification to the in-principle
publicity of the Absolute Good. However, the difficulty of access to
that good involves a de facto privacy of a deeper sort, beyond the
socially subjective publicity of the everyday world of the cave. The
apparent clarity of the everyday world is habit based, semilight
semidark, confused with the clarity of the Ideas which appear in that
everyday world as relatively opaque. But though light and clarity
dominate in Plato's imagery, the final reality is like darkness to the
limited capacity of the human mind itself. The last word in Platonism
tends toward an ultimate darkness. The reality of the physical is
revealed most deeply when it is seen as image of the intelligible, but
even more deeply as image of the Good/One which is not seen but
aspired toward. In such aspiration human desire is explicitly extended
to the whole. Lovers of the Good/One become lovers of the mirroring

of the Good/One everywhere, but especially in those instances of mirroring that are relatively self-disposing and thus capable of ever clearer mirroring: in other humans. Corresponding to the total thrust of human Eros, this involves all humans; but corresponding to the incarnate conditions of humanness, that involves anchorage in the here-and-now of encounter with those with whom we have our every-day dealings. Love for the farthest thus returns us to the dialogical situation.[39]

The approach, presented in the *Republic*'s treatment of the Cave, to the Good as the final object of the mind's thrust for the eternal is contained within an overall context that continually denies our ability to reach the Good itself, because "the impulse that propels us there is insufficient."[40] Though, in the context of the cave, Socrates refers to the sighting of the Good itself, he also speaks of such sighting as his "dream."[41] And the use of the sun as metaphor for the Good itself suggests a necessarily indirect approach, as we already said. A similar image is evoked in the *Laws*, where the Athenian exhorts that we avoid creating darkness at noon by seeking to stare directly at the sun, when we ought rather to focus on an image of it, the intelligible order generated by orientation toward a single point.[42] But the context of Book X presents the Good as a living soul, a mind initiating motion in things.[43] The Good/One is here not simply a principle but a living mind, hence a personal ultimate. The same is true of the *Sophist*, where the Athenian stranger asks rhetorically, "Are we really to be so readily convinced that change, life, soul, understanding have no place in that which is perfectly real . . . ?"[44]

The *Timaeus* makes a similar linkage: the god fashions a world outside himself because, being good, he is not jealous and did not wish to keep his goodness to himself.[45] The *Timaeus* presents itself as "a likely story,"[46] and the argument of the *Laws* seems deliberately to hold open other options, while the *Sophist* makes a rhetorical appeal. All seem to point us back to Socrates' intellectual autobiography in the *Phaedo*.[47] Here he describes his early interest in explanation through determination of the material elements that enter into the composition of bodies. But he was puzzled especially by the problem of what constitutes the unity of multiple elements in a given body, and in general, how the one becomes many and the many one. The discovery of the work of Anaxagoras signified a turning point, for Anaxagoras claimed that mind is the basic cause of the composition of the elements. Socrates was thrilled since he considered that mind would arrange things for the purpose of achieving the good, both in individual beings and in the universe at large. So an analysis into elements would only give us necessary conditions, but the basic cause would be the arrangement of the elements for the good of the whole. This parallels contemporary analysis of the distinction and relation between action and motion, where the latter can be understood in terms of mechanisms and reflexes, while the former is intelligible in terms of understanding the purposes aimed at by the action.[48]

However, Socrates was disappointed with Anaxagoras, for after his intriguing suggestion, Anaxagoras continued to explain things in terms of elements and mechanical combinations. And Socrates himself claimed that the discovery of mind arranging things for the good was beyond his power. But the notion itself led him to develop a "second best" way, a "makeshift method," a "second sailing" positing the Forms, participation in which makes bodily beings intelligible.

Laws X returns to the same situation. There are those who claim that the elements are first and constitute the nature of things, and that mind with its creation of laws and production of art is secondary. The Athenian suggests the opposite: elements can ultimately be understood as the product of mind, and thus as objects of its lawmaking and artistic activity. It is this which Plato seems to have as his major purpose throughout his work: to show our mind as the key to the ultimate character of Being. Our mind's arranging things for the purposes we project, requiring the determinate matrix of material elements to realize its purposes, is itself the prime analogate for a World-Mind organizing the universe as a harmonious whole.[49] The One/Good as impersonal principle is, at least in intention, an outside view of what is aspired to as a Person, a Mind, the One God. Plato's historical task is to prepare the way for that.

* * *

Figure 7.1 shows the transition from Parmenides' notion of Being to Plato's.

Parmenides' Being (*estin*), correlate of the heart and beyond the realm of *dox,a* is preserved by Plato as the One/Good/Beauty. But, led by the atemporal character of mathematics, Plato interposes the realm of the Forms which links the One to the realm of *doxa*; and he positions the Receptacle at the base of the realm of *doxa* to account for the plurality of mutable individuals participating in their respective Forms.

Being for Plato is a hierarchically scaled totality topped off by the One which is Good Itself and Beauty itself, the correlate of human Eros fully conscious of itself. It is the most manifest region of (participial) being (*on*). Below it stands (substantive) being (*ousia*), the region of the Forms, all of which are divided from the One by partici-

Figure 7.1 TRANSITION FROM PARMENIDES TO PLATO

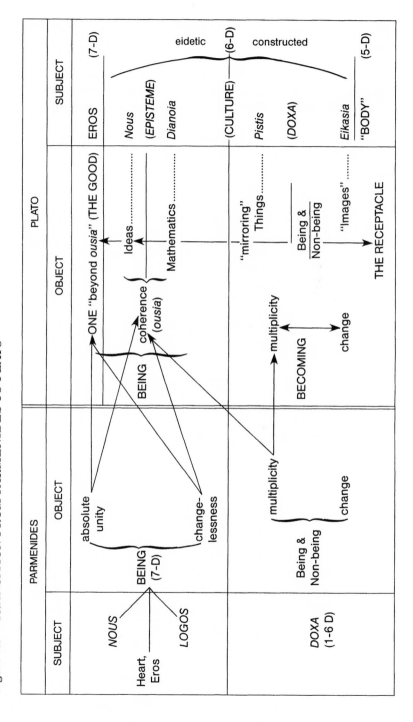

pating in a type of non-being, the form of Otherness, but unified as a coherent, intelligible whole by participating in the One. Below the region of *ousia* stands the realm of Becoming (*genesis*), the material world, each member of which *is* insofar as it mirrors the Forms as a coherent unit, and *is not* insofar as it is subject to change and imperfect realization of the Form of its type. All such things participate both in the Forms and in the negativity of the Receptacle, the restlessness of space-time. Human being spans the hierarchy and is the single locus in the material world where the whole becomes conscious of itself.

Epilogue on Plotinus

Platonic Renaissances reoccur throughout the history of Western thought—usually in conjunction with attention to the greatest of the Platonists after Plato himself: Plotinus (fl. A.D. 3d c.). Through Plotinus's influence on Augustine, and, before Augustine, on the Greek fathers of the church, Western thought and Western spirituality were given a powerful otherworldly turn. Plato's otherworldliness always has a this-worldly side—even, in a sense, a this-worldly ground, for Plato was ever interested in the foundations of political-social order, even in his most austere metaphysical moments.[1] But Plotinus always desired to be "There," and was ashamed of being "Here," in an embodied condition.[2]

The center of Plotinus's thought may be most easily approached if we attend to the character of mathematical insight once again. We apprehend the truth of a geometrical theorem not by gawking at figures or by measuring, but by reflection upon what a given geometrical figure involves in principle. And such reflection is a movement back into the mind, where we see the universal truth occasioned by the particular example. That is the first point: the truth, being universal, is seen "in the mind" by a "turn within" from the "outwardness" of sensory observation. But secondly, such a truth, far from locking us in the privacy of our own mental processes "inside," frees us from sensuous immediacy which operates in terms of bodily need, frees us from the here-and-now of the sensory surface, and opens us to truths that hold universally, for all instances, like the figure that occasioned the insight into the principle. The flowing stream of colors, sounds, kinesthetic feelings—tingles, itches, strains, pains—memories, fantasies, desires, and moods that constitute my privacy is surmounted by reaching the public space of the universal truth. For such truth holds, not only for any similar instances, but also for any rightly disposed mind, that is, for anyone able to follow the evidence. "In the mind," then, (not sensorily "outside") I see a universal truth (not simply a particular instance) accessible in the same way for all rightly disposed minds (not simply for my private awareness).

149

What then is this level of mind that transcends my privacy, that surmounts the flux of consciousness in a changeless, universal object? What is it that, being in me, yet contains truths which transcend me? Or maybe "I" at this level am no longer the private, isolated ego, conceived of on the model of my individualized, separated, clearly circumscribed body. Maybe here I become or I am taken over by an encompassing Mentality that contains the universal truths. Perhaps when I am raised above my privacy in this way I attain the Common Ground of all minds: I become in some way identified with a World Mind.³ This is Plotinus's essential move: to see a universal truth in the mind is to be identical with a World-Mind or to have the World-Mind dwell in me. This clarifies Parmenides' dictum: "Thought and being are one."

Plotinus is fortified in this move by traveling a different but related path, or perhaps by following the same path further in a different manner. He follows Plato's "upward way" from the multiplicity of axioms and postulates in the differing areas of mathematics towards "the One" from which all could ideally be deduced, in the manner in which all the theorems of a region of mathematics are deduced from the axioms and postulates of that region. What is the reality-status of myself, insofar as I ascend beyond the plurality of truths in the World-Mind and attain to "the One"? Porphyry, Plotinus's friend and biographer, reports that four times during his life Plotinus was seized by the One, identified with It, and experienced simultaneously his own absolute unity with the Oneness that is the Source of all things.⁴ Parmenides's "Thought and Being are one" is here understood, in terms of the peculiar character of Plotinus's mystical experience, as an absolute identity between the individual human and the Absolute One from which everything, the entire plurality within and without the self, is seen to flow. Even the plurality involved in the distinction of subject and object at the level of the World-Mind is here surmounted.⁵ "Going into the self," one reaches at this level a maximal transcendence of the privatized self in the stream of consciousness. One indeed becomes "alone with the Alone," but in such a way as to reach most deeply into the heart of things through reaching experientially their most inward Ground.

This inward and upward path is opened through an initial turning back from the flowing distractions of a biologically immersed, extroverted pattern of experience. It requires a rigorous restraint of "bodily appetites," a *purgative way* "out of the body."⁶ Led initially by the object focus of a theoretical discipline like geometry, we are brought along the *illuminative way* when, in reflecting upon the strategy of geometrical proof, the ontological status of the objects of geometry, and, above all, the structural levels of the self involved in the doing of geometry, we cₔ me to understand better our cosmic position and to see our initial cavelike situation for what it is.[7] But the final step is to follow the upward path to the One, no longer simply theoretically (orthotically), but with our whole inward substance, until we are grasped aletheically by the One, until we are at one with the One at the summit of the *unitive way*.[8] These three "ways" became the staple description of the levels of development of the spiritual life in the Middle Ages.[9]

The levels of the self thus unveiled are correlated with the great levels of the universe in which the self is embedded. The plurality of the parts of the the body is unified at one level by the presence of soul, vivifying, synthesizing the material parts into a functional whole. But at this level, conscious life is split and carried by varying stimuli arising from without and from below. The body becomes the tomb of the mind. But there is, corresponding to the animating level of the self, a level of the cosmos that Plotinus calls the "World-Soul," which makes the material plurality into a living universe. A higher level of humanness is reached when, like the poet, we develop sensitivity to an encompassing felt unity that makes the world as a whole seem alive, shot through with felt affinities.[10] (This exhibits remarkable parallels to the vision of Chinese Taoism.)[11]

At the next level, the level of mind, the self becomes gathered into the unity of a detached subject viewing its theoretical objects. To this corresponds the World-Mind. And to the level of the experience of the absolute unity of the self corresponds the One, Source of all. The world cascades from the One as progressive (or regressive) levels of multiplicity, unified in a coherence that is immobile at the level of the World-Mind, shifting but continuous through the work of the World-Soul in the reproductive and nutritive activities of individual organisms and in the ecosystem as a whole throughout time. At last multiplicity dominates at the level of sheer matter, the negativity of the Receptacle.

Plotinus offers the image of the One as a source of light trailing off until it reaches absolute darkness. The dimming of the light as it proceeds from the Center is a progressive invasion by the darkness of multiplicity, rooted ultimately in "matter." The universe flows out, "emanates" from the One as fall from unity until it reaches the ultimate dispersal of "matter."[12] In man, however, as one who can "return to himself" from the flow of bodily based life, the universe is brought back into progressive unity. Man attains to the light insofar as he learns to integrate the scattered plurality of experience. He becomes light insofar as he finally reaches "the still point of the changing world" in the One.[13]

One might also symbolize this situation by the same diagram we used in the chapter on metaphysics and practicality: The movement within to more concentrated and progressively higher levels of unity in the self is correlated with a movement to increasingly broader, more unified levels of reality outside the self. (See Figure 7.2.) What has to be surpassed in this vision is not only the overtness of the observable "body," but also the inwardness of a consciousness "in here," both in some sense localizable in space.

Figure 7.2   PLOTINUS'S VISION OF BEING AND HUMANNESS

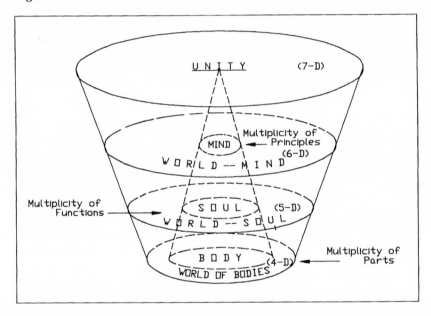

Augustine (d. A.D.470) said that he discovered in Plotinus everything of Christianity except that the Word was made flesh.[14] The light shining in the darkness, the One as Father of all, mirrored in the Word (the *logos*) as the World-Mind, locus of the intelligible patterns in accordance with which the world has been created, and the life-giving Spirit, "brooding over the waters." He read of a Fall and of a redemptive return to the Father. But he read further of a kind of dualism, an otherworldliness and contempt for the body and the world that ever since affected, and perhaps infected, Christianity, essentially a religion of incarnation, with a fundamentally non-Hebraic vision. And since Christianity's core is the Incarnation and Resurrection, what Augustine did *not* see in neo-Platonism was Christianity! It took a Franciscan revival of sensitivity for natural things and an

Aristotelian revival of interest in nature to balance off the strong dose of otherworldliness that Plotinus provided for the West. It was especially through Plotinus that Christianity became Hellenized.

8 Aristotle

Empiricism and the Principles of Changing Being

Aristotle has been called an empiricist by reason of his assertion, contrary to Plato, that all human knowing begins with the senses. But he has also been called a rationalist because, like Plato, he claims that humans are capable of grasping invariant principles. The empiricist orientation might be connected with the fact that Aristotle's father was a physician and Aristotle himself founded scientific biology as systematic investigation, classification, and explanation of living forms. Similarly, Plato's rationalist orientation is connected with his deep interest in mathematics. (Affinities with Plato are displayed by mathematicians again and again throughout history: in the Middle Ages, the mathematically oriented School of Chartres;[1] in the Renaissance, Nicholas of Cusa;[2] in the modern period, Descartes, father of analytical geometry and modern philosophy;[3] and Leibniz, codiscoverer of the calculus;[4] and more recently, Whitehead, coauthor of the *Principia Mathematica*, for whom the history of Western thought is a series of footnotes on Plato.[5]) Aristotle's empiricist starting point and his rationalist conclusions amount to a "domestication" of Plato's Forms, bringing them into the world of our sensory Cave from their state of eternal separation from sensorily experienced things. For Aristotle, the universal appears, so to speak, in the plane of the sensed particulars. Later Aristotelianism roots it in a process of abstraction of the universal from the particular, though careful Aristotelians like Aquinas will see abstraction as simultaneously related to a "conversion to phantasms," that is, to developed sensory experience.[6] As Aristotle himself put it in his *Posterior Analytics*, seeing the universal is like the reestablishment of the battle line during a rout: at first all are fleeing; then one man takes a stand; then the others gather about him until the entire line is reformed.[7] Later psychologists will refer to this as the formation of a *Gestalt*.[8] Today, the philosophy of science has been rethought along Gestaltist lines (cf. Michael Polanyi, Thomas Kuhn, Marjorie Grene, Errol Harris).[9]

To begin with sense experience is not, as in the modern empiricist tradition, to begin with isolated sense-data.[10] It is rather to begin with *things* showing themselves in various ways. They are colored, sounding, smelling, having various textures, resistances, temperatures, flavors; are of definite sizes and shapes and weights; stand in various relations to one another; they act and are acted upon; are in certain places and at certain times; have different relations between their parts; and are in various conditions. These comprise nine of the ten *categories* or ultimate universal classes (also called "genera") into which the objects of experience can be divided: quality, quantity, relation, action, passion, when, where, posture, and possession.[11] All these different features are modes of being, but peculiar modes in that they do not exist in themselves, that is, they occur in, accrue to, follow from, and thus are only intelligible in reference to, the things that they show in various ways. They are the conjugates, *symbebekota*, Aristotle's Greek expression, which was translated into Latin as *accidentia*, befallings or "accidents," some of them incidental, some of them essential to the things in question.[12] For example it is essential to a material being that, when it shows itself to the eye, it shows itself as colored, though it may be incidental that it be *this* particular color. And in any case, color does not exist except in virtue of something whose color it is: there is no "color in itself," but only colored things—men, trees, clouds, and so forth. Aristotle calls the colored thing *ousia* (one of Plato's terms for the Forms). He also calls it *hypokeimenon*, that which underlies or sub-stands, which the Latins translated as *substantia* (to grasp which would be under-standing).[13] "Substance" exists in itself and functions as ground of the accidents. The accidents in turn exist only in substances by actualizing the potentialities of the substances.

What is immediately given is actuality within the sensory field. That actuality is the simultaneous actualization of the potentialities of the sensible substance for being perceived and of the potentialities of the perceiving substance for perceiving. According to a later Scholastic adage: "The sensible (thing) in act is the sense (power) in act."[14] Aristotle thus stands between a *naive realism*, often attributed to him, according to which the sensory qualities exist outside the presence of the perceiver just as they are perceived, and a *subjective idealism*, according to which the sense-qualities belong only to the perceiver as effect, inside the chamber of the mind, of the physical events that cause them.

Considering colors and sounds as relational and not absolute properties of things does not make them merely subjective, any more than the perspective of a thing gained from a point of view and the horizon established from that point of view are merely subjective. When I look, the horizon is actually "out there" as the objective limit of my field of vision in the objective world. But it is not there *as horizon* unless there be a situated perceiver. Likewise the perspectives of the things that I see while I look out the window are the things' real perspectives, though again, not without the presence of a perceiver. Sense-qualities, the perspectives within which they appear, and the horizon that surrounds the field of perception are subjective-objective, relational structures, modes of access to others on the part of a biologically situated knower. The sense qualities are *modes of manifestness*, essentially relations to awareness on the part of physical things. As such, they are *real* properties, though not, like quantity, absolute properties. Martin Buber later puts it more poetically: things wait upon perceivers to flower forth in the splendor of their sensory features.[15]

The potentiality involved on both the subject and the object sides of the relation of identity in perception between thing and awareness is not an immediate given because the sensorily given is actual, and potentiality, by definition, is not. As Sartre observes, the immediately given world of objects is full, like an egg.[16] Potentiality is known by a reflective act that requires a pulling back from the Now in which perceptual actuality occurs in order to infer the potential.

The notion of potentiality seems pedestrian enough until we reflect upon its status and the conditions for its apprehension. Potentiality is a condition of universality. The see*able* thing is seeable by an indeterminate number of seers. And the power of seeing in any one of them is a general orientation to an indeterminate number of seeable objects. But the power of seeing is actuated only by particular seeable things, whereas the apprehension of power-as-such involves being actuated by a nonsensible object. The recognition of potentiality involves a backing off from the sensed actuality, a reflection or "bending back" that is made possible by the intellect as oriented beyond the here-and-now of the sensed activity. One discovers potentiality, universality and intellect at one stroke. And one comes to see that the spontaneous tendency to take sensed actuality as the model for being-as-such fails to account for the non-sensorily-actual features thus discovered. So the underlying or sub-stance displayed in the actual *percepta* involves potentiality. And potentiality, like the pastness and futurity it involves, has the odd status of both being and not-being. Potentiality is a non-being in-and-toward being, an actual modification of a being as oriented toward actuation.[17]

As we are actuated by the sensory showings of things, we catch the things in process of actualizing some of their potentialities. But the things are in relative stages of unfolding, maintaining or losing various actuations toward whose full actuation the processes of the thing tend, until the weight of negativity pulls them down. The central determinant of the kind of process and the perfection of its unfolding Aristotle calls "Form," which translates both *morphe* or shape (from which we get morphology as the study of the various "shapes" of living things) and *eidos*, another term for Plato's Ideas or Forms as objects of "eidetic intuition."[18] What we come to grasp is the *eidos* immanent in the thing, a form or *Gestalt* that gradually shows itself in and through the flowing display of the various accidents throughout a temporal process. The accidental forms show the substantial form as actuation of the underlying substance. Stressing the tendency toward fulfillment, Aristotle calls the form *entelechy*, having (*echeia*) in itself (*en*) its end or aim (*telos*) toward which the process is directed.[19] Goal directedness is thus referred to as *teleology*. 'End' in this case does not signify *any* termination—then dissolution would be the 'end' of all things. Rather it signifies the full unfolding of the form. (Aristotle seems to view the unfolding as normally occurring in such a way as to actualize the potentialities, without any basic potentialities remaining unfulfilled. This seems to square with his notion of the fixity of the species, even though evolution of species was surmised by Empedocles who reflected upon fossil remains.)[20] As actualizing agencies, the forms are called *energeia*, operating (*ergeia*) within (*en*) themselves; but as not fully actualized they involve *dynamis* or potentiality.[21] *Dynamis* stresses the nonactual side, *energeia* the actual side of the dynamic-energetic process entelechically engaged in taking on various accidents. The entelechy is also called *phusis*,[22] a coming into the light, which the Latins translated as *natura*, a being-born, thus an immanent principle of development toward and a resting in full actualization of innate potentialities.

Potency is twofold in Aristotle's view: active and passive. The former is linked to the developing character of a substance, the latter to that which makes the things in experience essentially mutable.[23] Ultimately, Aristotle attributes mutability (and several other features we will shortly examine) to a principle termed "prime matter."[24] Prime matter functions in a way similar to Plato's Receptacle: as a kind of existent negativity ingredient in things that makes the things such that they must change, moving from potency to the full actuation of their form, and from that actuation to the de-actuation of dissolution. Things that emerge give way to other things that are continuous with them: elements become plants which become cows which become men which become elements again. And the elements have their own forms, which also must change. Prime matter is the substrate in which such transmutation occurs. As such, it is not a "stuff," for all determinate stuff, as changeable, is composed of *energeia* and *dynamis*. Prime matter is rather *the principle of materiality*, not directly observable, but like all potentiality, inferred as requisite for the character of changing things.

Aristotle's "matter-form" doctrine is called *hylomorphism* (from *hyle* = matter and *morphe* = form). Its original derivation is from an analysis of artifacts, for example, a bed, where "bedness" is the form (= shape) given to wood as the material (= the shapable).[25] The form here is an exterior imposition, but it enters into the composition of the thing, not as another thing, but as a principle or coprinciple. (This will have significant implications for Aristotle's doctrine of soul as form, which we will examine below.) As imposed principle, such a form is an "accidental" or conjugate form belonging in the category of quality as the boundary of quantity.[26] To grasp Aristotle's doctrine we have to extend the notion of form significantly.

Bedhood is imposed on a "matter" that has its own "form," more properly described as its immanent *logos* or formula that determines the proportion of the elements (fire, air, earth, and water) that make the material to be wood.[27] The elements, in turn, have their own *logos* as certain proportions of the elementary qualities: for example, the hot or cold, the dry or moist.[28] These qualities are forms at the lowest-common-denominator level: *energeia* as determinate actuality, though, as essentially mutable, these qualities are coprinciples with a level of matter, "prime matter," as principle of change. From the *logos* of wood and the elements to the *energeia* of the elementary qualities, "form" is not "accidental" but "substantial," coconstituting the underlying being-in-itself of the things in question.

At each level there is a corresponding "matter," related to "form" as determinable to determining. At each level except the most basic, "matter" is still, in itself, a determinate-determinable. Later Aristotelians will call it "secondary matter," to distinguish such a principle from "prime matter," the underlying coprinciple of the existent elementary qualities, fundamental non-being in-and-toward being, ground of mutability, the indeterminate determinable.

Things in an Aristotelian view are individual compositions of substance and accidental forms. But substances, changing in and through their accidental forms, are, in turn, compositions of substantial form and prime matter. The substantial form is an energizing, an actuality aiming at its full unfolding. Form and matter, teleology (final cause) and agency (efficient cause) constitute the basic principles of explanation, the "four causes" of the Aristotelian universe.[29] These relations are expressed in figure 8.1.

There are two basic aspects of act and potency: the most fundamental aspect of the nature in question and the derived aspect of that nature's development. At the former level, the "first act" is the

Figure 8.1   ACT-POTENCY RELATIONS IN ARISTOTLE

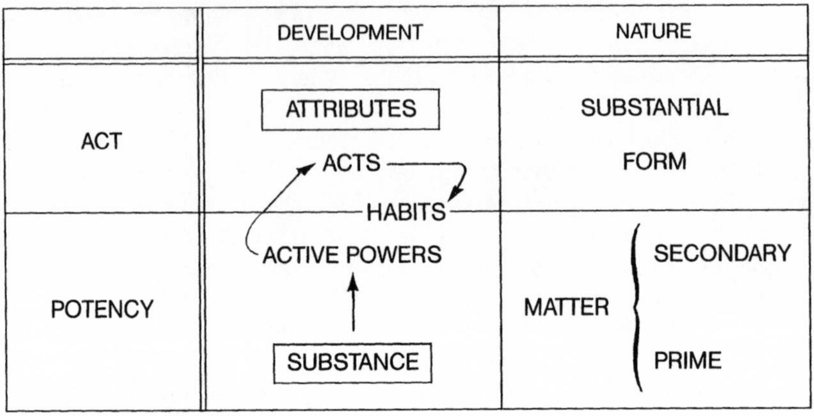

	DEVELOPMENT	NATURE
ACT	ATTRIBUTES ⟍ ACTS ⟶ ⟍ HABITS	SUBSTANTIAL FORM
POTENCY	ACTIVE POWERS ↑ SUBSTANCE	MATTER { SECONDARY / PRIME

"substantial form," that is, the actual determination of the kind of nature in question in any given thing. But since it is a kind in the realm of *phusis*, it is necessarily involved in change, the ultimate principle of which is "prime matter," the determinable indeterminate. But the form organizes the elements as "secondary matter," that is, matter already relatively determinate. Matter and form together comprise the substance. At the level of organic forms, the substantial form is a complex of active powers that, through their acts, form habitual tendencies to act, beginning with the vegetative acts that produce the organs for the sake of the release of the higher powers. We will not have begun to understand the full amplitude of these notions until we attend more carefully to the hierarchy of being and include *knowledge itself* centrally within such notions. (See figure 8.2.)

The Hierarchy of Changing Being

Locating these principles within the fuller context of Aristotle's world will allow us to understand his basic conception of being as form. To do that we will have to lay out the various meanings of causality, establish a hierarchy in experience, and analyze the notion of form as involved in knowing. This will prepare us for the inference Aristotle makes to Pure Form as Final Cause.

The Aristotelian notion of the four causes is initially derived from reflection on the activity of *techne*. An artisan (efficient cause) gives shape (formal cause) to some material (material cause) having previously envisioned the shape of his artwork (*telos*) in order to feed his family (final cause). To explain why the object is as it is, one

Figure 8.2   AN ARISTOTELIAN APPROACH TO CHANGING BEING

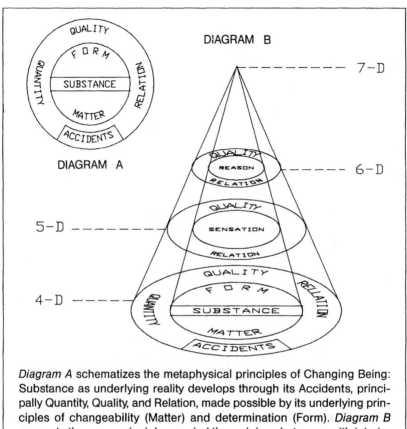

Diagram A schematizes the metaphysical principles of Changing Being: Substance as underlying reality develops through its Accidents, principally Quantity, Quality, and Relation, made possible by its underlying principles of changeability (Matter) and determination (Form). *Diagram B* suggests the same principles carried through in substances with interior dimensions, each successive set of determinations having different modifications of the basic accidents.

needs these four different but related answers in the form of "because," which are thus the four "(be)causes." One has to hear all these resonances when Aristotle speaks of cause (*aitia*) and not simply bring to mind the efficient cause, especially not simply the modern reduced notion of regular temporal antecedence and consequence linked by contiguity. The artisan functioning as source is ever so much more a cause than the latter. The final causality involved here is dual: on the one hand, the finished product he has in mind is a goal that has sometimes been referred to as *extrinsic formal cause*—the idea of the shape of the tool prior to its being given to the material. On the other hand, there is the reason why he wants to make such a product: to make money to feed his family.

This preliminary analysis is used to get a grip on the work of nature (*phusis*) that constitutes the frame within which the artisan operates, for both he and his materials are provided by nature. In the case of the material, though *telos* may be difficult if not impossible to determine—or even irrelevant—the material does have a natural form, the proportion (*logos*) of elements that makes it granite rather than wood. And the elements (*stoikeia*), in their turn, are of different types (Aristotle distinguishes fire, air, earth, and water), as we noted above. The *logos* principle is the basis of modern chemistry, which expresses the proportion in mathematical formulae; the *stoikeia* principle is developed in modern physics. But the *stoikeia*, being differentiated and mutable, are also determined by the principle of form as basic, determinate actuality (*energeia*) and a principle of determinability and thus mutability, which Aristotle terms *prote hyle* or "prime matter." The same *stoikeia* exist in different proportions in the artisan where they are shaped into organs as instruments for the realization of the various levels of potentialities constituting the artisan.

Thus overlaying and subsuming the level of the material elements are the organic forms. Such forms are the basic actualities of bodies as instrumental complexes, incarnate purposes linked together for the achievement of the integrity of the organism as a whole. Aristotle describes the substantial form of organisms as "the first act of an organized body."[30] Such a form is called a "soul" or *psyche*, a term employed here with greater amplitude than in modern psychology, which limits it to life forms that are conscious. *Psyche* originally meant breath (as the Latin *spiritus*), the "breath of life," animating principle (Latin *anima*). It is to be conceived of not as a thing, but as a form within Aristotle's more general theory of form. In its higher reaches, the deeper dimensions of conscious life, supported by minimal psychic life (the life of the vegetable), form becomes the capacity of being "informed." The "fifth dimension" opens up, linked to the manifestation of what is outside as the four-dimensional structure of the observable organism. Here Aristotle notes that if the eye were a complete organism (and not an organ within an organ complex), its soul would be the power of seeing, a nonseeable completion of the organ.

To articulate it further: it is the *power* of seeing that is the guiding *telos* for the formation of the observable organ (the eyeball). That power is the "first act" of the organ capable of seeing. The organ as seeable is the observable actuality whose power of vision is *not* observable. But that first act is completed in the "second act," the full actuation of the power in the act of seeing as a nonseeable termination. *Psyche* as providing the *telos* of the developing organism is understood on an analogy with the artisan imposing a form on some material by reason of his preconception of the form. The completed artifact is the end in view that sets in motion the steps toward that completion. Of course, in the case of organic development, the end in view is not "in view," that is, not a matter of conscious viewing. Awareness projects ends in view, having itself been projected as an end of the process of embryological development. The eyeball is a material organ informed by the power of seeing to whose actuation the process of embryonic development heads and which is fully actuated in actual seeing. Actual seeing, in turn, is "material" shaped by intelligent observation that admits of progressively higher actuation through more penetrating insight into the being of the seen object. Reflection upon seeing and the seeable thus introduces us to a hierarchy of forms, from the inanimate (the elements) through the vegetative (the eyeball) and the sentient (seeing) to the rational (insight).[31] (See figure 8.3.)

We should emphasize here that the conception of soul as "first act" or substantial form of the organ complex means that the very "material" actuality of "the body" as we observe it is the soul in one of its moments. It is the soul in its exteriority relative to an organ-based percipient which so apprehends it.[32] There is thus no dualism of soul *and* body, but the unity of a multidimensional entity with inner and outer dimensions, the highest inner dimension being the intellectual. (Our seven-dimensional model was developed in chapters 2 and 3 to make this Aristotelian view more plausible by making it conceivable.)

Knowing and Being

Our next step in approaching the full amplitude of Aristotle's notion of being as form is to describe knowing in terms of form. Aristotle describes knowing as "the possession of form without matter."[33] That means, negatively, that what one "has" in knowledge is not the "stuff" of the thing: the thing is not divided or diminished by being known by one or many. "Matter" here seems to be a kind of incommunicable opacity (which is true both on the object- and the subject-side of an awareness of material things). 'Form' immediately suggests 'shape', which Aristotle himself relates when he compares knowing with the imprinting of the form of the signet ring in wax. But think more of the related terms in English: 'information', 'formation' (whether in a military exercise or in the "shaping" of character), 'formal' (as in a "formal affair," that is, one governed strictly by

Figure 8.3 CAUSALITY: *PHUSIS* AND *TECHNE*
(An Aristotelian Analysis)

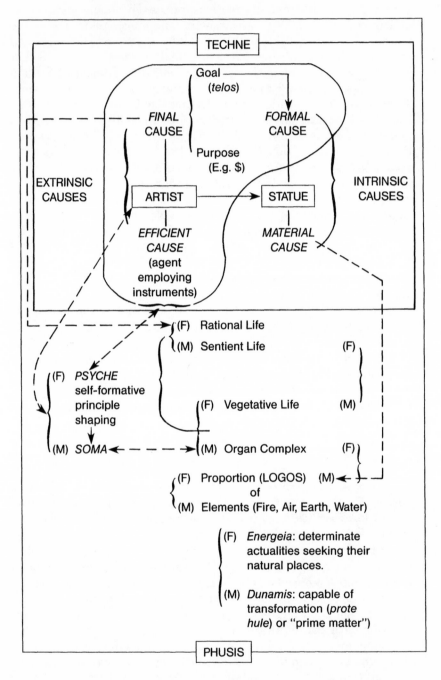

rules). The reader will do well to focus on these derivatives of 'form' and, as much as possible, prescind from the connotation of 'shape'.

Perception, though imperceptible by reason of the inwardness of the knowing form, is internally linked to the complexity of a material organ. Form in both cases is the same, though differently apprehended: the complex form of the organism apprehended as sense-object "from without"; the inwardness of the knowing form apprehended through awareness of awareness "from within." That is, the same actuality that is aware is the actuality of the complex perceptible organism. Unlike the Cartesian conception[34] that governed modern thought since the middle of the seventeenth century and even to this day, there is no mutual exteriority of two clearly and distinctly perceived substances: a completely inward perceiving and a complete outward material extensity. Rather, the single entity is articulated in several dimensions—in the case of the perceiver, in five dimensions.

Similarly, perceiving involves, as well as an identity between perceiving and organism, an identity between the act of perceiving and the perceived quality: "The sensible in act is the sense in act."[35] Though both ends of the perceiving process are anchored in self-existent units of being, in substances, their respective accidents here (the act of perceiving and the act of being perceived) are identical, so that, through their accidents, perceiver and perceived form a single system.[36] This contrasts significantly with the modern tradition since Locke, for which perceiving is a purely inward event causally related to a quite different event occurring in an unknowable material substratum.[37] The external relationship between mind and body and between perceiving and perceived in this modern tradition is basically at odds with the Aristotelian view of the unity of perceiving and organism on the one hand and of perceiving act with perceived quality on the other.

But there are two levels of cognitive form possession in human experience: at the sense level, the form is possessed "with the conditions of matter," and at the intellectual level, without such conditions.[38] "Matter" was posited as the principle that makes change possible both at the accidental and the substantial levels. One of the conditions of matter is thus change. And change itself is correlated with both space and time. Space is the exteriority of part outside of part that dissolubility involves: a kind of inner division and exterior relatedness.[39] And time is the measure of change.[40] The materially qualified form is thus not only changing, but is also always an instantiation of the form of a type located in a spatial "here" and a temporal "now." Platonic Forms or principles are characterized not only by their eternality over against the changing things that mirror

them, but also by their universality over against the multiple instances
that display the given form throughout space and time. Space and
time are later referred to as "principles of individuation."[41] And they,
in turn, are rooted in "matter" as the underlying principle of change.
A deeper penetration would have to show how sense-perceptibility as
well is one of the "conditions of matter," since the intelligible form
(sixth dimension), as universal, is not sense-perceptible—nor, indeed,
is the perceptual act itself (the fifth dimension). There may be a link
here between exteriority and passivity. Sensory forms are potential
and doubly dependent for their actuation: the sense quality is dependent upon a perceiver for its actuation, as the perceiver is dependent
upon the sensible thing for its actuation: "The sensible in act is the
sense in act." Thus, "the conditions of matter" within which sensing
operates are: change, immanence in the here-and-now, sense-
perceptibility, being an individual of a class—to which we will add
self-opacity or self-absence when we consider the transcendence of
the conditions of matter on the part of a knower. For Aristotle, intellect grasps form "without matter and without the conditions of matter," but it grasps such form in and through sensory experience as
the principle of the sensed individual. The individual substance, given
immediately in the senses, remains the locus of being for Aristotle.
The Platonic Forms thus have a certain derivative status as the intelligibility of bodily individuals.

Aristotle locates Plato's *ousia* or the realm of Forms under the
One/Good, in the "between" of intellectual apprehension of sensibly
given things. Plato's *ousia* is Aristotle's "secondary substance" or
abstract universal, derived from *ousia* in the primary sense of the
term, which is always individual substance, be it a mind or a nonmental
thing.[42] It is the peculiarity of mind in individuals and the peculiar
relation of individual nonmental things to mind that makes possible
the actuated intelligibility, the abstract universality of the sciences.
Thus likewise at the intellectual level, for Aristotle: The intelligible
(thing) in act is the intellect in act.[43] Abstract universality exists in
the relation between mind and things because the mind exists as a
"concrete universal" (to use Hegel's expression), because it "is, in a
way, all things,"[44] and because things are referred to it. Any substances
separate from matter would be such "concrete universals" to which
any abstract intelligibility would be subordinate. Mind and not Ideas,
person and not impersonal principles, would have absolute priority.

As in the case of sensory knowing, once again, here at the level
of intellectual knowledge, knowledge of principles, Aristotle stands
between extremes. The *extreme realism* of Plato held to the absolute
priority of universal principles, to their being "the really real."

Nominalism is a position invariably connected with atomism and with emphasis on the individual (Greek. *a-tomos* or "uncuttable" is etymologically identical with Latin *in-dividuum* or "un-divided"). Nominalism locates the universality of principles only in names (*nomina*), individually locatable things referred by the mind to other locatable things: only individuals exist.[45] *Conceptualism*, a later position held by Occam in the late Middle Ages and by Kant in modern times, locates the universal as a concept in the mind, either as natural effect of things outside the mind[46] (Occam) or as a form of the mind itself (Kant).[47] Aristotle's *moderate realism* has affinities with all the other positions. Like Platonism it maintains the transcendence of circumstance, the "eternal" character of the objects of science, only it locates that "eternality" in permanent instantiation and in the permanent possibility of being understood scientifically that belongs to changing, sense-perceptible things. Aristotle's position also has affinities with Conceptualism: the universal does only exist as universal "in the mind." It likewise has affinities with Nominalism: only individuals truly exist. But existing "outside the mind" is existing as an intelligible individual; existing "in the mind" is existing as an actuated intelligibility. The abstract intelligibility "in the mind" is the intelligibility of the thing "outside the mind." The intelligible in act is the intellect in act. (See figure 8.4 for the parallelism between sensory and intellectual knowledge.)

Such a view establishes the foundation for scientific knowledge. Things and persons are not simply individuals: they are intelligible individuals. That means they bear in themselves signs of a universal order: their "form" is common to many and fits within an overarching structure. And mind is not a private chamber but a referent to that overarching, universal order. I am not confined to gawking at things, but I can come to understand them. When I come to understand a specimen I am examining, I understand more than it: I understand its *kind* of being and all analogous kinds.

The presence of a form in the senses, in the case of human experience, is simultaneously the presence of the form in the intellect, so that anything perceived is also understood as an instance of a universal form. In the individual sensible substance, the form is a *logos* or gathering or, as the Latins translated it, a *ratio*, a proportion, a set of relations, which shows itself only through a series of temporal displays. A natural unfolding in the perceiver leads to such gatherings in discriminating active centers from their accidents and from their surroundings. But the presence of an intellectual form related to the totality (the seventh dimension:"The human soul is, in a way, all things") makes possible a deliberate search for an universal order

Figure 8.4   BASIC EPISTEMOLOGICAL OPTIONS

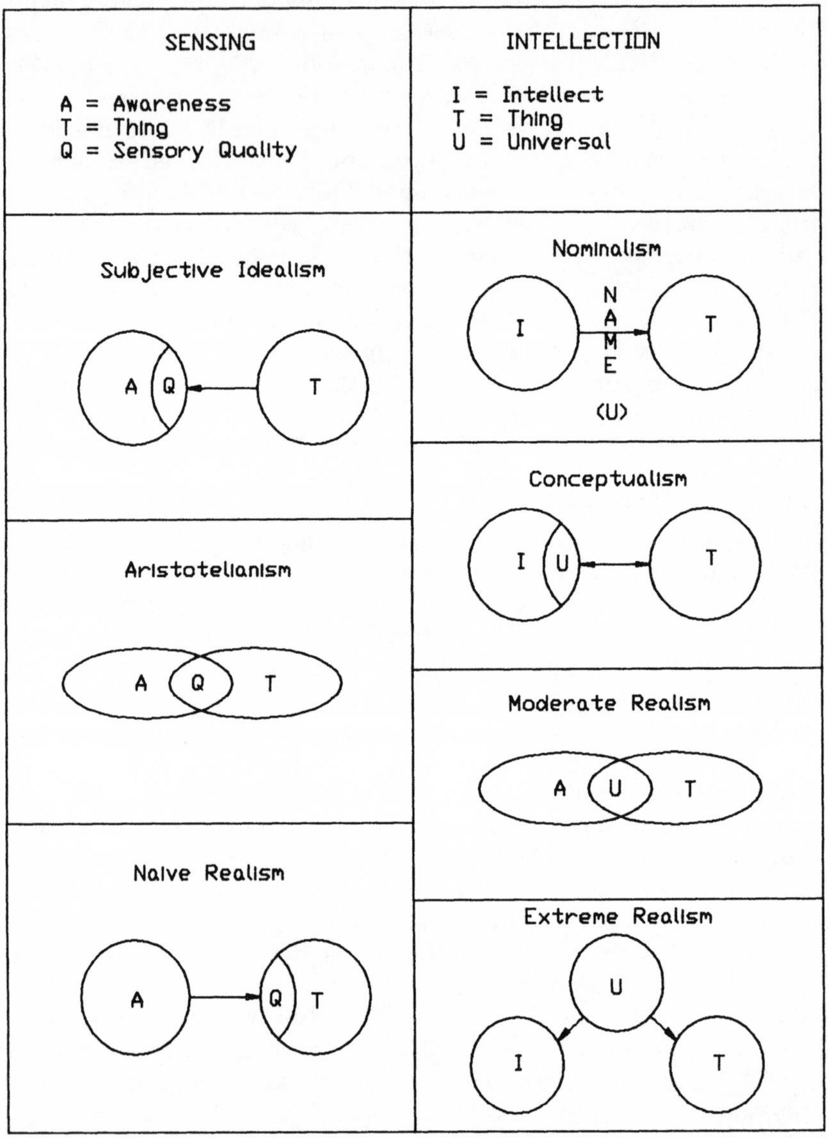

SENSING	INTELLECTION
A = Awareness T = Thing Q = Sensory Quality	I = Intellect T = Thing U = Universal

through the formation of an intelligible *Gestalt* built up by observations and inferences from the regular showings of different kinds of substances. Logic or reasoning as inference is rooted in the grasp of the *Gestalten* of regular occurences within the sense-field, and is aimed at the grasp of the (substantial) "reasons" (*logoi*) of things within the "reason" of the whole.

It is important to see that what makes possible cognitive "possession" of form is the transcendence of "matter" within the one who knows.[48] Sensory knowing involves a transcendence of "here," that is, the given boundaries of the knowing organism, in relation to "there," that is, the otherness of the sensory given; and a certain transcendence of the "now" in relation to the "then" of the recalled associations of the Other. The form of the sensory knower is thus less "matter immersed" than the form of the nonknower, which possesses only its own form and perhaps also the physical impressions of other things (e.g., mirrors and cameras), though not "as other." Otherness is manifest only to a "self," not to an isolated function. And a "self" And a "self" is a psychic, organ-informing whole, shot through by desire in function of its *telos*. A photoelectric cell hooked up to a computer would thus not be a knower, but a knowledge simulator.

But intellectual knowing involves a transcendence also of the "conditions of matter" because it involves a grasp of the universal, of that which obtains throughout the whole of space and time—and, as we shall see, in the case of reflective knowing of knowing, of that which transcends space and time as eternal and immaterial Form. Intellectual knowing involves a power which stands beyond the matter-based senses. But since this matter-transcendence allows the Other to be revealed *as other*, it involves a self-presence as the point of reference, other than which the Other is revealed. The final "condition of matter" is thus *self-opacity*, lack of presence to itself on the part of a "matter-immersed" entity. However, the Aristotelian insistence that our knowing is perpetually rooted in sensory experience and that the forms apprehended are the forms of sensory things safeguards the unity of the human being as "the living being that has the logos."[49] There is no human self-presence, no intellectual apprehension of the universal without sensing, and therefore correspondingly without an organ complex subsuming chemical elements that makes sensing possible. Self-presence for a human necessarily involves the self-absence of material organization.

Intellectual knowing as the highest act of an organic being, as the deepest way the human organism is alive is, however, only realized insofar as the human being is simultaneously "political animal" or one distinguished from other animals by the publicity of "words and deeds" or by language and action.[50] *Logos*, translated as "reason," is initially "word," so that reason as capacity of the universal only comes to itself within the context of the *polis* or human community structured by words and deeds. Antecedent to the emergence of the "rational" individual, there are the sedimented "words" of the community, its structures of language, and its general structure, its *ethos* as the sedimented "deeds" of a tradition. "Reason" is not then the property of an isolated individual "rationally" mastering the world in the solitude of his *cogito*—the first act in the modern drama of philosophy initiated by Descartes. It is more something "objective"— over against the individual who first confronts the *logos* given him by the community.

Such reason is first of all a capacity, based upon good upbring-ing, to find the mean between extremes of conduct in situations struc-tured by the interplay of the self and the other within the matrix of a tradition and of nature.[51] Where the action is one of legislation, what is to be done is to achieve the interplay between the ideal and the capacity of the community to bear the ideal.[52] The establishment of the universal in the community rests upon the recognition of the universal in the nature of things human. The transition, however, from the recognition of the ideal to the situation involves a function of reason other than the recognition of the universal. Recognition of the universal is a function of "speculative reason," assessment of the situation a function of "practical reason" (*phronesis*)[53] or what later is called "prudence."[54]

But the ideal in Aristotle is not far from the ideal in Plato:the constitution of a state in which "the best" rule, where 'best' involves the capacity to have an eye on the ideal. The ideal for humans is the life of contemplation, ultimately the contemplation of Pure Form, the Unmoved Mover.[55] The ideal is thus the ideal of the metaphysician, not simply involving the ability to make inferences as to the ultimate principles of being, but involving also and primarily the sense of contemplative vision toward which we directed attention in chapter 1.

The locus of being, we have already indicated, lies for Aristotle in the individual substance. However, when we press for what is "really real" about the individual, it is not the matter (as a kind of nonbeing) but the form that is more fully being. Matter is a restriction of form, which restriction is only grasped by that kind of animal whose own form is not restricted to its own physical boundaries nor to the here-and-now, but is oriented toward the whole, "is, in a way, all things." The reality of the material individual turns out to lie in its ability to actualize the form fully (to realize its full potentialities as an individ-ual of a kind); but even more radically, to keep the species or form eternal through reproduction.[56] Whatever of being matter has, it has by reason of its being informed: whatever of being accidental forms have, they have by reason of the substance in which they inhere; and whatever reality the substance has, it has by reason of the substantial form which is a kind of temporal participation in an eternal species—which however is not found in some separate Realm of Forms, but is carried by individuals.

Revisiting the One and the Good

But Aristotle sees a deeper dimension to being. The very nature of time involves its always being: any Now is inconceivable without a Before and an After.[57] We are forced to think in this way. If we think that "In the beginning, God created heaven and earth," and thus created time, we then ask, "What did He do *before* that?" If we think that in the end God will be all in all and this temporal world will end, we then ask, "What will we do *after* that?" If any temporal Now involves necessarily a Before and an After, and if these three temporal dimensions are necessarily ingredient in the world of changing being, such a world cannot have a beginning or an end: it always was and always will be. But as a changing world, each element in it has the potentiality not to be: as changing, everything is composed of matter. Given, then, the infinity of time past, the possibility not to be for each thing that has that potentiality would have been realized; and then there would be nothing. Since there is something, there must then be, connected in some necessary way with changing things, something that does not have the potentiality not to be.[58]

What kind of being would that be, and what would be its connection with the changing world? Not changing, it must not be matter but Pure Form. As Pure Form, it is pure knowing. This is essentially connected with the central notion that thought involves remotion from matter: a possession of form without matter in proportion to the degree of remotion from matter in the substantial form of the knower. As a thinking that involves dependency upon matter in the formation of sensory experience and that can only grasp the intelligible in and through such experience, the human intellect is involved necessarily in the changing world. Its object is being as found in sensible things and what is necessarily implied in such things. Our thought is thus dependent upon being informed by sensory things, that is, things that necessarily change. But Pure Form and thus a thinking-knowing that is without implication in matter cannot be dependent upon changing things for its specification, else it would have matter in its makeup. Hence, thinks Aristotle, it can only know itself: it is knowledge of knowledge, *noesis noeseos*, or absolute self-presence without presence to what is outside itself.[59]

In Abbott's *Flatland* one of the characters is the inhabitant of Pointland, the sole content of whose consciousness is "I am I!" This sounds much like Aristotle's Pure Form, except that the self-enclosure of the point is enclosure within the least conceivable reality, whereas Aristotle's Self-knowing Knower inhabits the other end of the hierarchy: it is fully actual, absolute perfection, containing everything desirable in itself in absolute unity. It is thus Parmenides's One Being and Plato's One/Good, though advanced over the latter in that it is not a principle and thus impersonal, but a self-presence and thus a person of sorts; and advanced over Parmenides' notion in having, like Plato's One, a significant linkage with the world of change, and in having the nature of the oneness of thought and Being more clarified. As we have noted earlier, that oneness in Parmenides admits of interpretation either along the lines of an absolute identity or along the lines of a relation between two disparate relata, the Being-pole in the latter case seemingly impersonal. What might have been a person in Parmenides and what perhaps substituted for a person in Plato, is in Aristotle clearly a person, that is, consciousness and not simply a principle.

However, the relation to the world of change bears certain similarities in all three cases: the changing world has everything to do with the Fullness or Height of Being, mirroring it, striving to be like it, even, in the case of the human being, striving to be at one with it in contemplation. But Pure Form has nothing to do with the world of change, at least not in the sense of knowing it, and (for the same reasons) not in the sense of doing something to it either. But we need a distinction here. Doing something to something else in the sense of throwing a ball, carving a statue, and so on, involves a reciprocity between cause and effect. Like Newton's third law, for every such action, a reaction. Acting is also being acted upon. I am myself changed in acting upon something other than myself. This kind of doing Aristotelians call "efficient" causation, in the sense of acting and being acted upon. Such acting is not possible for the Pure Form because it would then have to have potentiality in its makeup. But there is another kind of "doing something to something else" that does not involve being also acted upon: Aristotle calls this "final" causality. It is the kind of causing an apple does when it causes the hungry appetite to drool. "Final" here refers to end or purpose. The Pure Form is connected with the world of changing things in a one-way relation of being desired by that world. However, the desire involved here is, unlike that of the appetite for the apple, not for something the desirous one could consume, but for something whose perfection the desirous one imitates according to its capacities. Thus Pure Form for Aristotle explains why a world, all of whose members are able not to be, but whose very notion as temporal involves the infinite duration of that world, does not lapse into the nonbeing to which it is potential: all things desire eternal perfection. That means, for such beings, full actualization within their form; for all organic beings, that means, in addition, contributing to the eternality of the species, since they cannot hold their own actuality perpetually; and for rational beings, it means, as well, contemplation as a conscious participation in the eternally perfect. Whether this implies individual immortality of the rational individual for Aristotle is a highly debated issue.[60]

Being thus ultimately means the perfection of self-presence, and that implies relationlessness, self-sufficiency, independence, transparency, unruffledness, and eternal self-possession. Thought and being, once more, are one. The multiplicity of beings is a shattering of the image of such self-presence in the brokenness of negativity, the nonbeing of "matter." Matter links each being up in a web of spatial and temporal relations, of dependency, of mutual causality, of vulnerability, but also of self-opacity. Matter is thus a principle of lack of self-presence, in the sense of the need for temporal unfolding for full actuation of any substance; in the sense of constant threatenedness and inevitable dissolubility; and in the sense of relative self-opacity and limited self-disposability. But eidos is ingredient in any substance, and to the degree that it dominates in the substance, there is a participation in that which exceeds the confinement of the substance to the here-and-now and to its being dominated from without: in that which is eternal and actual, immediately as the embodiment of a species, but more deeply as a mirroring of the eternal actuality of Pure Form, Self-knowing Knowing, in contemplation.

Platonic Forms are static principles modelled after geometric theorems. Aristotelian forms are active principles modelled after organic processes. They are *entelecheia*, *energeia*, principles of self-formation aimed at an end which would be actually what early stages of development are potentially. Full being for any form of being in the realm of *phusis* would be full actualization of all its active potentialities. What Platonic Forms describe in Aristotle's world are not a separate realm, much less a superior realm; rather they are activations of the potentialities of the rational soul in relation to sensorily given substances. They do indicate superiority, though not *their* superiority. It is rather *mind's* superiority that they manifest. For Aristotle, substance in the primary sense is always individual; abstract universals have a derived status and are substance in a secondary sense. However, there are "concrete universals" that are being in a fuller sense than other individuals, namely, minds, which are, in a way, all things and are thereby able to grasp abstract universals. And Mind in the fullest sense, Mind which always embraces the fullness of Being in itself, Mind as pure Form, is Being in the fullest sense, is God!

*   *   *

Figure 8.5 shows the transition from Plato to Aristotle and should be related to the diagram at the end of the chapter on Plato linking Parmenides to Plato. Parmenides' One/Being is preserved in Plato's notion of the One/Good, and both are preserved and developed in Aristotle's notion of the Pure Form, the final Good as Unmoved Mover, but also as Self-thinking Thought. In Aristotle, Plato's Forms sre located in the realm of *phusis* as relations to intellect, as the intelligibility of things. Though the Pure Form, like the One and the Good, is the final end of human development, nonetheless it is reachable for Aristotle only by intensive penetration into the things that belong to the realm of *phusis*. Hence that realm attains to a nuanced, hierarchical articulation. Prime matter translates Plato's Receptacle as the lowest level, always informed by the elementary qualities (hot-cold, dry-moist), yoked in turn by the forms of the elements. Vegetative forms, in their turn, yoke the elements into organs that, in animal and human forms, are material for the form of sensation. And, in the case of human beings, sense experience furnishes materials for the work of the agent intellect that grasps the intelligible forms in, and grounding, sensorily given things.

Figure 8.5 TRANSITION FROM PLATO TO ARISTOTLE

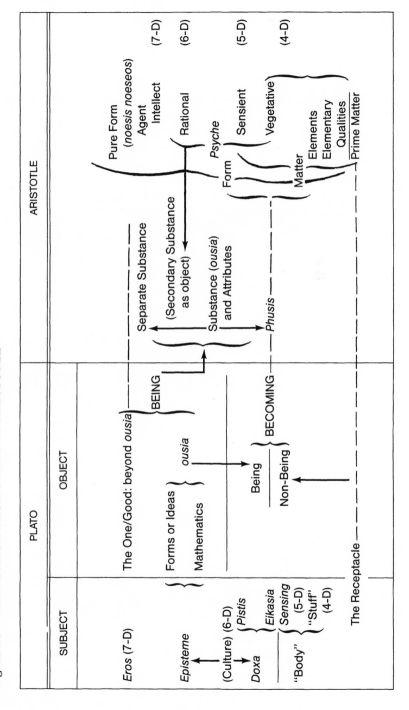

9 *Aquinas*

Thomas Aquinas appeared in the midst of a religious culture saturated with a neo-Platonic hermeneutic of the Hebrew-Christian tradition, especially via the writings of St. Augustine (d. A.D. 430) and Dionysius (a fifth century A.D. Syrian monk). The former, we said, saw in Platonism the whole of Christianity except that the Word was made flesh. And during the Middle Ages the latter's works were viewed as almost canonical, since he was for centuries considered to be St. Paul's disciple and therefore close to the sources of Christian revelation.[1] However, outside of the beginning portion of Plato's *Timaeus*, almost nothing of either Plato or Plotinus was directly available. Proclus (sixth century A.D.) who systematized the neo-Platonic tradition, was translated in the late thirteenth century, while Plato was not directly available in the West until Ficino's translations near the end of the fifteenth century.[2]

The century of Aquinas was also the century of the appearance in Latin translation of the entire Aristotelian corpus.[3] The neo-Platonic otherworldliness and dualism of soul and body assimilated by the Christian tradition held in great suspicion the works of a pagan who argued that the human being was essentially bodily, a (seven-dimensional) psychophysical unity. But Aquinas assimilated Aristotle whole. By way of theological apology, he argued, in effect, that Augustine's remark about Plotinus's writings containing the whole of Christianity except that the Word was made flesh actually meant that Plotinus left out the very center of Christianity: the Incarnation of the Word. And even that is not the whole story. Christ's bodily resurrection and ascension completed his life, prefiguring the end of history when He will come again and all bodies will rise.[4] Though resolving the problems involved in Aristotle's tangled teaching on the intellectual power of the soul in the direction of personal immortality, Aquinas nonetheless held that "the human soul in separation from the body is less God-like, because less able to perform its own proper acts, than the human soul in the body."[5] One who maintained the "pure spirituality" of Plotinian salvation would find that unintelligible, and the reincarnation of the soul in the body a punishment rather than a fulfillment.

Being and the Sensorily Given

Aquinas's philosophical starting point is Aristotle's: sensory experience as "illumined" by the active intellect.[6] Such illumination involves the immediate intuition of Being. For Aquinas, "that which first falls under the intellect's grasp is Being. [7] Though the sensorily given individual is the permanent anchor of human knowing, it functions as a kind of material cause in relation to the activity of the intellect, which sees the individual "as being," and thus in terms of the "first principles" that flow immediately from Being and are seen as having application throughout the whole range of Being.[8] Such principles are, for example, that a being cannot both be and not be at the same time and in the same respect (the principle of noncontradiction); that every being is identical with itself throughout its temporal span; that everything that comes into being has an efficient cause; and that every agent acts for an end.[9] Based upon these principles, we stitch together the sensorily given within a coherent system of inferences such as we have seen operative in the thinkers examined so far.

The mind is thus present to the whole (our seventh dimension); as in Aristotle, it "is, in a way, all things,"[10] and thinks throughout the whole in terms of the first principles operative beyond and within the here-and-now sensorily given. Hence Aquinas observed that it is no wonder that human knowing extends beyond the senses, since the senses are material causes in relation to the formal causality brought to bear upon the sense-experience by the intellect.[11]

Sensory knowing considered by itself (and it does not exist by itself in our ordinary experience) is the result of the actuation in relation to the sensory power of the potentialities of the thing to be sensed. The sensory powers are receptive to the influence of things, but in such a way that the sensory knower is "outside himself." The light of the intellect, bringing to bear a relation to the totality, involves the "return of the subject into himself" from the initial exteriority of sensory receptivity.[12] A human being can back off from the flow of immediate sensation, opening his relation to the whole and thus also to the whole of himself, which thereby makes possible the appearance of the sensorily given (initially an identity of sensing and sensed) *as other* than the now self-present self.[13] Such recollective return of the self to itself makes judgment possible and, with judgment, responsibility, self-disposability.

In the Aristotelian-Thomistic tradition it is said that abstraction of the universal from the particular occurs through "the agent intellect illuminating phantasms."[14] Phantasms may be defined as unified coordinated sense-experience. The term "phantasm" is etymologically related to the Greek *phainomai* "I appear," and is the chief subjective-objective feature that makes manifestation possible. Things show themselves, beyond the immediacy of the single, perishing, perspectival sense experience, through the mediation of past experience. In order that things appear, even the most immediate experience requires the inwardness of temporal extension whereby the first split second of experience is carried over to the last. But beyond that, we learn to expect, for example, that the front of an apple will be followed by a similar perspective as we rotate it before us, that these perspectives will cohere with a certain texture within a range of textures from moderately soft to moderately hard, with a certain taste within a range of flavors, and so on. The sedimentation of past experience through the different senses enters into the way I experience the apple now before me. It is the principles connected with this rich matrix of sensory experience—only abstractly considered here because in actual experience it is shot through with eidetic apprehensions— that we grasp through the illuminative action of the agent intellect.

As we have interpreted it in part 1, chapter 3, "the light of the intellect" is the reference of human consciousness to Being as such; it is the movement of the mind toward the Totality, toward all actual or possible instances.[15] Whatever appears in sensory experience appears against the background of that reference. The mind seeks for that in the thing which can be referred to all actual or possible instances, both at the level of the most fundamental metaphysical principles and at various levels of the abstract sortings of experience. In the process, the notion of Being, implicating all actual or possible instances, is contracted to all actual or possible instances of the kind specified by the sensory experience, and the intelligibility immanent in the sensory experience is abstracted from the sensory matrix and extended to all actual or possible instances of the feature focused on in the experience: redness or color or perspective or apple or thing or being, and so on. Indeed, all the observations made about the character of the developed sensory matrix are matters of abstract focusing. Thus we learn to fill the space between the empty intention of the Totality and the "concreteness" of the sensory matrix with eidetic and constructed structures.

Different general types of speculative knowing are capable of being abstracted out from this original experiential matrix. Recall again our observations in ch. 2. Human awareness in its typical functioning is a matter of attending through sensations (5-D) to bodily individuals (4-D) as instances of universal meanings that apply throughout space and time (6-D), against the horizon of Being as the Totality (7-D). A first general level of sciences is gained by abstracting general meanings from the particularities of their individual instances; so we can have, for example, general sciences of changing being (physics) and of living being (biology). Such meanings as are operative within these sciences are "wholes" insofar as classes of perceptible things are what we investigate. This is to be contrasted with another set of sciences that are based on abstraction of a certain form, the form of quantity: these are the mathematical sciences.[16] It has been suggested (following with significant modifications the Kantian position) that mathematical abstraction disengages the reference to the whole of space and time involved in the grasp of the universal forms of sensible things as realizable throughout space and time.[17]

The concepts developed at these two levels of abstraction are at progressive degrees of "remotion from matter." The first level abstracts from this or that material individual (from "signate matter," sensorily designatable), but deals with "common sensible matter," that is, involves a necessary reference to perceptibility. The second level abstracts from the perceptible character of things and develops idealized notions (e.g., absolute triangularity) that involve reference to matter, but only to the "intelligible matter" of quantity, abstractly considered as the common feature running through all the sensory aspects.

However, there is a third general type of science beyond the physical and mathematical sciences that deals with notions that completely transcend material reference, namely metaphysics. It is based upon the disengagement of the infinite orientation of the mind toward Being from its engagement with Being found in sensory things. Aquinas calls the process whereby this is accomplished "the negative judgment of separation." Being is seen as not restricted to being material or to being intellectual but finite, but can be absolutely unrestricted. Though the concepts we form of Being found in sensorily given things (and of ourselves as sensorily engaged) are adequate (at least by comparison with our metaphysical concepts), there is no proper concept of Being. Rather, we arrive at the notion of Being by negating the limitation, found in the beings of experience, of the full plenitude of Being given as the in-finite horizon of all our dealings with things. The very way we express the notion of the infinite, as not finite, embodies one negation. But this allows us to see the negation built into the positive affirmation of the finite from which we began.[18]

Metaphysics is thus concerned with the full amplitude of the meaning of being: not being as changing or as living or as quantified, etc., but Being as *being*. And we have seen samples of how that meaning is developed in Parmenides Plato, Plotinus, and Aristotle. Things in experience *are*, but they are not the fullness of Being. They are a hierarchically graduated scale of approximations to that fullness that is realized only in a single instance. Aquinas's approach both assimilates this line and transforms it.

Essence-Esse and God

Aquinas's central distinction is that between essence and the act of existing, the latter of which he calls *esse*, the infinitive form of being, meaning "to be." Aquinas especially assimilated all of Aristotle's basic distinctions (substance and accidents, matter and form, the nature of knowing, and the four causes), but he places under them, so to speak, his own distinction and radically transforms the whole Aristotelian view.

There are several ways in which his distinction can be approached. I suggest (following Coreth)[19] that we approach it by way of our interpretation of Parmenides. I do this in order to see the new question that Aquinas was in effect asking. Following out the logic of Being and non-being, Parmenides had concluded that the pure nature of Being must be absolutely one and unchanging. The changeless unity was a unity of absolute plenitude, complete fulfillment, absolute perfection, but finite. Parmenides' follower Melissus pushed the logic one step further: if outside Being there is nothing, nothing could limit Being, and thus Being itself is limitless. The equation of perfection and finitude was broken, but only for a moment, for in Plato and Aristotle the dominant Greek view reasserted itself. Aquinas, in effect, sides with Melissus. If the nature of Being— Being conceived as a pure nature apart from all non-being—is infinite, then the factual existence of finite beings (unquestioned in the dominant Greek view) itself requires explanation. Not only why things are as they are, but *that they are at all* is what must be explained. If Being in its pure nature is infinite, how is it factually limited in the things of experience and in our experience of them? (Note, this is not the way Aquinas actually approaches it; but I think it brings us to a sharpened insight into the question he implicitly raises and thus shows his difference from the Greeks so far considered.)

The new question Aquinas was asking was actually stimulated by the Hebrew account of creation, for that account not only claimed to explain, as Aristotle's notion of the Pure Form so claimed, why things change by reason of their imitation of that Form as supreme exemplar, as the full, actual and self-present plenitude of Being. Creation also explained how things can be at all as such imitations. The nature of God implied in that explanation—Pure *Esse*—is likewise suggested by the burning bush episode in Genesis: "I am Who am," which Aquinas takes to mean, "I am one whose essence is to be," or "I am Being as a nature."[20] Aquinas 's metaphysics is thus rightly characterized as the metaphysics of Genesis,[21] interpreting the core of the book, inspired by it, yet claiming independent grounding in philosophic reflection on the implication of the way the relation between human experience and its objects occurs.

Prior to Aquinas, Anselm developed what Kant was later to call an *ontological argument* for the existence of God, that is, an argument developed from the concept (*logos*) of being (*to on*). It is a three-step argument:[22] (1) The starting point is the notion of Being as "that than which no greater can be conceived." We have met it before: it is Parmenides' Pure Nature of Being developed along the lines of Melissus as Infinite Plenitude. I can think of the absolutely Infinite. (2) The second step is an observation: That which exists outside of merely being thought about is greater than that which is merely thought about. My actual daughter is greater than (more real than) the thought about my possible daughter thirty years ago. (3) The conclusion is that this peculiar notion of the Absolutely Unrestricted must contain the note of existing outside of merely being thought about. In Anselm such a proof is couched inside a prayer. Hence we rejoin the Parmenidean context in another way: not the sheer *logos* of the notion of Pure Being, but the aletheic presence of Being, the being-apprehended of *nous* is the prior ground of logical proof.[23]

Aquinas seems unimpressed by the argument. All it proves, he says, is that we have to *think* that than which no greater can be conceived as existing outside of merely being conceived. It does not prove that Pure Being has to be outside. For Aquinas, one must *begin* with what is given outside: sensorily present things. Hence his approaches to God always have that starting point.[23]

There is a way to "redeem" Anselm's argument in the context of Aquinas's thought. For Aquinas the intellect itself "is, in a way, all things" because it grasps whatever it meets "as being," thus "in the light of the agent intellect" which makes knowing possible. The notion of Being expresses this prior structure of the intellect in such a way that, for Aquinas, all knowers *implicitly* know God, though not as God. Our reference to Being is our reference to God. Our actual existence as intellect is the "ontological argument."[25] But for Aquinas this can only be rendered explicit through the presence of the sensorily given other (whence the unity of humanness as a mind one with the body in order to become fully a mind). Descartes picks this up by claiming the need for God as cause of the idea of Perfection in us.[26]

One might also consider the ontological argument, in the face of the principle invoked by both Aquinas and Kant[27] on the impossibility of moving from concept to existence, as a meaningful hypothesis, like a scientific hypothesis, that must be referred to "experiment," that is, to the presence of actual things. The experimental proof of the ontological hypothesis is the mystical experience that figured centrally in Parmenides and Plotinus, but also in Plato's experience of the real presence of Beauty Itself. But this is an aletheic explanation of what Aquinas considers only orthotically: the transition from the initially empty knowledge of Being as being, founding all intellectual (and volitional) operations via actual experience, to God as the Absolute Plenitude of Being.[28]

Aquinas's famous "five ways" to prove the existence of God are just that: five *ways* and not five separate proofs, five ways of showing one thing: that finite beings require the sustaining causation of the Infinite Being for them to be.[29] Some of the ways involve the alleged inconceivability of an infinite series of "moved movers," of caused beings, in their turn, causing others. This is all too often misunderstood in terms of causal series such as that of a father and mother, having been generated, generating their children, and so on. Such a series, as infinite, is actually unimaginable, but not inconceivable. One can clearly *conceive* the differing infinities of number series: for example, the infinite series of positive integers and the likewise infinite series of negative integers; of fractions between any two integers; of even numbers or of odd numbers, positive or negative. Aristotle's argument from the intelligibility of the Now as always requiring a Before and an After shows at least the possibility of a past infinity of successive beings linked in a causal chain. The alleged proof of the beginning of the universe from the evidence leading to the "Big Bang" theory is itself only conjectural. It admits of the theoretical possibility, as Empedocles long ago proposed, that the universe is like an eternal accordian process of dispersal and return to unity.[30]

Though in his attempt to infer the existence of a God, Aristotle used as his premise the inference from the nature of time to the necessary eternality of the universe, Aquinas tones down the insistence on the universe's *necessary* eternality to its conjectural *possibility*.[31] Thus he cannot use as premise in any of his own attempts to show that God exists the claim that an infinite series of moved movers succeeding one another in time is impossible—in fact, he expressly repudiates such a premise. In the arguments where he invokes a similar principle of the impossibility of an infinite series of moved movers or caused causes—often misunderstood to mean that theoretically the world could not always have been—what he means is what he calls a *"per se* series," that is, a series operative in any here-and-now.[32] For example, the words on this page are caused by the keys which are being depressed by my fingers, which are being moved by my nerves, which are being moved by my brain, which is being moved by my desire to express my thoughts, which desire is a concrete articulation of my nature as an intelligent being directed toward the fullness of Being—all in one simultaneous series. In such a series, we cannot go to infinity, that is, to an infinite number of moved movers. The termination of the series, involving finite processes all the way along, demands a single Infinite Ground, the unlimited Plenitude accounting for the factual limitation in the series and in all its members. Recurring back to our observations, in our chapter on Plato, regarding the "causality" of axioms in relation to theorems in geometry, we should distinguish here, by way of parallel, a "horizontal series" stretching backward and forward in time (potentially infinite in both directions) and a "vertical series" always anchored in God, no matter what the status of the temporal series regarding its beginning or end.

Aquinas's "five ways" to prove the existence of God involve differing observations of the limitation, the finitude of beings in experience. Things move, things affect one another because they have "matter," a kind of non-being, in their makeup; things occur that need not occur; things are more or less perfect; things are directed to goals they did not choose or have not yet realized. Motion, efficient causality, contingency, hierarchy, and teleology in the things of experience show that things involve negation of the plenitude of being. Only a being in whom there is no negation, functioning as the perpetual ground of finite beings, could explain this factual negativity. Aquinas's way of saying this is that essence or what-things-are limits the *esse* or the "to be" or the act of existing.[33]

The distinction in question is expressed in various ways: essence and *esse*, essence and existence or act of existing, what-is and to-be, substance and being. 'Essence', 'what-is', and 'substance' are themselves each to be taken in a certain sense. 'Essence' is here not to be taken to refer to the universal as distinct from the individual, for example, when we speak of ourselves as "in essence" human, though differing as individuals. Nor is 'essence' to be considered as the core in distinction from the nonessential, as when we speak of a person as "in essence" good, though not without faults. Again, 'substance' is not to be considered here apart from the attributes but as actualized in them. Both substance and 'essence' here, as distinguished from *esse*, refer to the wholeness of what-is in any given case. Every aspect that can answer the question "What is this?" is included in this meaning of 'essence' or 'substance': "This is a brown, seven-foot, 280-pound, intelligent (and so forth) man." And what-is, in any case, is a restriction on the plenitude of *esse* by a finite type.

This *esse* is not simply the being-outside-of-nothing that is common to all things in the same way. Rather, *esse* is the "act of all acts and the perfection of all perfections," "form" even with respect to the deepest Aristotelian form of things.[34] Being is not then some addition, the finishing touch or final property of an essence, but the fullness of what any given thing is. But that fullness is itself a limited imitation of *the* Fullness. That limitation is the essence, more or less limiting depending upon the dominance of form over matter—and that means, following Aristotle, of thought over nonthought. But even an Aristotelian Pure Form, thought of thought, as finite, would be limited. And in fact, in Aquinas's universe, the locus of such a Form would be among the angels as pure subsistent intelligences.[35] Such intelligences, being finite, would require an explanation as to why the unlimited perfection of Being is factually limited in their case. And if Pure Form is related to lesser forms as exemplary cause, the further question would be how it is that imitations of such perfection can be as imitations. Creation is again the answer, though not by a Pure Form, but by an Infinite Who is not simply a highest instance of being, but the Pure and Infinite Nature of Being.

In the case of the Pure Nature of Being required to explain the factual limitation of beings, one could either say that He is One Whose essence is identical with the plenitude of existence or One Who has no limiting essence or One Who does not *have* but *is* existing.[36] It is of the utmost importance here to see that the Nature of Being or Being as a Nature must be conceived of intensively rather than extensively. On this reading, one could not say, like Spinoza, that God cannot be both transcendent and the fullness of Being because, granted even one creature, there would be more to the plenitude of being when there is God plus a creature than there is when there is only God.[37] That plenitude is rather an intensive plenitude—and so, I think, Parmenides's being has to be understood.

Following Aristotle, Aquinas views beings as more intensively realized in "remotion from matter and [thus] change."[38] But such remotion *is* awareness, and awareness is ultimately self-presence. What could it mean to be fully self-present as a plenitude if it does not include that which is other than itself? God is eternal, self-illumined self-presence. In the world of our experience, self-thinkers are known in terms of their capacity to include a wider range within their awareness in terms of possessing, in addition to their own "forms," the forms of other things as well.[39] Thus certain animals are aware of the immediate environment (in terms of their own needs, since "whatever is received is received according to the mode of the recipient"),[40] beginning with those who have only the sense of touch, while others add perhaps memory and imagination. But human knowers constitute a "leap to another genus" as being related to the fullness of

Being and thus, beyond the need-based appearance (though in and through it alone), related to the whole of each encountered being. Is there sense then in a subsistent Fullness of Being that does not include all that is? Aristotle would probably say that the Pure Form includes everything else by being fully what each other thing is in a lesser degree of intensity, without, however, the Pure Form's being aware of anything but itself.

One can bring into clearer view Aquinas's basic distinction between essence and *esse*, which grounds his notion of God, by relating it to the basic Aristotelian distinctions of substance and attribute and matter and form as three levels of potency and act relations.[41] At the level of immediate encounter with things, the processive patterns of the sensed surface are actual expressions of the underlying powers of the substance encountered. The substance itself is the nature it is because of its substantial form, *able* to develop because it is the actuation of prime matter, *having* to develop for the same reason, and thereby also condemned to destruction. An organic enmattered form begins as primarily a locus of active potencies, set upon articulating for itself a complex of organs as instruments for the functioning of its higher potentialities by yoking already formed matter (secondary matter) to itself as its "body." Thus far Aristotle. In Aquinas, all this, considered in itself, is a *possibility* for being. Being could exist in any finite mode only if there is a Ground that is not in the finite mode, whose essence, does not limit *esse*. Hence any finite mide is an essence, a determinate limitation of the plenitude of *esse*, not *Esse* Itself.

These relations can be summarized in Figure 9.1.

Figure 9.1   ACT-POTENCY RELATIONS IN AQUINAS

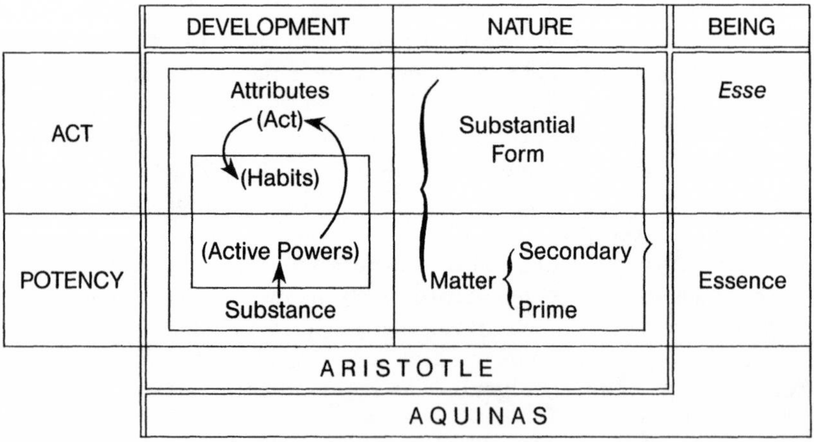

	DEVELOPMENT	NATURE	BEING
ACT	Attributes (Act) ← (Habits)	Substantial Form	*Esse*
POTENCY	(Active Powers) Substance	Matter { Secondary Prime	Essence
ARISTOTLE			
AQUINAS			

Assimilation and Transformation of Aristotle

Aquinas's distinction of essence and act of existing in relation to their nondistinction or identity in the Creative Ground of all finitude both assimilates and transforms Aristotle's position. The intensive Fullness of Being for Aquinas is indeed the final or exemplar cause, but that is rooted in His being more basically the efficient cause. That means that He gives being to what is; and since it is the very finitude of the finite that needs explanation, He must give it perpetually and not just "once upon a time." If this is so, there is nothing to preclude His knowing what is outside Himself, for that would not involve His dependency upon it (as would be the case with Aristotle's Pure Form), for the situation is the reverse: creation means total dependency upon Him of what is. His knowing is thus not objective, i.e., encountering something standing over against Him upon which He is dependent for His knowing of it; rather, His knowing is projective i.e., giving reality to what He causes to be by His knowingly willing it. His self-knowing would thus *explicitly* include what is other than Himself. As Aquinas says, in knowing Himself, God knows all the ways in which His perfection is imitated and imitatable among finite beings.[42]

At the same time the doctrine of creation transforms Aristotle's Pure Form from something simultaneously too immanent in the world and too transcendent of the things of the world to One Who is absolutely transcendent *and* absolutely immanent. Aristotle's God is too immanent in that He is still part of the finite, though the highest instance. Aquinas's Creator is absolutely transcendent because absolutely infinite—not infinite in a mode like the infinity of different number series or of conceptual space or time past or time future or the extension of any category to its possible particulars. In Him essence does not limit the act of existing: He is thus unlimited in perfection. Thus all finite beings are, in a sense, equidistant from Him insofar as the finite is infinitely distant from the Infinite, no matter what the hierarchical distance of the finite from each other. God as Infinite Being—and that is the same as One Whose essence is to be—is thus wholly Other than all His creatures.

But as Creative Source, He is at the same time wholly immanent. The same reason that leads to the positing of an Absolutely Infinite as the ground of the finite leads to the doctrine of the proximity of the Infinite to the finite. To be is to be self-identical, but self-identity is a relative term. Immersion in the dispersal of materiality involves relative lack of self-identity, being at the mercy of that which is outside oneself, directed relatively from without, though to

be at all involves a certain self-direction—at least the direction of
maintaining self-identity against the forces that impinge from without. Self-identity or self-possession for the conscious being always
involves both a self-identity over against others *and*, at least in the
case of finite awareness, relative self-opacity; and that means a certain distance from oneself. The "return of the subject into itself" either
cannot be a "complete return" or it cannot yield transparency, but
only *concern for* one's totality.[43] What do I know, after all, here and
now, of what particular events are occurring within my body? What
do I understand of how the motor mechanisms work, connecting hand
and brain? Of how thought connects here-and-now with language? I
do not even know when beginning a sentence how it will end! The
imperative "Know thyself!" makes sense only for a creature that is
carried by processes, natural and social, of which he is largely igno-
rant and which he ought to come to understand. But granted creation, granted that Infinite Being thinkingly makes to be whatever is,
then the whole of each finite being is wholly transparent to the divine.
Hence St. Augustine: "God is more intimate to me than I am to
myself."[44] Full presence to self would be impossible in principle for a
finite being since to be at all for finite being is to be a relation to the
Infinite. But since we can only understand relations if we understand
the terms, finite being remains relatively opaque, both to itself and
to others.[45] But that opacity concerns only finite knowers. Each is
totally transparent to the Infinite; and in the case of the Infinite
alone, total self-presence occurs as the basis for such total presence
to the Other. Prayer to such a God is not only admiration directed by
finite intelligence toward the Highest (as in Aristotelian and Platonic
contemplation), but a personal interchange in which the divine is
both aware of and capable of acting upon the finite. This would not
violate the purity of being in the Highest, since it does not make God
dependent in knowing and doing. Creation is rather a one-way dependency of the creature upon the Creator.[46]

Such a view also involves attributing potency to God. Now passive potency clearly involves imperfection: it is intrinsic vulnerability, lack of self-direction, self-opaqueness. Active potency suggests
future completion and thus present lack. However, active potency as
noncompulsive *habit*, as *skill*, is completion. Exercise of a skill perfects another, and it also allows its possessor to possess it more perfectly. If we exclude the need to come into possession and to develop
further involved in the lack characterizing ourselves and the things
that surround us, eternally perfect Act would possess active potentiality—and that in an absolute way: God is omnipotent. His acting
perfects others.[47] This follows Plato's insight in the *Timaeus* expressed

in the later medieval axiom: *Bonum diffusivum est,* "Good is diffusive of itself."[48]

Such a view does not absorb all causality into the single causality of God. The causal relations between creatures remain as a kind of horizontal series, but such a series is perpetually intersected by a vertical causality that is sui generis, consisting of the permanent, sustaining creative action of the divine.[49] The free causality of human agency is itself rooted in the peculiarity of the human relation to the Infinite, as a participation in the vertical causality that is the creative action of the divine. Living out of the horizon of relation to the Infinite, and thus as "the light of Being" or "the image of God," the human being at the deepest level is in principle pried loose from every finite specification and thus is free in relation to everything finite — indeed, even in relation to the Infinite insofar as He is not directly encountered, but viewed only as non-finite, as negation of the negation of plenitude found in the finite.

God's existence is thus implied in the unfolding of "the light of Being" (our seventh dimension), which is fundamental to humanness, so that "whoever knows, implicitly knows God."[50] That knowledge only comes to light in illuminating the sensorily given Other, for the proper object of intellect, that with which the human being is most at home and can know best, is being found in material, sensorily given things.[51] The full being of the sensory Other is its being creature, i.e., its being a perpetual rootedness in the Creative Source. To understand relations we must understand the terms, yet one term of the relation that is createdness is Infinite. So Aquinas concludes both that "We do not know the essence of a single thing, not even a simple fly"[52] (simple before microbiology got to work!) and that "He who knows best about God knows that he does not know about God."[53] He knows *that* God is as identity of essence and existence, and *that* He precontains all perfections He produces in things; but *what* it is for all perfections to be contained in infinite identity, he knows not at all. All things remain shrouded in the ultimate Mystery. Things are thus capable of being understood because they are thought-created — are, as it were, the congealed thoughts of God (and this is the great truth of philosophical idealism). And we can understand them because we are a kind of "participation in the divine light,"[54] a reference to the Infinite. But because things are rooted in the Infinite, they are in principle unfathomable, closed to our ultimate encompassing of them in knowledge. Creation thus grounds both the intelligibility and mystery of things: they can be understood because they are created by thought; but because they are created, they are unfathomable.[55]

"The Mystical"

No interpretation of Aquinas should fail to keep constantly before our mind's eye the fact that Aquinas was a mystic, in the sense of one who strove to live perpetually in the presence of God and who, from time to time, was caught up in that Presence.[56] But what could that mean: living in the presence of God? Surely not simply arriving at being in the judgment of existence and being able to infer that there is a Fullness of Being corresponding to the full intension and extension of being actuated in the judgment. What "faculty" is there whereby we "live" in the "presence" of God? I think presence and living have to be understood correlatively. I think, too, that the Aquinian notion that being apprehended in the judgment as an act exceeding all the forms we can clearly and distinctly apprehend opens the space for and also is on the way toward comprehending the possibility of living presence. "Living" is a matter of the whole self, the habituated self that has a feel for the depth underlying and announcing itself in the immediate sensory givenness. It is a matter of developed "phantasms," enriched experience, sustained commitment and consequent action, sets of habits clarified by judgments and inferences, by *ratio* or reason as inferential movement, but fulfilled in *intellectus*, a "seeing into" things according to Thomas's etymological suggestion.[57] But it is a "seeing into" that can be more or less intensive, more or less revelatory of the hidden depth, the mystery of things that exceeds and grounds our penetration. To exercise our judgment fully is to point to that which exceeds our concepts and to live off of that. (There is, I think, a connection here between the teaching of the "impressed species," which corresponds to the richness of our relation to things and the "expressed species," which corresponds to the clarity of conceptual expression.[58] To exercise judgment fully is to understand that no matter how deep our penetration, "the essential principles of things remain unknown to us," and "we do not know the essence of a single thing, not even a simple fly."

Perhaps in Aquinas the equivalent of Platonic Eros and its migration into Christian thought in Augustine's *cor*[59] is *intellectus* so understood. "For intellectual beings, to be is to understand."[60] And being in its full sense is the total self-presence of intellect, though in the case of the finite, it is intellect related to the Mystery of being, intellect pointed beyond lucidity to a depth that is darkness for us (In-finite) but full Light in Itself. The statements, arguments, connections that the great philosophers lay out for us are ways of articulating in a common space of understanding the depth of *intellectus*, the profundity of luminous presence that generates the propositions and connections.

Analogy and the Transcendentals

Aquinas's thought can be grasped in the fuller grandeur of its sweep and implications if we conclude our exposition with a consideration of analogy and the transcendental properties of Being. This will also serve to relate our considerations back to Plato and Parmenides and to the culmination of our reflections in part 1.

In one sense, the doctrine of the transcendentals is the capstone of Aquinas's metaphysics, because it allows us to understand in a rich manner the notion of the hierarchy of Being, for the transcendentals are properties which are found throughout the hierarchy, but are more intensely realized as we move up the hierarchy.

Transcendentals are distinguished from *categories*. The categories are the ultimate classificatory units into which Being can be divided. Thus Being, considered in terms of its various types, can be ultimately divided into substance (being-in-itself) and accidents (being-in-another). The accidents in turn are divided into types: quality, quantity, relation, action, passion, when, where, posture, and possession. The categories divide Being and exclude each other. Each of the categories has its own Porphyrian Tree, articulating the relation between the higher and lower species under the genus. On each branch of the Tree the lateral members exclude each other as, for example, do men and brutes under the genus of animals as sentient organisms. On the other hand, transcendentals cut across, or literally "climb across" the categories (from the Latin *trans*, here "across," and *scandere*, "to climb"), applying to them all.

Now, in order to understand the significance of the doctrine of transcendentals and hierarchy, we have to preface our considerations with a treatment of the differing modes of predication or usage of terms. Terms can be used univocally, equivocally, or analogically.[61]

In *univocal* predication, the term is used in the same way in each of its instances; for example, in the mathematical understanding of 'one' as a numerical unit, each time 'one' is used, it is used in the same way. In *equivocal* predication, on the contrary, a term is used in different and unrelated ways; for example, 'bark' said of a tree's outer layer and of the sound a dog makes, or (from the point of view of sound) 'sun,' 'son' said of the source of daylight and of a male offspring. Equivocal usage, however, is reducible to two different univocal usages, for 'bark' is used in the same way of all instances of the integument of a tree, and in turn, in the same way of all instances of the sound of the dog.

In one way of understanding 'Being,' we could speak of it as being used univocally. That is the usage of the term in its lowest-common-denominator significance, namely, as being-outside-of-nothing which all things share in common, from the lowest level of matter to God. But 'Being' has more than a lowest-common-denominator meaning: it englobes everything. Being is thus not only being-outside-of-nothing, but also that outside of which there is nothing, the englobing perfection, or—as Aquinas puts it—the act of all acts, the perfection of all perfections, "form" even with respect to form (the supreme act, in Aristotle's universe).

We need another mode of predication for Being—and also (as we shall soon indicate) for the transcendental properties of Being. The third mode Aquinas considers is the *analogical* mode, in which the meaning (analogue) in question is realized in partly the same way, and partly a different way in the instances (analogates) of which it is predicated. But we must distinguish three types of analogical predication, only the third of which is adequate to the predication of Being and its transcendental properties. The first type is the familiar *metaphorical* type. Here we have a transfer (from the Greek *meta* meaning here "over" and *phorein*, "to carry") of an analogue from a primary analogate of which the meaning is properly (and univocally) said, to a secondary analogate on the basis of a kind of *resemblance* of the second to the first. Thus 'tiger' is transferred from the wild, striped jungle beast to the man who fights or mates like a tiger. To call him "tiger" is obviously to consider him, not as having claws, massive incisors, a tail and stripes, but as possessing a certain wildness in mating or a ferocity in fighting which suggest a resemblance to the beast. The predicates belonging to the real tiger that do not fit the transfer are suspended and those that do are retained. The aura surrounding the beast is affixed to the conduct of the fighter or the "lover."

Metaphorical analogies may be suggestive, even furnishing fruitful models for scientific exploration. They may enrich our metaphysical sensibility; but they are not properly metaphysical, for the analogue in the case of the metaphor belongs properly only to one instance, but the notion of Being and its properties are intrinsic to every instance of Being.

A second type of analogy is the analogy of *attribution* wherein the analogue is transferred from a primary to a secondary analogate on the basis of a causal connection. Thus "healthy" is predicated primarily and intrinsically (and also univocally) of an organism. But it is transferred to healthy climate and healthy food, though only on the basis of the capacity of the climate and the food to cause health in the organism, not on the basis of the health of the food or the climate themselves. Aquinas also speaks of a healthy urine specimen as an effect caused by (and thus as a sign of) health in the organism. But again, since Being is intrinsic to each thing that is, and attribution involves a transfer from an instance in which the analogue is intrinsic to a causally related instance to which the analogue is extrinsic, attribution cannot be the proper metaphysical analogy. Though it has been argued that after the notion of creation has been introduced, a transformed version of attribution can be employed.[62] Though Being and the transcendentals are intrinsic to each thing that is, from the elementary qualities to God, they are said of creatures in a secondary way on the basis of their perpetual causal connection with the Creator of Whom Being is predicated in the fullest and most primary sense.

The third and most basic type of analogy — the one that describes the mode of predication of Being and the transcendentals — is the analogy of *proper proportionality*.[63] Analogy, we said, involves a mode of predication in which the analogue is used in partly the same way, partly a different way in instances related analogically. In Aquinas's metaphysics, each being is the same insofar as it involves an essence-*esse* relation: in the case of God the relation is an identity; in that of creatures, a difference. The essence-*esse* relation is intrinsic, constitutive of every being from the elementary qualities to God; but it is realized differently in each instance. And 'in each instance' here means not simply realized in the two great modes of being, finite and infinite, paralleling the primary and the secondary modes of the other analogies. 'Each instance' refers to each individual being in the massive complexity constituting the hierarchy of Being — not only the hierarchy of species, but also the hierarchy and/or lateral distribution of the differences of individuals within the same species. Each creature is a peculiar limited variety of Being, its essence limiting the degree of its being. But its essence is not, in this case, its 'core' considered apart from its 'accidents'. Rather, as we have said before, its essence here is the entire 'what' of the thing, everything that can be said about it, the total way in which being is realized and limited by the peculiarity of the being in question. Given the complexity of things, *each individual thing* then realizes a *different* proportion of the *same* principles, essence and *esse*, in a proper and intrinsic way.

The use of such analogy transcends other types of analogy that amount to the linkage of two or more univocal concepts: for example, 'tiger' and 'ferocious fighter' or 'wild lover'; 'healthy' and 'health-producing food or climate' or 'health-caused urine specimen'. In the case of proper proportionality, we have a concept of the essence-*esse* relation applied differently via judgment in each case to different individuals. This underscores the priority of the individual existent in

Aquinas's view without lapsing into the lack of an overall intelligible order that haunts nominalism in its focus upon individuals.

Being and its transcendental properties are thus predicated in each instance in a way partly the same (being an essence-*esse* relation) and partly different (being a different delimitation of Being) in each case. Thus Being and its transcendental properties are said analogously, by an analogy of proper proportionality. The fuller implications of this will be seen immediately as we treat the transcendentals proper, which are said to be coterminous with Being, *i.e.*, they are the same as Being, manifest in its richness, through different relational properties.

The doctrine of the transcendentals has its historical roots in Plato's doctrine of participation. The objects of ordinary experience mirror or participate in various ways in the intelligible realm of transcendent, eternal Ideas. Plato's thinking in the realm of the intelligible focuses on a hierarchy culminating in the One, the Good, and the Beautiful as convergent meanings. The ultimate Good to which all things seek to relate, each in its own way, is the One, radiating source of coherence as that unity compatible with multiplicity both in the intelligible and in the sensory realms. "In the light of" seeking to be like as well as to relate ourselves directly to that transcendent One, we come to grasp the relative coherence in our overall understanding of things as constituting a *universe*, a multiplicity turned toward (*versus*), pivoting harmoniously about, the One (*unum*). Beauty is the harmonious feature found throughout the hierarchy in its total articulation and "in itself" as a transcendent Idea peculiarly present in, and shining through the particulars as no other transcendent Idea does. The latter feature gives Beauty a special power of evoking the wholeness of our attention (Eros) and of breaking the crust of ordinary "dashboard" relatedness.

Aquinas follows in the Platonic tradition, attempting to clarify the relation between the transcendental properties, and grounding them ultimately not in Ideas considered as impersonal principles, but— according to Plato's own deepest intention—in a personal God conceived as *Ipsum Esse Subsistens*, the Selfhood of Subsistent Being.

Three principles must be held constantly in mind when attempting to penetrate Aquinas's teaching on the transcendentals: (1) the essence-*esse* relation in the two modes of essence-limiting-*esse* (creatures) and essence-identical-with-*esse* (God), (2) the hierarchy of being determined by the progressive transcendence of form over matter, (3) the latter transcendence determined through the levels of intentionality. Such consideration will serve to bring the whole text to a climax at this point.

The transcendentals Aquinas considers are thinghood, unity, otherness, truth, goodness, and beauty. They all apply according to the formula: each thing that is, insofar as it is, is one, true, good, other, beautiful and "thingly."[64] It is of the utmost importance to realize what is at stake here. It follows from the denial that Being is merely univocal being-outside-nothing—in Nietzsche's expression, "the last trailing cloud of evaporating reality."[65] Being is rather, more fundamentally viewed, the englobing reality of any being, hierarchically realized. To say that some things *are* more than others is to say that they occupy a higher rank on the hierarchy of Being; that they more approximate to, or, in the case of God, are identical with, the fullness of being; that what they are (their essence) is a more or less limited realization of, or an identity with, the fullness of Being. In a case of living beings, i.e., beings whose essence involves development, the developing phase is a more limited realization of the developed phase, and each developed instance of a species is a more or less perfect realization of the species.

Aquinas articulates the transcendentals according to figure 9.2.

Figure 9.2 OUTLINE OF THE TRANSCENDENTALS

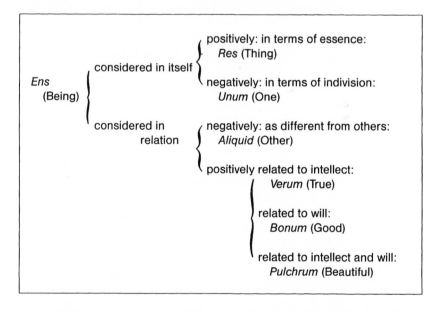

What is to be divided is Being (*ens*, the participial form of *to be* as *esse habens*, possessing *to-be*). And it can be considered in itself or in relation, both of which are further considered positively or negatively.

The absolute properties involve the inner structural principles of any being: considered according to the essence that either limits *esse* or is identical with it, each being is some sort of Res, or "thing."

Thinghood seems to be a kind of oddity among the transcendentals, for though, in ordinary language, we might say that God, angels, men and elementary particles are among the 'things' there are, we tend to reserve the term 'thing' more properly for "mere things," those which are "only things," nonliving, nonconscious, "merely physical."[66] Thus it seems a reversal of the other transcendentals: each 'thing' that is, insofar as it participates *less* in the fullness of Being, is a thing. And that means its essence is more constrictive, dominates, as it were, its *esse* in such a way that the kind (essence considered as universal) becomes more important than the individual. As we move up the hierarchical line, the individual existent takes on greater importance. Even biologically, on the lower levels nature is more prodigal with individuals, producing thousands and destroying thousands (e.g., in the case of fish-spawn) to satisfy both their subservience to other members of the food chain and to the survival of the species, which could not occur without such prodigality.

The constriction of Being by essence involves, at the lower levels of the hierarchy of Being, a subservience of the individual to the species, of the particular to the embodied universal, of the existent to the general essence.

Each thing that is is a thing (*Res*), i.e., possesses an essence. And it is a thing in proportion to the dominance of essence over existence. In the human case, by reason of the infinite orientation of the mind (though constricted by necessary embodiment in a material context in order to develop as human), we are free to "create our own essence." We ex-sist first. And to ex-sist is not only to stand out of nothingness, but to stand related to the Infinite; and for the human existent, to be constituted by the peculiar mode of "standing out" toward the Infinite involves the possibility of a free relation to the Infinite. As humans we ex-sist and then have to choose what we are to make of the determinate materials we have to work with, formed by our genes, our culture and by the sedimentation of past choices. The creation of our concrete individual essence transcends the general essence common to all members of the species. And so we participate in the creative movement of the universe as made in the image of God.

Aquinas speaks of *Unum*, or "Oneness," as a negative property of any being, viewing it in terms of its lack of dividedness. This property, however, would seem to be identical with what one would presume to be the positive property of integrity. But what Aquinas may have in mind in speaking of the negative character of Oneness is the negativity of our mode of apprehension, somewhat parallel to our negative mode of apprehending in-finity. As each thing that we can positively identify is finite, and the in-finite is known by a negation of the limitations involved in finitude, so also each thing we know is relatively divided, composed of a plurality of parts, and capable of corruption, or coming apart, so that we know its unity as a relative negation of dividedness.

It is this property that especially allows for the comprehension of the hierarchical character of Being. Each thing that is, insofar as it is, is one, is relatively undivided. Organic beings, for example, are within their kind insofar as they "have their act together," have achieved maturity and maintain their healthy functioning. As we move from the lower to the higher kinds of living beings, what a unit of Being is comes more clearly into focus, for at the lower levels—plants and certain kinds of worms—one may slice them in two and have two plants or worms. But as we reach the level of more integrated organisms—especially those with a spinal column and a progressively more highly integrated brain—the unit of Being comes more clearly into focus. And here we join our reflections on the progressive dominance of existence over essence as we move up the line of things, and the regressive dominance of essence over existence as we move down.

However, even at the higher levels of the primates, though they are each relatively sealed and self-contained, the organisms are still in necessary continuity with their environment and their genetic line. At the human level, by reason of the reference to the Totality, there is a distantiation from organic integrity-within-continuity, and the capacity to determine itself and establish in itself a progressively higher level of unity. Our capacity to "create our own essence" has its achievements measured by the degree of integration realized by such creation. The ideal integration would be a psycho-somatic integration linked to union with the Totality, identification with things and with all people of goodwill moving toward fuller identification with the good, the true, the beautiful and the one. Indeed, since oneness is wholeness, one might suggest that it is equivalent to *holiness* according to the Greek etymology of the term for holy, *holos*, or "whole." Such is the common general structure involved in the great religions.

The height of humanness would seem to be the realization of psycho-somatic unity in union with the All. Culture enters the picture here as a necessary matrix for the kind of spirit that can achieve itself only on the basis of a material objectification of mind in institutions, and thus on the basis of a tradition—a higher level of continuity with our kind, though mediated by the free creation of the past, and grounding the free, creative assimilation and transcendence of the tradition on the part of individual human beings. If there would be another order of finite beings above the human whose members have no dependence on material continuity—pure spirits or cosmic intelligences or angels—they would be much more fully integrated individuals, more truly units of being. The higher the level of integration, the higher the level of Being: each thing that is, insofar as it is, is one.

It is of crucial importance to realize that the achievement of the higher levels of unity is not to be conceived of primarily in terms of the apparent self-sealed character of material individuals, such as rocks or other mineral structures in which the unit of being is problematic, but in terms of the kind of unity realized by the higher orders of Being—the profound and openly developing unity of a conscious being with the objects of its attention. At the human level again, there is a breaking out of the realm of sense appearances correlated with our organic needs, a transcendence of relation to the Other-for-me, in the direction of a relation, capable of indefinite growth in depth, to the Other as Other-in-itself, from being-as-appearance toward being-as-being. By reason of the character of intentionality, progressive manifestation of and identification with the Other as other is both founded upon and develops in a dialectical circle the increasingly integrated possession of the self-as-self, other than which the Other is manifest.

These considerations lead immediately to the relational property of *Aliquid*, or "Otherness." Each thing that is, insofar as it is, is other, for unity is a function of relation to the Other, and one's own unity is progressively other than all else as relationship to Being deepens. The unique otherness of a person develops, not in terms of mere conformist actions, following routinized patterns of response (though not without them—e.g., in the use of language), nor in terms of following the quirks of impulse and cultivating "individuality," but in terms of a transforming contact with the interiority of another person or sacramental presence to things, or penetration to the environing impersonal inwardness within which the plurality of things is embedded or in relation to the final personal inwardness of the Godhead.[67] God as both the top of the hierarchy and its ground is Wholly Other, being infinitely infinite. But precisely that Otherness is linked to His absolute Presence to all things.

The positive relational properties of Being involve relationship to those capacities that are themselves directed, not to appearance, but to Being, namely, intellect and will. *Verum*, or truth or intelligibility, is Being as related to the intellect. Once more, each thing that is, insofar as it is, is intelligible. Intelligibility follows the depth of

Being. The lowest levels are least intelligible because least real, least full, least perfect, and can be better understood in terms of broader generalizations.[68] In them essence as general kind dominates existence. The higher levels are more intelligible, but also more difficult for us to penetrate, least capable of generalization because increasingly unique and superrich in intelligibility. But their presence to themselves is their intelligibility and their self-presence is their awareness of the universal order concretely realized in other existents, particularly other *human* existents.

Aquinas considers Verum to involve a relation of conformity between intellect and things that runs in two directions. The intellect's correspondence to things is termed *logical truth*, the truth of our constructions, our inferences, as measured by the progressive unveiling of things. But logical truth is founded upon *ontological truth*, the truth of things and the truth of our own being as referred to the Being of things, insofar as that Being corresponds to the mind of God. Things are "false" insofar as they do not reach the full measure of their unfolding. Human beings especially have to take responsibility for their own falseness. There is also another mode of correspondence of things to mind at the level of *practical truth*: the written word corresponding to the intention of the author, the work of art to the idea of the artist. At this level, man participates in the creation of the truth of things.

Bonum, or "Goodness," involves the relation of Being to the will. Aquinas defines it, following Aristotle, as that which all things seek.[69] At every level of changing being, it involves the *telos* of each being as the love for Being Itself in the limited mode capable of being mirrored by that being. At the subhuman level, it involves other things, not in the integrity of those things, but as they satisfy the needs or the appetites of the one who desires them. This is not to be read as ignoble, since each such being follows the order of nature laid out by God. Other things *are* means to the completion of a given nature. Aquinas distinguishes at this level *bonum delectabile* and *bonum utile*, "the good which pleases by satisfying the appetite," and "the good which is instrumental to satisfying some other desire." But there is another level, the level of *bonum honestum*, "the intrinsic good of a being." It is that to which the human mind, as appetite for Being as Being, is directed.[70] We can learn to appreciate the harmonious functioning of other beings as seeking their ends, even though it may be at our expense. We can marvel at the intricacy and efficiency of a mosquito as it sucks our blood. We can respect the courage and dedication and even the nobility of our enemy in time of war. We can learn, like the American Indians, to show reverence for our natural prey: they developed rituals and prayers of apology to the buffalo which they hunted, but which they did not destroy wantonly, beyond necessity. We can learn to appreciate people not only for the satisfaction or utility we can derive from them, but "for their own sake," because they are the marvelous beings they are.

But once more, the goodness of things, their intrinsic value (and not merely their extrinsic, functional relationship to the appetites of another creature) is linked to their position on the hierarchy of Being. Each thing that is, *insofar as it is*, is good. It *is* insofar as it reaches the fullness of its kind; it *is* insofar as the kind occupies a higher rung on the hierarchy of Being; and, in the case of ourselves, we *are* insofar as we are related, in a progressively deepening mode, to Being as being, to Being as a whole, in and through relations of increasing depth with the beings we encounter.

Finally, *Pulchrum*, or "Beauty,' is defined generically by Aquinas as "that which, when seen, pleases," involving a simultaneous relation to apprehension and appetite. He further develops the notion, by suggesting three properties of beauty: integrity, proportion and clarity or splendor of form, possibly related to the central transcendental properties of unity, goodness, and truth respectively.[71]

But we have to distinguish and relate sensuous and ontological beauty. In the case of subhuman types and relative to us, sensuous beauty is immediately related to the perfection of the being in question as the expression, within the circle of our perception, of its perfection in its kind. But in the human case, by reason of the peculiar transcendence of the mind and therefore its freedom to "create its own essence," sensuous and ontological beauty can be separated— though not entirely. We must distinguish here the beauty of sensuous form and even of observed performance in certain situations from the sensuous display of evil dispositions in conduct; consider, for example, a beautiful ballerina who sadistically beats her grandmother. On the other hand, ontological beauty may coexist with hideous sensuous form and graceless movement, for example, a saint who looks like Quasimodo, through whose conduct, nonetheless, the splendor of profound interiority shines. Each thing that is, insofar as it is—i.e., once more—reaches maturity in its type and occupies a high-level type, is integrated, fulfills its end, displays the splendor of its form to those who have eyes to see.

Each of the transcendental properties is a way of unfolding the richness involved in the Being of things. And each property—as is the case with Being itself which all of them unfold relative to us—finds its culmination in God, Who is Being Itself, the top of the hierarchy of things, infinitely surpassing everything else: the Holy One, the

Wholly Other, Goodness Itself, Truth Itself, Beauty Itself, Whom we seek in all that we seek.

Presence to Being

Fulfilling its transcendental thrust, for human consciousness, is learning to live in the presence of God. But learning such living is learning to become sensitive to the "more" in things and persons than what fits within our current modes of attending: the relative superficiality of our everyday dealings; the deeper attention to the opening up of the observational surface through scientific investigation, usually unintegrated with everyday relations both at the orthotic and especially at the aletheic levels; intellectual attention to the inferrable ground of things, again usually unintegrated with both scientific understanding and everyday relatedness. But sufficient sensitivity, developed through meditation, provides conditions for the occasional fusion of these differing horizons. However, the fully integrated human is one whose life is lived "in the presence of God." And it is out of this presence that Aquinas developed his philosophy.

In this way we rejoin our meditations in chapter 1. But we also lay hold of the ground for the hierarchy of values in chapter 4. The final value in relation to the Sacred is fulfilled, not in intellectual apprehension of the most universal principles, nor even in intellectual inference to the most actual Ground of Being, but in sensitive attention to the "more" in our encounters with persons and things, leading to the overarching presence of God. It was this to which Buber called attention in his contrast of the I-Thou and I-It relations, the former opening out to relation to the Eternal Thou.[72] Buber's attempt to ground these relations in the "primordial distance" of the structure of humanness groped back toward the fuller analysis presented in the line of thinkers we have been examining, culminating in Aquinas.[73] But Buber's descriptions present the basic experiential contrast through which the fuller human significance of this development can be understood.

If being human is directedness, in and through appearance, to Being as the fullness of all and each being, and if Being is revealed most fully in the perception of ontological beauty as the fusion of the transcendental properties, then being human is more deeply fulfilled in perception of ontological beauty. But that means aletheic dwelling in the mystery of each being within the Mystery of Being.

By considering the notion of intellect as oriented toward Being, we can place in proper perspective the claim that intellect is distinguished from the senses by its apprehension of the universal. Being is both the most universal and the most concrete, including as it does all that is. Such universal orientation makes possible not only the apprehension of universal meanings, but also the apprehension of one's own individuality and the individuality of any encounterable Other by an intellectual act of return from the outwardness of absorption in sensory appearance to the self as oriented toward Being.[74] Such "return" would ground the deepened presence to the self developed in chapter 1. It would also ground our relation to the Other *as other* than the self that has returned to itself—culminating in the deeper presence of the self to the whole otherness of the Other as a being in itself, revealed and concealed in sensory appearance. It would ground the lived experience of the presence of God in things. The relation of our wholeness, in the fusion of the faculties at the single root of the soul's powers, to the wholeness of the encountered Other fulfills the reference to Being only emptily referred to in the judgment of existence. One, as it were, "moves into" the ultimately inconceptualizable *esse* as the fundamental and full being of the Other. But in so doing, one meets it at the level where it receives the creative influx of Unlimited *Esse*. The I-Thou relation opens out to relation to the Eternal Thou. One learns thus to live in the presence of God through the world experienced as theophany.

* * *

Figure 9.3 summarizes the relation between Aristotle and Aquinas. It should be studied in relation to the diagrams near the end of the chapters on Plato and Aristotle to show the continuity of the tradition we have been studying.

Aquinas assimilates Aristotle to the Christian tradition by developing a new and most fundamental distinction between essence and *esse* (to be), where *esse* is, in its own nature, absolutely infinite as well as self-present (Aristotle), the ultimate Good (Plato), the absolute One (Parmenides), Pure Being. But the very finitude of Being for the Greeks requires an infinite Ground for Aquinas. Hence the Greek God, as finite, would occupy the place of (philosophically hypothetical) angelic minds in Aquinas's view. God's essence is *Esse*; in everything else essence, limiting *esse*, is other than *esse*. In Aquinas, the line we have been examining attains to a kind of completion as a fusion of Greek philosophy and Hebrew-Christian revelation, for which an Aristotelian philosophy of human incarnation furnished the best vehicle.

Figure 9.3 TRANSITION FROM ARISTOTLE TO AQUINAS

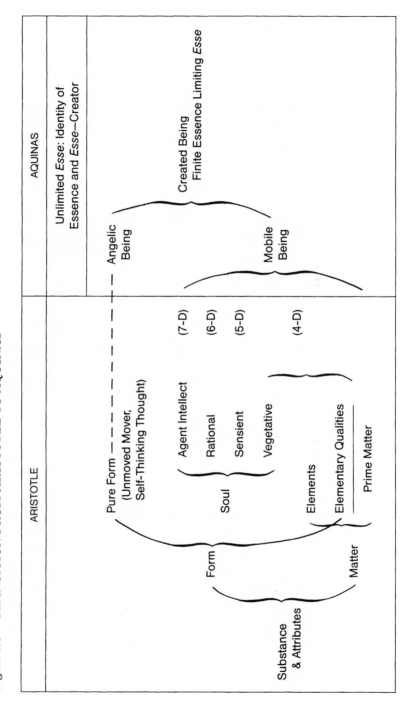

Section B

THE MODERN TRADITION

Many who exhibit the kind of sympathy for ancient and medieval philosophy displayed in this book are adamant foes of anything "modern." From Descartes to Heidegger, they see nothing but a series of mistakes, a regressive sinking into the swamp of subjectivism and relativism. They deliberately seal themselves off from anything modern and inoculate their students against its noxious influence. Their case can be made, and made with some justice; but it is an extremely one-sided view, based in fact on the subjectivism of personal preference (perhaps a mixture of dogmatism and the need for security as two sides to the same coin). It thus falls prey to the very subjectivism that the return to the past was supposed to escape. What I want to stress is both continuity with the past and the genuine advances over the past—together with the possible deficiencies—of the line we will examine. It is at this point that the text alternates between exposition and assessment, making explicit comparisons with ancient-medieval thought and relating back to the positions developed in part 1 that were based upon a deliberate wedding between the ancient-medieval and the modern traditions.

The thinkers we have selected are the continental rationalists, treated as a developing line, from Descartes through Spinoza to Leibniz. Though they strike out in novel directions, stimulated by the rise of the new science of physics, all three are in significant continuity with the tradition we have examined thus far. Leibniz in particular attempts an explicit wedding between ancient and modern in accordance with his general project (in anticipation of Hegel) of reconciling opposed positions.

Conspicuous by their absence are the empiricists: Locke, Berkeley, and Hume. I have omitted them not only in order to limit an already large task, but also because I have been impressed by Hume's acute display of the skepticism that results from understanding the sensory starting point the way these three have. I have presented what I take to be essential for a critique of the starting point of this line of thought in part 1, chapter 2.

Kant, Hegel, Whitehead, and Heidegger round out the list of moderns we will treat. Kant is the real watershed in the tradition. Kantian philosophy is in many respects a needed corrective and forces attention to the phenomenon of metaphysical pluralism, which every serious student of philosophy must face as in some respects the central problem of the history of philosophy. Hegel moves us beyond Kant and in many respects back to the tradition whose pluralism he attempts to assimilate in a developmental view. But he forces us to develop philosophy in all its aspects from the point of view of the history of its unfolding, and thus is a clear antecedent to the historical approach taken in this work.

Whitehead both explicitly returns us to Plato and assimilates the new physics and evolutionary biology. In the process of doing so, in the line of Leibniz, he transforms our understanding of matter and raises basic issues about traditional monotheism. Heidegger, finally, affords a good bit of the basic perspective from which this work has been written. His thought is an attempt, in the line of Kant, to get back to the ground of metaphysics; it is an attempt, in the line of Hegel, to think that ground in its operation through the history of philosophy; and it is an attempt to relate that history to the arts and to the tradition of "spirituality," of attunement to the Sacred that has been a major theme throughout this work.

Heidegger, Hegel, and Leibniz together reinvoke the notion of philosophy as a dialogue and send us back to the tradition as The Great Dialogue. But that has conditions for its own possibility, some major facets of which we have attempted to work out in part 1 and to which we will return in our final chapter.

* * *

10 René Descartes

René Descartes, considered with Francis Bacon to be one of the fathers of modern philosophy, is praised and blamed for having centered thought on the conscious human subject as its pivot. He is praised for having brought out the priority of subjectivity in the impersonal cosmos,[1] blamed for having supposedly locked the human subject up inside itself, prying it loose from the cosmic order and thereby also introducing a dualism of mind (subjective inwardness) and body (mechanical extension).[2]

However, a case can be made that both assessments involve misunderstanding. What he attempted to do was to rescue thought from arbitrary speculation and set it on the way to the most rigorous objectivity. In a paradoxical way, his centering upon subjectivity opened out to the possibility of an intersubjectivity that does not depend upon having accepted without thought the tradition within which one was raised. Such traditions grow spontaneously without criticism of their own presuppositions and issue necessarily in an incompatible and often antagonistic plurality. Cartesian critical grounding in evidence secured by methodical procedure makes possible an in-principle worldwide community to which anyone can gain entrance because of the character of the evidence founding such community.[3]

Methodic Doubt and the Cogito

To achieve such community, Descartes tried to sort out levels of certitude within experience. The methodic device he used to achieve such sorting was a *methodic* doubt.[4] It is most important to keep in mind that the doubt is methodic; it is a means of sifting through experience, not an existential claim. Descartes puts into methodic doubt everything subjectible to even the wildest theoretical doubts, beginning, for example, with my hand in front of my face, than which, for ordinary thinking, nothing seems more evident. The evidence of the sensorily given seems indisputable, so strong is the immediate impression it makes upon us. Yet, in a dream state what I "see" and "feel" and "hear" presents itself in the immediacy of the dream with a sense of evidentiality similar to wakeful life. I cannot believe that I am not

207

really seeing and doing and undergoing the things I seem to be seeing and doing and undergoing. When I dream it seems that I am experiencing "the real world." So, the "immediate impact," the "sense of reality" appealed to by "realists" as the index of "reality" cannot be taken as unshatterable evidence. It is important to note here that Descartes will return, at the end of his *Meditations*, which are initiated by methodic doubt of the evidentiality of the immediate sensorily given, to what is the relatively—and strongly—indubitable element in wakeful sensory attention, as contrasted with the dream state. The evidentiality of the wakeful world will be shown in its true and not its merely supposed ground.[5] "Common sense realism" is confused on the nature of the evidence with which it operates.

Comparison with the dream state casts doubt on the allegedly absolute indubitability of my hand in front of my face. Mathematical evidentiality has a different status.[6] If we might rejoin our reflections in the chapter on Plato, in this case the object of experience is not just passively given. The mind actively engages in a reconstruction of experience, reducing empirical regularities gained through experience in measuring the land (*geo-metria*) to the axioms necessarily presupposed in those regularities, and deducing those and others—potentially infinite—as theorems grounded rigorously; step-by-step, in the axioms. It was the necessity, universality and eternality of such evidence that guided Plato in his separation of experience into a realm of *doxa* correlated with the objects of *genesis* or becoming (a mixture of being and non-being) and a realm of *episteme* that he regarded as pure Being.[7]

Descartes himself was a geometer of note, having enunciated the basic principles of analytical geometry and thereby having the Cartesian coordinates named after him. He was impressed with the rigor of mathematics. But, like Plato, he was also concerned with the framework within which it occurred. Methodic doubt is exercised even here in order to let that framework stand out. Here he introduces another methodic device, the wild hypothesis of an *evil genius*, a deceptive divinity.[8] How do I know that the evidence of geometry is not merely the trick of such a genius tampering with my mind, beguiling me into thinking that I had followed the chain of evidences properly? In order to carry out the geometric demonstrations, I must remember the past evidentiality—more immediate or more remote—of the axioms, deductions, and theorems that led to the conclusion. What ultimate guarantee do I have that my memory is not being tampered with as I *think* that I am carrying out the demonstrations? One way is to check with other people. But with methodic doubt of the evidentiality of the outer sensorily given world goes methodic doubt of the evidentiality of other minds against whom I can check the reliability of my own rational procedure. I am thus apparently reduced to the solipsism of the present moment. My ordinary recourse is to run over the supposed demonstrations again, step-by-step, in my mind. But I have no absolute guarantee that the more immediate pastness of my demonstration of a supporting theorem five minutes ago that grounds the present demonstration of a succeeding theorem now is nondeceptively in my memory. Of course, I can repeat it at will. But the mediated character of geometric demonstration has the same dubitability as the immediate evidentiality of the sensorily given.

Note that the notion of an "evil genius" is an extremely wild hypothesis that no one, Descartes included, would take seriously as a real proposal. It is part of the methodic sorting device Descartes is using to bring foundational evidences into prominence, obscured as they are in our ordinary experience. An extension of the methodic doubt, it is like the stain biologists employ to allow certain aspects of the sections they are examining to come to the fore. Descartes wants to give methodic doubt full reign. He does not really, i.e., for practical purposes, for carrying on the ordinary activities of human life, doubt his everyday experience or his mathematical ability. But he sees they can be theoretically or hypothetically put out of play to achieve the grounds he seeks.

Well, there would seem to be nothing left when we bring such a doubt into play. But there is. Like Augustine before him, Descartes sees that even if I am deceived about the objects of my thought, I must be given to myself as thinking, present to myself in the state of being deceived. *Cogito, ergo sum*, "I think therefore I am,"[9] no matter what I think about, no matter how confused or uncertain or deceived or dubious I am about the object of my thought. My being, the fact that I am (*sum*) is given with every act of thinking, every act of awareness (*cogito*). The *ergo* here would not be the sign of an inference from something present (*cogito*) to something not present but implied (*sum*), but a sign of immediate coimplication of evidences.[10] So unshatterable is this evidence that the attempt to question or doubt it exhibits it.

Descartes installs himself within the three internal dimensions (5-7). The *cogito* includes within itself all wakeful states and acts: feeling, sensing, desiring, remembering, and imagining as well as understanding, judging, and choosing. It is the total field of awareness within which everything else appears.[11]

What is given here is the necessary self-presence of a thinking being to itself. The necessity of that self-presence indicates a truth that is not a matter of a private episode in the life of René Descartes, but an *eidetic* feature of consciousness-as-such. And the apprehension of that feature eidetically exhibits clearly an essential structural feature of what we have called the sixth dimension. For any consciousness it is true that it cannot really (though it obviously can verbally) doubt its presence to itself. So we have a singular existent—each of us given to himself or herself—in the act of thinking/doubting, exhibiting an eidetic feature that is therefore true beyond the confines of this conscious act and this conscious subject in any of its acts. It is given as true of all possible thinking subjects (though at this point one might hypothetically doubt if there are any other such actual subjects). But that coincidence between an essential feature and an existing being involves the recognition of "being" contained in the *sum*. And "being" is a meaning applicable to all actual or possible instances of whatever kind. As we suggested in part 1, it is the ground of our ability to recognize an *eidos* transcending the Now of the single act of thinking.[12] Being provides the "intelligible light," the "*lumen naturale*" of the principles that stabilize the *eidos* and that make possible coherent thought about the situation of the *cogito* exercising methodic doubt and grasping eidetic features.[13] It is our seventh dimension. The self-presence of the *cogito*, existing as the locus of the *lumen naturale*, is the initial indubitable for Descartes.

Being and God

Descartes proceeds to search among the contents of his consciousness and picks out the idea of perfection.[14] We have met what seems to be the equivalent of this in the idea of Being as a nature in Parmenides[15] and in the notion of that than which no greater can be conceived in the ontological argument of Anselm that Aquinas attacked.[16] Perfection of a kind is defined as the completion of a nature, absolute perfection as the completeness of Being itself as a nature, with no negation, no non-being within it. Descartes considers this notion as an a priori notion, incapable of being derived from imperfect things and therefore incapable of being derived from the self which is so imperfect he can easily be deceived and led into confusion. It will turn out to be "the sign of the Creator in the creature."[17]

This notion of Being will furnish the way out of the initial methodic closure of the *cogito*. Descartes develops it basically in two ways. One is by a causal argument that determines the only adequate cause of the idea of perfection. The second way is through a variation on the ontological argument. The latter argument by itself terminates in a perfect existent; the causal argument links it to the self in a twofold way, as the Creator of the idea and of the self that has the idea. There are some obvious long leaps here. If it works, Descartes's causal argument does not arrive at a "Creator of heaven and earth," i.e., of the totality of the finite, but only at a Creator of the self and its peculiar idea. The ontological argument, without further elaboration, terminates in the objective existence of the absolutely greatest, but that does not immediately imply creation or, for that matter, even awareness on the part of the absolutely greatest at this point.

Descartes's move terminates in God as conscious creator of all, characterized, because perfect, as the opposite of the hypothetical evil genius: as being essentially nondeceiving. Thus He would not create beings such as us who can be and frequently are deceived in "following our nature" unless He also provided a remedy for such natural deception.[18] The theoretically misleading character of the senses and the passions that are tied to the sensory world is rooted in the factual conditions for biological adjustment. The character of the mind, however, is such as to be able to discover this, provided we do not let the will side of the mind, which is oriented toward the totality of being, run ahead in its assent to the intellect side, guided by the *lumen naturale* of the evidence which the intellect is able to gather. We must learn to restrain our tendency to give a too ready assent before we have considered adequate evidence. The criteria to which Descartes appeals are "clarity and distinctness," such as he saw operative in bringing the *cogito* into focus as well as in discerning the axioms and the logical steps in geometric procedure.[19] Such criteria applied to the material world yield quantitative physics. As applied to the *cogito* they yield an eidetic psychology implicating a perfect, nondeceiving creator-God as the ground for the possibility of the apprehension of the *cogito* and of the evidentiality of the principles of operation in the development of the cosmological , psychological, and theological sciences. So much is Descartes convinced of the evidentiality of God that he claims the knowledge of God is more certain even than the evidentiality of the *cogito*, because the *cogito* is made possible by the *lumen naturale* and the *lumen naturale*, via the ontological argument, necessarily implicates the existence of God as the absolute fullness of Being.[20]

World

Having established the unshatterable ground of thought, we are ready to come to terms with the world of the senses, which was the first region challenged by the methodic doubt.[21] The senses are to be understood primarily as pragmatic instruments yielding effects in us useful for our biological adjustment. We learn to sort out the reliability of the everyday sense-world from the unreliability of the dream world or illusions or hallucinations by resting upon the principle of coherence. We discover we have been dreaming or hallucinating or subject to perspective distortion, not in the momentary experience as such, but in retrospectively checking the coherence of any given object of experience with the coherence of the waking world. It is not then the immediate impact of things that is the criterion to which we factually appeal by resting faith in our sensory experience, but apprehension of the coherence of our repeated sense-experiences—the result of a process that works automatically in ordinary experience. We check the apparent bentness of the oar in the water by bringing it out of the water, by feeling it in the water, and by going under the water to observe it in a different medium. We might even go further and develop our understanding of the laws of refracting media and come to understand why the oar *has* to appear in exactly the way it does appear. Here the ordinary world is not only recovered but also explained. In this case we have moved from description to explanation, getting under, as it were (and therefore under-standing) the givenness of the everyday. For theoretical purposes, i.e., as involved in the search for the ultimate truth of being, for "the really real," the senses have to be worked over with principles derived from the "light of Being" and stitched together into systems of intelligible coherence before they become indicators of something other than the "dashboard" we learn to control and to which we have learned to adjust.

Further, the very character of the way that world presents itself—as colored, sounding, smelling, hot or cold or tepid, sweet or sour, hard or soft, rough or smooth—is understood in responsibly reconstituted experience as rooted in the character of our receptive organs and the relation between them and the inner chamber of our awareness. Sensa are not absolute properties of things but subjective effects in us of what are objectively measurable, extensive properties. In fact, for Descartes (and here he follows the tradition set in motion by Galileo and Kepler), the very reality of what we call "matter" consists in extension or that which corresponds to our measurements.[22] Physics studies the reality of matter, not what was formerly considered the abstract quantitative aspects.

Now, as we have already noted, Aristotle at one level anticipated this position, but not in the self-contradictory form it has assumed. Aristotle maintained a distinction between the proper and the common sensibles.[23] The proper sensibles are *relational* and not absolute properties of material things. Red comes into being as actually red only in actuating the sense power of a perceiver. The common sensibles are the quantitative features that run through all the senses.

But the quantitative features are available only because the sensory features are not simply subjective effects but real relations of manifestness set up between subjects of knowing (who are also subjects of being) and subjects of being (who may or may not be subjects of knowing). Berkeley noted the contradiction that, since we have access to the common only through the proper, subjectivization of the latter subjectivizes the former as well. However, he concluded to the subjectivity of both proper and common sensibles or, in more modern terms, of secondary and primary equalities.[24] He was followed in this by David Hume.[25] But a subject of material being for Aristotle is not identical with its extensive properties. It is also guided by a nature or form that is the ground of the powers that it uses to realize its *telos*, its perfected condition toward which it tends in development and which it struggles to maintain in achievement. All that metaphysical substructure dissolves in Descartes's reduction of material things to extensive properties operating in accordance with invariant laws. The picture of the *mundi machina*, the world machine, is no longer viewed as an abstraction that allows certain features of the world to stand forth (those determined by measurable and invariant laws) but which has to be modified in the light of the full concreteness of experience from which it had been abstracted. Matter is no longer viewed as a variable level of reality modified by the kind of principle or form that animates it and for which its lower-level operating principles provide the limits of operation. It is now a sealed-in ontological region, absolutely other than the *cogito*. Such a view raises the problem of the possibility of free intervention by the *cogito* into such a sealed-in region. Spinoza follows with his notion of thought and extension as two sides of a single reality in a completely deterministic world.[26] Leibniz suggests a preestablished harmony between them.[27]

Cogito, World, God

Living things thus appear not as distinct but related ontological regions subsuming the lower level of "matter" into themselves, but as mechanical variations within the overall system of physics. One consequence is this: the howling of an animal writhing in pain (let us say under the knife of a seventeenth-century Cartesian biologist) is not really an indication of pain as we experience it when we are in similar situations. It is strictly analogous to a steam whistle blowing off under a certain level of pressure.

By contrast, the *cogito* is the luminous field of consciousness characterized by private inwardness, self-presence, self-directedness, but structured in such a way that, though seemingly cut off at one level from the inward reality of things by its biologically based senses, it is yet open to the absolute totality of being through the *lumen naturale*. When the mechanical base of sensation and physical operation is destroyed through death, the *cogito* as a self-contained substantial reality linked only externally to the completely different mechanical base, could continue to exist. The human being thus appears in a new Platonic guise, not as a pure inwardness buried or imprisoned in the body, but as a pilot in a newly conceived vehicle: an angel or devil—or, in any case, a ghost—in a machine. I say "appears" because Descartes explicitly denies the pilot conception and claims an "intimate connection" between the two substances, even though his way of distinguishing them makes their unity extremely problematic and the pilot conception more plausible.[28]

So we have the following coming into focus of the most fundamental levels of certitude within the field of experience: God as the unfolding of the notion of Being is the most certain (what is more certain than Being as the fullness?); the *cogito* as indubitably given but as grounded in the *lumen naturale* that implicates the principles of Being is pivotal; mathematical demonstration is third, developed by following the principles of Being and spilling over into a mathematicized reconstruction of the experienced world in the new physics; fourth is the consistent world of ordinary experience, the world of dashboard knowledge within which other minds make their appearance; and last is the idiosyncratic world of feelings, fantasies, illusions, hallucinations, and dreams. The fourth is essentially a world of adjustment to, rather than knowledge of the reality of sensorily present things. The third is linked to the exercise of power over nature. Indeed, even metaphysical insights are viewed as grounding the new physics.

Descartes represents the situation in terms of the old image of the Tree of Knowledge[29] (hearkening back to the Tree of the Knowledge of Good and Evil in the Garden of Paradise, the eating of which would make men equal to God). The roots of the tree are metaphysics, the trunk is physics, and the branches are mechanics, medicine, and morals, the fruits of which are the practical payoff in the exercise of power, controlling each of three areas: nature outside us, nature within us (biology) and our relations with each other. The purpose of the tree is the fruit. Contemplation, mental return to the divine, though appearing for a brief moment at the end of Meditation III (as we indicated in chapter 1), actually becomes secondary in a vision aimed at the exercise of power.[30]

Descartes's Tree of Knowledge and Bacon's claim that "human knowledge and human power meet in one"[31] present the same view. According to Bacon, we obey nature only in order to control her: we put her on the rack and torture her until she yields up her secrets.[32] Human-kind puts itself in an adversary relation to nature, coming to know only in order to bring her to heel for its purposes. Descartes's bracketing of the tradition in favor of the clear evidentiality of reason led to the En-lightenment's attack on tradition, even and especially the traditional religion which Descartes himself claimed to follow with devotion.[33]

But perhaps we dwell too much on the image of the Tree and the way Descartes's influence occurred in subsequent decades. One might come at his thought in an entirely different way and consider his meditations as a variation on the Ignatian *Spiritual Exercises* that lay in the background of the Jesuit education he received.[34] One begins by withdrawing from the world and turns within, removing the mind from its usual preoccupations. In the *Exercises*, meditation on the Four Last Things (death, judgment, heaven, and hell) performs the function of putting out of play our ordinary functions and granting us final distance from them by running ahead to the absolute end of our being-in-the-world, the this-worldly side of which we highlighted in chapter 1. The methodic doubt performs a similar function. The turn within culminates, both in the *exercises*, and in the *Meditations*, in discovering the presence of God above the mind illuminating our awareness. After this discursive or "orthotic" discovery, Descartes invites us, at the end of the third meditation, to contemplate this God "aletheicly," as we might put it, following our earlier distinc-tions. Dwelling thus in the presence of God, we are led in the *Exercises* to make our fundamental decision as to what way of life we are to choose. Descartes speaks of the basic decision to restrain the will so that it gives its assent only to that which is responsibly, i.e., method-ically, arrived at. Only then can we "return to the world" to recon-struct it. And the major point of the reconstruction is not theoretical but practical: guided by compassion for our fellow men[35] and living in the presence of God, we learn to develop mechanics, medicine, and morals. Discovering the presence of God "above the high-point of the soul" (to cite Augustine in whose line Descartes clearly stands),[36] one is sent forth for a mission to the world. In this life we are called upon to work, to "earn our bread by the sweat of our brow." Though there may be Sundays of contemplation, the contemplative life is reserved for the final end where the *cogito*, in its own nature a complete sub-stance fully distinct from the body, will go to its final reward.

Response

It may well be the case, as proponents of the Aristotelian-Thomistic tradition have argued, that we are aware of the *cogito* only on a rebound off of sensorily given things, but it is equally true that we are aware of anything at all—sensorily given things included—only insofar as we are present to ourselves as the Other in contrast to which the otherness of the given is given. Those opponents of Descartes speak of the sensorily given other as "real being," seeming to forget that awareness is no less—indeed, in a sense is more—"real being" than the sensorily given. In the sixth meditation, Descartes makes clear the character of the givenness of the sensorily given other: that it is a *constituted* givenness, having been spontaneously constructed in terms of principles of coherence that sort out the veridical from the illusory. Kant and, following him, Husserl further clarify the constitutive work of the cogito.

Husserl also reemphasizes, in the Aristotelian-Thomistic-Kantian line, the intentionality of consciousness, its essential directedness to an other in the mode of manifestation as coimplicated with its own self-presence. He follows the Cartesian line in attempting a methodological purification of the field of consciousness. This involves a bracketing of theoretical claims that go beyond the immediately given, thereby eliminating the presuppositions, insufficiently grounded theoretically, that insinuate themselves into everyday life as well as into philosophy. Such presuppositions insinuated themselves into Descartes's thought by his acceptance of deduction as the mode of development of thought—a presupposition followed by Spinoza. Husserl picks up the clue Descartes offers in the *Meditations* when Descartes observes that, whether the objects of consciousness are as they seem to be or not, they still *seem* to be, and seeming itself has a describable structure.[37] Seeming is presentation to consciousness, and the discipline of phenomenology emerges as a descriptive inventory of the various modes of seeming and the various acts of consciousness correlated with those modes. The modes include the structure of inference that would allow us to move from the immediately given to the mediately implied. Such a discipline is a permanent prolegomenon to any philosophy, which attempts to locate the immediately given within the character of the not-immediately-given whole of Being.

On the debit side, Descartes's notion of matter and its relation to awareness seems most questionable. Matter considered as mathematically measurable extension and awareness viewed as a substantial reality are abstract reconstructions of the concrete field of experience. Though the field of awareness has the virtue of being really, concretely given, Descartes's substantialized view of it leads to a neglect of the fact that, in our experience, indeed *as* our experience, consciousness brightens and dims, goes on and off like a light. Descartes's view of matter, by contrast, lacks the immediate givenness of the field of experience and leads to our having to look away, first of all, from the immediate givenness of physical beings. Following the conditions for external givenness, the modern subjectivization and the naive realist objectivization of the sensa, as we have indicated, should give way to a relational view: sensa are relations of manifestness tied to the biological needs of the organism as well as to the ontological character of the sensorily given other. The principles of coherence that lead to a sorting of the veridical from the illusory within the sensory field interplay with a self-presence dialectically tied to the manifest other. And that other appears in various *Gestalten* as a hierarchy of types oriented, at the level of the living, toward their full unfolding. Descartes's matter is an abstracted portion of that fuller field of givenness.

More crucially, Descartes's notions of mind and matter lead us to look away, especially at the level of the higher forms of life, from the immediate givenness of beings that give every evidence of being aware, namely, the whole animal kingdom. For Descartes animals are nothing but machines, and only humans are aware. However, if we maximize the descriptive givenness of both poles of the subject-object relation—on the object-pole through the convergence of the data of evolution focused upon the *Gestalten* of living beings, on the subject pole through attention to the phenomenon of unconsciousness and of the preconscious lived body (as we indicated in chapter 5), argument could be made for restoring the Aristotelian notion of soul along evolutionary lines. Not only the externality of sensory *Gestalten*, but also the internality and unconscious, grounding character of soul would serve to link the two regions abstractly separated by Descartes.

However, we should underscore two positive aspects of the *cogito*. First is the coimplication of an essential insight with a concrete existent. As we observed, the *cogito* is not simply Descartes's awareness at the moment of his initial claim, but it involves a claim to have uncovered a truth for any awareness. The second aspect of the *cogito* as Descartes presented it—something that often seems to have been overlooked—is that the necessary self-presence of the *cogito* in any of its acts involves the even more basic necessity of the *lumen naturale* as the light of Being relating us to the whole. This provides the grounds for the principles of inference. We have suggested that it also grounds the possibility of essential insight that moves from the individual given in experience to the whole field of the possible instantiations of the essential structure seen in the individual. It further provides the necessary bridge that enables us to move from the finite to the infinite in any putative proof of the existence of God.

And for Descartes, that move is so important that he claims God's existence to be even more certainly known than the *cogito*.

If we follow that direction, Descartes, viewed in terms of our last set of remarks in the main part of this chapter, seems to stand strongly in the line of Christian philosophy, whose dissolution he is considered to have largely initiated. The restraint of the will's consent only to that which presents itself with clear and distinct evidence, combined with the methodic doubt, appears to many to have corroded the Christian tradition—indeed, all tradition.[38] But just as the ordinary world returns at the end of the *Meditations* with its mode of evidentiality clarified, so the tradition may also return, but sorted and clarified. Indeed, one might see Descartes as standing in the line of Aquinas, the patron saint of Catholic orthodoxy, for whom grace does not cancel out, but rather presupposes and perfects nature.[39] And in us, nature involves the realized perfection of reason, standing on its own ground, aware of its limitations, and still operating—yes, for Aquinas, *having* to operate also, and perhaps especially, when one accepts the faith. As such, Descartes's approach may serve to purify tradition as a whole and the faith tradition in particular by clarifying modes of evidentiality, especially the mode of evidentiality proper to religion, setting it off from credulity, superstition, general irrationality, and social convenience.

11 *Baruch Spinoza*

Spinoza proceeds from Descartes and very much exemplifies the line of thought that came out of Plotinus.[1] The procession of things from the One as a kind of deductive implication modeled after geometrical demonstration as well as the identity between our minds and the World-Mind reappear in Spinoza and will be carried, following Kant, into German idealism. The thesis of the identity between God and creation led to his being alternately designated as an atheist and as "the God-intoxicated man," just as the identity thesis used to overcome Cartesian dualism led to his being considered alternately a materialist who identified mind with matter and a spiritualist who identified matter with mind.[2] This peculiar polarization of assessments is typical when it comes to judging nondualist thought.

Being as a Single Substance

It is important in reinforcing our earlier observations on metaphysics and practicality to note that Spinoza's metaphysics is contained in a book entitled *Ethics*. His work is a matter of finding *and learning to dwell within* "man's place in the universe." One has to begin with an inventory of the differing levels within the self as correlated with the differing ways in which Being shows itself in order to discover what is deepest within the self. But the discovery and the dwelling therein go hand in hand: *nous* and *logos* feed upon each other. The clues that exist within ordinary experience point to the possibilities of understanding that are fortified by dwelling therein. Spinoza proceeds through a rough phenomenological inventory of the levels of experience in a way that remarkably parallels Plato's Cave and Line.[3]

The first level of experience is a level of confusion (dreams, hallucinations, illusions). The second, the level of ordinary communication, operates pragmatically (dashboard knowledge). The third is the level of investigation in natural science and mathematics (outside the Cave) that grasps partial intelligibilities. It focuses features of our sixth dimension. The fourth and final level is the level of intuition, which is referred to and identified with Being, the Whole, outside of which there is nothing (our seventh dimension again). It is the deepest

219

level, pushing us beyond the paths of our own private dreams, beyond
ordinary life in common, beyond the limited intelligibility of various
scientific ventures, toward the Whole. Such a drive, which carries all
other levels of consciousness, is a desire for "God," for Being Itself in
its fullness. It is the "intellectual love of God."[4]

According to Spinoza's diagnosis, philosophy has gotten into
problems by trying to construct the totality from abstractions,
whether they be the usually understood abstractions of general ideas
or the not usually understood abstractions of sensory-experience. He
suggests that the only adequate starting point is the most concrete
of all ideas, that which constitutes the horizon of all our dealings: the
idea of Being.[5] It is most concrete because it includes all—the sensible and the intelligible, the finite and the infinite, the apparent and
the real, the actual and the possible. By contrast, any other content
of consciousness abstracts from the whole to attend to some part,
some aspect, whether some particular *attribute*—in part or as a
whole—running through the totality (like extension or thought)[6] or
some particular *mode* of being like a dog or a tree or you or me.[7]

Beginning with the idea of Being, Spinoza develops a variation
on the ontological argument. In effect, that than which no greater
can be conceived is not a single Source from which all proceeds (*natura
naturans* or Nature giving birth) conceived of, along Plotinian lines,
as containing the whole region of intelligibility, the eternal truths, as
the *Logos*. For, granted even the least item of *natura naturata*, of
nature born of and governed by the intelligible Ground, there would
be a greater than "God", namely, the system constituted by God-and-
the-creature. The only truly concrete existent, the fully necessary
Being, than which no greater can be conceived, is the entire system
of things and principles organized into unity and following deductively
from the One: *Deus sive Natura*, God or Nature, call it what you will.
It is that Totality to which our minds are directed at base.[8]

The ultimate groundlessness of the realm of principles or of the
realm of things when conceived of as disconnected from the Ground
leads to the notion of a single Substance.[9] Descartes had defined
substance along the lines of Aristotle as that which exists in itself.[10]
Spinoza radicalizes that principle in such a way that there can be
only one true substance, one complete self-existent. All other things
and principles exist as modes of that Substance. They are Its (in
Aristotelian terms) "accidents," i.e., they only exist "in" It, have their
mode of being, not "in themselves," but "in another." Here Spinoza is
following the long tradition that holds to the necessary and perpetual rootedness of all single existents in a single, encompassing, immu-
table Ground. Here he reinvokes Plato's notion of the participation of

individual things in the Ideas, Aristotle's view of all natural things exhibiting the exemplarity of the Pure Form, and Aquinas's notion of creation as perpetual grounding. The "horizontal causality" of every temporal series is perpetually intersected by an eternal "vertical series" of intelligible causality, each principle of which is deductively related to "the One" principle from which everything flows. Being Itself, the Whole to which we are referred at the deepest level of our being, is the single system of principles and things flowing from the One.[11]

Nothing finite exists in itself, stands wholly in itself. Certainly, relative to "accidents," there are relatively self-standing centers. Aristotelian analysis bases itself on this enduring observation. There are experientially given "substances" that are distinguished from their "accidents," which only exist as based upon those substances. But these "substances" (*modes* in Spinoza's terminology), in turn, stand upon the primordial Ground and do not exist at all apart from so standing. They are themselves "accidents" of the single self-standing Being. Spinoza recovers powerfully the notion of the perpetual rootedness of *natura naturata* in *natura naturans*, of the temporal in the eternal that lies at the heart of classical metaphysics. He also recovers profoundly certain facets of freedom (while significantly eliminating others).

Freedom

His basic conception of freedom integrates two facets: freedom from outside coercion and freedom for the unimpeded fulfillment of nature. The former is the central focus in most discussions of political freedom. And in the age when Spinoza lived (midseventeeth century) it was a particularly burning issue. Spinoza himself became an apologist for the freedom of the Dutch Republic and an antecedent of the Glorious Revolution.[12]

The second facet of freedom, the freedom of a nature for its unimpeded functioning, appears in the free flight of a bird and the free fall of a rock. The human case is complicated by the fact that human nature is multileveled, and the free flow of the lower levels, uninhibited by the higher, chains the higher. The free soaring of our spirit toward the Totality is enchained by the free flow of our bodily passions. Spinoza's concern for freedom is not only concern for freedom from tyranny, especially the religious tyranny he himself experienced in his expulsion from the synagogue in Amsterdam,[13] but, connected with this, also and especially, concern for the ultimate freedom that consists in union with the Whole, the completion of our "seventh dimension," the consummation of authentic religiousness.

Within this vision of freedom, God turns out to be the only totally free existent because there is nothing outside Him (It) to inhibit Him (It).[14] But that is linked with the notion of the Totality as a system governed by absolutely necessary principles. Spinoza accepted Descartes's notion of the mechanically determined world of extension and extended that to the inner world of thought, since both regions are patterned after and governed by the necessary deductive system of *natura naturans*. Nothing is free, including God, in the sense of not being determined any antecedents, but all is governed inflexibly by principles. Even for God, there is no real freedom of choice in the way that is commonsensibly understood. We tend to think of free choice as absolute initiation of a line of causality. But when we do so we always have to add a motive, even if the motive is "because I felt like it." Of course, the next question will always be, But why did you feel like it? or, in case a clear reason is offered, why was the motive you presented the actual 'motor' for your choices? In both cases, the answer has to go back to prior conditions, physiological, psychological, and sociological. Freedom at the level of *natura naturata* is self-determination in the way an organism is presumably self-determined over against its environment. Programmed by its genetic code, it struggles to unfold itself against the obstacles placed in the way of its free functioning by its surroundings. The Totality is such an organic system, but it is without anything outside it to resist its free functioning. God is that system. He alone is therefore totally free.

At the human level of the system, we are not actually free to choose a shift of levels in us from the lower to the higher, since all occurs by necessity. If such a shift and the realization of final freedom as identity with the All occurs, it is by a happy coincidence of determined principles. The more we come to understand why people are the way they are, the more we see they are victims. Hence Spinoza suggests that we approach everything, human conduct included, in the way we would approach lines and planes and triangles.[15] Hence he advises us not to laugh at human foibles, nor to weep over human tragedy, nor to become enraged over human violation.[16] To understand all is to forgive all. And as we become more detached from indignation and revenge by coming to understand, we become more grateful that what determines us who are able to see things *sub specie aeternitatis*,[17] "from the point of view of eternity," is what is deepest in us. We are thus the privileged ones, the elect, called by God (or Nature), freed in the deepest dimension of our being.

Spinoza's development of this position runs parallel to two differing movements within the seventeenth century. On the one hand, there was the development of the conception of the world machine, heading from Kepler, Galileo, and Descartes to Newton. Though each of these thinkers placed the human mind outside the world machine, already in Hobbes (seventeenth century) the human mind is assimilated to the machine as a species of motion. Spinoza attempted to overcome from within Descartes's dualism of an inner, free, thinking substance and an outer, determined, mechanical extension.[18] On the other hand, there was the Calvinism of the Quakers and the Illuminists with whom Spinoza himself lived after his expulsion from the synagogue.[19] That we are each predestined from all eternity by the absolutely sovereign God is a dogma of Calvinist faith that claims ancestry in Augustine and in the Hebrew-Christian notion of creation. If the total being of things is "made" by God Who Himself remains unchanged, omniscient and omnipotent, there really is no room for free choice. Humans are all predestined by God's inscrutable design for salvation or damnation.[20] Now the unimpeded sovereignty of God becomes the unimpeded functioning of the world machine. "Election" involves the fortunately free release of higher levels in certain philosophic types who achieve beatitude in "the intellectual love of God."

Unity

Spinoza maintains the closest bond between the *cogito* — isolated in the first moment of Cartesian philosophy — and the totality. It is a relation of conscious identity at the deepest level of the mind. However, such unity is a matter neither, following Plotinus, of being alone with the Alone, nor, following what might seem to be an Aristotelian notion of philosophic contemplation, of apprehending fundamental principles. It rather involves more and more detailed awareness of individual things in whom the divine is fully realized.

Spinoza likewise maintains the closest bond between the two substances of Cartesian man, thought and extension, or mind and body. For Spinoza, the two are one, related as inside to outside.[21] Thought and extension are two known attributes of the divine, manifest to us through our own self-experience as embodied awareness. But God is the absolutely infinite, not, like differing number series, relatively infinite. Hence His complete set of attributes, by reason of the infinitely infinite character of Being, are infinite in number.[22] Thus, for all the rationalism of Spinoza's approach to things, we find ourselves involved, at this level, in a final mystery. But we do have access to thought and extension. Thought, however, is not limited to consciousness, for there is thought within everything, namely, intelligibility, instantiation of networks of universal principles[23] In us, factually and by reason of the hierarchical tiering up of empirical complexity, thought becomes conscious thought, the "inside" of a complex, hierarchied, centralized "exteriority."[24] As in the case of Zen Buddhism, Spinoza's vision culminates in psychophysical integration with the Totality.

As a corollary to such a vision of unity, this rational mysticism is at the same time a defense of sensual joy. Contrary to the ascetical tendencies that followed the neo-Platonic tradition, Spinoza celebrates the joys of sensory satisfaction. Mind and body, the rational and the sensory, the natural and the divine are fused in Spinoza's philosophy.

Spinoza touched a deep spot in the western psyche. The initial reaction was mostly violent rejection of him as atheist and materialist. However, a little over a century after his death, he began to come unto his own and was hailed as "the God-intoxicated man" who spiritualized the universe of modern science. Through Lessing and Goethe[25] he had a decisive impact on German Idealism. To Schleiermacher he became St. Spinoza.[26] And in our own day Einstein recognized his metaphysics as the system most in keeping with contemporary physics.[27]

Response

From the point of view advanced in this book, there is much that recommends itself in Spinoza. First, there is the link between metaphysics and ethics. Spinoza's metaphysics appears in a work entitled *Ethics*. It follows the ancient claim, expressed in Parmenides, that "thought and being are one," or, expressed in Aristotle, that "the human soul is, in a way, all things." In both of those cases, as well as in the case of Spinoza, intensified awareness of the totality (contemplation or *theoria* or "intellectual love of God") is the fulfillment of humanness. It corresponds to the notion of "final freedom" developed in the first part of our book. This cannot mean simply having a concept or even carrying out a demonstration, but rather, as in Plato, having one's whole being magnetized by "an inconceivable Beauty" that encompasses and pervades the totality. It involves, as in Nietzsche, a Yea-saying to Being and a letting oneself be carried by the admirable, the prerequisite of which state is a whole way of life actively pursued.[28]

For Plato, dualistic tendencies to the contrary notwithstanding, this involves, as his notion of the identity of Eros implies, a psycho-somatic unification. For Spinoza, it involves, more explicitly, an experience of psycho-somatic identity that his dual-aspect theory of the mind-body relation explains: awareness is the inside of which the complex body is the outside. This overcomes Cartesian dualism by grounding the two modes of evidence to which Cartesians appeal, namely, the two modes of presentation involved in any presentation:

the presence of a materially given other to consciousness and the self-presence of consciousness. As Schelling put it, reality splits into subject and object in order that its fundamental unity can not only *be* but, as the completion of its being, can also be *manifest*.[29] Philosophical dualism is a stage in rendering the meaning of the whole more articulate.

Contemplation or "intellectual love of God" underscores the notion of "final freedom," but Spinoza's commitment to a deductive system (*Ethica ordine geometrico demonstrata*) eliminates the notion of free self-determination and thus also personal responsibility. It thus eviscerates ethics as usually understood. As Kant underscored later (and as we shall see), autonomy is the presupposition of all ethical conduct. The notion of final freedom does sustain the notion of a nature with a distinctive *telos*, in spite of Spinoza's criticisms of teleology; however, we would claim with Kant, such a *telos* can only be reached through a history of choices.

The geometric style of philosophizing points one toward first principles as *Natura naturans*, Nature giving birth to the system of individuals as *natura naturata*. It also suggests a model that remains at the level of theorems, that is, universals deductively entailed by the first principles. However, for Spinoza as for Plato, geometry remains at the third level of knowing. The highest level for Spinoza (but presumably not for Plato) lies in the concreted knowledge of the individual within the Totality. This underscores the individual and the immanence of the divine in the individual. Buber later emphasizes the same (though far from following the geometric order) in his claim that the Eternal Thou is made present through the presence of the finite Thou (whether person or thing or work of art or source of inspiration).[30] And the possibility for that is provided by Aquinas's notion of the perpetual grounding of creatures in God. Yet the divine for Spinoza is *Deus sive Natura*, "God or Nature, call it what you will." The world is God's body and God is not independent of nature, nor (contrary to Buber) does He choose to create or not. This is linked to Spinoza's implicit reading of the implications of the ontological argument: that than which no greater can be conceived is God and finite things, not God supposedly alone. In Spinoza we have a kind of *imago Dei* doctrine in which final freedom is union with God that brings the self to its psychophysical wholeness and simultaneously identifies the self with the finite other. At the same time, however, the complete identity of mind and body advanced by Spinoza is paralleled by the complete identity of God and World and the lack of choice in man is paralleled by an equal lack of choice in God. That seems a very high price to pay.

12 *Gottfried Wilhelm Leibniz*

Perhaps the most attractive image Leibniz uses to speak of his thought is that of the great symphony of being wherein everyone plays the score that belongs to him alone and, whereby, because of the wisdom and direction of the Composer-Conductor, the richest harmony results. Even dissonances are resolved in the overall complexity of the score.[1] Leibniz reinvoked the Platonic notion of harmony within the greater complexity of the early modern age. But on the surface, that age was anything but harmonious. It was a field of tensions. Protestants and Catholics still were killing one another in the name of the Prince of Peace. Modern mechanism struggled with ancient teleology. Spinozist monism was challenged by Gassendian atomism. Oriental culture was infiltrating the West and Catholic missionaries were fighting over assimilating Catholicism to Chinese modes of thought and custom in the rites controversy. Of course the usual overt political battles continued, hot and cold. Leibniz was deeply involved in all these struggles, striving to bring about some sort of harmony both theoretically and practically in each case and throughout the whole.[2]

The Monad

Theoretically, he saw a way to sythesize Spinoza's conception of the unity of the whole, which conceived of the individual as a function of the total system of Nature,[3] and Gassendi's atomism, which failed to consider the unity of the whole.[4] To begin with, this was the age of the invention of the microscope when biologists like Leeuwenhoek, Malpighi, and Swammerdam were beginning to discover worlds within each organism.[5] Gassendi saw this as indicating the ultimate atomic structure of matter that the ancients Leucippus, Democritus, Epicurus, and Lucretius had espoused. That view, taken by itself, reduced the macroindividuals of ordinary experience (including the experiencer) to a surface play of similar elementary particles differing only in spatial shape and arrangement. In so doing, it destroyed the intelligibility provided by more encompassing wholes both at the macrolevel of ordinary experience and at the ultimate level cultivated by

Spinoza.[6] As Leibniz saw, each individual, in order to exist at all, must be compossible with everything else that exists and thus must contain within itself the whole from its point of view.[7] The ultimate atoms, now called *monads* (from the Greek *monas*, meaning "one"), were not quantitative at all, but were essentially qualitative units perspectively mirroring the whole.[8] Quantity is the way things appear to external perception at a certain level of magnitude. Body thus is not equal to extension, but is rather the point of view of the monad on the whole.[9]

Obviously, this is not something that one can read from sensuous inspection. What sensuous inspection yields are *phenomena bene fundata*, well-founded appearances of extended individual bodies relative to the perceptual equipment of the perceiver.[10] But the inner (what Kant would call *noumenal*) reality is a perspectival mirroring of the whole. Thus the world is comprised of ultimate individuals, as in atomism; but each contains the whole "representationally" and thus stands in harmonic relation to the whole.

In our chapter on Parmenides, we noted Melissus's criticism of viewing the One as literally spherical,[11] for any material extension involves distinctions between periphery and center, between any two points on the periphery, between any peripheral point and the points lying upon a straight line to the center and between any and all of these points, thus involving the non-being of otherness in the purity of Being itself. Leibniz, in effect, applies this to the plurality of atoms. Compound bodies he takes as evident: but the compound presupposes the simple. The simple, however, cannot be quantitative or extensive since it can always be at least theoretically subdivided and thus cannot be ultimately simple. Following the lines of the calculus that he invented, Leibniz suggests an actual infinity of points between any given termini of any extensive unit, like the infinity of fractions between any two contiguous whole numbers.[12] But he also introduced the notion of force to supplement the Cartesian notion of extention as identical with matter. If extension were the sole property of matter, there would be no resistance in the propagation of motion from one body to another. Resistance indicates the intrinsic force or energetic character of any body.[13] The notion of force can be viewed simply at a mechanical level. But mechanics is based upon a series of abstractions. Leibniz considers the force of passive resistance to be an abstract limit-condition of the essential *conatus* of each being striving to unfold all its pregiven relations.[14] Each such *metaphysical point*, as we have said, qualitatively contains the totality from its own position within that totality. Each is thus full and infinitely articulated within its absolute unity. But each is also dynamically unfolding, and that by reason of the fact that it is a finite perspective on an infinite totality. The tension between the finitude of the perspective in each case and the infinity of the orientation drives each monad beyond its current state. Leibniz generalizes this into a metaphysical principle: for a monad, to be is to act; being is process. Monads are thus not only representational, they are also essentially dynamic.[15]

The monads constitute an absolute plenum. The ancient objections to a void as existent non-being separating the atoms can be brought to bear here. If non-being separates them, then they are not separate; for non-being cannot exist. Leibniz, in effect, accepts that, claiming that spatiality is an abstract consideration: there is no real "empty container," no real void within which separate atoms exist. Between and around any two empirically given points an infinite plenitude exists. The whole is an absolute plenum.[16] Leibniz thus rejects Aristotle's argument as to the impossibility of an actual infinite. [17]

Leibniz likewise rejects the possibility of any two monads being identical. He speaks here of the principle of "the identity of indiscernibles."[18] Each individual monad is thus not merely an identical instance of a class, like dimes from the mint; but each individual is really unique, a variation on a theme rather than a mere identical repetition. Both Cartesian mathematical points and Gassendian atoms are regarded as useful fictions, abstractions from the concrete uniqueness of even the least monadic entity. Though each individual is an instance of the general metaphysical principles (its being is its acting, it is a monad having a perspective on the whole, etc.), each individual is a kind of concrete universal over against the plurality of its features. Leibniz speaks of "the law of the series" as a rule of transition from one state to another governing the uniqueness of the monad.[19] An individual would thus not only be an intelligible subject of several general sciences, beginning with metaphysics and continuing through physics, chemistry, and biology, but it would have an intelligible Gestalt of its very own, irreducible to the general laws that would only set its boundary conditions. The same would hold good for comprehension of a culture or an epoch. With this notion of the law of the series, Leibniz lays the groundwork for the distinction, later expressed in Windelband's terms, between *nomothetic* sciences on the hunt for laws of recurrence and *idiopathic* sciences, which seek the unique physiognomy of an individual person or epoch or culture.[20]

All finite things are composed of such monads which are, however, internally related to those that form the systems we call organisms and those more loosely related aggregate structures of preorganic types. As such, the notion of organism is in a sense extended to everything, for everything is internally related to everything else, the way the cells and organs are internally related to the total system of the organism. At the same time, contrary to the ancient view of atoms, such monads, as we have said, are not static units, internally changeless. They are units of force, energy units striving to unfold all their relations. Thus, like organisms, they are conceived of teleologically.[21] In a reversal of ancient (and modern) atomism, far from being a surface play of mechanical causes that eliminate the need for teleology, monads are the actual teleological causes of which mechanical causes are the surface play relative to the human field of perception.

Hierarchy

The universe, we said, is an absolute plenum. This is the case not only "horizontally," so to speak, as in the case of Cartesian matter, but also "vertically." That is, the universe is composed not of a single extension or of unileveled individual atoms, but of a continuous gradation of monads from the lowest to the highest, as in Aquinas's speculative angelology. There is no gap in the hierarchy, no missing link in the chain. The hierarchy is determined by the perspectives becoming richer and the tendencies more dynamic as we move up the line.[22] This is clear at the macrolevel as we move from the forms we can most rudimentarily distinguish from the nonliving to those living forms that are increasingly more complex and possess more and more integrated and developing forms of experience. The hierarchy would continue throughout humankind. Thus humans are hierarchically graduated in terms of their ability to come to terms with more and more aspects of experience in a more and more integrated manner within the totality of their lives. Plurality and integration together measure the rank in the hierarchy, as Nietzsche later noted. Yet he went on to add that there is a limit: all living things need a limited horizon within which to live, else plurality will tear them asunder.[23] Characteristically, Leibniz presses at the upper limit of human horizons.

The hierarchy is spelled out externally by graduations of organic complexity and integration. Such integrated complexity pivots around a "soul-monad." Each organism entails such a central monad as its ground, whose inner perception and appetition involves a clustering of other monads to form organs, as a gathering of "material" elements, to spell out the concrete perspective of the central soul-monad.

That some of the monads are significantly different we know, not only by inference from external observation, but also and especially from within the field of our own self-awareness, which Leibniz calls "apperception."[24] Here we have the highest level of soul-monads, which not only gather others about themselves to form organs into an organ system, but also gather perceptions around themselves in order to achieve awareness of the universal order. Now our field of awareness is at least partially constituted by *petites perceptions,* "tiny perceptions," such as that of the sound of a drop of water falling over a cliff. Imperceptible in itself at a distance, the sound becomes part of the roaring waterfall when it joins with billions of others. Leibniz deduces from this that the *petites perceptions* must be unconscious perceptions—a notion which, apart from such an observation, might seem contradictory.[25] Thus just as the Cartesian extended body is overcome in the nation of the monad as qualitative dynamism, so the Cartesian conscious soul is overcome in the notion of unconscious perception. Leibniz links this to the notion of the qualitative character of all monads and arrives at the claim that all monads are characterized by perception and its correlative, appetition, or *conatus.* Hence, in contrast to the essentially dead universe of mechanism; Leibniz conceives of a universe alive in all its monadic parts, taking his point of departure not from the externality of the objects of perception, but from the interior character of perception itself.

Though all monads are entelechies, goal-oriented souls composed of perception and appetition, and though they fill out a continuously graded hierarchy, they exist on four great levels. The first and lowest are those that have no organic system clustered about them, but rather are capable of being annexed to an organic system. Though still characterized by life in a rudimentary sense, by perception and appetition that mirrors the whole in a dynamic way, they are more like slumbering mind characterized by *petites perceptions* that are never combined to form conscious perception. The same is true for the lowest levels of identifiable life forms, except that they are possessed of a "central monad" whose "clearer perceptions" involve closer proximity to other monads organied around the center and, as a consequence, a more distinctive and more dynamic "view" of the whole.[26] Animal forms, involving greater complexity, also involve such "clarity and distinctness" of perception that the *petites perceptions* are raised to the level of conscious perception and desire. Animal life thus organizes itself not only unconsciously at the vegetative level, but also in terms of regularities empirically established from their own conscious centers. Animals are "true empirics," as is true of human beings three-fourths of the time, arranging their lives in terms of the association of reoccurring sequences.[27]

But the human case is distinctive. Not only is there vegetative and empirical organization, there is also the capacity to lay hold of necessary connections in logic, in metaphysics, and in mathematics.

Such necessities, transcending the limitations of empirical instantiation, ground the recognition of an enduring *I* that can take responsibility for its own actions.[28] The human central monad rises to the clarity of the principles that govern the whole and thus exists as "the image of God."[29] Humanness reaches its height in the disinterested love of God, which provides the greatest of pleasures.[30] However, in keeping with the general principle that to be is to act, the highest levels of humanness are characterized not only by the broadest and deepest perceptions, but also by the most intense and broadest range of activities. That implies an essential wedding of theory and practice, for activity unillumined by theory is cramped and self-defeating; and theory unrelated to practice is inadequate to its human condition. Indeed, the interplay of theory and practice is an instance in the human case of the general monadic condition of the interplay of perception and appetition. Leibniz applied this to his own life, for his motto was *Theoria et Praxis*, and he lived it most intensely.[31] The intensity of his own life and the depth of his sense of the divine love at the heart of things supported the visionary sense of the whole as an infinite sea of life.

First Principles

The fundamental principle in the Leibnizian universe is the *principle of sufficient reason*. Indeed, "sufficient reason" describes what is meant by "principle" in the first place. There are two ultimate specifications of that principle. The first is the *principle of noncontradiction* operative in the necessary truths of logic, metaphysics, and mathematics.[32] But then there are matters of fact, contingent truths. They are governed by the *principle of fitness*. In either order, it is true that everything that occurs, everything that exists, must have its sufficient reason either in itself or in another. If in another, then the same reasoning applies, until we reach something which has its sufficient reason in itself. Along these lines Leibniz argues for the existence of God both by a cosmological and an ontological argument.[34]

The necessary truths, contrary to Descartes, Ockham, and others, do not have their ground in the will of God, but belong to the divine intellect.[35] If the former, they would not be necessary truths. But as necessary, they cannot not be so. Hence they are independent of any, even a divine choice. Contingent truths are matters of fact that could either have been or not have been. The existence of the factual universe is itself a contingent truth. As such it must have its sufficient reason. Prior to its coming to be, it was one among an infinite number of possible universes, each constituted by systems of compossibility. Its existence is the result of the divine will, but a divine will following infinite wisdom. The only sufficient reason that would follow such wisdom would be that of the *best possible* from among the myriads of possible universes, that is,the one in which goodness would be maximized.[36] And for Leibniz that is possible through the maximum of factual plurality compatible with the simplest unity of principle. The criterion is not anthropocentric.[37] It is geared toward maximum richness and unity ("the greatest variety along with the greatest order")[38] in the universe as a whole, and human beings are a part—though a high-order part—within that whole.

Of course, the immediate problem that this generates is the problem of the existence of evil, both physical and moral. In his *Theodicy* Leibniz offers several reasons for the existence of evil. Paralleling Aquinas, Leibniz considers moral evil, first of all, to be a necessary corollary of human freedom. Freedom being significantly better than nonfreedom, and yet freedom involving the possibility of moral evil, the best of all possible worlds must include the possibility of moral evil.[39] Again paralleling Aquinas, Leibniz argues that physical evil is accounted for by the finitude and complexity of the world. Given a world that realizes the maximum of gradations of monads, clashes are inevitable.[40] Furthermore, the physical evil generated both by moral evil and by the physical system itself are accounted for in two ways. First, there is the purification of the human soul, the wisdom that comes through suffering seen by Aeschylus as well as by the biblical authors. Suffering is an invitation to move to a deeper level of existence.[41] Secondly, there is an aesthetic reason: evils are like shadows in a painting which enrich the whole. If we could see the whole, we would understand its deeper beauty.[42] This parallels Augustine's remark that "God writes straight with crooked lines." It also is linked to the Book of Job where God says to Job: "Where were you when I laid the foundations of the world?"[43] In effect, "If you could grasp the grounds of the whole, you would understand why there is evil. As it is, you cannot."

Response

Difficulties occur at several points. We might begin by highlighting the difficulty that lies in relating the notion of free self-disposition with the notion of the preestablished harmony of the monads. In order to satisfy compossibility, to square with his conception of the identity of subject and predicate expressed in his claim that the monads are "windowless" by reason of their self-containedness, and presumably to defend the traditional position of divine omniscience and thus foreknowledge of all events, Leibniz developed a notion of freedom that would seem to be restricted, like Spinoza's, to freedom from outside coercion in following out the "law of the series" of one's own predetermined states. Preestablished harmony, considered in terms of the images of clocks wound up to keep the same time, or of musical scores synchronizing all the instruments of the orchestra, would seem to leave no room at all for any but a *seeming freedom* of choice among possibles, for initiation of novel lines of causality only partially specified by antecedent conditions. Along with Spinoza, Leibniz seems to leave no room for ultimate self-determination.

But the notion of the "law of the series" for each individual has much to recommend it. Though linked up with the problem of predetermination, such a view does allow for the intelligibility of the individual—whether a person or institution or culture, and indeed also a work of art or even a thing—as having a unique *Gestalt* that is a concrete "one over many." There is an empirically verifiable law of the series in the genetic code, though its unfolding is subjected to the accidents of the environment. There is a kind of physiognomy of an institution or a culture, but it is dialectically tied to the less determined but relatively self-determining character of persons who sustain or develop or erode the institution or culture. An individual person, conditioned by genetic endowment, by institutional participation, by interpersonal pressure and example, and by the history of his or her own past choices, tends, as time passes, to fall more and more into an instance of a type, though a unique variation on a type, that gives him or her an intelligibility. Nonetheless, one is always capable of aspiring to alternative intelligible patterns, even as the possibility of the realization of some of them becomes more and more remote.

We should say something, at least in passing, about the windowless character of the monads. The way Leibniz conceives of preestablished harmony, the law of the series for each individual absolutely determines its entire temporal unfolding. As we have indicated, that seems to make merely apparent our experience of freedom as the capacity to initiate lines of causality from real antecedent possibilities. It also renders merely apparent the causality we exercise upon others and that others exercise upon us. If one test of the adequacy of a philosophy is how it clarifies rather than explains away the character of our experience, Leibniz's notion of preestablished harmony and the consequent windowless character of the monads would fail on that score.

But to return to more appreciative responses, the notion of *petites perceptions* allows for the paradoxical notion of unconscious perception and thus for anticipation of higher, more complex and conscious forms of life in lower, less complex and unconscious forms.

This breaks down the rigidity of the Cartesian conception of the distinction between awareness and extension and opens up the possibility, which Leibniz himself did not envision, of an evolutionary view of living forms. Indeed, it points in the direction of a notion of "matter" as "frozen spirit," that is, as the early and enduring beginning of a process that will terminate in the emergence of conscious, self-directive mind, as was suggested in part 1 and as will be developed in Hegel and in Whitehead. Further, Leibniz's notion of the ground of dynamism in any monad's relation to the totality may provide a basis for the directionality of evolution along the hierarchy of complexities sustained in ever wider circles of unity with the whole, though now rendered diachronic rather than only synchronic.

From the point of view of one sensitive to the fact that in the history of philosophy, no one thinker or school has been able to overcome or convince all other equally competent thinkers, Leibniz's perspectivism also has much to recommend it. For him it led to the notion of a worldwide conversation in which differing perspectives would be compared in the search for a *philosophia perennis*. In his own studies, Leibniz sought to penetrate to the unique *Gestalt* of each philosopher and to incorporate each view. He held that philosophers, insofar as they are intent upon refutation, are usually wrong in what they deny; but insofar as they are constructive, they are usually right in what they affirm.[44] According to Leibniz's intent, a philosophic dialogue carried on according to his principles would unite ancients and moderns, Catholics and Protestants, East and West. Each individual person or group or culture follows "the law of the series" that is uniquely its own. But by reason of its peculiarly human directedness toward the totality that affords reflective self-direction, each can and should expand the limitations of his or her monological perspective by entering into dialogue with others. Such dialogue is more than a possibility built into the structure of humanness; it is a transcendental imperative, an imperative coequal with the requirement of being in the truth. Such a dialogue is an even more pressing practical necessity in an age of expanded and instantaneous communications, weapons capable of exterminating all human life, and the interrelation of institutions that is global in scope. Earlier ages, as ages of relative or even well-nigh absolute separation of the peoples of the earth, could afford dogmatic closure. Today, survival itself is at stake. As if in response to this situation, such dialogue is also the deepest aspiration of thinkers today, like Gadamer, Habermas, Rorty, and others.[45] Leibniz provides at least significant elements for its metaphysical grounding and exemplifies its reality in his own practice.

13 *Immanuel Kant*

Immanuel Kant's thought constitutes a great watershed in the history of philosophy in general and of metaphysics in particular. The view he developed indicated the necessity of metaphysics as an aspiration, but the impossibility of metaphysics as an achievement. According to Kant, we are necessarily referred to the totality, so that our "seventh dimension," our being referred to being, our being "in a way all things," is underscored; but because we have adequate access to, that is, can prove, only what pertains to a restricted range of phenomena, we cannot know but can only think what lies beyond that range. Now, most of the philosophers we have examined also explicitly hold some form of limitation on human knowledge: for Plato we can only develop *philosophia* and never reach *sophia*, only pursue the completed picture, not possess it, because the latter is reserved to the gods. For Aquinas as well as for Descartes, there are truths of faith that lie beyond the range of our ability to prove. For Spinoza we have access only to two of the infinite attributes of God/Nature. For Leibniz we cannot grasp the connection between what appear to be contingent truths of fact and necessary truths of reason. But for Kant, the restriction of human knowing explicitly excludes most of what the thinkers just mentioned claimed to be able to know. Everything turns upon the character of Kant's restriction and the affiliated notion of 'phenomena'. Kant places the whole enterprise we have been examining within a different framework that would retain the descriptive basis out of which the tradition works but block off the claim that it reveals the inner reality of things.

The Ground of Kant's Thought

Many approaches to Kant focus on his first great work, *The Critique of Pure Reason*,[1] often not attending to it in toto but selecting certain key passages, and/or examining the subsequent moral writings, usually *Foundations of the Metaphysics of Morals*,[2] and *Critique of Practical Reason*.[3] What results is a truncated approach to Kant. Kant, as any great thinker, must be read as a whole.The question, then, is one of starting point. I suggest we begin at the very end, which is, literally and figuratively, located on the ground of his thought. I suggest beginning with his tombstone on which stand the words, "The starry skies above and the moral law within."[4]

The epitaph is taken from the fuller text in his *Critique of Practical Reason*, which reads: "Two things fill me with awe: the starry skies above and the moral law within."[5] The starry skies, with their clocklike regularity, represent the model for the science that Kant's first major work, *Critique of Pure Reason*, aims to ground. The moral law within is the object of his second critique within which the quotation is found. But Kant's thought—abstract and austere, presented in a prose style that is often turgid, filled with technical jargon, complex and at times seemingly impenetrable—is sustained by a profound emotional state: the state of awe that occasionally burst into brief poetic passages. In his third critique, the *Critique of Judgment*, he presents a description of awe as constituted by a tension between the two poles of attraction and repulsion whose correlate is the sublime.[6] This is parallel to, and perhaps the inspiration of, Rudolf Otto's notion of the Holy as *mysterium tremendum et fascinans*, as "the mystery that produces tremors of fear yet simultaneously binds our attention."[7]

In the presence of the starry skies, one is crushed by the thought of own's own insignificance in that grander, vaster scheme that he contemplates, but at the same time one is drawn up to a sense of exaltation which Kant takes to be a sign of our supersensuous destiny that exceeds all that external grandeur. Such a destiny is linked to our moral call, which presents us with the only reasonable point to the entire cosmic process. Moral awareness awakens us to our freedom from the law-governed world of bodies and impulses in which we find ourselves, and to our membership in a self-determining kingdom of ends, a network of autonomous persons sustained as a network by free adhesion to "duty," rising above the causal network that operates automatically in nature both within and without us. Commitment to the moral order awakens us to the presence of God (as ground of the whole process of nature) and freedom in their interplay because He is required as guarantor of the moral end of the whole.[8] The grandeur of the starry skies thus becomes a symbol both of the exalted freedom of moral agency and of the encompassing grandeur of the God who sustains and fulfills both the order of nature and the order of freedom. Kants thought must be viewed in that total framework of necessary causality, freedom, the moral end, and the emotions that sustain us in steering through the complexity of our earthly life.

Kant's project is guided by a distinction between what he calls *phenomena* and *noumena*, or appearances and realities. or things-for-us and things-in-themselves. (*Noumenon* is a Greek term related to the term for mind, *nous*, whose object for Plato is not particular things found in the sensory world, but their universal principles or archetypes.) The distinction expressed in these different sets of terms is linked to (but by no means identical with) Aquinas's contention, alluded to above, that we do not know the essence of a single thing;[9] and both are related (though more tenuously, I think) to what we have termed, in part 1, "sacramental sensibility."[10] For the latter, the character of the sensory world is a symbol and mask for an inner reality that is totally different from the sensory object. Orthodox Catholicism claims that the Eucharist is in reality the body and blood of Christ, though the sensorily given appearance (*species*, which in Latin, means "outward display") remains that of bread and wine. Were a scientific test to be performed, the molecular structure would be identical with the nonconsecrated bread and wine. As Aquinas wrote: *Praestet fides supplementum sensuum defectui*, "Faith alone the truth supplying where the feeble senses fail."[11] However, as far as Kant's conception of a humanly unknowable *noumenon* and Aquinas's disavowal of knowledge of the essential principles of things are concerned, the distinctions involved appear to operate for both primarily at the orthotic level, the level of objective thinking, not the level of presencing, the aletheic level. But Kant's awe and Aquinas's mysticism indicate a deeper psychological root. What we "know" in the strong sense constitutes "dashboard" knowledge, revealing things relative to us, appearing in terms of our conditions. For Aquinas, "whatever is received is received according to the mode of the recipient."[12] But Kant pushes that point much further than Aquinas, though I think Aquinas pushes it very much further than some of his naively realist interpreters think.

For Kant, the *noumena/phenomena* distinction is rooted in a distinction between two modes of knowing. One mode (in principle inaccessible to us, except by a kind of symbolic analogy)[13] would be an intuitive, divine mode whose knowing would constitute the very being of things. Divine *nous* would have as its exhaustive correlate the noumenal reality of things. Such a symbolic analogy is based upon the knowledge an inventor would have of the projected form of the things he invents. The prime analogate here would presuppose the material upon which it projects its form. But the divine mode would constitute, by its projective knowing, the matter upon which the human inventor operates as well as the inventor himself. By contrast, our theoretical knowledge of the reality of things is necessarily receptive, based upon fleeting sensory experiences that are given to us rather than made by us; such knowledge is therefore discursive, having to be built up bit by bit.[14] Again, Aquinas would claim something very similar, except that for him we can demonstrate the existence and some of the attributes of God, whereas for Kant we can only think them.

The latter claim is linked to what Kant calls his "Copernican Revolution" with regard to the framework within which we make our basic distinctions.[15] Usually inquirers simply ask questions within the framework of a discipline that investigates a given region of objects (natural or human sciences); about the objective principles constituting the framework within which a given discipline operates ("philosophy of. . ." a region of being); or about the framework within which all disciplines operate (philosophy of being or metaphysics). As we have suggested, Plato, by attending to the framework of mathematical demonstration, arrived at a specific object for philosophy above the mathematical level and then pressed on toward the ultimate notions of motion/rest, same/other, being and the good, the one and the receptacle. Now, Kant wants to shift the framework within which we carry on these inquiries. Earlier in the history of modern science Copernicus had suggested a construal of celestial motions that took the sun rather than the earth as point of reference, claiming that the earthly position of our observations really circled around the sun rather than, as it appeared, that the sun circled around our earthly position. Similarly, (though in a reverse manner) Kant suggests that things cognitively revolve around us rather than that we revolve around them. It appears, in a naively "realist" mode of thinking, as if the things around us presented themselves just as they are and that we have simply to "circle around them" and be informed of their "reality." But, Kant observes, the apparent independence of the appearance of objects in experience is really as much a function of the peculiar structure of the observing subject as it is of the thing observed. The Copernican revolution in thought involves a "transcendental turn," the "turn to the subject" of knowing and thus a move beyond exclusive consideration of objects. Kant inquires into the conditions in the observing subject that make possible the way the observed object has to appear. Put another way, Kant asks for the principles of operation involved in the discursive character of our knowledge, the principles involved in our having to build up by association and inference what we think the character of any given object or region of objects is. How can a thing be an "ob-ject" at all, that is, stand over against a knowing subject?

To concretize the approach: seeing this paper seems to be an immediate act involving intuitive obviousness. As a matter of fact, Kant claims, the so-called immediate is actually mediated by the past of our experience, which sediments according to certain principles into a world of familiar objects.[16] Recall our observations in chapter 1 on the threshholds within which our sensations occur. Kant accepts that observation, but extends it further to the character of the things as they appear through the senses.

Sensibility

On this question Kant, actually functioning in the Aristotelian-Thomistic line, claims that the starting point for all human knowing is sensing. Sensing, for Kant as well as for Aristotle and Thomas, is the "matter" of all our knowing. However, Kant assumes the Cartesian-Lockean position that sensations are subjective effects in the chamber of our minds which place us from the start one step removed from things. Recall that the Aristotelian alternative is that the mind is, to begin with, not locked within itself in sensing, but just the opposite: it is ec-static through its senses. And the sense qualities are the thing's own blossoming forth into actually being sensed by drawing out the ecstatic potentialities of the being capable of sensing for actual sensing. Heidegger, commenting on Kant (and on this point opposed to him), remarks something similar: our very nature is "being-in-the-world," outside the supposedly private container of our minds.[17]

However, the matter of sensation in this Aristotelian-Thomistic-Kantian line never appears except in terms of "forms" contributed by the mind, so that resultant appearances are constituted by a twin movement from things to the mind and from the mind to things, each side making its own distinctive contribution.[18] In Aristotle and Aquinas the forms are minimal, namely, being and the "first principles" of identity and noncontradiction.[19] Anything given in sensation is given "as being," that is, in terms of being an instance within the whole, being identified with itself and nonidentified with what is not itself and thus being such that it cannot both be and not be at the same time and in the same respect. These principles make possible the inferential operation of the mind in logic. Kant takes that as an important clue and, as we shall see, provides a large inventory of forms beyond the Aristotelian-Thomistic minimum we have mentioned. In Kant the extended list of forms falls into three groups: the forms of sensibility,[20] the categories of the understanding,[21] and the ideas of reason.[22] They constitute a hierarchy of modes of integrating "the booming, buzzing confusion" of the streaming plurality given in sensation. Without the forming power of the mind, sensations are merely blind affections of our awareness. But without the sensations, the forms of the mind are mere empty shells.[23]

Sensations are integrated, first of all, by being immediately given within a spatiotemporal framework that appears to be something existing outside us. However, Kant suggests that space and time (and indeed all three levels of form) are, in effect, like rose-colored glasses that make the world in itself seem to have qualities that are really contributions made by our viewing structure to the world as perceived. Space and time are given as necessary parameters of the objects immediately present in the field of sensation. But we "know" that, for example, space as such, exceeds the space given within the perceived horizon and does so indeterminately; and so also with time, both past and future. There is a spread that in each case emptily extends beyond any empirical filling. Kant calls space and time *the forms of sensibility* and claims that they are given as individual wholes in a single act of (projective) intuition.[24] We immediately intuit them by their being projected upon sensory experience through our natural observing apparatus and as the context within which such experiences are possible. It is an eidetic feature of the field of sensory givenness that nothing can appear as sensory object except within a spatiotemporal content. Space is the basic framework within which objects external to consciousness appear; time is the framework within which *states of consciousness themselves* appear; and because spatially exterior things appear through consciousness, they also appear in time.[25]

With this suggestion Kant is able to handle the phenomena at the base of Plato's metaphysics in a novel way. Plato saw that the universality and necessity of mathematical principles could not be accounted for in terms of the particularity and contingency of sensorily given things. He saw that we can develop mathematics by using the sensory as only an initial example in relation to which we then reflect upon and construct (follow, deduce) "in the mind", the principles involved. As we saw, that observation had implications for one of the first Western monastic ways of life in the Pythagorean societies and in the Platonic Academy. Both were based upon the separation of the reflective pattern of experience (henceforth referred to as a substantial mind) from bodily extroversion, from spontaneous community based upon a tradition immediately interwoven with bodily need, and from preoccupation with shaping the external environment tied initially with bodily needs, but extended through artistic refashioning. "The body," tradition, and art all fall under censure. Kant follows the Aristotelian critique of Plato which grounds all our knowing in sensory experience and therefore in the essentially embodied character of human intellection.

Plato noted that, *mirabile dictu*, the theorems developed in the mind were such that, once they were proven to follow from the axioms, there was no need to recur back to the sensorily given to validate them further. It is recognizably foolish to set about to disprove the Pythagorean theorem by proceeding to measure every right-angled triangle we find so as to discover an exception. The theorem runs ahead of experience and applies to all actual or possible instances. Plato thought that this meant one was thereby present to an eternal realm above things and above the mind in accordance with which from the very beginning things have been made and the mind informed.

Kant's counterproposal is that we see the forms "in the mind" and apart from things, though applicable to things beyond present and past experience, because we are grasping the purely *mental conditions*, logically prior to experience (hence a priori), for the perception of things, not the ontological conditions for the being of things. We meet phenomena relative to us, not *noumena* or things-in-themselves supposedly present to an intuitive *nous*. Mathematics reflectively analyses the "glasses" though which sensory things are given to us.[26]

Categories

The categories of the understanding, as a second level of a priori mental forms, constitute a higher level of unification. They are not individual concrete wholes like space and time, but abstract universal structures under which our knowing apparatus arranges, as a world of objects, the sensory experiences located within the spatiol-temporal framework. Things are not only present as here-now-white-lack, but, that is, as a page in a book (and indeed also *as* here and now and white and black, that is, as instances of meanings relating to the whole of space and time). Even more generally, they are given *as things*. What is it to appear to human awareness as a thing? The first part of the answer is that any object can only appear to human awareness as an instance within the whole of the field of space and time (providing part of the basis for a theory of apprehension of universal meanings as referring to the whole of space and time).

Kant's clue, we said, was logic, which has remained in place since Aristotle first elaborated it as an inventory of the structures implicit in any conceptual, judgmental, or inferential operation in however primitive and un-self-reflective a state.[27] A being is not a set of inference chains; but because of the identity/noncontradiction character of what is, inference relates back to the things from which we initially derived the data upon which we exercise our reason. Inference chains are developed wholly "in the mind," but they do have reference to being "outside the mind." This conventional way of speaking is somewhat misleading since it suggests that Being is restricted to being "outside the mind," whereas in fact Being also includes the mind (an important point to keep in mind when considering Descartes's thought). Being "only in the mind" actually refers to un-self-reflective thinking which may or may not be validated in that to which it refers. As reflected upon, what is "in the mind" is that to which we then refer. Indeed, the aim of Kant's philosophy is to make explicit what is "in the mind" as the structure of reference for the structure of inference.[28] What principles does our mind employ in stitching together the continuously streaming plurality of sensations into an objective, intersubjective world, as distinguished from a melange of private experiences, dreams, and constructs?

We seem to have two problems here: the problem of linking experiences together and the problem of reference for the structures of inference. But are they really two? Logic is a way of linking, but it is itself not a way of referring. Referring is a way of sorting erperiences, for experience involves dreams, hallucinations, proprioceptions, imaginings, memories, perceptions, thoughts, and the like. Not all of them refer, and those that do, do not refer in the same way. In effect, Kant follows Descartes's suggestion in Meditation VI that in the perceptual world the veridical is sorted out from the illusory or the dreamy by its consistency with the experience of the past, so that the real criterion we employ as "reality test" is not "immediate impact" or "sense of reality," but coherence with past experience.

Still, what is it to be a coherent object? Here Kant picks up a clue from logic and suggests that for each type of logical judgment there is a "category" of reference that we follow in building up our objective world. The judgments we make upon things have certain parameters to them that have been objects of traditional logical inventory. Basically they fall into the general classes of quantity, quality, relation, and mode.[29] In traditional logic, these are the forms that the mind brings to bear in its thinking. But as every beginning student of logic knows, the analysis of logical form yields only conditions for the *validity* of inference. Without reference to objects via true propositions, such conditions are empty. Kant thus proposes to develop another dimension to logic, a logic of reference that he calls a *transcendental* logic providing the rules we follow in organizing the sensory materials into an objective world.[30]

Sensing provides the material of our experience that can be isolated by analysis from the structuring provided by the mind. For Kant, sensing is an effect caused by events outside the field of awareness. That means that the originally given, the "received" aspect of experience, is an "inner" event, not the presence of an "outer" thing.

Some sensations are caused by "exterior" things, some by events internal to our own physiology. It is this material that the mind sorts and stitches to build up the appearance of enduring objects. To appear as an enduring object in what would otherwise be a "rhapsody" of sensory impressions, a thing must appear in terms of the rules for appearance. It must have some extension or quantity and it must exhibit some degree of sensory quality. It must also present itself as a substance enduring through the variations in its sensory accidents (like the subject of predication in the categorical judgment); as linked to its causal antecedents (like the If/then linkage in a hypothetical judgment); as reciprocally related to the things that coappear with it (like the mutual exclusiveness of the components in the either/or relation of a disjunctive judgment). But even as so considered, the object is only an object of thought of which judgment has to be made as to its possibility or impossibility, factual existence or non-existence, necessity or contingency. We arrive at such modal determinations by employing the rules in relation to actually given sensory impressions. This we do by linking the categories with sensations through various determinations or schemata of time,[31] since everything ultimately appears in terms of time. This is required because of the divergence between the generality of the rules and the particularity of the encountered objects. *Schematism* is the product of "an art hidden in the depths of the soul," the work of the imagination that provides that link.[32]

Objects are precisely the appearance of things "over against" (Latin *ob*) a self-present subject. Such enduring appearance presupposes an enduring subject which Kant terms, in typical jargon-laden fashion, *the transcendental unity of apperception:*[33] "transcendental" because it transcends particular objects and provides conditions for the appearance of any objects; "apperception" (a term used by Leibniz[34] as an immediate antecedent to the tradition out of which Kant operates) because it involves an addition (Latin *ad-* or *ap-*) to our perceptual focus on particular objects. The very character of this self-presence (the "I think" that accompanies all representations) is to stitch together, to synthesize the over-againstness, the objectivity of things. This it does, claims Kant, via the categories of the understanding that correspond to the list of judgments considered briefly above. Just as the forms of space and time are the conditions for any exterior sensation to appear, so the transcendental unity of apperception is the condition for any category being employed. The self-presence of the knower and the over-againstness of appearing things emerge together as the knower follows rules built into his very constitution to stitch and sort sensory impressions via schematisms into solid objects given as other than the knower.

Reason

There are other principles involved. Again, logic is the clue. Not only is there the logic of the judgment, which we have hitherto considered, there is also the logic of the connection between judgments in reasoning processes expressed in syllogisms.[35] The general types of syllogism are determined by the kinds of propositions that form the initial premise in each case. So there are categorical, hypothetical, and disjunctive syllogisms. Corresponding to them Kant claims three transcendental functions, which he calls *ideas of reason*. Reasoning leads us from the perceived world of objects and our perceptions to more inclusive wholes that can be inferentially connected to the perceived world. Reason moves in that direction guided by certain anticipations of totality. Kant names them *Soul*, *World*, and *God*, which he links, rather quickly and somewhat unpersuasively, to the categorical, hypothetical, and disjunctive syllogisms respectively. 'Soul' is the basic experiential subject for which everything that appears is a kind of predicate (all appearances are *my* experiences). It is never given as a whole, but as an idea it constitutes the ever-receding horizon at which we aim in attempting to put together all our inner experience. 'World' is the total object within which all outer things appear. It is the sum total of all things linked together with their conditions (a suggestion derived from the If/then conditional character of the hypothetical syllogism). 'God' as an idea, finally, is the idea of the Ground of the systematic unity of everything subjective and objective into an inclusive totality (suggested by the inclusiveness of a disjunctive syllogism). Such ideas are, in a sense, the very opposite of the categories of the understanding which supply the rules that constitute the objects of experience, for the ideas are not constitutive, but merely regulative functions. The categories are always filled by a world of appearing objects. God, Soul and World never appear, but draw us on to move in a more comprehensive fashion toward completion in experience.

So considered, ideas still serve phenomenal and not noumenal functions, extending and linking experiences together, but not moving us into the heart of things-in-themselves. However, we are continually tempted to take them for noumena and thus are drawn to metaphysics as the attempt of reason to operate in a pure fashion, independent of experience. What has happened historically is the generation of antinomic positions regarding the World, paralogisms with respect to the Soul, and inconclusive inferences regarding God.[36]

Antinomies consist of conflicting ultimate claims that can be advanced by apparently compelling argumentation offered on both sides of the opposing positions. We have already seen some of the cosmological antinomies. In Leibniz, for example, we have seen argument for the infinite divisibility of extended things, in the atomists for an ultimate quantitative dividedness, the uncuttable *atomos*. In Aristotle we have presented the argument for the eternity of time.[37] In Aquinas, as perhaps the first to grasp one of the antinomies as such, we have argument for both a beginning and a nonbeginning to time that leaves it as an open question philosophically. Aquinas accepts the beginning of time only as a matter of revelation. But then, of course, he has to move against the entirely reasonable argument of Aristotle that the eternity of time is absolutely necessary and its opposite "ridiculous," since Now is only intelligible as the end of the past and the beginning of the future.[38] Aristotle also argued for the finite character of the extended universe; Descartes and Leibniz for its unlimited character. Rationalists argued for the existence of an absolutely necessary being; empiricists for an entirely contingent universe. Another antinomy for Kant concerns the claim, such as that advanced by Spinoza, of a fully necessitated universe versus the more frequently advanced claim of a need to introduce the causality of freedom.

Kant accepts the antinomies of space and time as insoluble and draws from this the inference that reason is not made to deal with the ultimate issues but only to stitch experience together consistently. But he sees that his grounding distinction between noumenon and phenomenon provides the direction for a solution to the antinomy of necessity and freedom.[39] The exploration of the outer world terminates in the ever-developing conception of a clockwork universe in which the notion of causality as necessary connection of antecedents and consequents is central. According to this conception any condition of the world at a given time is in principle, and more and more fully in fact, explainable in terms of derivation by necessary laws from antecedent conditions of the world. Of course such a view reduces human freedom, as in Spinoza, to only apparent self-determination. If I say I do something freely, that means that I do not feel coerced. But I do what I do for a reason. The question then is, why this reason rather than another? We are then moved to consider my past states, and so on. Free acts, on this reading, are themselves determined by antecedent conditions. But if all this is only within the realm of phenomena, it is at least theoretically possible that the noumenal realm is a realm of freedom having the capacity of radical initiative, of new beginning outside the temporal chain of determined events. We will return to this notion shortly.

Behind the antinomies lies the experience of awe in contemplating "the starry skies above." Physics in the century before Kant pushed the perceived distance of the stars from the vast but surely very limited view of an overarching dome perhaps as far as several hundred or even a thousand miles away (that is how it still looks to the untutored eye) to an almost infinite distance. This was linked to the Copernican view and the phenomenon of the fixed stars. If the earth moved around the sun in an orbit whose diameter is some 186,000 miles, and if the so-called fixed stars did not undergo a parallax shift in our perception of them on either side of our orbit, that is, they appeared to occupy the same relative positions, they must be a breathtakingly far distance removed from us. The starry skies suddenly expanded by light years. At the same time, their clocklike regularity furnished the primary instance of a mechanism that whirled on necessarily in utter indifference to human beings and led to the expansion of the mechanical conception from the heavenly bodies to terrestrial bodies, and from the inorganic to the organic and thus to man himself. The entire world of outer experience became "the clockwork universe" and any other view was considered "anthropomorphic." But this very attempt put cosmology on a collision course with our typical self-experience, which suggested our free self-determination.

When we try to go beyond the patient stitching together of our experience of the outer world into an ever more inclusive tapestry and to decide on the ultimate character of spatial and temporal limits, on ultimate freedom and necessity and on ultimate necessity and contingency, we run up against unmediatable claims and counterclaims. When we consider the inner world, something similar occurs.

In the case of so-called rational psychology, for Kant all its propositions are derived from a single given, namely the "I think" that must accompany all our representations. It is that for which everything else appears as object; as such, it cannot itself be an object. This singular difference from all things, its presence as enduring identity through all the changes of experience and through the alternations of sleeping and waking, again and again rising up as the same subject, leads us to think of it as a self-contained substance, simple because having no other content than being a locus of manifestation, and therefore incapable of coming apart. With the dissolution of the complex body, such a subject is thought of as continuing to be.[40]

Kant's observation about such procedure is twofold. First, its value lies in the fact that it does away with naive materialism by attending to the radical difference of the thinking subject from all that people understand by 'matter', that is, objects appearing in the outer world, since such objects are only objects-for-subject. But while it does away with materialism, it fails to see that the cogito is still part of the realm of phenomena, being, as it were, the origin of the field.

That leaves open the possibility that both matter and 'mind', that is, the exterior objects and the thinking subject, are expressions of a more basic noumenon or noumena whose real character we are not fitted out by nature to know.[41]

As far as reason's attempt to reach the primordial Ground of things is concerned, there are, according to Kant, three types of attempted theoretical proofs for the existence of God: the ontological, the cosmological, and the "physico-theological" (teleological) arguments.[42] In reverse order, they rest upon a determinate experience (i.e., the experience of goal-directedness), or upon indeterminate experience (i.e., any experience), or upon abstraction from all experience. The last argument involves consideration of the idea of a "most real being" and to it Kant gives the name by which it will subsequently be known: *the ontological argument.* Kant parallels Aquinas in rejecting the possibility, which the ontological argument presupposes, of moving from concept to existence.[43] He goes on to claim that the other two arguments clandestinely presuppose the ontological argument. But he rejects attempts like that of Aquinas to move from experience of contingent or goal-directed things to a Cause that transcends the order of contingent, finite things. A cosmological argument by itself only infers a necessary being, leaving undetermined whether that being is even aware. We could call it, following Spinoza, either "God" or "Nature."[44] A teleological argument seems more persuasive in that it infers an intelligent ground; but even this is insufficient for establishing the existence of God as infinite, omniscient and omnipotent, loving and just, and so on. Indeed, as Hume pointed out in a devastating critique of typical ways of viewing the teleological argument, one could just as well infer a team of cosmic but finite intelligences.[45] And many aspects of the world suggest that at least some of them should be considered demons rather than divinities. Schopenhauer later infers the basically contradictory, vicious character of the Ground.[46] But Kant was not finished with arguments for the existence of God when he finished the first critique. He returns to them again from another direction in his two later critiques.

The battle has been raging for centuries over the ultimate nature of the world,the ultimate nature of the soul and the proofs for the existence of God in a discipline that claims to be the highest form of knowledge (i.e., metaphysics), providing scientific knowledge of final reality. The inability of metaphysics to reach substantial consensus on these issues contrasts strongly with the steady growth in the intersubjectively compelling sciences of mathematics, logic, and, since Galileo and Newton, physics.[47] Mathematics and logic unfold the structures of our own thinking, while physics applies the categories to sensory experience. This strong contrast between the unsettled character of metaphysics and steady progress in these other fields suggests that the mind is made for dealing with the sensory and with the conditions of its own thinking about the sensory. Metaphysics is a kind of hubris leading to transcendental illusion when one takes the ideas of reason as anything more for theoretical knowledge than ideal lures for integrating our human, all too human, experience that belongs, to the phenomenal order existing "this side" of noumenal reality. Kants own philosophy is neither metaphysics nor mathematics nor logic nor physics, but *critical* or *transcendental* philosophy, which lays out the conditions for the possibility of these other disciplines.[48] The mind is so constituted that it naturally tends to fall into illusion the way the interplay of vision with certain physical conditions produces the illusion of water on the road ahead on a hot day or the way in which mirages appear in the desert. The illusions do not disappear; but when we fully explore them, we discover that they are indeed illusions and learn to discount them. However, in our own case there is more to be said for them, but that requires considerations of another sort. (See figure 13.1 for a synoptic summary of the basic distinctions involved in the first critique.)

The Moral Order

As we have said, the distinction between phenomena and noumena allows Kant to handle the central problem that had gained special prominence in the time within which he wrote: the problem of freedom in a necessitated universe. In relation to that problem the experience of awe before "the starry heavens above" met that same experience in relation to "the moral law within." Spinoza's vision of a wholly necessitated universe had its parallel in the Newtonian clockwork universe that, in thinkers like d'Holbach and La Mettrie around the middle of the eighteenth century, was taken to include human beings as well. If human freedom is conceived of as freedom from inhibiting conditions, there is complete compatibility between such freeedom and a wholly determined universe: it is the free functioning of a mechanism. But considered as responsible self-determination and therefore as the ground of moral accountability that would determine reward and punishment, such freedom disappears in the clockwork universe. And as the bulk of his work testifies, Kant was interested in the moral order above all.[49] As a matter of fact, the point of his whole project was essentially moral: to show the limits of reason's claims to know the Totality, restricting its reliable knowledge to the phenomenal order in order to make room for "faith," i.e., for reason-

Figure 13.1   THE STRUCTURE OF IMMANUEL KANT'S CRITIQUE OF PURE REASON

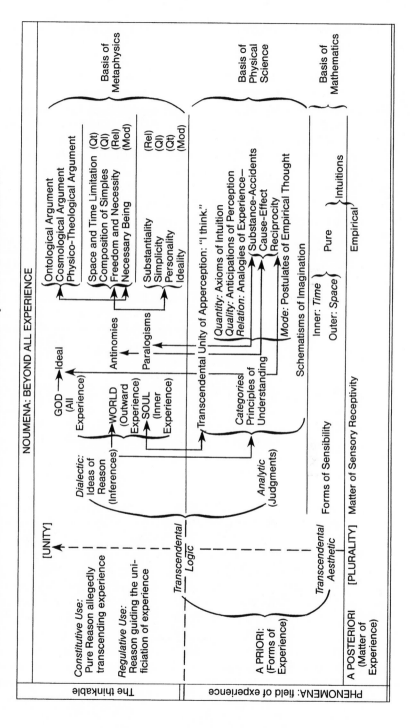

able (though noncompelling) acceptance of the implications of the moral order, as distinguished from the irrationality of fanaticism and superstition.[50]

The distinction between phenomena and noumena was calculated to do just that. Because of the necessities involved in what we can reliably know, the whole of the phenomenal world shows itself as a necessary chain of causes and effects in which antecedent conditions wholly account for all consequents. But that leaves open the possibility that the noumenal world may not be so determined. Our own experience of moral obligation reasonably implies that we must be ultimately free to do or not do.[51] In fact, it is moral obligation that awakens us from the freedom of spontaneity, i.e., the spontaneous welling up from within of certain urges, and allows us to discover a capacity to determine ourselves against those urges.

But what constitutes moral obligation? Kant himself rejects, at least as starting point, any conception of teleology according to which moral goodness is a function of fulfilling an end. Such conceptions involve *hypothetical* imperatives: Do X in order to reach Y. Moral obligation is rather a *categorical* imperative: Do X, period! Such obligation is not conditional upon anything else.[52] It involves the experience of that imperative that fills him with an awe akin to that which he experienced in the presence of the heavens.

Kant formulated it in several different ways. The first is a formal strategy for testing moral sincerity. It is a principle of universability for moral norms: "Act only according to that maxim by which you can at the same time will that it should become universal law."[53] A second formulation seems entirely different and unrelated, but supplies content to the merely formal character of the first formulation: "Act so that you treat humanity, whether in your own person or in that of another, always as an end and never as a means only."[54] But the relation to the first formulation is contained in the notion of humanity, which involves precisely the ability to act in accord with principles. Things of nature are *heteronomous*, that is, they act in accordance with the laws of nature and cannot do otherwise. Human beings act in accordance with a conception of laws. The conception of laws gives us distance from the immediacy of being determined by laws and thus allows us to give ourselves laws. We thus have the ability to be *autonomous*.[55] Acting autonomously is our dignity. But the very foundation of that dignity lies in our viewing ourselves in accordance with our universalizing capacity as an instance of humanness, and thus to treat the humanness of all humans as an end in itself. Thus the third possible formulation: So act as if you were always through your maxims a law-making member in a universal kingdom of ends.[56] The kingdom of ends is the togetherness of autonomous agents acting in accordance with universalizable principles. The first and objective principle gives us the unity of the form of the will; the second and subjective principle gives us a plurality of material ends ('material' here signfying, in opposition to 'formal', actual content); the third and foundational principle presents the systematic embodiment of the first two principles as ground of the moral order.[57]

Kant goes further. The frequent non-coincidence in this life of following our moral duty with the experience of happy fulfillment—that fact that good people often experience suffering, and evil people often find satisfaction—points to the need, in justice, of an afterlife where the injustice will be redressed and happiness will be realized in proportion to one's deserving to be happy.[58] Non-coincidence points also to an omniscient Being Who can judge the hearts of men, and an omnipotent Being Who is able to see to the eventual coincidence of happiness and morality.[59] So Freedom, Immortality, and God are reasonable postulates of a moral faith, made possible by the distinction between phenomenal determinism and dissolution on the one hand, and noumenal freedom and possible immortality on the other. God and Soul, as ideas of reason, thus function not only as ideal lures for stitching together our phenomenal experience, but also as pointers to the noumenal realm that we enter, not through cognitive experience, but through moral experience. Kant takes the inconclusiveness of the claims of pure reason attempting to operate in independence of experience as an indication that we are not made for a theoretical end in this life. But the moral interest we have in the ultimate theoretical ideas points to a moral end.[60]

Following the moral "proof" of the existence of God, the other attempted proofs are then correlated with each other and made to pivot about the moral proof. The cosmological argument, if it proves at all, terminates in a necessary being (*Deus sive natura*). The teleological argument concludes to an intelligent cause or causes, which, based solely upon the evidence of teleology in nature, may turn out to be demonic. The ontological argument infinitizes the object of the proofs. But it is the moral argument alone that shows the object to have the predicates of "God": omniscience, omnipotence, absolute justice, providence, and so on. The end of nature is the moral good of man, the only known being who, by reason of Reason, is an end in himself. And the moral good of man generates the notion of the *summum bonum* as coincidence of nature and moral freedom in happiness based upon the deservedness to be happy. Awe before the sublimity of the moral law is linked to awe before the all-wise, infinitely perfect Lawgiver, Ground of nature and provider of its end in the moral man.

Critique of Judgment

Critique of Pure Reason attempted to lay out the conditions for
the possibility of sorting out and stitching together experience through
time in order to ground the possibility of things appearing as enduring entities in a consistent world as objects for human knowing. Such
an analysis, however, indicates nothing about the differentiations
among the things that make their appearance within such a world. To
that end we must be receptive to the differing specifications made
through differing collocations of sensory experiences.[61] The a priori
givenness of space and time as a whole makes possible the apprehension of whatever appears as repeatable within that whole. So we have
first of all the differing *sensa*—colors, pitches, textures, resistances,
heat ranges, smells, flavors, sounds. But unless we consult experience, we have no way of knowing that these appear in regular collocations to establish natural species that are linked together in a system
of genera and species, nor that some such entities and/or their combinations would have the properties that we associate with the notions
of beauty and sublimity and their opposites, nor that some are so
constituted as to be unintelligible without the notion of directedness
toward an end. We can arrive at these notions only by attending to
the differences that present themselves among the things that appear
as empirical objects. They are determined a priori in their *ob-jectness*,
that is, their over-againstness, by the categories analysed in the
first critique. But they are determined in their specific *content* a
posteriori by their differing collocations within the sensory field.

Kant's reflections in the *Critique of Judgment*, as indicated by
the full title of the work (*Critique of Aesthetic and Teleological Judgment*), center upon two regions that jut into prominence when we
pay attention to such empirical differences. However, what at first
sight appear to be two somewhat unrelated considerations turn out
to be so related that the aesthetic and the teleological appear as
subspecies of the more general notion of *finality* or *purposiveness*, as
we shall see.

Aesthetic experience occurs in relation to two different kinds of
objects: the beautiful and the sublime. The beautiful shows itself in
forms that are clearly delimited and are perceived as beautiful through
the experience of the harmony of our faculties brought about by a
perception of the form of the object.[62] Such experience is made possible by a certain detachment from what merely gratif ies our animal
appetites and by a defocusing of attention from our satisfaction to
the fine qualities of the beautiful thing in that unity Kant terms
"form." He calls such experience "disinterested."[63] One might clarify

what is involved here by distinguishing an erotic experience in relation to a painting of a nude from an aesthetic experience of that same
painting. The former is focused upon one's own gratification, the latter upon the qualities of the object detached from one's animal appetite. There are, of course, intermediary forms of experience, but Kant
attends here to the two pure types.

Kant sees two features of such experience that help to bring
together what the first two critiques seem to have broken apart,
namely, the outer, deterministic world and the inner realm of moral
freedom. The appearance of the beautiful object is such that it appears
as if it were there to bring about the harmony of our faculties. The
beauty of the object and the harmony of our faculties are involved in
a relation of mutual causality. The beautiful object brings about the
harmony and the harmony makes possible the perception of the beautiful object. Kant calls attention to the appearance of a goal-directed
character in such an object by the paradoxical expression "purposiveness without a purpose."[64] This indicates, first, the fittingness of the
object to the harmony of the faculties ("purposiveness"), and, secondly, the impossibility of discovering any conception of a purpose,
any conscious intent in such an appearance.

At the same time, the appetitive detachment involved in achieving the "disinterestedness" of aesthetic perception is linked, in another
relation of mutual causality, to the moral end of man. Since morality
involves detachment from our impulses in order to bring about their
subordination to the moral imperative, and aesthetic experience
involves detachment in order to let the aesthetic object appear as
such, morality and aesthetic experience support one another. So the
aesthetic, as experience of a realm of objects that appear within the
outer world, seems to exist to support the basically interior moral life
of man.[65]

The other kind of object that provokes an aesthetic experience
is the sublime.[66] The sublime object and the experience thereof stand
in a certain opposition to the beautiful object and the experience of
it. Where the beautiful object is limited and brings about a harmony
of the faculties and thus a sense of repose, the sublime object appears
as exceeding typical limits and as provoking a powerful response of
emotional unsettlement in us. "The starry skies above" appear as
overwhelming spatial magnitude, the stormy sea as overpowering
dynamic force. In both we are simultaneously repulsed because of the
sense of our own empirical tininess and powerlessness, but also
attracted and uplifted to the sense of the even more sublime character of our supersensible destiny through the moral order.[67] The starry
skies above and the moral law within call out to one another in the

sublime experience that constitutes the ground of Kant's philosophy as a whole. Here again, the aesthetic object appears as if it were there precisely in order to remind us of our moral goal. An object appearing in determined outwardness is thus linked to the essentially interior moral order.

This same conclusion is suggested by Kant's observation that in aesthetic experience we often attribute moral qualities to beautiful things.[68] For example, we call trees majestic, landscapes joyful, colors innocent, as we call the mountains, the storms, and the starry skies above sublime. This suggests that aesthetic objects are symbols of morality that excite moral feelings in us.

(We might add a further consideration suggesting a moral end to aesthetic experience in relation to the beautiful. The experience of the harmony of our faculties momentarily heals the rift opened up by the moral imperative between our appetites and our duty, and thereby gives a foretaste of that *summum bonum* at which all morality is bound to aim: the coincidence between happiness as complete satisfaction and deservedness to be happy through adhesion to duty, a coincidence that is only finally achievable in a life beyond this.)

The beautiful and the sublime are both found in fine art as well as in nature. The origin of fine art is the genius, who produces not simply according to rule, but so as to originate new rules.[69] Antecedent conditions do not account for the exemplary novelty he introduces. His aesthetic ideas bring about a peculiar togetherness of elements that are objects of immediate apprehension, perhaps linked to concepts, perhaps suggesting concepts, but not reducible thereto. Over and above the play between understanding and imagination involved in the judgment of taste, there is the creative source that Kant calls "spirit," which generates the ideas as impulses to create objects characterizable metaphorically as alive, organic, vital, fresh, in contradistinction to works that are dead, mechanical, stale. Spirit is indicated as the supersensuous ground, the source of an art, hidden in the depths of the soul: through which nature gives the rule to art.[70] Nature here is not the system of phenomenal mechanisms, but the supersensuous source with which the genius is in contact. That ground is the basis for the fact that both natural objects and art objects bring about either the harmony of the cognitive faculties through forms with moral qualities or the movement of our facilties in the direction of our moral destiny.

The directedness of aesthetic objects to our moral end dovetails with consideration of those other forms appearing in the outer world, which, to begin with and apart from consideration of their purposive relation to us: exhibit both interior and exterior teleology. Such are living forms, the appearance of which not only fits into the cause-and-effect mechanism necessary (for Kant) to the appearance of any object, but also leads us to consider them as organized for certain ends, on an analogy with our own purposive action guided by the concept of a project.[71] Thus the very term *organ* means "instrument," that is, tool organized to fulfill a function; and the term *organism* involves the conception of a complex or system of such instruments. But the essential difference between humanly produced instruments and the instrumental complex that is a living organism is connected with the self-formative, self-repairing, and self-reproductive character of the latter.[72]

The internal teleology of living things is matched by their external teleology. This occurs first of all internal to a given species in those forms that multiply by sexual reproduction.[73] Here the sexes are oriented toward one another for the sake of the propagation of the species. Secondly, there is a teleology of individual organisms to goals external to the species itself whereby, for example, plants are present as food for the herbivores; and herbivores are, in turn, so present for carnivores.[74] Nonliving forms likewise appear as conditions for the possibility of the living. And, it would seem, at the top of the chain are human beings who, by reason of their ability to project purposes and knit them together to form civilization, can use all the rest as their material. But just as carnivores can be viewed as moderators of the choking growth of vegetative life, so carnivores can be viewed as balancing their prey's relation to the environment, thus benefitting the species (though obviously not the individual). Human beings can also be viewed as fulfilling a similar reciprocal function in the ecosystem.[75]

However, the categorical imperative that founds the moral order gives expression to an end that is not reciprocally means: humanness. Human beings, in their moral character as legislating for a kingdom of self-governing persons, present themselves as the end of the whole of external nature as they work toward the final end of the *summum bonum*. Nature appears in a second guise, no longer simply as a mechanical system a la Newton, but as a system of ends with human beings operating under moral laws as the final purpose and the achievement of the *summum bonum* by human beings as the supreme end.[76]

The cap of the Kantian system is the notion of nature as the product of divine art, where Newtonian mechanisms are subsumed under the goals of living forms and living forms subordinated to the moral end of humankind developed through the advancement of science, the fine arts, and the political formation of the human species as a whole.[77]

However, Kant is insistent that the "purposiveness without a purpose" of aesthetic forms, the teleological reflections on living forms, and the projection of immortality and God are all in the mode of "as if." All purposiveness outside of our own self-directedness through concepts is a projection upon experience that makes sense out of it *for us*. In fact, for Kant this is the *only* way we can make sense out of the whole of experience and establish the unity of reason. But it is ultimately a matter of what Jaspers later calls "philosophical faith," as distinguished from all fanaticism and superstition.[78] It is a way of limiting the omnivorous claims of mechanistic science and trimming the exesses of religion[79] while opening the way for a moral view whose lack of an apodictically compelling character calls forth our moral efforts to sustain it.

Response

Kant's philosophy, taken as a whole, is concerned with the metaphysical. But his critique attempts to set limits to what can properly be achieved theoretically. He develops what Paton calls a "metaphysics of experience," that is, an analysis of the ultimate presuppositions constituting the phenenomenal circle, the realm of the appearance of beings relative to our biologically grounded, finite awareness.[80] As such, this might be called a phenomenology. So Ricoeur remarks that Kant founded phenomenology and Husserl developed it.[81] And it is phenomenology that is the basic approach employed in this work. Hence the prominence of Kant in this study. But Kant also attempts to show the impossibility of a "noumenology," that is, a science of what stands in itself beyond the phenomenal circle.

One might ask for the conditions of the possibilty for making the crucial phenomenal/noumenal distinction. In considering the antinomies, Kant remarks that, since being itself cannot be antinomic or contradictory, the antinomies tell us of the limits of human knowledge vis-à-vis beings-in-themselves.[82] That really reinvokes the single a priori allowed by the Aristotelian-Thomistic tradition: the light of the agent intellect which brings the principles of identity and non-contradiction, in their unrestricted applicability, to bear upon the presentations of sensory experience. Thus, in spite of himself, Kant claims, however thin, a grounding knowledge of noumenal reality. The presence of the light of being in us has an indeterminate reference to the totality of what is. It is this that permits the distinction between the noumena (the full being of things) referred to by this light and the phenomena (appearance conditioned by our biological and finite cognitive powers) on which we have more familiar hold.

Further, to hold that there is an unknowable thing-in-itself under-lying and causing the sensory material of experience is actually con-tradictory and transcends the limits Kant intended to impose on the use of the categories. For Kant claims to know of this supposedly unknowable that certain categories are true of it, namely *existence*, *causality*, and *substantiality* as it substands and therefore endures through the fluctuations of the appearances that it co-causes with the forms of the mind. The limitation is thus an arbitrary restriction that cannot he sustained on Kant's own terms.

Kant's restriction of knowledge cuts short a too-confident ration-alism that pretends to "penetrate to the very essence of things" and march into the heart of divinity. Thomists especially all too often do not take with sufficient seriousness Aquinas's remark that we do not know the essence of a single thing, not even a simple fly; or that we know best about God when we know that we do not know about God. Yet we are indeterminately referred to the full being-in-itself of all things, which appearance both reveals and conceals. Moral and aes-thetic indicators, linked to that indeterminate reference, allow us to learn to dwell in relation to final reality without providing a fleshed-out knowledge of that reality.

Further, we should underscore the self-cancelling position that Kant, together with many since the rise of modern science, takes towards the status of *sensa*. Based on the observations of physical and physiological phenomena, that tradition concludes to the posi-tion that *sensa* can only be subjective effects of objective, measura-ble causes. And, as Berkeley pointed out, since we only have access to the facts of physics and physiology through the *sensa*, "the facts" are as subjective as the *sensa*. We have contended several times that the only way to preserve "the facts" (outside of a naive realism that cannot handle all the facts) is to view the *sensa* as *modes of manifestness* that, like perspectives and horizons, are objective-subjective phenomena, relational phenomena connecting subject and object. They would not therefore be *mere* phenomena, but ways of showing. Thus, commenting on Kant's complaint of the scandal that we have not yet found our way out of the *cogito*, Heidegger claims that the scandal lies in even considering this a problem because of the fact that we are always already outside the *cogito* and with things (and persons).[83]

The *sensa* put us in touch with the "outer" world, but as medi-ated by our biological needs. However, the *sensa* are always also medi-ated by a mode of interpretation that reveals something of the character of the things we encounter (while also concealing other ways of "taking" the *sensa*). The lived-through interpretations we spontaneously give are—at least relatively—culture bound; but they draw us near to things. And so we are closer to things than we are to *sensa*. So much is this the case that we have to "listen away" from the airplane outside overhead in order to hear simply auditory phenomena. A key question here, and one that Kant claimed to be able to answer, is whether the categories of interpretation are *all* culture bound or whether some are conditions far the possibility of any objectivity.

Some kind of blend of Leibnizian perspectival dialogism (minus the larger Leibnizian metaphysical claims) with a Kantian critique (minus the absolute restriction of knowledge to phenomena) would seem to be the desideratum. Such a view would, like Kant's, move between a complete relativism, which cannot be formulated without contradiction, and a non-self-critical dogmatism. It would attend to the conditions for the possibility of any human experience that defines a nature whose fundamental structure generates culture. Biologically grounded sensory experience by itself yields things-for-us. Reference to Being relates us to things-in-themselves and in totality, but in the mode of questioning and as governed by the principle of noncontradiction. Culture emerges necessarily as, among other things, a way of situating the biologically given, immediate appearance in relation to the whole of Being and the wholeness of each being. Hence the necessarily historical character of human existence governed by the transhistorical structural principles that make history possible, as we indicated in chapter 3.

One might question also whether Kant's somewhat surprising claim in the third critique that freedom is the sole noumenal fact does not compromise his whole system. Admittedly, he qualifies that by saying that such a fact is not accessible to theoretical but only to practical knowledge. But what finally does that mean? The recognition of freedom as self-determination, involving the capacity to do otherwise than we in fact do, is the ground of theoretical as well as of practical knowledge. The theoretician commits himself to truth and eschews falsehood in principle, restrains his tendency to groundless assertions, respects the evidence, and strains for consistency in his claims and thus rejects in principle all inconsistent claims. Reflection upon this connected set of facts available only through practice nonetheless yields theoretical knowledge of what is involved in practice. One has then to rethink the way in which the causality of freedom inserts itself into a world of mechanism. But that would involve a revamping of Kant's view of how the categories actually work.

From the theoretical point of view of the causality of freedom, mechanism has to be viewed as a peculiar sort of abstraction. I would suggest it be reinterpreted as setting certain boundary conditions within which self-determination can be achieved. In a hierarchy of structures such as that analysed by Aristotle and refined by Hegel and Whitehead, the successive higher levels would determine by their own causality which of the options left open by the laws of operation of the lower level are actualized. The higher levels themselves may be governed by their own mechanisms; but at the top of the hierarchy we know in our own cases of the noumenal fact of free self-determination within the limits set by genetic endowment, biological-psychological developmental turns, cultural shaping and the sedimented history of past choices made on the basis of these factors. Following Aquinas in this matter, we have suggested that the ground of such free self-determination is precisely the reference to Being that pries us loose from all limited manifestations and sets the transcendental task of humanness to build an historical world in pursuit of the broader picture, with respect for the dignity and freedom of all humans, ourselves as well as others.

Respect for the dignity of others as linked to their freedom and rationality points to a significant gap in the Kantian system: the lack of any sustained treatment of the appearance of the other person. The first critique presented conditions for the possibility of the appearance of any object to us; the third critique pointed out that this leaves open the question of what types of object presented themselves. It goes on to treat of aesthetic and organic objects but fails to consider the ob-jectivity, the appearance over against us of the other subject, the other person. In the look, in the gestures, and in the speech of the other person we are presented with the exhibition *ab extra* of the causality of freedom within the general conditions of the appearance of objectivity. If Kant's restriction of knowledge to phenomena is eroded from within through his introduction of the sole noumenal fact of freedom, the extension of that fact to other persons erodes it from without.

Again, following Kant's lead, we should extend the transcendental task of developing the world-for-us in the direction of the aesthetic as well as the intellectual and moral: it should include beauty as well as truth and goodness. We might consider uniting suggestions from Kant with some from Leibniz and Aquinas here. We might explore the lines indicated by Kant's notion of the perception of form as involving the fusion of faculties, we might link that with Leibniz's notion of the law of the series and Aquinas's of the priority of *esse*. The latter is always individual, for which considerations of essence delineate the limit-conditions. Leibniz's law of the series traces those limit-conditions. The intellectual task of description and explanation in terms of universals arises from and should lead back to perception of the individual *Gestalt*, whether of a person or institution or culture or work of art or even of a "mere" thing. But our primordial relation to those individuals is in the mode of indwelling whereby the intellectually determined stands out in its arresting presence by reason of its peculiar *Gestalt*. That is the basis for our introducing this text with meditations aimed at awakening to that mode of presence.

But if we make a break through the Kantian phenomenal order by the moves indicated previously— following the unrestricted character of the principle of noncontradiction, adopting a more adequate notion of *sensa*, and allowing the recognition of the noumenal fact of freedom to impinge on our notions of mechanism and causality and to extend into our relation to other persons—then one might reconsider expanding the notion of form perception to link the sensory form to the total *Gestalt* of other persons and of the ingressions of meaning into sensory form in the various art forms. When we do that, we move very near the thought of Martin Buber, who claims to fall in the Kantian line. We also move close to Martin Heidegger, whom we will consider in the final chapter of this part and whose thought has in several respects remarkable affinities to Buber's.

Our response so far has been primarily critical, transforming Kant's thought at several key junctures. However, as we indicated in the beginning of this response, we have devoted so much attention to Kant because he has helped to open up the region of phenomenological exploration. He makes one more acutely aware of the problem of appearance and reality by reason of making the transcendental turn, focusing upon the conditions of the knower, and establishing the limited framework of ob-jectivity. He links the metaphysical with the moral and the aesthetic and thus points to a fuller relation to being than that of the abstractive intellect. If, in spite of all manifestness, things-in-themselves, that is, in their fullness, remain deep wells of mystery, our reference to Being draws us forth to those other modes of relation. The indication of the invasion of that mystery into the core of our own being is the sense of awe, whether it be at the starry skies above or the moral law within or the presence of the other person or the arresting character of a work of art or "sunlight on a maple twig and a glimpse through to the Eternal Thou."[84]

14 *G. W. F. Hegel*

G. W. F. Hegel can be viewed, first of all, as attacking the intrinsic difficulties with Kant's critical limitations of the scope of theoretical knowledge. Kant's proposal to examine the mind as the instrument of knowledge presupposes that we already know.[1] His knowledge that self-consciousness is the pivot of all knowing transcends the limitation of knowing to subsuming sensorily given particulars under categories.[2] Its appearance to itself is its self-transcendence. In his treatment of the antinomies, Kant finds it inconscionable that things could be contradictory, but is willing to accept this of the far higher reality of the mind. It gives witness to the fact that the underlying reference to Being at the base of the mind pushes beyond all restrictions to include the Whole. According to Hegel, "The truth is the whole."[3] Like Spinoza, Hegel takes his fundamental position from that reference to Being—though in the *Phenomenology of Spirit* he arrives at it slowly, beginning with the immediate sense-datum and showing how we are forced to move beyond it through the introduction of ever more inclusive frameworks until we have arrived at the position of the Whole that he calls "the Absolute" or the truth "absolved" from its self-obscurity in the darkness of Nature and the finitude of human understanding throughout history.[4]

The Comprehension of Christian Revelation

The character of Hegel's central vision may be better understood if we approach him as a Christian theologian who arrives at his view of being guided by the Christian claim to Revelation, but not developing from it as a starting point. He follows Lessing's claim that Revelation was given in order to become rational.[5] Now, the core of that Revelation is that the Word was made flesh, that is, that there is an identity in Christ between the finitude of humanness and the infinitude of divinity, that the two ultimate contrary modes of Being are brought together in Him. But for Hegel, that only reveals what *everything* is as coming to its self-awareness in humankind. The identity of opposites is also the content of the Trinitarian conception of God: the Son as Logos is the Other of the Father, united with Him in the love of the Spirit—an identity-in-difference that is the pattern of all beings. According to the prologue to John's Gospel, "In the beginning was the Word (*Logos*), and the Word was with God; and the Word was God." Creation itself is an otherness of God through the Logos made possible by the inner-Trinitarian othering that the Logos itself is. "All things were made through Him, and without Him was made nothing that has been made." The extra-Trinitarian othering of Creation makes possible the union of the inner-Trinitarian Logos with Creation in the Incarnation. "And the Word was made flesh and dwelt among us." Through the incarnation, death, and resurrection of the Logos, He sends the Spirit of love into the Church as the gathering of the faithful. And through the grace of the Spirit the faithful are drawn into the inner life of the Trinity as the bond of love comes to pervade their lives.[6]

All this for Hegel is true, but it is a way of speaking based on images (*Vorstellungen*) and must be brought to the level of the concept (*Begriff*).[7] The identity-in-difference formulation, announced in the Incarnation, realized eternally in the Trinity, and found in us in the life of grace whereby we finite beings live with the life of God himself—this Hegel saw early in his career as the essence of love, "a union of union and non-union."[8] Love is not mere merging, but an identity based upon and promoting the difference of the partners. In the terms developed in our part 1, this is only the full realization of the nature of intentionality, for intentionality involves being the other as other, identifying with what is other, realizing ourselves in that identity, and promoting thereby the fuller otherness of the other. But the foundation of such relation to otherness, that is, to the full being-in-itself of any other, lies in our reference to Being, to the encompassing whole that includes everything in its scope, sensory surface and ontological depth, individual and universal, finite and infinite. By reason of this founding reference to the Totality, such intentionality has to be read within a context where it operates dynamically, moving from a minimal identity-in-difference toward that maximum where one's identity as different from all else is realized insofar as we identify with all others within the otherness of the absolute Totality.[9] The founding reference is initially an empty orientation toward Being that itself is initially given as the emptiest of all notions. Yet as a notion, the notion of Being at the same time is all-encompassing, because outside of Being there is nothing at all. This is, from the point of view of the human subject, in the line of Plato's mythical analysis of Eros in the *Symposium* as born on the birthday of Aphrodite, goddess of love, when *Penia* (Poverty) laid down by *Poros* (Plenty). By reason of its origin, Eros therefore is always hungry, always empty, but always having designs upon plenitude. Literally transcribed, we are, at base, Eros as metaphysical emptiness longing for the plenitude of Being.[10]

We can come at Hegel, then, from the twin perspectives of the abstract notion of Being and the ultimate reference of the mind, which is itself a kind of subjective emptiness corresponding to the emptiness of the notion. Empty subject faces empty object. But both forms of emptiness must themselves be arrived at by beginning from where we all always find ourselves, from the already concreted world of everyday experience. We have undertaken our analysis in this book from the side of the subject, beginning with an everyday judgment and working out the levels of intentionality involved in it with a view toward arriving at a preliminary understanding of the reference to Being which appears as a reference to the totality and sets up the dialectic between appearance and reality in experience.

Following Parmenides, Hegel's basic move regarding these two poles is to claim a final identity: the mind at base is Being at base.[11] Both Being and the mind are emptinesses driving toward fulfillment. Hegel, in effect, is following at the conceptual level the path taken by the mystics who claim an identity with the All. Mind as oriented toward the All is oriented toward the concrete filling of its empty anticipation; Being as identified with non-Being in Becoming (Being as Process) is oriented toward its concrete development in and as the Totality. The latter process Hegel develops in the *Logic*, the former in the *Phenomenology of Spirit*.

The Phenomenology of Spirit

In the *Phenomenology* Hegel begins with the first candidate for the "concreteness" of Being, namely, the sense-datum as object of Conciousness, the title of the first major part of the work. He proceeds to show that it leads us to the level of conceiving it as expression of the not-directly-sensible reality of which it is an appearance, and then to the universal frameworks within which the apprehension of the sense-datum itself occurs, while simultaneously implicating the *I* as the locus of manifestation. "Here, now, red spot" involves reference to other "heres" and other "nows," other "reds" and other "spots". We always observe whatever we observe *as* something, that is, in terms of an indeterminate number of possible particulars that instance a given property. "Intellect" is thus immediately involved in "sensation". But the reality of things is not fully revealed in the interplay of *sensa* and formulation, or *sensa* and concept. Things also exhibit themselves as resisting our attempts to assimilate them, and thus as being forces as well as underlying intelligibilities.[12]

Up to this point, the world is still *my* world, yielding to me, and I am only implicitly aware of myself as the understanding-acting center of that world, viewed however, up to this point, only theoretically. However, *I* do not begin theoretically, as a conscious center exploring a world of potentially intelligible *sensa*. I begin as a needy organism, experiencing itself as the desire to be and to develop. The *sensa* are attractive or repelling or else they fade into insignificance.[13] But it is only when the encountered other is another person, setting up a struggle of world constructions, that I become aware of myself explicitly as an I. However it is not initially in theoretical world construction that this occurs, but in the practical realm of struggle for power that involves the risk of one's life. The possibility of violent death at the hands of another human awakens us to ourselves. By a "law of opposites,"[14] the encounter with a resistent other as well as with my own absolute otherness in death, joined in the threat to my life posed by that other, awakens me to genuine Self-Consciousness, the title of the second major part of the *Phenomenology*.

Now, in the context of person-to-person domination, it is possible for both sides to realize that there is a center in the self that stands beyond domination. Human beings are in essence free, free to think, free to take up an attitude, though existentially they may be severely hemmed in as far as overt action is concerned. *Stoicism* is based on the discovery of this truth: whether on the throne, in the person of Marcus Aurelius, or in chains, in the person of Epictetus, the human being as human is free.[15]

But this is an empty assertion, involving the loss of the entire world of practical activity, a kind of empty (though important) posture as a pivot by which the world might be manifested and an attitude assumed. Stoic freedom is merely abstract freedom. *Skepticism* involves a similar cancelling out of the world; but not in one fell swoop and therefore abstractly as in Stoicism. Rather, Skepticism cancels the world bit by bit, judgment by judgment, and therefore concretely. *Skepsis* in Greek means "careful inspection," and very careful inspection leads to the suspension (*epoche*) of judgment, since nothing in the world presents itself apodictically.[16]

A third response to the situation is neither cancellation of the world practically within the immanent circle of our freedom nor theoretically in the concrete skeptical judgment, but the location of our meaning beyond the world, in a transcendent Object. Hegel calls this response "Unhappy Consciousness." It is the ground of otherworldly religion.[17] Hegel's analysis here is the immediate historical background for Feuerbach's projection theory of the nature of God. Classical theism, on this reading, involves the projection, to the ultimate term of the human reference to Being as such, of the human ideals of complete knowledge, control, justice, love, and so forth. One gives up striving for these ideals in favor of an Other, beyond this life, Who will allow us to participate in His knowledge, power, justice, and love in the next life.[18] Such awareness is unable to affirm this life as such and thus finds itself in a "valley of tears." Schopenhauer will take this to be the essence of higher religion and recommends escape from the horror of existence.[19] Nietzsche will accept this view of religion, claiming that it involves a slander on this life, a failure to say Yes to being.[20]

The general movement of the *Phenomenology* is from the "abstractness" of the *sensa* to an increasingly concrete assimilation, through ever more comprehensive frameworks, of the Totality toward which the mind is directed. Kant's transcendental unity of apperception furnished the point of view in the section on Consciousness. The perspective was expanded to the factually antedating and underpinning desirous organism that gives a flesh-and-blood locus to the abstract subject of consciousness and turns it, via encounter with a threatening human other, into a *Self*-Consciousness. The latter, rejoining the abstract theoretical considerations of the first part, becomes Reason concretely assimilating its total world. The next great move then is to recover the world rationally from the point of view of the observer in the interiority of consciousness. In relation to the sensory surface, the struggle with things, and the power struggle between human beings, as well as the tendency to flee unhappily to another world, Reason next realizes its ability to penetrate the world concretely and make it its own in empirical science and in the realm of praxis.[21]

At this stage, the analysis has to undergo another significant expansion. So far the whole development took place from the point of view of the human individual. But the individual only comes into being and perdures on the basis of a tradition. A new encompassing sphere is now added. Enter the realm of Spirit, the fourth major part. Spirit is understood here first of all in the line of expressions like "team spirit" or esprit de corps, as the spirit of a people. It involves their sense of the whole, a simultaneous intellectual, practical, and affective matter. Spirit is the cultural world, the world of institutions, of living tradition that factually and implicitly supports the whole human enterprise from the very beginning. Law, the family, education, the struggle of education with faith in the movement of the Enlightenment, and the securing of the foundations of the principles for action reflectively within the interiority of the self: all this makes explicit the historical genesis of Reason laid out previously in a more abstract way as synthesis of Consciousness and Self-Consciousness.[22]

　　　The final concreteness, however, is opened up through a consideration of religion, which factually provides the concrete articulation for a people of the way in which the ultimate framework of all thinking and doing occurs.[23] The comprehension of the Totality on the basis of this last concrete movement of the mind reaches to Absolute knowing, and history is in principle fulfilled, when philosophy becomes Hegelian philosophy.[24]

　　　In this way, the subject of knowing, who in the beginning of the analysis was supposedly filled with the "real concreteness" of the sensory object, is shown to have been an empty orientation toward the Totality which is filled only by arriving at a full in-principle coincidence between that orientation and the Totality now brought to full consciousness. At this point we might consider the notion of Being that was the correlate of this empty orientation from the very beginning, even though unknown to itself at that stage.

The Logic of the Logos

We might approach Hegel's notion of Being the way we did in our Introduction by moving up the Porphyrian Tree of "substance." Beginning from the world of things around us as concreted through our experience up to this moment of reading, we can begin to sort them into classes. The classes admit of logically higher classes, that is, universals of greater extension, and these in turn of still higher classes. As we move up the line, the extension of concepts becomes broader and broader as their content becomes thinner and thinner. "Animal" is more comprehensive than "human," but for that very reason it is less articulated, abstracting from the rich diversity of animal species, including the human, and from all the individual variations of each species. At the level of the ultimate categories, substance as being-in-itself and accidents or attributes as being-in-another, we have almost evacuated all content and have arrived at two notions that appear to divide the Totality. One more step will abstract Being from "in-itself' and "in-another" to yield the pure notion of Being that englobes everything. Hegel claims this englobing notion is identical with utter emptiness or Non-Being, that is, Being is identical with its own opposite.[25] Nietzsche termed it "the last trailing cloud of evaporating reality."[26] But the realization of the coincidence of Being and Non-Being is what we have come to recognize through Parmenides, Plato, and Aristotle as Becoming. Becoming is a mode of being that includes the non-being of the no-longer and the not-yet: to become is to be in such a way that one is no longer that which one was and not yet that which one will be. The ultimate grounding of all things is thus not the simple unity of Parmenidean Being, but, as the Christian tradition has proclaimed, a Trinity as the identity in Becoming of the extreme difference of Being and Non-Being. Being therefore is essentially process.[27] It is thus not simple identity, but identity-in-difference. Indeed, the difference exists so that the initial identity be not flat, dull, one-dimensional and thus impoverished, but precisely that, through difference, a richer, more articulated identity might be achieved. Identity itself is dead; identity-in-difference, more fully articulated, is life. That will furnish the "genetic code" for all reality and, right from the beginning, indicates the teleological character of Being itself.[28]

Such a base, however, far from being identical with the fullness of Being in the Christian notion of the Trinity, is rather the emptiest of forms. It translates into the conceptual mode what Trinitarian theology presents in basically imagistic form as Father, Son, and Holy Spirit. Being, conceived of as Becoming, is itself the ultimate Eros as emptiness aimed at plenitude. Hegelian cosmic Eros, rather than a feature of the universe other than the changeless One and the changing world, linking the changing to the changeless, as it was in Plato, moves into the heart of Being: God is love.[29] However, such love is not Christian agape, or gift-love as a surplus spilling over of the plenitude of God through divine choice. For Hegel, "God Himself" as primordial Ground is needy, and His creation beyond Himself is His own striving for fulfillment. The divine totality therefore drives from this minimalist state of Being toward the full plenitude of Being as including the completed set of concepts and the completed totality of things within a single system. Such a system is similar to Spinoza's, exept that for Hegel the whole is a developing System whose *telos* is its own manifestness through the emergence and development of mind.[30] It is thus not simply Substance but, more fundamentally, Subject.[31] It is the very emptiness of this primordial Trinity that furnishes the reason for creation as the otherness of the totality of particulars in relation to their universal grounds. The pure notion of Being produces from itself, first of all, an increasingly complete system of notions, articulated down to the lowest species described in Hegel's *Logic*. It is the ancient Logos developed as an abstract set of possibilities of instantiation in individual substances and of comprehension in those substances that are individual subjects of consciousness. The system is teleologically arranged to establish the conditions for the possibility of progressively more complex and integrated forms that both create in more complex and integrated ways and comprehend more and more completely the systematic whole within which they operate and whose meaning they constitute.[32]

The *Logic* begins with the identity of Being and thought. It was the task of the *Phenomenology* to arrive at that identity. Our analysis of the Porphyrian tree of substance in the Introduction arrived at an empty notion of Being, but precisely qua notion Being involves thought, Being *is* thought. The ambiguity of Parmenides's statement on the unity of thought and Being is resolved, along the lines of Aristotle's Pure Form, as an identity, a self-presence. But quite the opposite of Aristotle and the classical theistic position, Hegel conceives of this identity as initially pure emptiness. Full self-thinking thought is the chronological and teleological end of the process.

Hegel considers the emptiness of the notion of Being at this point as equivalent to its appearance as exteriority.[33] This is confusing, since one would have thought that its identity with thought would have made it the most interior. But indeterminate thought, thought that has not penetrated the concrete richness of experience, merely abstract thought, is superficial. The interiority correlated with empty Being is the extreme periphery of the interior life: merely being-there. But precisely because it is there for mind, being-there must involve plurality, otherness, and not blank identity. But again, such otherness is entirely empty because it is of such extreme generality. It requires a process of becoming a more articulated generality.

The basic direction of such articulation is to develop the surface of quality, quantity, and measure,[34] but then to see these as expressions of underlying essences,[35] and further to see the relation of surface to essence as calling for the presence of Mind as their comprehension and thus their completion in the Notion.[36] The realm of the Notion in its turn is ramified into the various levels of Nature outside Mind as the conditions for the possibility of the emergence of that which, comprehending them, will be their own fulfillment, namely actual, individually instantiated, culturally developed Mind.

The complex analysis through which this is developed presents Hegel's view of the Logos though which and in accordance with which everything has been made as having intelligible structure. In the Logos, however, the whole exists only as a system of universals, and thus as a system of mere possibilities for instantiation in an actually existing world. If the empty, grounding trinity of Being/Non-Being/ Becoming, by reason of its very emptiness, had to spill over into an articulated system of universal structures, the still empty system of possibilities must spill over further into a system of plural instantiations, outside the Logos, of the principles of possibility within the Logos. Again, unlike Plato's notion, shared by the Hebrew-Christian tradition, of the generosity of God in creating outside Himself a world He could have chosen not to create, the needy, erotic Hegelian divinity *must* create a world outside Himself to bring Himself to completion. The articulated identity of the system of different universals requires the radical difference of the plurality of material individuals in order to establish a higher identity when Nature reunites with the Logos through humankind.[37]

Nature and Spirit

The first stage of the othering of the Logos is the instantiation of the physical system of spatiotemporal entitites as a kind of actually existent but slumbering Mind.[38] With its *telos* as fully alert Mind, the developing Mind of humanity carried by individual humans, such a system must advance to the point where it can return to itself reflectively. Living being is the first stage in the return to itself of the meaning of the whole, which is alienated but concretized in the material world.[39] The organism develops itself over against its environment, from which it derives the materials of its own articulation. Hegel does not share Kant's hesitation when Kant conceives of organic nature working according to a *telos* as a projected analogue of human goal projection and thus as merely *our* way of trying to make sense out of living form.[40] For Hegel, since conscious Mind, as it develops in each individual, derives from a "material" process, preconscious Mind is present from the beginning as the guiding *telos* of the process, allowing it to "return to itself." At the animal level, this return to itself is present to itself, though only in a diffuse way, in the pervasive life of feeling, which supplies the immediate basis of conscious Mind.[41]

Conscious Mind emerges as the truth of Nature that worked its way up to the immediate conditions for conscious Mind in the complex and centralized organism characterized by a central nervous system integrated by a high-order brain. Conscious Mind is an other to unconscious Nature, but is identical with that Nature in the individual human who alternates in his life between conscious and unconscious states. Chronologically, Mind emerges as the other of the self-identified body so that the intelligible order that the body symbolizes may be revealed and thus Mind might be united with body in a higher mode. Ontologically, teleologically, Mind projects the otherness of the body so that Mind may come to full but manifest identity with the body.[42]

The great tree of life has set down its roots and pushed up its branches to produce the bud of humanly conscious life. But this life, in turn, can only blossom on the basis of its own objectifications in the world of "objective Spirit."[43] Distinctively human awareness unfolds its potentialities on the basis of a set of institutions constituting a tradition, beginning with the tradition of language, and continuing through the organization of the family, economics, and politics. All this is required for the ripening fruit to begin to appear in the realm of what Hegel calls *Absolute Spirit* or Spirit "absolved," disengaged from all that obscures its true and final nature, which is to display and comprehend the presence of the whole in its parts.[44]

Absolute Spirit

The development of Absolute Spirit occurs first of all in *Art*, where the display is exterior.[45] Art passes through a Symbolic, a Classical, and a Romantic stage. Based upon the reference of the Mind toward the Totality that works necessarily through sensory givenness, all art is the display of the Totality in sensuous form. Whatever appears within the sensory field always appears against the background of the Totality. As in Plato, the attraction that beauty in anything exerts upon us is rooted in the "real presence" of Beauty Itself as the radiance of the fullness of Being in that thing. For Hegel Art, executed under the attractive power of Beauty Itself, thereby "absolves" that Totality from the darkness of Nature, from the immediacy and appetitive filtering of animal being, and from the limitation of finite conceptualization.[46] In what Hegel calls the *Symbolic* stage, especially embodied in architecture, the Totality is present as an infinite, mysterious and therefore conceptually empty Beyond. And the sensuous forms that give expression to it in, for example, Egyptian, Babylonian, and Hindu architecture, are distorted, often monstrous representations, corresponding to the relative barabarousness of the inner life.[47] What he calls the *Classical* stage was reached by Greek sculpture, where the gods that populated the encompassing Beyond were represented in human form. Here a certain balance was achieved between external expression and internal content, for the human body is by nature the exteriorization of the human Mind. The body is the condition for the possibility of the development of Mind which is essentially linked to the community and its traditions.[48] But the gods here are presented on a par with the mind's apprehension of its finitude. It is only with the Christian revelation that both the mind and Being are revealed in their essential infinitude. Hence art moves on to what Hegel calls its *Romantic* stage.[49] According to a principle of correspondence between the discovery of deepening inwardness and its exterior expression, and in keeping with the mission of art to display the Absolute in sensuous form, romantic art, like symbolic art, has to modify the sensuous appearance to show in more proper fashion that deepening of inwardness. The arts that especially express the

Romantic stage are those that use media that are progressively more removed from the immediate character of the three-dimensional objects of material existence employed in architecture and sculpture.[50] Those arts are painting, music, and poetry in that order. Painting, even in its most representational forms, reduces the immediate object to abstract two-dimensionality.[51] Music abstracts entirely from palpable dimensionality and deals with a medium that is purely temporal.[52] But in poetry, the medium is imagination itself in its concrete articulation of the Word. Of all the arts, poetry is closest to the ultimate inwardness of Mind.[53]

The development and discovery of the identity between the Mind and Being continues and turns inward in *Religion*, where the Absolute appears in the forms of the imagination in myth and in theological reflection upon myth.[54] The general medium of Art is sensuousness, though in poetry and in literature in general a transition is effected to the inwardness of the imagination itself which, though operative in all the arts, is itself the medium of Religion. It is here that Art touches Religion, whose expression is the story told of the object of the heart's deepest experience, rising up out of the ordinary affairs of life to the ever-encompassing Eternal.[55]

Religion begins as Religion of Nature, in which the sensuous appearances are read as manifestations of an underlying numinosity, whether all-encompassing or broken into a pluralism of forces.[56] In totemism the underlying Force is at the same time identical with the sacred bond of the community. Nature is alive and divine. It is only later, after the separation of Spirit from Nature, that Nature will appear as prosaic, dead and nondivine, matter-of-fact object for scientific comprehension and practical mastery.[57]

In a second great phase, the divine is manifest as Spirit in Its initial showing, as an inwardness absolutely other than Nature. This is the case in Jewish religion.[58] But Yahweh is hidden in darkness. It is only in Christianity that the final truth is revealed: that God is love. That means that He exists only for another and thus for being manifest: that is the truth of the Trinity.[59] But in Hegel's reading, the doctrine of the Trinity only describes an abstract, grounding potentiality. The in-principle self-comprehension of the Father, the Logos, had to be made flesh to show *ab extra* the truth at the heart of things.[60] But historical development was the precondition of such Incarnation, and creation is the precondition for history. However, this showing is itself only external and finite. Christ's death and resurrection indicates His divinity, His being more than a finite mortal. But His ascension into heaven was necessitated in order that He be manifest to the community "in spirit and in truth." He had to disappear as a finite mortal, albeit graced from above, in order that He might reappear through His Spirit in the heart of the community as their bond of love, a bond which, in principle, encompasses all humankind.[61] Such truth had to grow from the tiny mustard seed of its own beginning until it became a mighty tree that could hold all the birds of the air, that is, until all the potentialities of the human spirit could be contained within it in a unity not only aspired toward or merely felt, but grounded in the comprehension of its nature, preconditions, and necessity.

The process reaches its culminating phase when *Philosophy*, which arose among the Greeks, meets with Revealed Religion, which arose among the Hebrews, and develops the love-hate relationship that constitutes the deep history of Western civilization. Hegel sees the time of German idealism as a time of ripeness when the conditions are present for the whole process to be comprehended and the otherness of God and creation overcome. That he takes to be his historic mission.[62]

Now, he who does not have the core experience of Religion, that of rising in his heart to the encompassing eternal Spirit, will not have the starting point for philosophic comprehension.[63] Indeed, both religion and philosophy have the same object, namely, God. They differ, however, in their form, that is, the media and methods of approach to their object. But the difference in methods sets them at odds.[64] As philosophy, i.e., independent thought which spawns natural science as its own child, is set free, it tends to view religion as empty elevation of the heart that bypasses concrete comprehension of things.[65] But just as creation occurs as an otherness to the Ground of things in order that the Ground might rise to manifestness, so also philosophy appears as an other to Religion so that Religion may appear to itself in its full being. Indeed, this process at the level of Absolute Spirit is not only analogous to, but a completion of the general cosmic process. God projects His other in creation in order that, through human history, He might be absolved (Latin *absolutum*) from His mere potentiality "in Himself" as the Logos-system, from His concrete darkness in subhuman nature, from His merely implicit awareness in human nature, from his not-fully-self-present manifestation in Religion, and from His undeveloped self-comprehension in the history of Philosophy.

One aspect of Religion's insufficiency is involved in its being received from without, i.e., revealed. Indispensable as that is as a starting point for Hegel, like Lessing he insists that though Religion begins "irrationally," its task is to rise to rationality.[66] Revelation, like any other given, is given in order to become comprehended, and that means to furnish direction for Philosophy's development from its own resources.

Though this is the main line of development, the interplay between all the factors of subjective, objective and absolute Spirit has to pass through ever more adequate forms of development to reach maximum concreteness. Art and Religion begin crudely and barbarically and are progressively purified as different civilizations and different phases in each civilization take their place in this great development. Philosophy, as the final stage, begins late in history, and begins abstractly—first with the abstractness of sensuous conceptions of the Totality like water, air, and fire;[67] then with the conceptual abstractness of Parmenidean Being which is rightly identified with thought;[68] then with the elaboration of a world of abstractions in the Platonic Ideas.[69] In Aristotle ancient thought reached a high point. Thought is clearly installed within the world as its *telos* both at the cosmic level and at the level of human existence.[70] In the latter case, the organic phases of appropriation of the elements are shown as the preconditions for the emergence and development of Mind, which is no longer seen as an Orphic prisoner in the realm of matter, but as being fully at home therein. At the cosmic level, *Noesis Noeseos*, Self-thinking Thought, functions as the Unmoved Mover, Exemplar for all things, transforming the notion of the Good from that of a principle to that of a Mind. The third part of Hegel's *Encyclopaedia of the Philosophic Sciences* begins with the assertion that Aristotle's *De Anima* is a work unsurpassed in the history of thought. The *Encyclopedia* ends with the announcement of the culmination of cosmic development by a quotation, in Greek, from the twelfth book of Aristotle's *Metaphysics* on *Noesis Noeseos*, indicating Hegel's immense debt to Aristotle.[71] Indeed, one could equally underscore his enormous debt to Plato and to Parmenides as well. Parmenides's notion of Being and its identity with thought are securely located at the very ground of Hegel's System. Plato's Ideas, mediated by Plotinus and Proclus, furnish a good bit of Hegel's delineation of the cosmic Logos. However, Hegel sees them not statically, but developmentally, and not as randomly appearing, but appearing in a sequence of development. Each great philosopher presents the truth for his time, rising to the higher level possible with the materials available. Each is retained in the broader syntheses that subsequent development makes possible.[72]

Thought developed in the Middle Ages, but not with the independence it had among the Greeks. It stood under the tutelage of Hebrew-Christian revelation and was subordinate to that tradition. But it developed the doctrinal complex of Trinity, Creation, Incarnation, Redemption, Grace, Church, and Sacraments that contained for Hegel the final truth, though in inadequate form.[73]

With the age represented by Descartes, thought once again gained its independence and subjectivity entered the picture, though only extrinsically related to the body—a gain over ancient thought in the discovery of subjectivity, but a loss in the forgetting of the Aristotelian discovery of the essentially embodied soul.[74] Spinoza developed a systematic view of the totality, but only in the form of substance, i.e., after the model of things, with subjectivity swallowed up in what was essentially a dead, mechanical system.[75] Leibniz revitalized the whole, but in Hegel's judgment artificially, founded on the notion of abstract individuality.[76] Kant discerned limits to what he called reason (*Vernunft*), but which Hegel conceives of as understanding (*Verstehen*), i.e., Mind in its finitude.[77] Hegel's Reason is Mind discovering its infinitude, its all-encompassing character, and its mission to make explicit the undiscovered character of the Totality. With German idealism in general the Whole is once more penetrated and Spinoza's Substance is transformed into Subject, into the character of Mind, alive and developing as the Whole.[78]

As we have said, for Hegel each great philosophy is true for its time, i.e., satisfies the conditions posed for it by the level of life and thought at its time in clarifying the nature of the whole and thought's place in it. But the whole complex of human life continually shifts and interplays, posing new problems, calling for new and ultimately more comprehensive solutions—an idea of mental development parallel to that currently enjoying popularity in the philosophy of science.[79] Concrete thinking, that is, thinking that is adequate to the conception that is Being itself, the developing whole, is neither sensuous nor conceptual, but a total relation in which conceptual comprehension continually arises within and from the totality of our life-relations (See figure 14.1 for a sketch of Hegel's System.)

Response

After Hegel's death his followers split into two camps. The so-called Right Hegelians upheld a conservative interpretation of his thought, aligning itself with traditional religion and politics.[80] The Left Hegelians opposed both traditional religion and traditional politics. In Feuerbach "God" is seen as a future emergent, as the truth of Nature in humankind most fully realizing the ideals, built into human nature, of truth, power, justice, beauty, love, and the like. Given Hegel's identification (in difference) of God with the process of identity-in-difference of Nature and History, and with his conception

Figure 14.1 A SKETCH OF HEGEL'S SYSTEM

LOGIC
Spirit in itself
(the seed)

1–the idea of Being (outer being)

being ——┬—— nothing
      becoming

2–essence (inner being)
the joining of the categories

3–concept (synthesis of inner and outer being)
a) subjective traditional logic
b) objective: philosophy of nature
c) Idea: union of logic and nature
   i. life
   ii. cognition
   iii. Absolute Idea

(transition from thought to things)

The Science of Logic (1816) ("Lesser Logic" in *Encyclopaedia of the Philosophic Sciences,* 1817-1831)

NATURE
Spirit alienated from itself
(the plant)

1–mechanics

2–physics

3–organics
a) mineral (the corpse of the geological world)
b) vegetable
c) animal

(transition from nature to self-consciousness)

The Philosophy of Nature (developed in the *Encyclopaedia*)

SPIRIT
Spirit in and for itself

1–subjective spirit (the bud)
a) anthropology: soul
b) phenomenology: consciousness
c) psychology: mind

2–Objective spirit (the flower)
institutions:
Philosophy of Right (1820)
*Philosophy of History**

3–Absolute Spirit (the fruit)
a) art: sense-forms: *Philosophy of Aesthetic**
b) religion: myths: *Philosophy of Religion**
c) philosophy: pure thought: *History of Philosophy**

Phenomenology of Spirit (1807)

Philosophy of Spirit (in *Encyclopaedia*)

*lecture series published posthumously.

of person-to-person relationship as the completion of God Himself, does it really make a difference whether we call the final reality God or humankind, provided we understand humankind fundamentally as the species? This seems to confirm the Left's interpretation.

Hegel's developmental view of God (or Nature or Humankind) likewise poses the problem as to why the movement started at some time. An Aristotelian view holds for a fully realized divinity, Self-Thinking Thought, eternally outside and eternally luring the realm of *phusis* to develop and sustain itself in producing individuals who eternally instantiate different types. Humankind, in Aristotle's view, develops in and through the development of the sciences. But given an eternal universe, the intellectual development that he traces at the beginning of several of his works would have to repeat itself again and again as the sciences are lost and then found forever.[81] But with a developmental view of God Himself and creation as His own self-discovery through the emergence of philosophy, Hegel seemingly has no basis for holding a single, finite temporal development. In the Judaeo-Christian view of an act of creation "in the beginning" by a divinity Who is the fullness of Being eternally complete in Himself and of a final judgment "in the end" when all things will return to such a God, Hegel's view could be reappropriated as the development of Humankind in the image of God, rather than as the development of God Himself. Part of the *telos* of history is to produce the institutional conditions for the possibility of comprehending the conditions that make such comprehension possible, down to the structural conditions in Nature as a whole. Such comprehension, in the words of Einstein, would "trace the lines of God after Him,[82] only on Hegel's reckoning, and in reality, those conditions would have to transcend physics and especially include human structure, metaphysical grounds, and historical development. But to account for historical development, Hegel would seem then to have to come down either upon the Aristotelian side, in which case we would have a universe of eternal repetition, or upon the Judaeo-Christian side, in which case God would have to be seen as having a certain completeness both before and after the emergence of creatures. Any other position makes ultimate temporal beginning and ending unintelligible, in spite of the superrich intelligibility of the Hegelian achievement.

One of Hegel's achievements was to provide a direction for thinking internal otherness in a positive way. The Greek thinkers we have examined saw internal otherness as a sign of ontological inferiority; the One in its absolute simplicity, the Good, Pure Form—each consists of a final, undivided Reality, pure Being, without the non-being of internal otherness. In Aristotle, the Pure Form does include the forms of other things, but it is inclusion-in-absence and in principle. Aristotle's God is unaware of what is outside Him, though as Exemplar He includes in His own mode the principles imitated by things outside Him. In Aquinas, by reason of God's being Creator, His knowledge involves inclusion-in-presence and in the full concrete individuality of all creatures. Creation involves the ever-presence of things in their full constitution to the Thought-Will that constitutes them as finite modes imitating in their limited ways and from varying perspectives the infinite fullness of God's being. But even in Aquinas, from the point of view of philosophic inference, God in Himself is utterly simple because composition involves the nonbeing of internal otherness. From the point of view of revelation and in the case of those revealed truths not also accessible by reason, God is internally articulated: God is Trinity—Father, Son, and Spirit, Three in One. There is a mutual inclusion, a reciprocity. Here internal otherness is not negative or a sign of lower ontological rank. It would follow for the hierarchy of beings that the fuller the *reciprocal* inclusion of the other, the higher the being. That would also follow from the nature of intentionality unfolded into the interpersonal realm as the height of identity-in-difference. And that is precisely the center of Hegel's ontological vision. We would then have the possibility, from the point of view of a philosophy developed from within the framework of evidences available to anyone, believer or not, to expand the field of those revealed truths still also available to human reason, "after much time and with many admixtures of error," as Aquinas says of our access to those areas of truth where philosophy intersects with revelation.[83]

Another of Hegel's achievements was to teach us to think historically as well as systematically, i.e., to view philosophic propositions not only as reciprocally connected with other propositions in a given system, but also as bounded by the horizon made possible by the level of awareness available at the time the system is conceived. Hegel's own system appears to be one in which a final closure is claimed and the history of philosophy brought to an end. But, among other things, an the basis of Hegel's statement at the end of the *Philosophy of History* that "thus far the world-spirit has come,"[84] it can be argued that Hegel's thought comprehends the conditions for the possibility of a continually developing universe in which human creativity now plays the leading role. Indeed, something like this was involved in Marx's claim that history proper will begin the other side of comprehending what has hitherto passed for history; for then the kingdom of freedom will progressively drive back the kingdom of necessity posed by our uncomprehending relation to nature and to the dynamics of human culture.[85] "Philosophers have hitherto comprehended nature in various ways. The task now is to change it."[86] But changing it sets a further task for comprehension.

We might underscore another dimension to Hegel's thought; his close attention to the actual articulations of the field of experience. This is not only displayed in the *Phenomenology*, but also in his work generally where he is always intent upon achieving maximum concrete grounding for his theoretical claims. This is particularly true for his work on fine art and on religion. Philosophy for Hegel arises from a deepening experience, which remains the enduring ground of philosophy. If he is a severely "abstract" thinker, that is dialectically tied to his being one of the most "concrete" thinkers in the history of thought. The labor of the concept is the effort to move from the mutual abstractness of the sensory and the conceptual to an ever richer articulation of their togetherness.

* * *

The Existentialist revolt against Hegel was initiated by Kierkegaard and Nietzsche,[87] both protesting in different ways and with different emphases against the supposed swallowing up of the individual in the System. Kierkegaard's emphasis was upon any existing individual human; Nietzsche's concern was with the creative individual, the Overman. In Kierkegaard's interpretation of Hegel, what was lacking was "inwardness," "subjectivity," "indwelling," moments of decision, unique calling.[88] Hegel wrote as if the forward thrust of the universe was a matter of working out a pregiven program where the whole is like a single Leibnizian monad. Kierkegaard and Nietzsche both stressed the emergence of newness. That opens up the horizon for thinkers like Whitehead and Heidegger, to whom we will next turn, the former resting within a metaphysics developed on the basis of modern science but consciously returning to Plato; the latter critical of modern science and with it the history of metaphysics, whose culmination he regards as modern science and whose transcendence he proclaims through a thinking akin to art.

15 *Alfred North Whitehead*

In the first third of the twentieth century Alfred North Whitehead, mathematician turned philosopher, former head of physical sciences at Cambridge, England, and later professor of philosophy at Harvard, developed one of the most ambitious speculative visions on the contemporary scene. According to Errol Harris, his work brings us most of the way toward the categories we need to do justice to the whole of contemporary experience.[1]

In some respects like Hegel, Whitehead challenged the equation of Being with fixity and posited the priority of process. He thereby became, especially through his pupil Charles Hartshorne, the grandfather of contemporary process theology.[2] Again like Hegel and like Leibniz whom he resembles in many ways, Whitehead attacked the conception of the atomic individual, i.e. a person or a thing conceived of as having only external relations with others. He considered such a notion to be a prime instance of what he called "the fallacy of misplaced concreteness," and proposed a view of universal internal interrelatedness.[3] The latter follows the lead of modern physics, which rejects Newtonian atomism and the conception of classical law that involved. The new conception involves statistical law, describing (rather than prescribing) the regular but not invariant movement of particles that are no longer internally unchanging substances but pulsating events establishing themselves in societies of events that accumulate along certain routes that we call organisms.[4] This conception further involves an evolutionary view of nature, an emergentist view that requires a revision of our notions both of matter and of mind. Granted the evolution of mind from nature, Clerk Maxwell's vector equations turn out to be exteriorized descriptions of what, from the inside, turn out to have more of the nature of feelings, but are too diffuse to be conscious.[5] Along these lines Whitehead is able to unite science and the humanities in a single vision.

At the same time, revolutionary as his conceptions may seem, Whitehead considers his thought as an attempt to rewrite Plato in the idiom of modern physics.[6] In fact, he claims that the whole history of thought can be understood as a series of footnotes on Plato.[7] One way to approach his thought, then, would be through a comparison with Plato. Another would be to contrast it with the view against which he constantly does battle: the view of the universe promoted by classical modern (pre-twentieth-century) physics. We will begin with the latter.

Whitehead and Modern Physics

According to the Galilean-Newtonian view of classical modern physics, reality ultimately consists of atomic entitites, self-contained, conceivable in separation from one another, and internally unaffected by time or by other such entitites. They are located in an infinite spatial container and simultaneously in an infinite, regularly flowing river of time—both of which containers could conceivably exist independently of one another. The ultimate atoms operate according to inflexible laws imposed from without, for there is nothing in their internal structure that determines their operating the way they do. Such spatially and temporally located entities may or may not be related to a law-imposing God and a separate container-mind. If the latter is granted, it is generally conceived of as coming to know the atoms and their laws by way of sense-data that are formed by stimuli that come from without and that bear an extrinsic relation to the stimulus-source.[8]

Whitehead finds these views significant, part of the product of "the century of genius."[9] But he also finds them extremely confining, excluding as they do the most significant phenomena. "Science can find no individual enjoyment in nature: Science can find no aim in nature; Science can find no creativity in nature; it finds mere rules of succession."[10] But enjoyment, aim and creativity are the central characteristics of life, especially as manifest in our own self-experience.[11] Accordingly, science has to be relocated in the broader matrix of life as we experience it; but to achieve that, the presuppositions of Newtonian science have to be overcome.

Whitehead pursues that end from two different directions: from twentieth-century physics and from an analysis of the structures of experience. To take the former first: Particle physics has shown that, rather than being internally changeless substances, the ultimate components of the objects in the world of ordinary experience are rather to be conceived of as processes, as "vibratory entities," events, some of them existing only for a fraction of a second. This means that time, rather than being an extrinsic, flowing, riverlike container for atomic substances, actually enters into the internal constitution of things.[12] Further, such events are not isolated, but are functions within force fields. As functions, they are what they do.[13] They thus interpenetrate with other fields, ultimately with the space-time universe as a whole.[14] Thus space too is not so much a container of things as it is a total field of the internal relatedness of events. Again, the statistical character of the descriptive laws of particle behavior breaks with the classical model of invariant and imposed law and suggests a model closer to our experience of human habits which, once made, can be modified and are always subjectible to deviations in the case of individual acts.[15] Whitehead, following Peirce, speaks of "decision" at the level of elementary events, involving the continual possibility of deviation from invariant classical law.[16]

The fact that the extensiveness of the universe is dimensional, the fact that the number of spatial dimensions is three, the spatial laws of geometry, the ultimate formulae for physical occurrences [: t]here is no necessity in any of these ways of behavior. They exist as average, regulative conditions because the majority of actualities are swaying each other to modes of interconnectedness exemplifying those laws. New modes of self-expression may be gaining ground. We cannot tell. But, to judge by all analogy, after a sufficient span of existence our present laws will fade into unimportance.[17]

Here Whitehead moves in a Humean direction. Currently conceived "necessary connections" are merely factual regularities. He also goes beyond Husserl in maintaining that tridimensionality and even the laws of geometry are not "eternal truths" but limitations posed for current experience. But Whitehead's evolutionary awareness sees more broadly than Hume and leads him to make room, as Hume did not even in the case of human beings, for freedom as "self-creation." And Whitehead suggests that self-creation occurs even beneath the human level, all the way down to the level of the elementary events.[18]

The consideration of freedom here allows transition from consideration of physical science as a peculiar object to consideration of the structures of the field of awareness within which we exercise our peculiarly human self-creation. Whitehead attacks the view of sensism linked with the rise of modern science. Sensism typically claims to deal with sense qualities as inner, subjective qualities neutral to value and as the starting point for all thought. Whitehead rather points to the self-transcendence of awareness in its relation to other things in the environment via the sense-qualities, to the sense-qualities' appearing in function of the needs of the organic perceiver, to the essential entry of the past into the constitution of present perception and to the conceptual dimension of understanding, which relates the entities grounding the qualities to what he calls "eternal objects" as patterns of possible relatedness that individual events instantiate.[19] The event of encounter with things in the environment is an instance of basic togetherness, of the mutual inherence of one event in others. In awareness, the internal effect of other events on their others becomes "apprehension" when met and displayed, and "comprehension" when located and understood. By reason of evolution, mind as confronting and understanding, as apprehending and comprehending, reveals itself as an instance of events which, prior to their association into the society of events we call a conscious organic Being, are simply "prehensions" (without the ap- and com- of human awareness). Here again he follows Leibniz, who used a similar etymological turn to distinguish conscious acts of apperception from universal perception, though Whitehead's move rids us of the improper connotations of consciousness that attach to perception. (*Ception* would have been a more proper Leibnizian parallel to Whitehead.) Whitehead was fortified in moving this way by consideration of the Romantic poets.

A typical way of assessing poets like Wordsworth is to claim that they are affected by "the pathetic fallacy,"[20] by the projection of their own feeling (pathos) into natural objects and the reading of such feeling as a feature of those things. This all-too-common view is held in place by a theory of cognition as restricted to typical scientific knowing, leaving for poetic intuition only a subjective locus. Whitehead changes the perspective by asking, in effect; "When Wordsworth looked at nature, what did he see that Newton missed?" And his answer is that Wordsworth saw that nature itself is akin to feeling, indeed, *is* feeling! And the poet, by reason of his peculiar sensitivity, is more deeply aware of that than the typical scientist whose awareness as theoretician has been shaped exclusively by the abstract angle afforded by his scientific discipline. As in the case of Leibniz, the "dead nature" of the Galilean-Cartesian-Newtonian universe is brought back to life and poets are put back into the center of things.[21]

Whitehead's renewed anthropomorphism goes further. By reason of their instantiating eternal objects as well as their being internally related to other events, Whitehead considers all events to have a "mental pole" and a "physical pole."[22] Here he returns to Spinoza's conception of thought as ingredient in all things. Further, though each event is ultimately related to all events, its individuality is constituted by a principle of relevance that establishes a certain gradation of effect. Thus in our case, we only apprehend and comprehend other events selectively in terms of both organic, cultural, and personal relevance.[23]

Macroindividuals—human beings, birds, bushes, and flowers—are themselves maintained in being as continual processes of anabolism and catabolism. Formerly, such process was thought of as composed of particles that were internally invariant. But the particles themselves are now revealed as processes, pulses of energy, each element being a constant radiation of its own spectral lines. The pulsating events are determined by a principle of relevance to form "societies" as routes of transmission of patterns that mirror eternal objects. The complex organization of such societies constitute organisms, whose greater complexity forms the basis for the emergence of a field of awareness. This is a new type of society that constitutes a personality through the formation of memory linked to involvement with other persons.[24] Just as the organism apart from consciousness is a set of processive, relational patterns inconceivable apart from its implication in an environment, so also a person is a higher-order, conscious and self-conscious set of processive, relational patterns inconceivable apart from its implication, on the one hand, in an organic environment via its biological ground, and, on the other hand, in an articulated society of other persons formed by the transmission of the patterns of relatedness that constitute a tradition.[25]

Whitehead's processive-relational view of being seems to be one of his clearest departures from the tradition. It seems to be a rejection of the central notion of substance as the enduring ground of change and of relations. It is clearly a rejection of the old atomic notion of internally changeless elements and of the Leibnizian notion of sealed-in, monadic substances which, though relational and processive, are immortal. It is likewise a rejection of the Lockean notion of an inert substratum for macroindividuals[26] as also of certain Catholic views of the transubstantiation of bread and wine in the Eucharist that involve a purely extrinsic relation between substance and accidents. Original Aristotelian substance is, however, none of these; at least in the realm of the things of our experience and of our own selves, being is process. That is the very idea of *phusis* as that which strains to emerge and to sustain itself. Substances develop in and through their "accidents," their changes and relations. Accidents are the self-development of substances. Organisms are the clearest examples of substances, in Aristotle's view. They yoke the elements to themselves and the elements in their turn are proportions of elementary qualities that are more processes than anything else: heat and cold, dryness and moisture.[27] The equivalent of such a view of substance in Whitehead's world is a "society" as a pattern of events. Indeed, Whitehead says that "the concept of internal relations requires the concept of substance as the activity synthesizing the relationships into its emergent character."[28] It would seem that the difference between Whitehead and Aristotle on this score would be in Whitehead's making provision for those conditions that allow for the development of species. The "substantial form" or "social route of transmission of patterns of events" is not wholly determinative in Whitehead. At all levels, slight deviations from form allow for eventual changes in species and thus for evolution of species. Aristotle explicitly rejects the notion of evolution of species through pure random combinations proposed by Empedocles, who had examined the fossil remains at different strata of the quarries in Syracuse.[29] Whitehead accepts evolution on the basis of the vast accumulation of convergent lines of evidence and develops the conditions for its possibility.

It is important to note that, as one of the conditions of evolution, there is a dialectical correlative to the view of all events and societies of events consisting of relations to the totality of space-time and instantiating the totality of eternal objects by inclusion and exclusion through a principle of relevance. Individuality is not in this way swallowed up in the whole but is achieved through the centrality of 'decision'.[30] Somewhat like Hegel's, Whitehead's view of universal organicism includes the uniqueness of the human individual established by decision. But beyond Hegel and following Peirce, as we have already noted, 'decision' is extended all the way to the individual particle, and a fortiori to the individual organism. Again, though similar to Leibniz's view of the unique and dynamic mirroring of the totality by each monad established by a peculiar "law of the series," Whitehead's view escapes the determinism this suggests by allowing for the emergence of novelty. This is linked to the conception of cosmic law as nonprescriptive and relatively alterable, like human habits. Such a view also opens up the possibility of evolution as an openended modification of the laws-in-context by a slow, long-range shift in context that alters the species.

Whitehead's vision is completed by suggesting a locus for eternal objects, a continual lure for upward development (as having an unchanging perfection?), and a constant treasure house of past events that Whitehead calls God. Such a God seems not to be a creator, and is, contrary to traditional views, implicated also in process. He has what Whitehead calls an antecedent and a consequent nature.[31] The antecedent nature has a certain permanence apart from things, being the locus of eternal objects and thus being itself eternal. But the divinity also has a consequent nature that follows upon the occurrence of novelty in events. 'Decision', we have said, is a fundamental feature in the cosmos; and there is thus a certain unprevisibility of events belongs to their intrinsic character. A place is thus made for human free acts. In this way Spinoza is reversed. Freedom is not reduced to the unimpeded welling up of our inner nature that overpowers both outer and inner restraints, thereby preserving a certain divine omniscience that can know the future in advance of its occurrence. Rather, like Sartre,[32] Whitehead takes freedom conceived of as intrusion into the chain of causality, as the irruption of novelty, to be a radical given. But, unlike Sartre, he expands it into a cosmological principle. (Philosophy indeed is, for Whitehead, cosmic generalization of the categories of experience.)[33] Divine omniscience is preserved and yet restricted. It is preserved in that God can be taken to know everything that can be known: all that has been, of which God remains the permanent locus (thus grounding the "objective immortality" of events),[34] all that is possible as the realm of God's primordial nature, and all that now is. But his omniscience is nonetheless restricted in relation to traditional orthodox Christian views in that the future of decision-dependent events, of actual choice among the possible, does not yet exist and hence cannot be known. God thus has to wait upon events to be informed of them. In a sense, considerations such as these led Aristotle to hold that God only knows Himself and thus is radically changeless. For Whitehead, however, since God has to wait to be specified by the future of free decisions, God in his consequent nature is involved in process, is developing, and thus is sensitive to all other things. He can therefore, contrary to Aristotle's God, hear our prayers, and, with the Hebrew Bible and contrary to classical Christian theism, can grieve over the pains and sins of creation.[35] Both God and events are thus in the grip of a more primordial principle that Whitehead calls "creativity."[36] There is then a sense in which, by reason of its governance of all things, including God, creativity rather than "God" is God.

Whitehead and Plato

We have previously cited one of Whitehead's famous lines: that the history of Western thought can be understood as a series of footnotes on Plato. His own thought can be viewed in that light as an attempt to rewrite Plato within the idiom of relativity and quantum physics. And the Plato he rewrites is the Plato of his own reading of the later dialogues, a Plato for whom Life and Motion belong to Being Itself.[37] At one point Whitehead lists seven crucial Platonic notions: The Ideas, The Physical Elements, The Psyche, The Eros, The Harmony, The Mathematical Relations, The Receptacle.[38] A review of these notions will show the sameness and difference between Whitehead and Plato.

The Ideas find their place in Whitehead's thought in his doctrine of eternal objects, patterns of possibility and compossibility constituting God's primordial nature that cannot be simultaneously realized and which therefore necessarily involve sequentiality. However, as patterns of possibility, they cannot be the "really real" that they are in Plato's thought. Fixity is not the basic characteristic of Being. Being is presentness as creative process. Fixity belongs to the possible as permanent antecedent to creativity and to pastness as generated by creativity.

In Plato, the elements are mathematicized, on the one hand, and, on the other, embedded in the restless medium of "place" (*chora*) called The Receptacle or the "nurse" or "matrix of becoming."[39] In Whitehead, the elements are mathematized as well; but their mathematicization is even more temporal than spatial. For Plato, the elements are regular geometric solids; in modern quantum theory, they are "vibratory entities," pulses of energy, as much wavelike as particulate. Space-time constitutes the single matrix in which every such event is located as "almost exactly Plato's Receptacle."[40] And for Whitehead, as we have said, it seems that creativity is an even more primordial principle than the space-time matrix, being the ground for divinity as well as for material process.

In Plato's later dialogues, Psyche is not restricted to the human being or to its possible transmigration into subhuman natural forms. It is a feature of the structure of the cosmos as a whole. There is a World Soul which contains the whole, the realm of becoming as well as the realm of the forms. The whole is alive and in motion by reason of its ensoulment.[41] Whitehead's philosophy is, in its entirety, a philosophy of organism.[42] In the microdirection, its elements are events having the inner character of feelings. Such feelings involve the prehension of the totality of other events in a gradation of relevances. In the macrodirection, the character of the societies of events and the complex regularity of their routes of transmission bring into being evolutionarily the entities we recognize commonsensibly as organisms. And at the other end of the macrodirection, God involves the clear comprehension of the whole as cosmic ground, as cosmic memory, and as cosmic exemplar.

Eros for Plato is the design of the mortal upon the immortal, the urge to produce, beyond the fleeting existence of the individual, an enduring pattern.[43] It is aroused by the perception of beauty or Harmony of pattern and is consummated by the production of Harmony of pattern. Its obvious instance is in sexual love; but in both Plato and Whitehead, its instantiation is cosmic. For both as well, in its human form, it is the lure toward civilization in all its highest forms.[44] Of course, in Whitehead the dimension of evolution on a cosmic scale transforms the Platonic (and basically pre-eighteenth-century) vision by establishing diachronic as well as synchronic relationships of differing patterns (species) and suggesting a perhaps greater open-endedness and diversity of the possibilities for human development. Contrary to the Greeks in general, Whitehead's thought allows for a large and fundamental aspect of adventure, of novelty, and, linked to that, a greater appreciation of human individuality in its contribution to the overall symphony of Being Whitehead conceives.[45]

The Platonic notion of the tension between persuasion and force in the universe as a whole and of the overall superiority of persuasion over force is buttressed for Whitehead by consideration of the statistical and descriptive, rather than prescriptive, nature of the laws that characterize behavior as such all the way down to the elementary level and especially by consideration of the human level (the prime analogate for understanding the whole of Being in Whitehead), in which persuasion achieves a greater richness of harmonic development than does force. "In the beginning" the demiurge brings about order from the chaos of the Receptacle by persuading it to take on harmonic form.[46] And in human society, force basically brings about external submission and never, without persuasion, leads to that inward aspiration that produces the rich harmony of higher civilization. Society itself is lured on by the prompting of the cosmic Eros.[47]

But in the whole process, for Whitehead God himself develops in his consequent nature, both as cosmic memory, locus for the objective immortality of events, and as possibly involved in an active way in providing a concrete lure for the novel complexity of patterns of events produced by the free decisions of the plurality of non-divine entities.

In these ways, Whitehead rewrites and consequently modifies Plato in the idiom of modern physics and biology. He underscores the emphasis upon life and movement as a characteristic of Being itself in Plato's later dialogues and reduces the privileged ontological position of the Ideas in the early and middle dialogues to a set of possibilities for instantiation into the flux of evolutionary, historical process wherein Being itself is to be found, even at the level of divinity.

Response

In our treatment of Whitehead we have stressed, in addition to the ways in which he is continuous with the tradition we have examined, the significance of his advancement in the direction of evolutionary theory, following paths opened up by Leibniz and Hegel on the continuity of forms. Through his doctrine of *petites perceptions*, Leibniz broke down the Cartesian conception of the external (though "intimate") relation between mind and body as establishing two sealed-in ontological regions. However, Leibniz still conceived of the hierarchy of monads synchronically. Hegel followed that direction and conceived of matter as, in effect, "frozen mind." But he viewed evolution of the higher from the lower as simultaneously involving an emanation of the lower from the higher by way of teleology. Following the evolutionary line, Whitehead's assimilation of an increasingly convergent mass of evidence for evolution leads to a radicalization of the Aristotelian notion of *phusis* by historicizing the hierarchy of being.

Such a view seems to me to be unavoidable. Geological, astronomical, palaeontological, genetic, and comparative physiological evidence continues to pile up and to converge in the same evolutionary direction. Our time conception has stretched from Archbishop Usher's biblically based estimate of creation as occurring in 4004 B.C. to something like eleven billion years. The time required for the development of geological strata and the simplicity of life forms found at the lower and thus earlier levels are pivotal lines of evidence. The development of genetics provides the grounds for a theory of how transformations occur. Comparative embryological studies show similarity in the early stages of development for all animal forms. Considerations following in this direction led to our incorporating evolution along Leibnizian-Hegelian-Whiteheadian lines in part 1.

The centuries-long process of data accumulation that led to the theory of evolution likewise causes us to resituate the philosophic principles established before the emergence and powerful confirmation of the theory. As we have said, the Aristotelian hierarchy of being has now to be historicized. This leads to a view of the dialectical relation between philosophy and empirical science, especially as practiced by Whitehead. For Whitehead not only pointed philosophy toward developments in empirical science, he also pointed science to philosophy via his analysis of the field of awareness and his historical retrieval of Plato. In recent times Errol Harris has followed that dialectical direction.[48]

To continue with evolution, the way Whitehead conceives of it, a certain open-endedness characterizes the process. Law is descriptive rather than prescriptive, conceived of on an analogy with the human process of habit formation. Nature is read in terms of humanness as well as the reverse. Creativity is an essential ingredient in things. In spite of many affinities with Hegel's view, Whitehead's stress on creativity opens the apparent closure of Hegel's system. Through the development of human science and technology, subhuman nature and human choice are increasingly coimplicated in determining the future of evolution.

Such a view likewise suggests the coimplication of the contemplative and the active lives over against the classical arguments for the priority of the contemplative life. We have followed this suggestion in part 1 in our notion of contemplative praxis or respectful attention to the qualities of things in our refashioning of them. The combination of Whiteheadian and Hegelian themes leads to a teleological view of the whole of nature that produces the grounds for its own self-comprehension as it continues to generate ever new forms, though at the current level of human history the creation of new forms is based upon that self-comprehension.

Though we have assimilated a good bit of Whitehead, the fundamental problem with his thought from our point of view lies in his notion of God as Himself in the grip of a more primordial creativity, making creativity more God than God. This is linked to the very great problem of divine foreknowledge and human freedom that has been debated for millennia. The classical Thomistic solution was to point in the direction of the distinction between time and eternity, the latter of which remains relatively inaccessible to us. An eternal view would be one that encompasses time without enduring through time. Hence there would be, not divine *pre*vision, but divine *co*vision, since God does not exist in time. Hence what occurs in time occurs precisely in accordance with the character of the natures that act in time. If they act with self-determining freedom, that is how God sees them in His eternal encompassment of time.[49] Whitehead's vision holds fast to the givenness of human self-determination and eschews Spinozistic determinism. It also aims at not denying to God one of the higher forms of human elation: the zest of adventure. But whether the former necessarily involves attributing a consequent and developing nature to God and whether the latter is "bad" anthropomorphism are questions that one may well raise.

16 *Martin Heidegger*

Situating Heidegger

In a sense Heidegger and Whitehead are opposites; in another sense they are complements. We have chosen Whitehead because he comes to terms internally with modern physics and biology and because he returns to Plato for his fundamental categorial scheme, thus demonstrating the enduring relevance of the tradition we have examined. Though Heidegger has had significant things to say about modern science,[1] he does not, like Whitehead, approach it from within. His focus is rather upon the interpretation of the metaphysical tradition, returning to the Greeks (and in this he is like Whitehead), but primarily as a critic of Plato rather than as his imitator. His vehicle is the hermeneutic of texts, but in the service of phenomenological attention to "the things themselves."[2] Thus he furnishes a primary model of the approach we have taken in this text.

In one sense, the phenomenological movement within which Heidegger operated can be viewed as a recovery of the full context described in Plato's cave.[3] Edmund Husserl, the founder of the movement, sought to establish the foundations of mathematics and logic beyond the relativism, cultural and psychological, that dominated at the turn of the century.[4] For Plato, mathematics was the first step out of the shadows in the cave of sensibility and shifting public opinion into the sunlit world of eternal truths. Max Scheler, collaborator with Husserl, explored the realm of values that, for Plato, stood above the value-neutral region of mathematics and was his major interest. At the same time, Scheler initiated the sociology of knowledge as an investigation of those factors in the cave of actuality that inhibit or promote insight into the ideality of truth, goodness, beauty, and the sacred.[5] The major focus of Martin Heidegger, pupil of Husserl and Scheler, was upon the "light" that made possible access to the intelligible, the light Plato had called "the Good." However, contrary to Plato, Heidegger saw that ultimate condition for the possibility of intelligibility to be a light that changes over time.

This direction of Heidegger's thought is also indicated by another metaphor, borrowed this time from Descartes, in the title of one of his essays, "The Way Back into the Ground of Metaphysics."[6] Descartes had invoked the image of the Tree of Knowledge: the roots are metaphysics, the trunk is physics, and the branches are medicine, mechanics, and morals, from which practical fruits are derived in all three regions. Heidegger continues the metaphor, asking what the soil is in which the tree is planted. What nourishes the Tree of Knowledge?

Descartes dug down to the roots by way of methodical doubt of everything hitherto accepted, until only the bare *cogito*, the "I think," remained as the immediately indubitable. From this Archimedian point he attempted to reconstruct the world theoretically, bringing all under methodically controlled concepts. There is an obvious sense in which the reflective *cogito* can become a pivot around which reconstruction can be attempted. But such an "I think" is always rooted in the soil of a chronologically prior and always enduring human reality that Heidegger terms *Dasein*.[7] In ordinary German, the term means "being-there" in the sense of "being pointable-to," a meaning that Heidegger transforms for his own purposes. Later he hyphenates the word as *Da-Sein* to indicate the transformation. English translations often simply retain the German term *Dasein* as an English neologism. As hyphenated, the word shows its etymological roots: *da*, meaning "there," and *Sein*, a noun form of the verb "to be." *Da-sein* indicates the prior and always enduring human reality as the "There," the place, the locus whose peculiar feature is to make possible Being's appearance. Through *Dasein* "there is"—literally "it gives" (*es gibt*)— Being.[8] Descartes forgets this prior condition of all thought, and in so doing he carries on the tradition of Western metaphysics, which is characterized, according to Heidegger, by forgetting Being. But what is this Being? That question is the pivot of Heidegger's thought.

Being, Truth, and Being-in-the-World

The tradition of metaphysics we have examined, in contrast to disciplines that deal with various regions of being, has been concerned with being qua being, i.e., with those features which follow, not upon some restricted mode of being, but upon being as such, and which are consequently realized throughout the whole gamut of beings and in the deepest, fullest, and most unitary way in God as the highest being. This is the onto-theo-logical nature of metaphysics first enunciated clearly by Aristotle: metaphysics deals with the "first principles" (*logoi*) of beings (*ontos*) and with the highest being, God (*theos*).[9] The focus is everywhere upon various beings from which we attempt to derive their principles. Hence Heidegger claims that metaphysics traditionally has actually dealt with beings as beings, i.e., with the hierarchy of entities (*Seienden*) and their principles (their being— *Seiendheit*). But it is precisely this focus that stands in the way of thinking Being (*Sein*) as what makes possible the disclosure of beings in this way. This distinction between beings (*Seienden*) and their being (*Seiendheit*) on the one hand, and Being (*Sein*) on the other, Heidegger terms "the ontological difference," which, he claims, has remained unthought in the tradition.[10] If this Being is neither beings (including God) nor their principles, what is it?

The ontological difference has its parallel in Heidegger's conception of two modes of truth, expressed by two Greek terms, both of which translate as "truth." We have mentioned them at the very beginning of this work: *orthotes*, or "correctness of representation," and *aletheia*, or "unconcealment."[11] The work of apprehending principles and constructing sets of propositions that correspond to what shows itself presupposes the object of such work coming out of concealment. Being, in Heidegger's sense, is involved in that aletheic mode. Being, thought along these lines, is the ground of metaphysics, the soil in which the tree of knowledge is planted. And human reality is the locus of the appearance of Being as the soil that nourishes the roots of the reflective *cogito*. Such prior reality Heidegger conceives of as basically Being-in-the-world.[12]

Prior to taking up a starting point deliberately, we are always already started, already outside the sphere of our deliberate control, already appropriated to a world of meaning that has developed through a tradition, already linked thereby to a peculiar disclosure of things and ourselves. 'World' means here not the sum total of things, but the way that totality is disclosed, not only theoretically, but also as affording paths for our possible action on and among things and even, or perhaps espcially, as evoking a peculiar "feel" for things. 'World' is a Way for a people, like the Hebrew World, the Greek World; the Chinese World. Heidegger develops Kant's notion of the a priori that allows things to appear to us in the direction of Hegel's reflection on the historical character of the a priori in the worlds of inhabitance, each one of which is summed up by the great philosophers who think at the level of the epoch in which they live. But the opening out of the whole of beings within such a world essentially involves, along with disclosure, a mode of closure to the whole of meaning and beings. For this reason, the unconcealment of Being is essentially historical, for *the* Totality and the totality of any given entity within the Totality are never fully revealed within the angle afforded by any given world. Each world is a kind of Leibnizian monad (though not windowless and not preprogrammed) as a perspective on the whole.

Such Being-in-the-world was indeed the starting point of philosophy for Plato, only it was primarily a negative starting point. The Platonic view of Being-in-the-world was contained in the image of the cave with its attendant enchaining of the mind in mere *doxa*, in opining-appearing which, in its continually changing character as public opinion, distorted the eternal truths that beings copied. Descartes continues the same mind-set. After attempting, through the employment of methodic doubt, to dissolve every feature of being-in such a world, he began his reconstruction of experience from the pivot of the surviving *cogito*. Methodically shorn of its world, the *cogito* itself had to furnish the materials for coming back to the world. Thus its task was to find a way out of its self-isolation. Kant had claimed that it was a scandal that modern thought had not been able to find its way out.[13] Heidegger claimed the scandal was that this had been taken as a problem.[14] As a matter of fact, when we first undertake to inventory our experience and to develop our understanding of things, we find ourselves already close to other people, already engaged in projects, already intertwined with things. In other words, before we begin philosophy, we have already "been begun" by a process we did not initiate and in which we are "thrown" among people and things.[15] Being-in-the-world means not only being in a culture but also being "outside" with others and with things.

Heidegger here follows and radicalizes Husserl's notion of intentionality, according to which consciousness, far from being an "inner" container in which contents are located, is always directed to an other, is always "outside" itself.[16] In Heidegger's radicalization, *Dasein* is conceived of as a more encompassing reality that sustains and pre-articulates the sphere of consciousness. Heidegger (unlike Whitehead — and herein lies Whitehead's complementary role) focuses next to no attention upon that reality conceived of in its biological features. This is presumably because, while physiology does remain a permanent substructure consituting an essential aspect of the framework of humanness, it is the most remote from the relation to Being that Heidegger is at pains to uncover. Heidegger thus stands between the unconscious physical ground thematized by Whitehead and the lucidity of consciousness attended to in the Cartesian-Kantian-Husserlian line. For Heidegger, consciousness as the area of focal attention by the human subject to clearly revealed objects is girt about by a fringe that conditions the modality of focus. That fringe constitutes the pervading "sense" of things that guides both ordinary focus and the methodically directed refocusing of theoretical attention. It is deeply linked to the pervasive and enduring support of character (*ethos*) which is, in its turn, functionally related to the world that has formed and continues to inform character. *Dasein* as inhabitance of a world is more basic than the conscious subject focusing attention upon clearly present objects. Inhabitance precedes theory.[17]

The Light of Being

As we have said, one of the dominant metaphors Heidegger uses to describe what constitutes *Dasein* as the locus of Being is the metaphor of light. At least since Parmenides, then throughout the tradition we have examined, the metaphysical search was considered in terms of a special kind of light. Plato suggested a parallel between the triplet, at the sensory level, of power of sight, seeable objects, and light, another triplet, at the level of intellect, of power of understanding, intelligible objects, and the light of the Good. Aristotle spoke of the light of the agent intellect as the basis for the universal intelligibility of particular sense-perceptible things. The Middle Ages called this the *lumen naturale*, which provides the first principles of identity and noncontradiction that allow us to order our sensory experience and draw inferences as to the character of the nonsensory intelligible whole within which the sensory as such is found. Descartes also invoked this *lumen naturale* to move out of the initial self-confinement of the *cogito*, but also (frequently overlooked, I think also by Heidegger) to ground the *cogito* itself.[18] The "ground of metaphyics" for Heidegger is a peculiar light, "the light of Being," which he also calls "the clearing" across which things can be seen. In fact, in his later writings he distinguishes the light from the clearing or "the Open" that makes the illumination itself capable of illuminating.[19] But even this Open has to be thought of in relation to the closed, to that which is not available, to that which withdraws before every illumination. That is "the mystery" whose withdrawal is linked to the essential finitude of any human mode of illumination.[20]

But why call this light or clearing or soil "Being"? Because it is in its light that beings can be disclosed in their own being. What does that mean? To begin with, beings appear within the thresholds of sensibility set up by our organic nature. They appear here and now as ostensively designatable individuals with clusters of sensory characteristics. In the terms employed throughout this text, that involves the manifestness of four-dimensional space-time objects to a sense perception that constitutes a fifth (and inward) dimension. A little reflection shows that this involves a mode of organ-related appearance and constitutes a very abstract aspect of the way things are present to us in everyday relatedness.[21] Beings are, through sensory presentation, present to us in their being *what* and *how* they are.

Even in the initial description of them from the angle of how they "appear here and now as ostensively designatable individuals with clusters of sensory characteristics," they present themselves as instances of nonostensively designatable universal meanings, such as designation, ostension, individuality, sense-perceptibility, which apply in any here and any now, past, present, and future. The individual beings encountered in the sensory field show themselves *as* something, as instances of universal meanings, and thus appear in terms of the sixth dimension of interpretation.[22]

But this showing, we said, was only an abstract aspect of the way they usually present themselves. They are usually manifest to us as men and women, as pages in a book, as dogs and trees, as cars and houses, as computers and typewriters, brushes and chisels, pictures and statues, rocks and clouds, sea and sky. We have to shift our attention radically to see them only as clusters of sensory presentations. Furthermore, in the disclosure of each specifiable *what*, there is also the disclosure of something of the *how* of its manner of change and thus of its shifting disclosure. In the Western tradition, the shifting disclosure concerns the "accidents," while the being so disclosed is the "substance." The latter is a kind of permanent presence in relation to the accidents, but its being (in the sense of what it is—man, page, dog, tree, chisel) is indeed also a kind of permanent presence in relation to the individual substance itself that must eventually pass out of being. Thus Plato with his ever-present Ideas as the real locus of being; thus Aristotle with his eternal, though always instantiated, species; thus Aquinas and the Middle Ages in general with their Ideas in the mind of God; thus Spinoza for whom individual substances in ordinary parlance are modes of the one substance, *deus sive natura*; thus also Hegel with his conception of the *Begriff* as the universal substance displayed, though itself developing from potentiality to actuality, in and through the individuals that instantiate it.

The being of a sensorily present being shows itself as an instance of a specifiable essence, a 'what,' which has its peculiar way of unfolding and thus of displaying itself, its own peculiar 'how.' But this mode of being is not simply an instantiation of a universal, for the universal itself means something only insofar as it is fitted into a world of meaning which interprets it.[23] Thus any 'here' means something only in relation to a 'there,' each of which is designated 'now' and also 'then' which, in turn, reciprocally implicate each other, until eventually space-time as a whole is involved, in the designation of any individual, as the ultimate backdrop of the individual's presentation. Thus also 'page' means something only in relation to 'writing,' which makes sense only in relation to ideas and desires and feelings and persons whose inhabitance of the world of communication makes recognition of such a thing as a page in a book at all possible.

Now the mode of presence of such a world, which makes possible the showing of the sensorily present individual entity *as* something, as what and how it is, is not initially the mode of conceptual explicitation that we began with in the preceding paragraph. It is rather the mode corresponding to prereflective inhabitance that is initially in play.[24] Such inhabitance involves the whole mode of being of the individual *Dasein* who belongs to that world. Body mechanisms, motor habits, natural drives, habituated feelings, and evaluations, the sedimented history of past choices and conceptual explicitations: all this and more constitutes the basic mode of inhabitance, of indwelling as the prereflective subsoil in which the tree of our explicit thought is planted. In virtue of that mode of indwelling, which we brought into focus in chapter 2 as the seventh dimension, we are close to some things and distanced from others in the mode of basic presence.

That mode of presence is not simply a matter of the individual, but a matter of the entire tradition as it entered, and continues to enter, into the ongoing life of that individual in interplay with his or her directly and indirectly present contemporaries. It is a matter of the world of a people within which the individual was raised and in relation to which he or she continues to be. Such a world, articulated into the subworlds of intellectual specializations, furnishes the horizon within which things appear as material for interpretation, both in the lived modality) of our enduring inhabitance and in the reflective modality of the various intellectual disciplines. But as worlds change, so do the ways in which things are manifest, so that they disclose themselves differently in what they are, in their essences. The being of things is thus revealed and concealed in the light of the world of meaning we inhabit.

Historicity and Authenticity

The context-dependency of all essences in their mode of appearance within human experience means, for Heidegger, that our understanding is essentially historical, for the contexts differ in different historical worlds. In the tradition, essence and being take on the character of the eternal Now, for which geometry furnished the paradigm. When Pythagoras enunciated the Pythagorean theorem, the theorem presented itself as a truth that had always been the case and that always would be the case, even if it should pass from the memory of humankind through the ever-present possibility of recurrence to barbarism.

Heidegger questions the ground of the predominance of the Now, which is, after all, only one—though a certain privileged one— of the three dimensions of time.[25] One might just as well speak of the Chess Game In Itself in which King's Gambit is an eternal truth. But the truth depends upon the initial creation of the game, as the truths of geometry depend upon the peculiar construction of the axioms of the system. In effect, for Heidegger such an observation cancels out the dominance of the geometric paradigm as a model of eternal truth in an eternal Now. Given the context-dependency of our understanding of the essential being of things, Heidegger seeks to ponder the peculiar relation between being and time considered in its essential three-dimensionality. Manifestness "now" depends upon a gathering of the past and an anticipation of the future that constitutes the horizon within which all definition and thus also all deduction occurs.

But the essential character of the human individual as *Dasein*, as the locus of the manifestness of the whole, directs the individual beyond the culture to the whole itself. This ground structure makes possible deliberately prying onself loose—or having oneself pried loose—from the sedimentation of the culture. This fact makes possible the reform of the culture. In a most fundamental way, it is being grasped by one's own being-toward-death that establishes the essential transcendence of the individual *Dasein* in relation to culture.[26] There is a kind of Cartesian moment here. One gains distance from one's essential being-in-the-world by being grasped by one's being-toward-death. But the latter remains a tensive moment within the former. No one fully escapes his own culture, but no one is also wholly its victim. Realization of one's being-toward-death pries a person loose and makes possible fully deliberate choice of those options available in the culture.

As we have said, to begin with, one lives as a kind of reflex of one's culture. This is completely true of children. It is more or less true of adults. In relation to the self-appropriation that is possible in the ultimate aloneness of one's being-toward-death, the typical situation is one of not-being-oneself. One is "inauthentic," i.e., not one's own (Greek *autos*) and flees from the thought of death. As Heidegger insists, this is not a moral observation.[27] One might be good— indeed, very good: honest, kind, hardworking, self-sacrificing—and yet still be largely a cultural reflex. Further, one always remains to some extent "inauthentic" in Heidegger's sense in that one remains necessarily bound to institutions, especially to that first of all institutions: language. Just as one does not give oneself language (and thus also thought) but enters into language, so one does not give oneself the world within which one thinks, feels, and operates. So much is this the case, that one never wholly escapes being appropriated to institutions.[28] "Authentic" existence emerges on the other side of that realization when one at the same time, in a "moment of vision," realizes one's being as a whole in the light of being-toward-death. (Hence we began our initial chapter on secular meditations with a meditation on death.) But this itself is rendered possible by one's own transcendent orientation, one's being toward the whole within which one's own being is found. Thus the horizon of all our dealings comes to light, advancing from perpetual fringe to explicit focus—not as a comprehended phenomenon, but as the basic question of being, one's own being as being within the whole. Such awareness allows one to "desediment" the tradition, to shake loose the encrustations of meaning, to arrive at the original phenomena, the get to "the things themselves" and to become capable of "letting things be," thankfully, thoughtfully. We are enabled to allow them to draw near in a deeper mode of presencing whereby we become aware of the horizon of their mystery and the mystery of global manifestness (the mystery of Being). Such "authenticity" allows us to be appropriated by the mystery of manifestness and concealment in its historical, eventlike character.[29] Here Heidegger plays upon the *eigen* in *Eigentlichkeit*, the *autos* in "authenticity" as parallel to the *proprius* in "appropriation." *Eigen*, *autos*, and *proprius* all refer to "one's own." And the event-character of the manifestness of Being is its *Er-eignis*, its eventful appropriation of *Dasein*. Open to the mystery, one dwells thankfully, thoughtfully, thus poetically.[30]

The Play of the Fourfold

Natural science gives us a world of meanings, but it is not a world of inhabitance. The horizon within which it operates reduces all encountered entities to equivalent energy units within a space-time grid that allows for exact measurement, correlation, and hence control. A world of inhabitance is a world of presences that appear at significant times and in a space of nearness and distance that transcend the space-time metric grid operative in natural science.[31] Even philosophy, in its attempt correctly to represent and explain, abstracts from presences. Presences arise out of what Heidegger calls, more than somewhat cryptically, "the play of the fourfold": Earth and Sky, Mortals and Immortals, the four regions that enter into a world of inhabitance.[32]

In an earlier work, "The Origin of the Work of Art," a lecture originally given in 1935, World was seen as in fundamental tension with Earth, somewhat as the open to the closed. But Earth is the closed which rises up as it meets World. And World itself, as opening the paths for human decision, likewise is exposed to the closure of our not being master, theoretically or practically, of the full context or of the consequences of our decisions. But when the essential tension of Earth and World comes to hold sway for a people, Earth becomes native ground and World a home for that people: significant presences arise. It is in the work of art that the essential tension of World and Earth is powerfully manifest as the work arises from and reciprocally occasions that essential tension that deepens presence.[33]

In Heidegger's later work, Earth is absorbed into world as one of the regions that constitute the fourfold of the World. Earth has to be understood here not as a location in the solar system and not as a chemical mass, for these are abstractions from native land; from the sensuousness of rhythm and melody that sound in our words, from the radiance of color, from our own lived embodiment. It is part and parcel of our speaking that it rises up from the sensuousness, the "earthiness" of language, not as that which we control with full deliberateness (we know how artificial "studied" style is), but as that which grows up in us. It is in the latter that Earth appears primordially as Earth. Language that rises up poetically from this Earth is foundational natural language, of which ordinary language is a sedimented resultant and scientific and philosophical language flattened out abstractions.[34] World that includes Earth so considered is a world for dwelling. That is why a scientific world is uninhabitable. That is why our literature is filled with the experience of alienation. Insofar as the world we live in is increasingly and totalistically a technologically reconstructed world, it is not a world that brings us to ourselves.[35] It is a world in which presences have become increasingly absent. Inhabitance shrivels through the priority of the work of the reflective *cogito* that has forgotten the soil in which it is rooted.

Earth always interplays with the second region, Sky, as the open expanse that allows Earth to appear and that sets the measures for our time on earth, generating the days and the seasons. It encircles our lives and by its vastness gives us a sense of our smallness and our simultaneous belonging to that vastness that animals could not notice. It is the region of Kantian awe: "the starry skies above."

Mortals are the third world-region. We humans belong to the earth: we come from the earth and are made of the earth. The human (Latin *humanus*) is humus, earth as soil. Biblically, human beings are made from the slime of the earth or from its clay. Earth in turn flowers forth in our speech and in our art. But we also return inevitably to earth. We are mortal. That, however, does not mean simply that each of us will one day fall apart, decaying into the earthly elements of which we are composed—though that is correct. Much more basically, we humans are "the mortals," i.e., those who live out of an awareness of having to die, out of an anticipation of the temporal termination of our being. Mortals are likewise distinguished as the ones who speak. Death and language belong together.[36] One for whom the whole speaks, for whom therefore there is language, is one for whom the wholeness of his own being as stretched from birth to death is opened up by a rebound from both terms and becomes the echo chamber of the Whole.

Called out from Earth and living under the Sky, mortals take the measure of their being from the Gods, the fourth world-region. Gods here are to be taken as messengers of what is highest, sources of inspiration regarding those things that set the measure, the Sacred, the inviolable. As mortals are linked to the Earth, so are Gods linked to the Sky, to that above us which measures us, which reveals what is most high, which encompasses us with its vastness. For Heidegger, the Gods are linked to the dimension of concealment manifest as such, i.e., as essentially concealed, by the sky which presents an essential unreachability. It is the domain of the hidden God.[37]

World is, for Heidegger, the interplay of these four regions: earth and sky, mortals and immortals. The peculiar character of the interplay differs in different cultures, and indeed in different epochs within a culture. That is why manifestness is essentially historical: *Seinsgeschichte*, history of Being, is the essentially perspectival, essentially mutable, essentially temporal opening up of the whole. When the four regions play together in our silent listening, when we are not intent on mastery, but are open, thankfully letting things be manifest, the poetic word arises. With this word things become significant presences, and with this play of things and word, world comes to hold sway.[38]

To emphasize the priority of the "speaking" of things over our use of language as expressive instrument of the dominating *cogito*, Heidegger speaks of things "thinging". He links this to the original meanings of the German *Ding*, which means "assembly."[39] Things are assemblies, and what they assemble is a world of meanings. World, in turn, "worlds," i.e., it actively takes hold of us and reciprocally takes hold of and is gathered by things that stand in the play of the fourfold. In one of Heidegger's most difficult expressions: things thinging bear world; world worlding grants things.[40] When the play of the fourfold is lost, things disappear as "thinging" and become mere equidistant data; they lose their "being," though they remain as objects at hand.[41] They are each placed at an equal distance when, with the rise of modern science, humans take to viewing them as composed of points of force governed by law in an overall space-time grid. Nearness disappears: everything is equally far for this mode of objectivity. But the payoff is that this pose allows things to be increasingly controlled. Things, and eventually even humans, are transformed into "standing reserve," sources of power to be used in achieving our projected ends.[42] Heidegger calls this the epoch of "enframing." His view here is wrongly considered wholly negative. Enframing is the mode of revealing that has us in its grip today, the way in which Being shows itself—and also the way it conceals. Fundamental thinking has as its task to ponder the peculiar mode of *aletheia* that operates here.

But there is, obviously, a strongly negative criticism involved. All modes of revealing make us prone to forget that—and what—their peculiar modality conceals. One of the peculiarities of the currently dominant mode of revealing, however, is that it is, in a sense, worldless. Clearly, there is the scientific-technological world; but it is not, as such, a world of inhabitance. We talk to each other in ordinary language, language laden with evaluation, feeling, command, committment, appealing to other humans as responsible agents dealing with the determined objects of science and technology, even as practicing scientists manipulating our experimental objects. The modality of that inhabitance, that dwelling in a world with other humans is better articulated in art than in science.[43]

Art speaks essentially to the heart, the center of *Dasein*, "where our treasure is," the "inner," "subjective" correlate to that which we view as the most commanding presence.[44] "Intellect" itself, as ordering and thus directing, controlling, is rooted in the most commanding presence. What has passed traditionally for "rationality" in the Western tradition was indeed, according to Heidegger, essentially in the service of the desire to dominate and control[45]—an insight brought to the fore by Nietzsche in his concept of the centrality of the will to power. The will to truth (as *orthotes*) is rooted in the will to power.[46] The meditative move, pondering the unconcealment that has us in its grip, is characterized, on the contrary, by "letting things be."[47] But that places the ground of metaphysics, not in the intellect, but in "the imagination." According to Heidegger, Kant divined that direction in the first edition of his first critique, but backed off from it in the second edition. Imagination opens the relation between intellect and sensibility through the schematism. However, this does not simply occur in a general way, but in the particular historical way of affording the lived configurations of the whole of which metaphysics is the conceptual expression.[48] "Letting things be" consists in heeding the gathering of the whole afforded by the epoch in which we exist. Responsible philosophizing links that to the successive epochs in the "history of Being" back to the Presocratics.

The History of Truth and the Return to Meditative Thinking

The history of the coming to presence of the manifestness of Being in the philosophic tradition begins with Parmenides, the father of metaphysics. In Parmenides the belonging together of thought and Being is proclaimed in such a way that it has to be wrested from non-being and brought to stand in relation to the changing realm of *doxa*. Thus it emerges into presence. Not the flat assertion "It is; and 'It is not' is not"; but the "mystical" presence of Being as an encompassing whole is at stake. This is the way of *aletheia*, unconcealment, coming out of the concealment of non-being.[49]

Heraclitus, especially since Hegel, has been traditionally posed as the antithesis to Parmenides, proclaiming Becoming over static Being. Heidegger sees them as equivalent. Heraclitus's *Logos* is Parmenides's *Estin*: the gathering of the whole whose depth comes to presence by the struggle of opposites. The gripping presence of the whole comes to light in the tension between life and death and between unconcealment and concealment. Heraclitus focuses the role of language in this gathering.[50]

With Plato presence itself comes to dominate as an eternal Now, and the presencing that includes concealment is obscured. Being migrates from the shifting process of revealing/concealing in the realm of *doxa* into the realm of the *eidoi*, the ideas or "intelligible looks" as correlative to intellect that leaves the Cave of Being-in-the-world. The light of the Good as an eternal shining lights an eternal stage of truth to which our formulations can now be made to correspond and which we can then come to dominate.[51] However, in Plato and in Aristotle, that which is present is object of wonder, of amazement that functions as the perduring ground of philosophy.[52] Contemplation of the radiance of the intelligible looks ranks higher than practical or logical mastery. Descartes initiates another chapter in the history of presence. Truth migrates from correspondence to certitude. Only that is consented to as finally true that can pass the test of apodictic evidentiality laid down by the *cogito*. Being-in-the-world is bracketed out. And things are allowed to show themselves only insofar as they pass the tests of objectivity. Such an approach is aimed at the fruit of practical mastery of nature. As we noted earlier, contemplation plays a minimal role in Descartes's thought, which is driven by the desire to control and extract practical fruit.

The historical process of the various understandings of truth reaches a high point in the contemporary world, the epoch of enframing, where things are no longer even primarily objects, but have "disappeared into the objectlessness of standing reserve." We are in the grip of a mode of revealing in which things are basically energy sources for our projects. Calculation governs our approach, which unlocks more and more of "the secrets of nature," but which "conceals revealing," and thereby *Dasein*, world and things, along with the Sacred.[53]

This line of "representative-calculative thinking" operates within the horizon of truth as *orthotes*, as correctness of representation, which corresponds to the manifest. "The saving power" lies in the direction of "meditative thinking," "thinking which recalls," a mode of appreciative reflection that allows the concealed to come to presence (though not to evidence) with the unconcealed. Relation to the concealed in the unconcealed involves a sense of the mystery that encompasses all things, that draws close and apprehends us. Thinking in such a way "lets things be" and is not intent upon mastery. Such thinking follows a "way" rather than a "method." The latter, especially made central by Descartes and modern science, allows us to "get somewhere," to "make progress" as more and more aspects of what-is come into our ken. But a "way" brings to presence where we always already are and which, in our haste to make progress, we are constantly forgetting. And in forgetting, we enter an era of homelessness.[54]

Metaphysics began with Parmenides and the "mystical" coming to presence of Being. It was "sustained by awe" in Plato and continued to be a matter of contemplation in Aristotle and Aquinas. But, according to Heidegger, the grounding of metaphysics itself in this coming to presence was not explicitly thought in the tradition. Metaphysics itself became a factor in the "forgottenness of Being" in Western thought. But its mode of coming to presence silently governed the various epochs in the history of metaphysics. The task is to return to the ground of metaphysics in the manner of revealing and concealing that has us continually in its grip. Pondering the history of the epochs of such revealing affords us the distance to see the one-sidedness that approach has involved. And especially in the modern era, we can come to understand the homelessness that can only be overcome when we learn meditative attention to our belonging to the mystery that surrounds all our modes of revealing.

Response

Heidegger has pushed us beyond typical metaphysical preoccupation with developing coherent systems of thought and arguing against their competitors and objectors. With Kierkegaard he has made us aware that "philosophers construct magnificent thought-castles but live in miserable shacks nearby." He has pushed us back "into the ground of metaphysics" in the historically shaped life-world that nourishes the tendency to develop our thought in certain directions. He has thus, like Hegel, taught us to think historically and thus to question ourselves first of all. He has made us aware of the hypnotic power exercised by geometrically patterned thinking in its self-presentation as inhabiting an eternal Now. He has made us aware, with Nietzsche, of the will-to-power that has guided Western thought, even in its more theoretical moments. And he has awakened us to the premodern tradition of meditation, Eastern and Western, that draws near to significant presences as a response to the Holy. Such a meditative mode of thought he considers much more fundamental than metaphysical construction.

But for all the significant refocusing Heidegger has provided us, there is at least one serious lack in his thought: attention to the personal Other. Platonic philosophy, in its neo-Platonic phase, aspired to be "alone with the Alone"; Heidegger's thought seems to be a this-worldly variant on that aspiration. Plato's own thought, however, was centered upon dialogue, taking Socrates as model. Martin Buber considered Socrates to be the exemplar of interpersonal relatedness. Socrates was a kind of humanistic psychotherapist who rooted his therapeutic practice in an understanding of the differing needs of each of his interlocutors, but who aimed to awaken in each a desire for integration into the Whole by orientation toward the Good.[55] In Plato's line, Aristotle saw contemplation of the Good, under the rubric of the Unmoved Mover or Pure Form or Self-thinking Thought, as reciprocally tied to friendship; the deepest friendship was founded on contemplation and led to contemplation. Martin Buber saw Heidegger's deficiency to lie in the minimal attention given to the personal Other in his thought.[56] Influenced by Buber, Emmanuel Levinas argues for the priority of "the face" of the Other as the ground of ethics and thus of "authentic" human existence.[57] Influenced in turn by Levinas, Edith Wyschogrod has recently called attention to Heidegger's focus upon the priority of the thing (neglect of the integrity of which is a conspicuous feature of modern technology), while yet ignoring the more conspicuous instances of the death camps and the growing nuclear arsenal that threaten the integrity of persons.[58] "The thing," to be sure, has metaphysical implications as dialectically related to the gathering of the whole in a world of inhabitance. But, as Buber, Levinas, and Wyshogrod argue, the personal Other ought to take on significant priority over the thing as the primary locus of the manifestness of Being.

Rather than being simply asserted, their position can be grounded metaphysically. As we have indicated, an analysis of the notion of intentionality, combined with Aquinas's position on the priority of *esse* (which is in every case individual) over the abstract universal, and his affirmation of the hierarchy of actual existents, would provide metaphysical ground for the interpersonal assertions of these latter-day Hebrew thinkers. It would also ground Heidegger's attempt to focus upon full participatory relations with actually existing things. Intentionality involves self-possession in function of the manifestation of otherness. The natural drive toward one's own completeness involves the inclusion of other beings by "letting them be" themselves and not simply subsuming them under our own projects, theoretical or practical. This stands at the center of ethics as we sketched it in the fourth chapter of part 1. The otherness of being is located in the individual reality of other beings, though manifest only in relation to the historically uncovered whole of Being. But other beings are hierarchically scaled, culminating, in our experience, in the personal Other. It is in learning to foster the real otherness, the full being-in-itself of the personal Other, that the meaningfullness of the whole draws near in a special way, that sacredness is experienced and that the claim of the Most High is heeded most profoundly.

Epilogue: The Metaphysical Basis
of Dialogical Pluralism

The history of thought on the notion of Being, like the history of thought on all philosophical issues, appears on one level as a battlefield of competing claims. Different thinkers arise and stake out differing claims that are then picked up by epigoni who spin endless arguments in favor of their school and against all others. The first question, when confronted with claims that appear to be incompatible with the school's philosophy, tends to be, What is the source of their error? There is an inclination to rush to judgment, all the more so insofar as the contemporary gurus of the school have already passed judgment. Where one would have expected to see the greatest dispassionateness, maximum detachment from their own predilections and from socially set conceptions, i.e., in those supposedly dedicated to the pursuit of wisdom, one too often finds petty wrangling, myopic vision, rationalization, and ideological fixation, especially if they think they have the backing of the divinity.

To minimize these faults, we have developed our view in part 1 in dialectic with a select portion of the classics of the metaphysical tradition as a whole. What makes the classics classics is in part the degree to which they exhibit the ability to rise above the limitations of psychological and sociological presets, to speak, beyond individual preference and cultural context, of "the things themselves." Of course, it is a truism to say that no one rises entirely above his own time and the constraints of his own individuality. But what classics give expression to are the least confining visions.

Our procedure has been to begin with meditative attention to certain key phenomena and to relate them to certain key problems in interrelated aspects of anthropology, ethics, and metaphysics. Our view of these matters was developed in part 1 by resting simultaneously upon the modern tradition from Descartes to Heidegger and the ancient-medieval tradition from Parmenides to Aquinas, but our focus was upon the phenomena and the problems they generate. The view that we developed provided the basis for a dialogical approach. Hence in part 2 we undertook an explicit dialogue with the tradition of metaphysics. We first considered the ancient-medieval tradition from Parmenides through Plato, Aristotle, and Plotinus to Aquinas as the progressive articulation of a single tradition, reaching maximum articulation in Aquinas. We approached the modern tradition from Descartes through Spinoza and Leibniz to Kant and on through Hegel and Whitehead to Heidegger both in relation to the premodern tradition and to the position we developed in part 1. Hence we followed each chapter on the modern tradition with a section responding to the thinker in question by relating his thought, by way of assessment, to the positions we took in part 1 and by way of comparison with the earlier tradition.

Progressive penetration into these sources, phenomenological and historical together, should permit one some distance to view the storms that rage on the contemporary surface and to test the depth to which they reach. This implies both great detachment from prior expectations and the establishment of a set of epicenters in oneself as the conditions for genuine dialogue.

But why detachment and why dialogue? Differing traditions preach detachment from oneself, but generally in favor of attachment to a tradition. Some preach detachment from one's tradition, but in favor of attachment to whatever one happens to think one's self is at the present moment. The fundamental claim underlying the present text suggests detachment from one's present self-conception in the first place, but also from one's tradition as well, and indeed, even from the tradition as a whole, in favor of "affirmation of Being." I am not the measure, nor is any tradition itself the measure, but only Being itself. Indeed, the deepest traditions make precisely that claim.

That claim points in the direction anatomized by descriptive phenomenology: the structure of the field of experience that both presents the enduring data base, and the grounds as well as the direction for theory construction. Phenomenology is the permanent prolegomenon to the philosophic penetration of any area of human experience. The claim is based upon the triple structure of intentionality analyzed in the pivotal chapter, chapter 2: *sensing* that manifests relational properties of things in the environment linked up initially with organic need; *interpreting* that is set in the tension between cultural immanence and cultural transcendence; and *presence to Being*, which refers us beyond biological immediacy and cultural mediation to the Totality and thus also to the totality of each thing within the encompassing Whole. The tension between cultural immanence and cultural transcendence is exhibited in the ability to recognize the triple structure itself as the condition for the possibility of interpretation. It lays the basis for the requirement of dialogue. We have developed that structure in part 1. We have relied upon it in the interpretative work of part 2.

There is a kind of Cartesian-Kantian-Husserlian move involved here in the emphasis upon the structure of the field of awareness as that which is known with certitude. But two significant modifications must be made. First, Ricoeur's admonition is important: though the *cogito* is indubitable, fully what the *cogito* is remains problematic.[1] Leibnizian, Hegelian, and Whiteheadian considerations suggest a reappropriation of Aristotelian form-matter coimplication in an evolutionary framework such as we have sketched in chapter 5. Cartesian "matter," the contrast term to "mind," would then be an abstraction from "slumbering mind" at the preliving level. And "mind" would itself be the emergent cutting edge of a universe in process toward greater creativity and comprehension. More immediately, apart from such suggestions for metaphysical construal, we do come to understand more and more of the field of experience and its implications as we carry on our inquiry. But to do so presupposes (1) initial data (whether construed as immediately given or as always mediated), (2) possibilities for interpreting or explaining, and (3) judgments, founded upon reference to Being, of the adequacy of our explanations to the convergence of data and theory.[2] Always we are referred to the as yet unencompassed but ever-encompassing Whole which appears only partially in the mediated immediacy of the things that appear and which thus always calls for more adequate explanation, linking the appearance to deeper and more encompassing understanding. Hence the need for dialogue with the full range of factually compelling visions.

Further, Hegel and Heidegger bring us closer to a concrete comprehension of our own *cogito* in examining the character of the *Zeitgeist*, in tracing the archaeology of the Western tradition and in surveying the life-world. Each makes us more aware of the extent to which our own *cogito* is tied to our age and upbringing. Each directs us to the historical a priori out of which we factually experience ourselves. Only Heidegger takes the archaeology one step further to reach beneath or behind philosophy both historically and synchronically to the lived sense of the Whole that underpins all our explicit judgments.

Secondly, when we begin philosophic reflection, we do not find ourselves locked up within the *cogito* and faced with the problem of winning our way out to the exterior world of other persons and things. As we have read Descartes, the problem is more one of explicating the criteria we actually employ for distinguishing between dreams or hallucinations or illusions on the one hand and real beings on the other. We begin by "being in the world" of other persons and things and "discover our own mind" on a rebound off of them. Kant's restriction of knowing to things-relative-to-us is a salutary corrective to the temptation to assume our possession of a divine mode of access to things. But our reference to Being, involving the principle of noncontradiction, and the ability to understand the distinction of phenomena and noumena render plausible Aquinas's notion of mind as *quaedam participatio luminis divini*, "a kind of participation in the divine light," provided the "kind of" is heavily underscored.[3] Ours is a discursive mode of understanding that begins with sense experience and an empty reference to the Whole which forces us to construct our knowledge of the character of the Whole that surrounds the field of descriptive phenomenology. However, when we begin to philosophize, we find the character of the Whole already constructed for us by our assimilation of a culture into a pattern of choices arrived at without full reflection on our part. We are thus invited to begin philosophizing as an ever-increasing purification of an affirmation of Being initially appearing as a cultural reflex.

Affirmation of Being as understood here involves a view of Being as hierarchically scaled. So much is this the case that the very denial of hierarchical structure is an instance of it, that is, the rejection of hierarchy as false involves the affirmation of the hierarchical superiority of truth over falsity. Hierarchy is given initially in the triple structure of intentionality as resting upon a biological matrix and as teleologically arranged in terms of the reference to Being. Following Hegelian lines as modified by Whitehead, this permits a hierarchical and teleological reading of the evolving world within which the self as oriented toward Being appears. This founds the possibility of an affirmation of Being that includes, contrary to Spinoza, negation of those factors that solicit our free choice to close off the teleological thrust involved in the founding reference to Being. But even the ultimate negation of other humans involved in war or in one of its microequivalents—for example, in the slaying of a sadistic killer threatening innocent children—still might involve a hope for their inclusion in the goodness of Being.

Orientation toward Being pulls us out of simple biological adjustment to environmentally available goods that satisfy our appetites. It also pulls us beyond the cultural mediation that situates the environment and our corresponding appetites within the Totality. It orients us toward the absolute Totality. As in Leibniz, the factual perspectivity of vision and the founding reference to the Whole make necessary the development of a dialogical view that seeks a reconciliation of traditions in their depths. But a mistrust of rationalism views that reconciliation as a synthesis only to be achieved in the ultimate future.[4] The lines of dialogue must be kept open and the focus of criticism directed at our own presuppositions as well as at those of our dialogical partners.

Reference to Being is not simply the reference of theoretical intellect. We have distinguished, following Heidegger, the orthotic disclosure of intellect from the aletheic disclosure of "the heart." We have attempted to discern the operation of the aletheic as the generative source of the speculative tradition we have examined. We thus began with Parmenides's mystical ascent to the *Estin* described in his proem. We underscored the erotic character of the ascent to the Good in Plato and the mystical experience of the One in Plotinus. We emphasized the priority of contemplation in Aristotle and the "hidden key" to Aquinas in his own mysticism. We offered the possibility of a reconfigured reading of Descartes based upon the moment of contemplation in the *Meditations*. We stressed the intellectual love of God in Spinoza and in Leibniz. We ferreted out the experience of awe as the basis of Kant's three critiques and pointed to the indispensability of "the rising of the heart toward the eternal" in Hegel. Finally, we stressed the priority of the poetic in Whitehead. Presence to Being functions as ground and as term of the emotional aridity associated with conceptual argumentation and systematization.

Presence to the being of an encounterable other is not summed up in his/her/its subsumability under an explanatory universal, any more than the being of the self is summed up in the apprehension of such universality. In us, reference to Being gathers up the whole of what we are. It is located more in the "sense of the whole" that leads us to interpret and argue and establish preferences and make decisions. Its correlate is not simply the theoretically subsumable Other within the theoretically comprehended Totality. It is rather the partially revealed and more basically concealed fullness of any encounterable other within the partially revealed and even more basically concealed totality of being. Dialogue would thus involve not simply interchange between diverse theoretical positions, but coaffirmation of the total being of any encounterable other. It would be a dialogue of life to life that attends to the totality of needs, an affirmation of the full being of the other as polarized by reference to the mystery of Being. Dialogue would include poetic relation to subhuman nature, flowering forth in artistic re-creation of natural materials as well as in poetic apostrophe of natural and historical things.[5]

Philosophy developing within such a matrix would be less tempted to partiality and imperialism, at least as much intent upon listening and learning as upon speaking and instructing. It would be keenly aware that what each of us knows or thinks he or she knows, and indeed what all of us collectively know or think we know, is but a small sliver of light in the darkness of the encompassing mystery of Being to which we are essentially oriented.

In this way, metaphysics as a conceptual discipline would come to terms with the factual plurality of its own history, with the fact that no school has ever been able to drive the others conclusively from the field. It would enter into dialogue based upon a genuine attempt to understand the partners in dialogue. It would locate itself within the full fabric of life and would not lock itself up in the proverbial ivory tower, repeating to itself the myth of its own superiority to ordinary mortals and their pursuits. It would dedicate itself to promotion of the legitimate concerns of other people, cultivate poetic sensitivity and artistic creativity, become a sympathetic student of the philosophic classics, enter into dialogue with colleagues across clannish lines, flexibly construct its own vision, and open itself to final Mystery. It might even help to sustain a tradition that has produced, and still, from time to time, could produce, philosophical classics that could emerge when dialogue might lead, at least for a time, to a powerful fusion of horizons.[6]

Abbreviations

AI	*Adventures of Ideas*, Whitehead
BN	*Being and Nothingness*, Sartre
BT	*Being and Time*, Heidegger
CAM	*Commentary on Aristotle's Metaphysics*, Aquinas
CJ	*Critique of Judgment*, Kant
CPR	*Critique of Pure Reason*, Kant
CPrR	*Critique of Practical Reason*, Kant
CUP	*Concluding Unscientific Postscript*, Kierkegaard
DV	*De Veritate*, Aquinas
EPS	*Encyclopaedia of the Philosophical Sciences* (3 vols.), Hegel
FMM	*Foundations of the Metaphysics of Morals*, Kant
FMS	*The Foundations of Metaphysics in Science*, Errol Harris
HCPMA	*History of Christian Philosophy of the Middle Ages*, E. Gilson
H&R	*The Philosophical Works of Descartes*, eds. E Haldane and G. Ross
IM	*Introduction to Metaphysics*, Heidegger
Logic	*Hegel's Science of Logic*, trans. A. Miller
LFA	*Aesthetics: Lectures on Fine Art*, Hegel
LHP	*Lectures on the History of Philosophy*, Hegel
LPR	*Lectures on the Philosophy of Religion*, Hegel
Med	*Meditations on First Philosophy*, Descartes
Meta	*Metaphysics*, Aristotle
MT	*Modes of Thought*, Whitehead
NE	*Nicomachean Ethics*, Aristotle
OWA	"The Origin of the Work of Art" in *PLT*, Heidegger
OWL	*On the Way to Language*, Heidegger
PLT	*Poetry, Language, Thought*, Heidegger
PM	*Philosophy of Mind*, Hegel
PP	*Phenomenology of Perception*, Merleau-Ponty
PR	*Process And Reality*, Whitehead
PrP	*The Presocratic Philosophers*, ed. G.S. Kirk and J.E. Raven
PS	*Phenomenology of Spirt*, Hegel
QCT	*The Question Concerning Technology*, Heidegger

Rep	*The Republic*, Plato
SCG	*Summa Contra Gentiles*, Aquinas
SMW	*Science and the Modern World*, Whitehead
ST	*Summa Theologica*, Aquinas
WBG	"The Way Back Into the Ground of Metaphysics" in W. Kaufmann's *Existentialism*, Heidegger
WCT	*What Is Called Thinking?*, Heidegger

Notes

Preface

1. Etienne Gilson, *The Unity of Philosophical Experience*, New York: Scribners, 1937.

2. Immanuel Kant, *Prologomena to Any Future Metaphysics*, P. Carus (tsl.), revised by J.W. Ellington, Indianapolis: Hackett, 1977, pp. 2-3; *Critique of Pure Reason*, B xxxi, N.K. Smith (tsl.), New York: St. Martin's, 1929, p. 30. (Henceforth *CPR*).

3. Robert E. Wood, *Martin Buber's Ontology*, Evanston, Ill.: Northwestern University Press, 1969.

4. Paul Tillich, *Systematic Theology*, vol. 1, Chicago: University of Chicago, 1951, pp. 12-14.

5. Martin Heidegger, "On the Essence of Truth," in *Basic Writings*, D. Krell, ed., New York: Harper and Row, 1977, pp. 117-41.

6. Martin Heidegger, *What Is Called Thinking?* J. Glenn Gray (tsl.), New York: Harper and Row, 1968, pp. 139-47.

7. Martin Heidegger, "Metaphysics as History of Being," in *The End of Philosophy*, J. Stambaugh (tsl.), New York: Harper and Row, 1973, pp. 1ff.

8. Stephen Strasser, *Phenomenology of Feeling: An Essay on the Phenomena of the Heart*, R. Wood (tsl. and intro.), New York: Humanities Press, 1977.

9. Martin Buber, *I and Thou*, W. Kaufmann (tsl.), New York: Scribners, 1970. See my "Buber's Notion of Philosophy," *Thought* 53, (1978), pp. 310-19 and "Martin Buber's Philosophy of the Word," *Philosophy Today*, (Winter, 1986), pp. 317-324.

10. Edmund Husserl, "Phenomenology," C. Solomon (tsl.) *Encyclopaedia Britannica*, vol. 17, 14th ed., 1927, pp. 699-702.

11. Edwin Abbott, *Flatland*, New York: Barnes and Noble, 1963.

12. Henri Bergson, "Philosophical Intuition," in *The Creative Mind*, A. Mitchell (tsl.) New York:Philosophical Library, 1946, pp. 107ff.

13. Robert E. Wood "Fernöstliche Themen in Bubers Werk," *Martin Buber: Bilanz seines Denkens*, Freiburg: Herder, 1983, pp. 340-66.

14. Cf. Wilhelm Halbfass for a critique of approaches to Indian thought in the western metaphysical tradition, *India and Europe*, Albany: State University of New York Press, 1988.

Introduction

1. This is implicit in Aristotle, *Metaphysics*, H. Tredennick, (tsl.) Cambridge: Harvard University Press, 1967, I, 1, 981b, 25. (Henceforth *Meta.*)

2. René Descartes, *Meditations on the First Philosophy*, in *Philosophical Writings of Descartes*, E. Haldane and G. Ross (eds. and tsl.), New York: Dover, 1955, vol. 1, pp. 131-95. (Henceforth *Med.* Reference to the collection will be H&R.)

3. Aristotle, *Meta.*, VII, 1028b, 3.

4. Cf. Joseph Owens, *An Elementary Christian Metaphysics*, Milwaukee: Bruce, 1963, p. 3, for a challenge to this view and a broad discussion of the history of the terms.

5. John Duns Scotus, *Philosophical Writings*, A. Wolter (tsl.), Indianapolis: Bobbs-Merrill, 1962, pp. 22ff.

6. Friedrich Nietzsche, *Twilight of the Idols*, R. Hollingdale (tsl.), Baltimore: Penguin, 1968, p. 37.

7. Aristotle, *Categories*, H. Cooke (tsl.) Cambridge: Harvard University Press, 1962., 4, 1b, 25f.

8. Bernard Lonergan, *Insight*, London: Longmans, Green: 1957, pp. 348ff.; Thomas Aquinas, *Summa Contra Gentiles*, vol. I, A. Pegis, (tsl.), Notre Dame, Ind.: Notre Dame University Press: 1955, I, ch. 25. (Henceforth *SCG.*)

9. Baruch Spinoza, *On the Improvement of the Understanding*, R. Elwes (tsl.), New York: Dover, 1955, p. 29.

10. G.W.F. Hegel, *Hegel's Science of Logic*, A.V. Miller (tsl.), London: George Allen and Unwin, 1959, pp. 82ff. There are two *Logics* published by Hegel, this and the shorter *Hegel's Logic* as part 1 of *The Encyclopaedia of the Philosophic Sciences*, William Wallace (tsl.), Oxford: Carendon Press, 1975. (Henceforth *EPS.*) To avoid confusion we will refer to the Miller translation as *Logic*, and the encyclopaedia *Logic* as *Logic EPS*, I.

11. Martin Heidegger, "The Way Back into the Ground of Metaphysics," in W. Kaufmann, *Existentialism from Dostoevsky to Sartre*, Cleveland: World Publishing, 1956, pp. 206-21. (Henceforth *WBG.*)

12. Sören Kierkegaard, *The Journals of Sören Kierkegaard*, Alexander Dru (ed. and tsl.), London: Oxford University Press, 1959, #583, p. 156.

Chapter 1. Secular Medititions

1. René Descartes, "Letter to Picot," *Principles of Philosophy*, H&R, vol. 2, p. 211.

2. Paul Ricoeur, *Freud and Philosophy*, D. Savage (tsl.), New Haven: Yale University Press, 1970, pp. 32-36.

3. This is Alexander Pope's epitaph, intended for Newton's tombstone, cited in Preserved Smith, *The Enlightenment, 1687-1776*, vol. 2 of *A History of Modern Culture*, New York: Collier, 1962, p. 49.

4. John Locke, *Essay Concerning Human Understanding*, 2 vols., A. Fraser (ed.), New York: Dover, 1959.

5. John Locke, *Second Treatise of Government*, Indianapolis: Bobbs-Merrill, 1952.

6. Descartes, *Med III*

7. Thomas Aquinas, *Summa Theologica*, Fathers of the English Province, (tsl.) New York: Benzinger, 1947, II-II, qs. 180-82. (Henceforth *ST*.)

8. D.T. Suzuki, *Zen Buddhism*, W. Barrett (ed.), Garden City, N.Y.: Doubleday, 1956, pp. 83ff.

9. Plato, *Theatetus*, in *Theatetus* and *Sophist*, H. Fowler (tsl.) Cambridge: Harvard University Press, 1977, 155d.

10. Martin Heidegger, *What Is Philosophy?*, Wm. Klubak and J. Wilde (tsl.), New York: Twayne, 1958, pp. 78-85. See Philipp Dessauer, *Natural Meditation*, New York: Kennedy, 1965, p. 89, on the origin of philosophy in meditation.

11. Aristotle, *Meta*, I, 11, 592b.

12. Plato, *Republic*, P. Shorey (tsl.), Cambridge: Harvard University Press, 1969, VI, 514a ff. (Henceforth *Rep.*)

13. Rollo May (ed.), *Existence: A New Dimension in Psychotherapy*, New York: Basic Books, 1958.

14. Wilhelm Dilthey, *Pattern and Meaning in History*, H.P. Rickman (ed.), New York: Harper, 1962, pp. 105ff.

15. Cf. *infra*, pp. 126ff.

16. Martin Heidegger, *Introduction to Metaphysics*, R. Mannheim (tsl.), New Haven: Yale University Press, 1959, p. 141. (Henceforth *IM*.)

17. Such is Plato's understanding of Sophism: see his *Sophist* for a typology. Cf. *Theatetus* and *Sophist*, H. Fowler, tsl. Cambridge: Harvard University Press, 1977. George Briscoe Kerferd's "Sophists" in *Encyclopaedia Britannica*, (Macropaedia, vol. 17, pp. 11a-14a) has a more sympathetic interpretation.

18. Thomas Aquinas, *Commentary on the Metaphysics of Aristotle*, J. Rowan, tsl. Chicago: Regnery, 1961. I, 1, 981b 25.

19. Bonaventure, *De Septem Donis Spiritus Sancti, Opera Omnia*, II, VII, I, A.C. Peltier, ed., Paris: Vives, 1866 vol. 7, 636a.

20. Aquinas, *ST*, II-II, 45.

21. Blaise Pascal, *Penseés*, #282 and 283, W. Trotter (tsl.), New York: Random House, 1941, pp. 95-97.

22. *The Encyclopaedia of the Philosophical Sciences*, 3 vols., W. Wallace (tsl.), Oxford: Clarendon Press, 1973-75.

23. Sören Kierkegaard, *Concluding Unscientific Postscript to Philosophical Fragments*, D.F. Swenson (tsl.), Princeton: Princeton University Press, 1941, p. 181ff. (Henceforth *CUP.*)

24. Henri Bergson, *Creative Evolution*, A Mitchell (tsl.), New York: Modern Library, 1944, pp. 218ff.

25. Gabriel Marcel, *The Mystery of Being*, 2 vols. G.S. Fraser (tsl.), Chicago: Regnery, 1960, vol. 1, pp. 260 and 95-126.

26. Martin Buber, *Daniel: Dialogues on Realization*, M. Friedman (tsl.), New York: McGraw-Hill, 1965, p. 64.

27. Martin Heidegger, *On the Way to Language*. P. Hertz (tsl.), San Francisco: Harper and Row, 1971, pp. 90ff. (Henceforth *OWL.*) T.S. Eliot, "Little Gidding," 5, *Four Quartets*, London: Faber and Faber, 1945, p. 12.

28. A.N. Whitehead, *Science and the Modern World*, New York: Free Press, 1967, pp. 83ff. (Henceforth *SMW*).

29. Martin Heidegger, "The Origin of the Work of Art," in *Poetry, Language and Thought*, A. Hofstadter (tsl.), New York: Harper and Row, 1971, p. 25. (Henceforth *OWA.*)

30. "Heraclitus of Ephesus," *The Presocratic Philosophers*, G.S. Kirk and J.E. Raven (eds.), London: Cambridge University Press, 1966, frag. 204, 205, 236, 239, 242, pp. 190-210. (Henceforth *PrP.*)

31. The "classical" statement of the view is in A.J. Ayer, *Language, Truth and Logic*, New York: Dover, 1946.

32. Bergson, *Creative Evolution*, p. 3.

33. Piere Teilhard de Chardin, *The Phenomenon of Man*, B. Wall (tsl.), New York: Harper, 1959, pp. 31-36.

34. This meditation is an attempt at concretizing the analysis presented by Heidegger in *Being and Time*, J. MacQuarrie and E. Robinson (tsl.), N.Y.: Harper and Row, 1962 pp. 278-311. (Henceforth *BT*.) Cf. also Paul Ricoeur, *Freedom and Nature: The Voluntary and the Involuntary*, E. Kohak (tsl), Evanston: Northwestern University Press, 1966, pp. 456-63. This section in the main originally appeared in my paper, "Experience and the Totality," delivered at the University of Dayton Symposium on Experience, *The University of Dayton Review* vol. 8, No. 1, (Summer 1971).

35. Karl Marx, "Economic and Philosophic Manuscripts" (1844), in L. Easton and K. Guddat (eds. and tsl.), *Writings of the Young Marx on Philosophy and Society*, Garden City, N.Y.: Doubleday, 1967, pp. 285ff.

36. The perennial import of existentialist philosophy is its recall and exploration of experience in its relation to thought and of thought in relation to lived experience.

37. A colleague once remarked that we all *know* we are to die but we do not *believe* it: that is the distinction I am struggling to illumine. (And that usage of the term "believe" could serve to throw light also on the real meaning of religious belief.)

38. Albert Camus, *The Myth of Sisyphus*, J. O'Brien (tsl.), New York: Random House, 1955, pp. 12 and 42-43.

39. Cited in Karl Jaspers, *Reason and Existence*, W. Earle (tsl.), New York: Noonday, 1959, p. 33.

40. Gisela Nass, *Molecules of Life*, D. Jones (tsl.), New York: McGraw-Hill, 1970, pp. 81 ff.

41. Richard Zahner, *The Problem of Embodiment*, The Hague: Martinus Nijhoff, 1964; Ricoeur, *Freedom and Nature*, pp. 88-134, 231-307, 409-43.

42. Kierkegaard, *CUP*, p. 256.

43. Dean Wooldridge, *Mechanical Man: The Physical Basis of Intelligent Life*, New York: McGraw-Hill, 1968, pp. 84-86, 158-162.

44. Martin Buber, *The Knowledge of Man*, M. Friedman and R.G. Smith (tsl.), N.Y.: Harper and Row, 1965, p. 63.

45. Lonergan, *Insight*, p. 356.

46. Cf. *infra*, pp. 104f.

47. This all-too-compressed treatment will be explored in some depth in the next, and pivotal, chapter.

48. Ricoeur, *Freedom and Nature*, pp. 444-82.

49. Max Picard, *The World of Silence*, Chicago: Regnery, 1956. This marvelous little book by the Swiss poet, together with Dessauer's book mentioned in note 10 and Suzuki's essays cited in note 8, are a fine introduction to the region of experience I have been at pains to delineate.

50. Cf. Marcel, *The Mystery of Being*, vol. I, pp. 251ff. on "presence."

51. See note 33.

52. See Edmund Husserl, *Phenomenology of Internal Time-Consciousness*, J. Churchill (tsl.), Bloomington: Indiana University Press, 1964.

53. Stephen Toulmin and June Goodfield, *The Discovery of Time*, New York:Harper, 1965, p. 76.

54. Errol Harris, *The Foundations of Metaphysics in Science*, New York: University Press of America, 1983, pp. 142-63. (Henceforth *FMS*.)

55. Cf. William Cannon, *The Wisdom of the Body*, New York: Norton, 1963, for an earlier breakthrough work in physiology.

56. William Storer, *Man in the Web of Life*, New York: The New American Library, 1968.

57. Harris, *FMS*, pp. 393-400.

58. Aristotle, *The Politics of Aristotle*, E. Barber, tsl. Cambridge: Harvard University Press, 1970, 1253a 1.

59. Heidegger, *OWL*. See also Robert E. Wood, "Heidegger on the Way to Language," *Semiotics, 1985*, J. Deily (ed.), N.Y.:University Press of America, 1987.

60. Strasser, *Phenomenology of Feeling*, pp. 374-75.

Chapter 2. The Many Dimensions of Humanness

1. Heidegger, *WBG*, p. 206.

2. Augustine, *Confessions*, W. Watts, tsl. Cambridge: Harvard University Press, 1977, X, 54.

3. Bonaventure, *De Septem Donis*, II, VII, I.

4. Hans Jonas, *The Phenomenon of Life*, New York: Dell, 1966, pp. 135ff.

5. Marshall McLuhan, *The Gutenberg Galaxy*, Toronto: University of Toronto Press, 1962.

6. Ludwig Wittgenstein, *Tractatus Logico-Philosophicus*, D. Pears and B. McGuinness (tsl.), London: Routledge and Kegan Paul, 1961, #7, p. 74.

7. W. Garrett, Introduction to Abbott, *Flatland*, pp. vii-x.

8. Karl Heim, *Christian Faith and Natural Science*, New York: Harper and Row, 1957, pp. 129 and 137.

9. C.D. Broad, *Scientific Thought*, London: Routledge and Kegan Paul, 1923.

10. J.R. Smythies, "Aspects of Consciousness," in *Beyond Reductionism*, A. Koestler and J.R. Smythies (eds.), Boston: Beacon, 1969, pp. 240ff.

11. "Life in Two Dimensions," *Newsweek*, Jan. 18, 1982, pp. 84-5.

12. Henri Bergson, "Introduction to Metaphysics," in *The Creative Mind*, M. Andison (tsl.), New York: Philosophical Library, 1946, pp. 162, 190.

13. Michael Polanyi, *Personal Knowledge*, New York: Harper and Row, 1964, esp. pp. 60-202; Martin Heidegger, *The Question Concerning Technology and Other Essays*, W. Lovitt (tsl.), New York: Harper and Row, 1977, p. 174 *et passim*. As Heidegger notes, what is concealed in modern science is the process of revealing. This is clear in all simplistic reductionism. It is quite clear in the epiphenomenalism of Wooldridge's *Mechanical Man*, (cf. ch. 2, n. 46).

14. E. Husserl, *Ideas: General Introduction to Pure Phenomenology*, W. Boyce Gibson (tsl.), New York: Macmillan, 1958, pp. 119ff; Jean-Paul Sartre, *Being and Nothingness*, H. Barnes (tsl.), New York: Harper, 1965, pp. 59ff. (Henceforth *BN*.); Karl Rahner, *Spirit in the World*, W. Dyche (tsl.), New York: Herder and Herder, 1968, presents an interpretation of intentionality ultimately in diametric opposition to the position developed by Sartre.

15. Cf. *infra*, pp. 105.

16. See Floyd Matson's clear and systematic historical account in *The Broken Image*, New York: Braziller, 1964.

17. G.W.F. Hegel, *The Phenomenology of Spirit*, A. Miller (tsl.), London: Oxford University Press, 1977, pp. 104-11. (Henceforth *PS*.) See also my "The Self and the Other," *Philosophy Today*, (Spring 1966), pp. 48-63.

18. Descartes, *Med.*, I.

19. Descartes, *Med.*, VI.

20. Kant, *CPR*, Bxxx.

21. Hegel, *EPS*; Heidegger, *BT.*.

22. Cf. Hubert Dreyfuss, *What Computers Can't Do*, New York: Harper and Row, 1979, for a critical account of the development of artificial intelligence that moves in a Heideggerian direction.

23. Martin Heidegger, "Letter on Humanism," in his *Basic Writings*, D. Krell (ed.), New York: Harper and Row, 1977, pp. 205ff.

24. Jean-Paul Sartre, *The Transcendence of the Ego*, F. William and R. Kirkpatrick (tsl.), New York: Noonday, 1957; Sartre *BN*, pp. 1-1vi.

25. Cf. *supra*, pp. 15f.

26. Heidegger, *BT*, pp. 78-90 and 377; Sartre, *BN*, pp. 171ff.

27. See Plotinus, *The Enneads*, Pantheon, n.d., S. MacKenna, tsl. New York: IV, 3, 20.

28. Locke, *Essay Concerning Human Understanding*, bk. II, ch. 11, 12, & 13; ch. 11, 17.

29. George Berkeley, *Three Dialogues between Hylas and Philonous*, LaSalle, Ill.: Open Court, 1945, p. 90; Berkeley, *Philosophical Commentaries, The Works of George Berkeley*, vol. 1, A. Luce and T. Jessop (eds.), London: Nelson, 1948, pp. 429-29a.

30. Maurice Merleau-Ponty, *The Structure of Behavior*, A. Fisher (tsl.), Boston: Beacon, 1963, p. 210.

31. Rahner, *Spirit in the World*, p. 117.

32. Michael Polanyi and H. Prosch, *Meaning*, Chicago: University of Chicago Press, 1975, pp. 48ff; Michael Polanyi, *The Tacit Dimension*, Garden City, N.Y.: Doubleday, 1966, pp. 14ff.

33. Maurice Merleau-Ponty, *Phenomenology of Perception*, C. Smith (tsl.), London: Routledge and Kegan Paul, 1962: on space, pp. 98ff and 243ff; on time, pp. 410, pp. 410ff. (Henceforth *PP*.)

34. Heidegger, *BT*, p. 189 ff.

35. Edmund Husserl, *Experience and Judgment*, J. Churchill and K. Americks (tsl.), Evanston: Northwestern University Press, 1973, pp. 121ff.

36. On Locke see n. 28; on Hobbes, *Leviathan*, M. Oakeshott, ed. New York: Collier, 1973. I, I; on James, *Varieties of Religious Experience*, New York: Modern Library, 1902, pp. 370ff; on Bergson, *Two Sources of Morality and Religion*, R. Andra, C. Brereton, and W. Carter (tsl.), Garden City, N.Y.: Doubleday, 1935.

37. See Aquinas, *SCG*, IV, 11; Rahner, *Spirit in the World*, pp. 117-20.

38. See Joseph Owens, *An Interpretation of Existence*, Milwaukee: Bruce, 1968, pp. 28ff.

39. Cf. my study of a similar development in Paul Weiss in "Weiss on Adumbration," *Philosophy Today*, Winter, 1984, pp. 339-48.

40. Buber, *The Knowledge of Man*, p. 157.

41. Lonergan, *Insight*, pp. 348ff; Rahner, *Spirit in the World*, pp. 183-186.

42. Merleau-Ponty, *PP*, pp. 348ff.

43. Merleau-Ponty, *Structure of Behavior*, pp. 60ff.

44. Aaron Gurwitsch, *The Field of Consciousness*, Pittsburgh: Duquesne University Press, 1965, pp. 110, 309, 336.

45. Michael Polanyi, *The Study of Man*, Chicago: University of Chicago Press, 1958, p. 32.

46. Cf., *infra*, pp. 10ff.

47. Wilfrid Sellars, *Science, Perception and Reality*, London: Routledge and Kegan Paul, 1963, p. 140.

48. Paul Feyerabend, *Against Method*, London: Verso, 1978, p. 67.

49. Heidegger, *BT*, pp. 91ff.

50. Cf. Jacques Maritain, *The Degrees of Knowledge*, G. Phelan (tsl.), New York: Scribners, 1959, pp. 119ff; Polanyi and Prosch, *Meaning*, p. 37.

51. Heidegger, *BT*, p. 98.

52. Ibid., p. 88.

53. Cf. Carl Jung (ed.), *Man and His Symbols*, New York: Dell, 1964; Paul Ricoeur, *Symbolism of Evil*, E. Buchanan (tsl.), Boston: Beacon, 1967, especially pp. 3-19 and 347-57; also by Ricoeur, *Freud and Philosophy*, D. Savage (tsl.), New Haven: Yale University Press, 1970, pp. 37-58 and 494-552.

54. Cf. Eric Voegelin, *Plato and Aristotle*, vol. 3 of *Order and History*, Baton Rouge: Louisiana State University Press, 1957, pp. 170ff. for a general discussion of myth based on an analysis of *Timaeus* and *Critias*. See Julius Elias, *Plato's Defense of Poetry*, Albany: State University of New York Press, 1984, for a discussion of the myths Plato uses.

55. Plato, *Symposium*, 203.

56. Marcel, *The Mystery of Being*, vol. 1, pp. 242ff.

57. Jacques Maritain, *Creative Intuition in Art and Poetry*, New York: Meridian, 1955, p. 48.

58. Bonaventure, *In Hexaemeron, Opera Omnia* vol. 5, II, 10, Quarrachi: College of St. Bonaventure: 1891, p. 338.

59. Heidegger, *BT*, p. 32.

60. William Blake, "Auguries of Innocence," in *The Complete Writings of William Blake*, G. Keyes, (ed.), London: Oxford University Press, 1966, p. 431; "Eternity," ibid., p. 179.

61. Buber, *I and Thou*, pp. 135-6.

62. Cf. Dionysius the Areopagite, *The Divine Names*, IV, C. Rolt (tsl.), London: SPCK, 1983, pp. 86ff. The work of Dionysius was one of the major sources of speculative mysticism in Western thought.

63. *The Little Flowers of St. Francis*, R. Brown (tsl.), Garden City, New York: Doubleday, 1958.

64. Augustine, *Confessions*, X, 28.

65. Heidegger, "What Is Metaphysics?" *Basic Writings*, pp. 100-101.

66. Buber, *I and Thou*, p. 58.

67. Cf. *supra* pp. 9ff.

68. *Meister Eckhart, a Modern Translation*, R. Blakney (tsl.), New York: Harper and Row, 1941, p. 220.

69. Buber, *I and Thou*, p. 61.

Chapter 3. Toward a Definition of Humanness

1. For a highly informed and perceptive account, see Lewis Mumford, *The Myth of the Machine: Techniques and Human Development*, New York: Harcourt Brace Jovanovich, 1967.

2. Ernst Cassirer, *An Essay on Man*, New York: Doubleday, 1944.

3. Wolfgang Köhler, *The Mentality of Apes*, E. Winston, (tsl.), New York:Harcourt, 1924.

4. Much has been made recently of the ability to learn sign language by Washoe the chimpanzee and Koko the gorilla. Cf. Francine Patterson, "Conversations with a Gorilla," *National Geographic* 154, No. 4, (October 1978), pp. 438-65, and Thomas Sebeok for an appraisal of the limits of such achievement in relation to human linguistic competence: " 'Talking' with Animals: Zoosemiotics Explained," in *Frontiers in Semiotics*, J. Deely et al. (eds.), Bloomington: Indiana University Press, 1986, pp. 76-82.

5. This is not Aristotle's definition but a later one in his school. He gives several definitions: "Man is a political animal" (*The Politics*, 1253a 1), and "Man is either desiderative reason or ratiocinative desire" (*Nicomachean Ethics*, H. Rackham, tsl. Cambridge: Harvard University Press, 1975. 1139b 4). (Henceforth *NE*.)

6. See *infra.* pp. 104ff.

7. Plato, *Phaedo* in *Euthyphro, Apology, Crito, Phaedo, Phaedrus*. H. Fowler, tsl. Cambridge: Harvard University Press, 1977, 97ff.

8. Karl Marx, *Writings of the Young Marx on Philosophy and Society*, p. 295.

9. G.W.F. Hegel, *Hegel's Philosophy of Mind*, (henceforth *PM*), in *EPS*, III, pp. 483-552.

10. Gilbert Ryle, *The Concept of Mind*, New York: Barnes and Noble, 1949, p. 16.

11. Heraclitus, *PrP.*, frag. 201, p. 189.

12. Aristotle, *On the Soul*, W. Hett, tsl. Cambridge: Harvard University Press, 1975 III, 5.

13. For a much more nuanced account that moves in a similar direction see Rahner, *Spirit in the World*, pp. 117-236.

14. Aristotle, *Meta*, IV.

15. A.N. Whitehead, *Process and Reality*, New York: Harper, 1960, I, III, I, pp. 46-47.

16. Aquinas, *ST*, I, 82, 2, ad 2; Sartre, *BN*, pp. 439 and 481ff.

17. Cf. Lonergan, *Insight*, pp. 607-33.

18. Sartre, *BN*, pp. 481ff.

19. Merleau-Ponty, *PP*, pp. 439ff.

20. Cf. Jacques Maritain, *The Degrees of Knowledge*, G. Phelan (tsl.) New York: Scribners, 1959, pp. 260ff.

21. Sigmund Freud, *The Ego and the Id*, J. Riviere (tsl.), New York: Norton, 1960, pp. 18-29.

22. Merleau-Ponty, *PP*, pp. 434ff.

23. Herbert Marcuse, *Reason and Revolution: Hegel and the Rise of Social Theory*, Boston: Beacon, 1960, pp. viiff.

24. Sartre, *BN*, p. 7.

25. Cf. *supra*, pp. 45 and 55.

26. Aristotle, *On the Soul*, II, 412b, 20.

27. Ryle, *The Concept of Mind*, pp. 15-16..

28. Cf. *supra*, pp. 49ff.

29. Plato, *Symposium*, in *Lysis, Symposium* and *Gorgias*, W. Lamb, tsl. Cambridge: Harvard University Press, 1975, 207Aff.

30. Eric Fromm, *Beyond the Chains of Illusion: My Encounters with Marx and Freud*, New York: Pocket Books, 1963, pp. 95ff.

31. Peter Weiss, *Marat/Sade*, New York: Pocket Books, 1965, p. 53; cf. Friedrick Nietzsche, *Genealogy of Morals* in *The Birth of Tragedy* and *The Genealogy of Morals*, F. Golffing (tsl.), Garden City, N.Y.:Doubleday, 1956, p. 11.

32. Ludwig Klages, *Der Geist als Widersacher der Seele*, 3 vols., Leipzig: J.A. Barth, 1929-1933.

33. Sigmund Freud, *Civilization and Its Discontents*, J. Strachey (tsl.), New York: Norton, 1961.

34. Sartre, *BN*, pp. 77-78, 619ff.

35. *Genesis 3.*

36. Plato, *Phaedo*, 66.

37. Ricoeur, *Fallible Man*, C. Kelbley (tsl.), Chicago: Regnery, 1965 pp. 139ff.

38. Hegel, *PS*, #144 and #207ff.

39. Immanuel Kant, *Critique of Practical Reason*, L. W. Beck (tsl.), Indianapolis: Bobbs-Merrill, 1956, pp. 114ff. (Henceforth *CPrR*.)

40. Arthur Schopenhauer, "On Man's Need of Metaphysics," *The World as Will and Representation*, E. Payne, tsl., New York: Dover, vol. II, pp. 160ff.

41. Sarvepalli Radhakrishnan and Charles Moore (eds.), *A Sourcebook in Indian Philosophy*, Princeton: Princeton University Press, 1973, pp. 274-78.

42. Friedrich Heer, *The Medieval World: Europe, 1000-1350*, J. Sondheimer (tsl.), New York: Mentor, 1963, p. 226.

43. Paul Tillich, *Systematic Theology*, vol. 1, Chicago: University of Chicago Press, 1951, pp. 12-14.

44. Several years ago, Huston Smith wrote a widely used text examining the diverse features of the great religions (*The Religions of Man*, New York: Harper, 1958). In a subsequent work (*Forgotten Truth: The Primordial Tradition*, New York: Harper and Row, 1976) he uses the notion of dimensions in much the same way this text does to elucidate the common ground of the great religions.

Chapter 4. Metaphysics and Practicality

1. The hierarchy is linked to Max Scheler's treatment in *Formalism in Ethics and Non-Formal Ethics of Values*, M. Frings and R. Funk (tsl.), Evanston: Northwestern University Press, 1973, pp. 104-10.

2. Epicurus, "Principal Doctrines," #V, XIV, XV, XVI, XX, XXI, in *Stoic and Epicurean Philosophers*, W.J. Oates (ed.), New York: Modern Library, 1940, pp. 35-36.

3. Plato, *Symposium*, 210ff.

4. R. M. Hare, *Freedom and Reason*, Oxford: Clarendon, 1963, pp. 91-93.

5. Immanuel Kant, *Foundations of the Metaphysics of Morals*, L. W. Beck (tsl.), Indianapolis: Bobbs-Merrill, 1959, p. 39.

6. Ibid., p. 47.

7. Kant, *CPrR*, p. 33-34.

8. Charles Stevenson, *Ethics and Language*, New Haven: Yale University Press, 1945, p. 210; Sartre, *BN*, pp. 625-28.

9. Friedrich Nietzsche, *The Gay Science*, W. Kaufman (tsl.), New York: Vintage, 1974 Bk. II, 107, p. 163.

10. Aristotle, *Politics*, IV, 1288b 21f.

11. Cf. Lonergan, *Insight*, ch. 18, pp. 595-633, for some parallel reflection on the metaphysical grounding of ethics.

12. Plato, *Meno*, in *Laches, Protagoras, Meno* and *Euthydemus*, W. Lamb, tsl. Cambridge: Harvard University Press, 1962, 82ff, see below, ch. 7.

13. Plato, *Phaedrus*, H. Fowler, tsl. Cambridge: Harvard University Press, 1977, 250d; *Symposium*, 210-12. See my "Art and the Sacred," *Listening* (1984), pp. 30-40, for an appropriation of these notions.

14. Augustine, *Confessions*, X, XXVII.

15. Michael Polanyi, *Personal Knowledge*, New York: Harper and Row, 1964, pp. 49ff.

16. Aquinas, *Summa Theologica*, I-II, 32, 3. I take that as a central insight in Plato's *Republic*: to find the rule-generating grounds in fundamental human structure. This is the pivot of Aristotle's *Nicomachean Ethics: phronesis* based on rightly oriented upbringing (*NE*, 1095b, 1107af.)

17. Cf. *supra*, pp. 10f.

18. Francis Bacon, *Novum Organum*, I, F. Anderson (ed.), New York: Liberal Arts Press, 1960, pp. 38-67.

19. Cf. Thomas Hobbes, *De Corpore*, Part 2, ch. 7ff, in T. V. Smith and M. Grene (eds.), *From Descartes to Kant*, Chicago: University of Chicago Press, 1950, pp. 177ff.

20. Merleau-Ponty, *PP*, pp. 174 ff.

21. Plato, *Protagoras*, in *Laches, Protagoras, Meno* and *Euthydemus*, W. Lamb, tsl. Cambridge: Harvard University Press, 1962, 357.

22. Bonaventure, *De Septem Donis Spiritus Sancti*, II, VI, VI, Peltier, vol. VII, p. 632b.

23. Plato, *Symposium*, 210.

24. Buber, *I and Thou*, pp. 61ff.

25. Plato, *Republic*, VII, 514ff.

26. Kierkegaard, *CUP*, pp. 325 ff.

27. Plato, *Symposium*, 210-212.

28. William Blake, "The Marriage of Heaven and Hell," *The Poetry and Prose of William Blake*, D. Erdman (ed.), Garden City, N.Y.: Doubleday, 1970, p. 39.

29. Immanuel Kant, *Religion within the Limits of Reason Alone*, T. Greene and H. Hudson, (tsl.), New York: Harper, 1960, p. 175.

30. Sören Kierkegaard, *Fear and Trembling*, W. Lowrie (tsl.), Garden City, N.Y.: Doubleday, 1954, pp. 22-132.

31. Matthew, 5: 27-30.

32. Paul Tillich, *The Courage to Be*, New Haven: Yale University Press, 1971, pp. 186-90.

33. Buber, *I and Thou*, p. 68.

34. See my "Buber's Notion of Philosophy," *Thought*, 53 (1978), pp. 310-319.

Chapter 5. Abstract and Concrete

1. Sartre, *BN*, pp. 303-59.

2. See our meditation on embodiment in ch. 1, *supra*, pp. 17ff.

3. Cf. Owen Barfield, *Saving the Appearances*, New York: Harcourt, Brace and World, n.d., pp. 28-35.

4. "Thales of Miletus," *PrP*, pp. 93-95.

5. Cf. Sartre, *BN*, pp. 252-302.

6. In modern times, it goes at least back to Buffon, Linnaeus, Mapertuis, and Diderot in the eighteenth century. Cf. Thomas Goudge, "Evolutionism," in *Dictionary of the History of Ideas*, Philip Wiener (ed.), New York: Scribners, 1973, pp. 174ff.

7. de Chardin, *The Phenomenon of Man*, pp. 53ff.

8. For a survey of positions, see Jerome Shaffer, *Philosophy of Mind*, Englewood Cliffs, N.J.: Prentice-Hall, 1968.

9. A.N. Whitehead, *PR*, pp. 139ff.

10. This is the Platonic position for which see ch. 7.

11. Hegel, *Logic*. See ch. 15.

12. Paul Ricocur, *Symbolism of Evil*, E. Buchanan (tsl.), Boston: Beacon, 1967, pp. 347ff.

13. Auguste Comte, *Cours de philosophie positive*, vol. 1, Paris: Editions Anthropos, 1968, pp. 2ff.

14. Nicholas Cusanus, *Of Learned Ignorance*, J. Hopkins (tsl.), Minneapolis: Arthur J. Banning Press, 1981.

15. J.B. Lotz, "Person and Ontology," *Philosophy Today* 7, no. 4, (Winter 1963), pp. 279-97.

16. Sartre, *BN*, pp. 221ff.

17. Genesis 1.

18. I John 2:15.

19. Sartre, *BN*, p. 115.

20. Michelangelo, cited in René Dubos, *A God Within*, New York: Scribners, 1972, pp. 10-11.

21. Martin Heidegger, *The Question Concerning Technology and Other Essays*, W. Lovitt (tsl.), New York: Harper and Row, 1977, pp. 23ff. (Henceforth *QCT*.)

Chapter 6. Parmenides

1. "Parmenides," *PrP*, frag. 342, p. 266. (All unnamed references in this chapter are to Parmenides.)

2. For a history of the analytic movement, see J. Cornman, "Philosophical Analysis and the Future of Metaphysics," in R. Wood (ed.), *The*

Future of Metaphysics, Chicago: Quadrangle, 1970, pp. 32-49; for a history of the phenomenological movement, see H. Spiegelberg, *The Phenomenological Movement: A Historical Introduction*, Phenomenologica 6, The Hague: Martinus Nijhoff, 1960.

3. See my Introduction to Stephen Strasser, *Phenomenology of Feeling*, pp. 3-14.

4. The father of this approach is, of course, René Descartes. See below, ch. 11 for the appropriate references.

5. *PrP*, frag. 342, p. 267.

6. Werner Jaeger suggests the same in *The Theology of the Early Greek Philosophers*, Oxford: Clarendon Press, 1960, pp. 10ff; see especially p. 98. Cf. also Eric Voegelin, *Plato and Aristotle*, in *Order and History*, vol. 3.

7. Heidegger, *IM*, p. 141.

8. *PrP*, frag. 2 (344), p. 269.

9. *PrP*, frag. 7 (346), p. 271.

10. Jaeger, *Theology*, pp. 102 ff. Cf. also his *Paideia:The Ideals of Greek Culture*, G. Highet (tsl.), New York: Oxford, 1945, vol. 1, pp. 174-76.

11. Aquinas, *ST*, I, 10, 5, and 2.

12. A. van Melsen, *From Atomos to Atom*, New York: Harper, 1960. See especially pp. 17-23.

13. Cf. Joseph Owens, *A History of Ancient Western Philosophy*, New York: Appleton-Century-Crofts, 1959, p. 96.

14. Melissus, cited in Aristotle, *On Sophistical Refutations*, in *On Sophistical Refutations* and *Coming-to-Be and Passing Away*, E.S. Forster (tsl.), Cambridge: Harvard University Press, 1955, 167b 13; cf. *Meta*, 986b, 19.

15. *PrP*, frag. 3-6 (282-385), p. 299.

16. *PrP*, frag. 3 (344), p. 269. Heidegger spends much time reflecting on this fragment: e.g., *IM*, pp. 136ff; *WCT*, pp. 241ff.

17. *PrP*, frag. 2, (344), p. 269.

18. "Mundaka Upanishad," *A Sourcebook in Indian Philosophy*, pp. 52-53.

19. *PrP*, frag. 1 (342), p. 267.

20. *PrP*, frag. 12 (358), p. 283.

21. *PrP*, frag. 1 (342), p. 267.

22. Frag. 15 in Philip Wheelwright, *The Presocratics*, New York: Odyssey, 1966, p. 100.

23. Ibid.

24. Such is Plato's basic assessment. Cf. especially his *Sophist*. For a more favorable assessment see George Kerferd, "Sophists," *Encyclopaedia Britannica*, 15th ed., Macropaedia, vol. 17, pp. 11a-14a.

25. See *PrP*, pp. 286-306 for texts and commentaries on Zeno and Melissus.

26. *PrP*, pp. 400-426, on Leucippus and Democritus.

27. Epicurus, "Principal Doctrines," pp. 35-36.

28. Paul Tillich, *Systematic Theology*, vol. 1, pp. 11-15.

29. "Milindapanha," in *A Sourcebook in Indian Philosophy*, p. 281-84.

30. Voltaire, *Candide*, T.G. Smollett (tsl.), New York: Washington Square, 1962.

31. *IM*, pp. 110-12, 136-39; *WCT*, pp. 170ff.

32. *BT*, pp. 279ff.

Chapter 7. Plato

1. *Rep.*, VII, 514ff. Unnamed references in this chapter are to Plato.

2. *Rep.*, V, 476 c.

3. Ascent and descent are the structural metaphors of the *Republic* as a whole. See my "Image, Structure and Content: On a Passage in Plato's *Republic*," in *The Review of Metaphysics* 40, no. 3 (March 1987), pp 495-514 for further interpretation of Plato. My analysis there and here owes much to the following: Eric Voegelin, *Plato and Aristotle* in his *Order and History*, vol. 3; Jacob Klein, *A Commentary on Plato's "Meno,"* Chapel Hill: University of North Carolina Press, 1965; Eva Brann, "The Music of the *Republic*," *Agon* 1 (1966), pp. 1-117; Allan Bloom's "Interpretive Essay" in his translation, *The Republic of Plato*, New York: Basic Books, 1968; John Sallis's *Being and Logos*, Pittsburgh: Duquesne University Press, 1974.

4. *Rep*, 476c.

5. *Theatetus*, 212.

6. *Theatetus*, 155dff.

7. *Rep*, VI, 509d-11e and 533e present the distinctions and the initial, surface meaning. Paralleling the line with the cave yields the metaphorical reading we are providing.

8. *Rep*, II, 372e.

9. *Rep*, VI, 493a.

10. *Timaeus*, R. Bury (tsl.), Cambridge: Harvard University Press, 1977, 41ff.

11. *Rep*, VI, 493a.

12. *Rep*, III, 403c.

13. *Rep*, VII, 533e.

14. Heidegger, *IM*, pp. 104-05.

15. *Rep*, VI, 511d.

16. *Rep*, VI, 509b.

17. Plotinus, *Enneads*, VI, 7, 34.

18. *Phaedo*, 100c.

19. This is typical Socratic procedure. Cf. *Rep*, I for the employment of this method on the question of the nature of justice.

20. *Rep*, VI, 505d.

21. Edmund Husserl, "The Origin of Geometry," in *The Crisis of European Science and Transcendental Phenomenology*, David Carr (tsl.), Evanston: Northwestern University Press, 1970, pp. 353ff.

22. *Rep*, VII, 525d-525a.

23. Albert Einstein, *Ideas and Opinions*, S. Bargmann (tsl.), New York: Bonanza, 1954, pp. 290ff.

24. *Rep*, VII, 533e-34a.

25. *Rep*, VI, 510a and 516a.

26. *Rep*, VII, 533e-34a.

27. *Timaeus*, 49b-53c.

28. *Symposium*, 206b-12c.

29. *Phaedrus*, in *Euthyphro, Apology, Crito, Phaedo, Phaedrus*, H. Fowler (tsl.), Cambridge: Harvard University Press, 1977, 251a-256e.

30. Ibid., 244a-245c.

31. *Sophist*, 256dff.

32. *Rep*, VI, 509b.

33. *Rep*, VII, 517b.

34. Aristotle, *Meta*. I.

35. *Apology*, in *Euthyphro, Apology, Crito, Phaedo, Phaedrus*, H. Fowler (tsl.), Cambridge: Harvard University Press, 1977, 23; *Theatetus* 150c; *Symposium*, 203d.

36. *Rep*, VI, 509d.

37. Cf. Norman Wentworth DeWitt, *Epicurus and His Philosophy*, Minneapolis: University of Minnesota Press, 1954, p. 291.

38. Ricoeur, *Fallible Man*, pp. 140ff.

39. On this reading, one "comes back into the cave," not out of coercion but out of concern for one's fellow men. The whole *Republic* is such a descent on Socrates' part for the sake of Glaucon.

40. *Rep*, VI, 506e.

41. *Rep*, VII, 517b.

42. *Laws*, X, 897d.

43. *Laws*, X, 896a-e.

44. *Sophist*, 428d.

45. *Timaeus*, 29e.

46. "The maker of all this universe is past finding out." "One ought to accept the tale which is probable and inquire no further." *Timaeus*, 28e and 29d.

47. *Phaedo*, 95e-100a.

48. Cf. Jerome Shaffer, *Philosophy of Mind*, Englewood Cliffs, N.J.: Prentice-Hall, 1968, pp. 77ff.

49. *Laws*, X, 891b-892e.

Epilogue on Plotinus

1. His two largest works suggest as much: the *Republic* in the middle of his life and the *Laws* at the end each surpass in bulk almost the whole of his other output. Voegelin argues that all of the other works have a political dimension: cf. his *Plato and Aristotle*.

2. Plotinus, *Enneads*, VI, 7, 34. Cf. Porphyry, *Life of Plotinus*, 1, in *The Enneads*. Unnamed references in this chapter are to Plotinus.

3. *Enneads*, V, 9, 5 & 13.

4. Porphyry, *Life*, 23.

5. *Enneads*, VI, 9, 3-11.

6. *Enneads*, I, 2, 4.

7. *Enneads*, III, 8, 8-9.

8. *Enneads*, VI, 9, 4.

9. A. Tanqueray, *The Spiritual Life*, H. Branderis (tsl.), Tournai, Belgium: Desclee, 1930, pp. 297ff.

10. *Enneads*, IV, 3, 8; III, 8, 4.

11. Thomas Merton, *The Way of Chuang Tzu*, New York: New Directions, 1969, pp. 75 and 80. Cf. Paul Weiss, *First Considerations*, Carbondale: Southern Illinois University Press, 1977, p. 114, n. 52.

12. *Enneads*, V, 1, 6.

13. *Enneads*, VI, 9, 3.

14. Augustine, *Confessions*, VII, IX, 13.

Chapter 8. Aristotle

1. Armand Maurer *Medieval Philosophy*, New York: Random House, 1965, pp. 71ff.

2. Etienne Gilson, *History of Christian Philosophy in the Middle Ages*, New York: Random House, 1955, pp. 534ff. (Henceforth *HCPMA*), Karl Jaspers, *Anselm and Nicholas of Cusa*, R. Mannheim (tsl.), New York: Harcourt, Brace, Jovanovich, 1966, pp. 27-182; Ernst Cassirer, *The Individual and the Cosmos in Renaissance Philosophy*, M. Domandi (tsl.), New York: Harper, 1963, pp. 7-72.

3. Cf. ch. 11.

4. Cf. ch. 13.

5. Cf. ch. 16.

6. Aquinas, *Summa Theologica*, I, 84, 7.

7. Aristotle, *Posterior Analytics*, H. Tredennick (tsl.), Cambridge: Harvard University Press, 1960, II, 19, 100a, 10-14. Unnamed references in this chapter are to Aristotle.

8. Cf. Harris, *FMS*, pp. 393-400.

9. Polanyi, *Personal Knowledge*; Thomas Kuhn, *The Structure of Scientific Revolutions*, 2d ed., Chicago: Chicago University Press, 1970;

Errol Harris, *Hypothesis and Perception*, London: Routledge and Kegan Paul, 1972.

10. For the clearest classical statement, see David Hume, *Treatise of Human Nature*, D. MacNabb (ed.), Glasgow: William Collins, 1978, Part I, Section 1, pp. 45ff. For a more recent statement, see Bertrand Russell, *Mysticism and Logic*, London: Longmans, Green, 1918.

11. *Categories*, 4, 1b, 25-32a, 4.

12. *Meta*, V, 1025a, 14ff.

13. On *ousia*, cf. *Meta*, VII, 1028a, 15; on *hypokeimenon*, *Meta*, VII, 1028b, 33ff.

14. *On the Soul*, III, 425b, 27.

15. *On the Soul*, III, 426a, 15-26; *Meta*, IV, 1010b 33; cf. Buber, *The Knowledge of Man*, pp. 156-159 for a similar but more poetically developed view.

16. Sartre, *BN*, lxvi.

17. *Physics*, P. Wickstead and F. Cornford (tsl.), Cambridge: Harvard University Press, 1980, I, 191a, 23ff; *Meta*, V, 1019a, 15ff and IX, 1045b, 25ff.

18. The terms are very frequently used together in Aristotle, e.g., *Meta*, VII, 1033b, 5; *On the Soul* II, 414a, 10; *Physics* II, 193a.

19. *On the Soul*, II, 412a, 20-30.

20. Empedocles, *PrP*, fr. 442-47, pp. 336-37. See Aristotle, *Physics*, II, 198b, 10ff. for a rejection of evolution.

21. *Meta*, IX, 1045b, 25 deals with act and potency. *Dynamis* is the term translated as potency; *energeia* or *entelecheia* as act.

22. *Physics*, II, 193b, 7.

23. *Meta*, IX, 1046a, 10ff.

24. *Meta*, IX, 1049a, 27.

25. *Physics*, II, 193a, 10ff.

26. *Categories*, 8, 10a, 10ff.

27. *Physics*, II, 193a, 18.

28. *On Coming-to-Be and Passing Away* in *On Sophisticated Refutations* and on *Coming-to-Be and Passing Away*, E.S. Forster (tsl.), Cambridge: Harvard University Press, 1955, II, 1, 329, 25ff.

29. *Physics*, II, 194b, 20; *Meta* V, 1013a, 24.

30. *On the Soul*, II, 412a, 1-413a, 10.

31. For a development of this notion, see Bernard Lonergan, *Insight*, ch. 8, pp. 245-70.

32. *On the Soul*, II, 424a, 18.

33. *On the Soul*, II, 424a, 25.

34. Cf. René Descartes, *Med.* (See ch. 11.)

35. *On the Soul*, II, 425b, 27.

36. Cf. Errol Harris, *Nature, Mind and Modern Science*, London: George Unwin, 1968, pp. 104ff.

37. Locke, *Essay Concerning Human Understanding*, bk. II, ch. 8, 7ff; 23.

38. This is Aquinas's development of Aristotle: *ST* I, 84, 2.

39. *Physics*, VI, 231 a, 21ff.

40. *Physics*, V, 220a, 24.

41. E.g. Schopenhauer, *The World as Will and Representation*, vol. I, #23, pp. 112ff.

42. *Categories*, 5, 2a, 111.

43. *On the Soul*, III, 430a, 1-25; *Meta*, XII, 1072b, 22.

44. *On the Soul*, III, 431b, 22.

45. Cf. Henry Veatch, *Realism and Nominalism Revisited*, Milwaukee: Marquette University Press, 1954.

46. Cf. Gilson, *HCPMA*, pp. 489ff.

47. Cf. ch. 14.

48. *On the Soul*, III, 429a, 10ff.

49. Martin Heidegger *IM*, pp. 141-42.

50. *Politics*, I, 125a, 2.

51. *NE*, II, 1107a, 1-3; I, 1095b, 6.

52. *Politics*, II, 1260b, 28; IV, 1288b, 25-30.

53. *NE*, VI, 1140a, 25-1141b, 22.

54. E.g. Aquinas, *ST* I-II, 57, 4 and 5.

55. *NE*, X, 1177a, 12ff.

56. *On the Soul*, II, 415a, 28ff.

57. *Meta*, XII, 1071b, 5-22.

58. *Meta*, XII, 1074b, 15-1075a, 11.

59. *Meta*, XII, 1072b, 1-5.

60. In *NE*, III, 1111b, 22 he refers to "impossible things like immortality." In *Meta*, XII, 1070a, 25, he suggests that perhaps something may survive death—perhaps reason but not the whole soul. In *On the Soul*, III, 430a, 20-25 he says the active reason is immortal, but we will not remember; cf. also 413b, 25.

Chapter 9. Aquinas

1. Gilson, *HCPMA*, pp. 81ff.

2. Paul O. Kristeller, *Renaissance Thought*, New York: Harper, 1961, p. 59.

3. M.D. Chenu, *Toward Understanding St. Thomas*, A. Landry and D. Hughes (tsl.), Chicago: Regnery, 1964, pp. 31-39.

4. Joseph Pieper, *Guide to Thomas Aquinas*, R. Winston and C. Winston (tsl.), New York: Mentor-Omega, 1962, pp. 106ff.

5. Aquinas, *On the Power of God (De Potentia Dei)*, L. Shapcote (ed.), New York: Benzinger, 1932-4, J. Rowan (tsl.), Chicago: Regnery, 1961, 5, 10, ad 5. Unnamed references in this chapter are to Aquinas.

6. Aquinas, *ST*, I, 85, 1, ad. 4.

7. *Commentary on the Metaphysics of Aristotle*, IV, 2 (henceforth *CMA*); *Truth (De Veritate)*, R. Mulligan (tsl.), Chicago: Regnery, 1952, I, Qs I, reply (henceforth *DV*); *ST*, I, 5, 2.

8. Jacques Maritain, *A Preface to Metaphysics: Seven Lectures on Being*, New York: Mentor, 1962, pp. 90ff.

9. Cf. *CMA*, IV; *SCG*, II, ch. 83 and III, ch. 2.

10. Aristotle, *On the Soul*, III, 4316, 22.

11. *ST*, I, 84, 3, ad 2.

12. *ST*, I, 84, 6.

13. *DV*, I, ad 9.

14. *SCG*, II, 76, 10.

15. Part 1, ch. 3, pp. 67ff.

16. Aquinas, *Commentary on Boethius's De Trinitate*, B. Decker (ed.), Leiden: Brill, 1965, Qs. V-VI; *ST*, I, 85, 1, ad 2.

17. Rahner, *Spirit in World*, p. 106, n. 30.

18. Cf. Emerich Coreth, *Metaphysics*, J. Donceel (tsl.), New York: Herder and Herder, 1968, pp. 92, 112.

19. Ibid., pp. 103ff.

20. *ST*, I, 13, 11; *SCG*, I, ch. 21 and 22; *SCG*, II, ch. 52.

21. Etienne Gilson, *The Christian Philosophy of St. Thomas Aquinas*, L. Shook (tsl.), New York: Random House, 1956, pp. 132ff.

22. Anselm, *Proslogion*, Ch. 2-4, *Opera Omnia*, Stuttgart: Friedrich Frommann, 1968, F. Schmitt (ed.), vol. 1, pp. 101-104.

23. Cf. especially Anselm Stolz, "Anselm's Theology in *The Proslogion*," in Hicks and McGill (eds.), *The Many-Faced Argument*, New York: Macmillan, 1967, pp. 183-206.

24. *ST*, I, 2, 1-3.

25. Cf. H. Ebert, "Man as the Way to God," R. Wood (tsl.), *Philosophy Today* 10, no. 2, (Summer 1966), pp. 88-106.

26. Cf. *infra*, ch. 11.

27. *ST*, I, 2, 1; Kant, *CPR*, A592/B620-A603/B631.

28. Cf. A. McGill "Recent Discussions of Anselm's Argument," in J. Hicks and R. McGill (eds.), *The Many-Faced Argument*, pp. 33-110.

29. Gerard Smith, *Natural Theology*, New York: Macmillan, 1951, pp. 86-88.

30. Empedocles, *PrP*, fr. 423, pp. 326-27.

31. *ST*, I, 46, 1.

32. *ST*, I, 46, 2, and 7.

33. *ST*, I, 3, 4; *SCG*, II, 52.

34. *De Potentia Dei*, VII, 2, and 9; ST, I, 4, 1, and 3.

35. *On Being and Essence*, A.Maurer (tsl.), Toronto:Pontifical Institute of Medieval Studies, 1983, IV, pp. 51-59.

36. *ST*, I, 13, 11.

37. Cf. *infra*, ch. 12.

38. *ST*, I, 85, 1.

39. *ST*, I, 78, 3.

40. *ST*, I, 84, 1.

41. Relate it back to the chart on p. 160.

42. Cf. *SCG*, ch. 54.

43. *DV*, Qs. 1, a. 9; cf. Heidegger, *BT*, p. 236.

44. Augustine, *Confessions*, X, 7, 17.

45. Joseph Pieper, *The Silence of St. Thomas*, J. Murray and D. O'Connor (tsl.), New York: Pantheon, 1957, pp. 53-67.

46. *SCG*, II, 12.

47. *ST*, I, 15, 1.

48. *Timaeus*, 29E.

49. *ST*, I, 84, 8.

50. *ST*, I, 2, 1 ad 1.

51. Aquinas, *CAM*, I, 1, 15; *On Spiritual Creatures*, M. Fitzpatrick (tsl.), Milwaukee: Marquette University Press, 1949, 11, ad 3; *DV*, IV, 1 and 8.

52. Cf. *SCG*, I, ch. 30.

53. *ST*, I, 84, 5.

54. *ST*, I, 79, 3.

55. Pieper, *Silence*, pp. 53-67.

56. See K. Foster, *The Life of Saint Thomas Aquinas*, Baltimore: Helicon Press, 1959, pp. 42ff.

57. *ST*, I, 8, 4.

58. Cf. J. Peifer, *The Concept in Thomism*, New York: Record Press, 1952, pp. 141-47.

59. On Augustine, see my Introduction to Strasser, *Phenomenology of Feeling*, pp. 17-18.

60. *ST*, I, 54, 2, ad 2.

61. *Meta*, I, 535.

62. Charles Hart, *Thomistic Metaphysics*, Englewood Cliffs, N. J.: Prentice-Hall, 1959, pp. 33-42.

63. The term is Thomas de Vio's (better known as Cajetan). Cf. G. Klubertanz, *St. Thomas Aquinas on Analogy*, Chicago: Loyola University Press, 1960, pp. 9ff; cf. *DV*, 2, 11.

64. *DV*, I, 1; *SCG*, II, ch. 41. This interpretation appeared earlier in my "The Self and The Other." For a collection of Aquinas's central texts on the transcendentals, see J. Anderson, *Introduction to the Metaphysics of St. Thomas Aquinas*, Chicago: Regnery, 1953, pp. 44-98.

65. Nietzsche, *Twilight of the Idols*, p. 37.

66. This analysis of thinghood follows, with modifications, Joseph de Finance, "Being and Subjectivity," in *A Modern Introduction to Metphysics*, D. A. Drennan (ed.), New York: Free Press of Glencoe, 1962, pp. 272-82. The modifications follow (with modifications) Jean-Paul Sartre's analysis in "Existentialism Is a Humanism," W. Kaufmann (tsl.), *Existentialism from Dostoevski to Sartre*, New York: Meridian, 1956, pp. 287ff.

67. Cf. Weiss, *First Considerations*; cf. my "Weiss on Adumbration," *Philosophy Today*, (Winter 1984), pp. 339-48.

68. *ST*, I, 5, 1: Aristotle, *NE*, I, 1, 1094 a. Cf. Michael Polanyi, *The Study of Man*, Chicago: University of Chicago Press, 1958.

69. *ST*, I, 5, 6.

70. *ST*, I-II, 27, 1, and 3.

71. *ST*, I, 39, 8. Cf. Mark Jordan, "The Grammar of *Esse*: Re-reading Thomas on the Transcendentals," *The Thomist*, (1977), pp. 1-26, for a suggestive analysis.

72. Buber, *I and Thou*, pp. 125ff.

73. Buber, *The Knowledge of Man*, pp. 59-71.

74. *ST*, I, 86, 1.

Chapter 10. René Descartes

1. G. W. F. Hegel, *Lectures on the Philosophy of History*, vol. 3, E. Haldane and F. Simson (tsl.), New York: Humanities Press, 1983, pp. 223ff. (Henceforth *LHP*.)

2. Jacques Maritain, *Three Reformers: Luther, Descartes, Rousseau*, London: Sheed Ward, 1950, pp. 53-89.

3. Cf. Edmund Husserl, *Cartesian Meditations*, D. Cairns (tsl.), The Hague: Martinus Nijhoff, 1960, p. 1.

4. Descartes, *Meditations on First Philosophy*, (henceforth *Med*), in *The Philosophical Works of Descartes*, E. Haldane and G. Ross (tsl.),

New York: *Med* I, pp. 144ff. All unnamed references in this chapter are to Descartes.

5. *Med* VI. Cf. *infra*, pp. 37ff.

6. *Med* I, pp. 146ff.

7. Cf. *supra*, pp. 137ff.

8. *Med* I, p. 148; *Med*, II, pp. 158-59.

9. *Med* II, pp. 150ff. The formulation "I think therefore I am," is actually from the *Discourse on Method*, Part IV, H & R, vol. 1, pp. 101-02.

10. On the *ergo* see S. V. Keeling, *Descartes*, London: Oxford University Press, 1968, pp. 102-04.

11. *Med* II, p. 153.

12. Cf. *supra*, pp. 67ff.

13. "Reply to Objection II," H & R, vol 2, pp. 34-35; also *Med* III, pp. 162 and 171; *Med* IV, p. 176.

14. *Med* III, pp. 165ff.

15. Cf. *supra*, pp. 125ff.

16. Cf. *supra*, pp. 182ff.

17. *Med* III, p. 170.

18. *Med* IV, p. 173.

19. *Med* III, p. 158.

20. *Med* V, pp. 180ff.

21. *Med* VI, pp. 185ff.

22. *Med* II, p. 155; *Med* V, pp. 179-180.

23. Aristotle, *On the Soul*, III, 1, 425a, 15.

24. George Berkeley, *Three Dialogues between Hylas and Philonous*, La Salle, Ill.: Open Court, 1945, First Dialogue, pp. 31ff.

25. David Hume, *An Enquiry Concerning Human Understanding*, Indianapolis: Hackett, 1977, p. 106.

26. Cf. *infra*, pp. 223ff.

27. Cf. *infra*, pp. 233ff.

28. Actually, the phrase "Ghost in the Machine" is Gilbert Ryle's in *The Concept of Mind*, pp. 15-16.

29. Descartes, Letter to Picot, Preface to *Principles of Philosophy*, H & R, vol. 1, p. 211.

30. The reference to contemplation is in *Med* III, p. 171.

31. Bacon, *Novum Organun*, I, 3, p. 39.

32. Ibid., I, XCVIII, p. 95.

33. Bishop Bossuet, in his funeral oration delivered at the burial service of Maria Teresa in 1693, named Descartes as the culprit and as the beginning of the universal dissolution Europe was facing. (Paul Hazard, *The European Mind, 1680-1715*, J. L. May (tsl.), New York: Meridian, 1971, pp. 212-14.)

34. Ignatius Loyola, *The Spiritual Exercises of St. Ignatius*, L. J. Puhl (tsl.), Westminster, Md.: Newman Press, 1959. For this interpretation, see L. J. Beck, *The Metaphysics of Descartes*, Oxford: Clarendon, 1967, p. 28.

35. *Passions of the Soul*, part 3, articles CLIII-CLXI on generosity, H & R, vol. 1, pp. 401-06. Cf. Richard Kennington, "René Descartes," in *History of Political Philosophy*, L. Strauss and J. Cropsey (eds.), Chicago: Rand McNally, 1963, pp. 379-96.

36. St. Augustine, *Confessions*, VII, X; X, VII.

37. *Med* II, p. 153.

38. Cf. Jacques Maritain, *The Dream of Descartes*, M. Andison (tsl.), New York: Philosophical Library, 1944, pp. 166ff; Paul Hazard, *The European Mind: 1680-1715*, pp. 212-13.

39. Aquinas, *ST*, I-II, 110, 1.

Chapter 11. Baruch Spinoza

1. Cf. *supra*, pp. 149ff.

2. Novalis called him "der Gottvertrunkene Mann." Harry Wolfson remarks: "his reported God-intoxication was really nothing but a hang-over of an earlier religious jag," *The Philosophy of Spinoza*, vol. 2, Cambridge: Harvard University Press, 1962, p. 348.

3. Benedict de Spinoza, *On the Improvement of the Understanding*, R. Elwes (tsl.), New York: Dover, 1955, pp. 8ff; cf. also Spinoza, *Ethics*, R. Elwes (tsl.), New York: Dover, 1955 part 2, prop. XL, Note II, p. 113. All unnamed references in this chapter are to Spinoza.

4. *Ethics*, part 5, prop. XV-XX, pp. 255-56; prop. XXXIII-XXXV, pp. 263-64.

5. *On the Improvement of the Understanding*, pp. 15 and 29.

6. *Ethics*, part 1, Definitions, IV, p. 45.

7. Ibid, V.

8. On *natura naturans* and *natura naturata*, see *Ethics*, part 1, Prop. XXIX, note, p. 68; also, part 1, Prop. XI.

9. *Ethics*, part 1, Prop. V-XV, pp. 47-59.

10. Descartes, *Principles of Philosophy*, part 1, Prop. LI, H & R, vol. 1, p. 239.

11. *Ethics*, part 1, Prop. XV-XVI, pp. 55-59.

12. *Theologico-Political Tractatus and a Political Treatise*, R. Elwes (tsl.), New York: Dover, 1951. Cf. L. Feuer, *Spinoza and the Rise of Liberalism*, Boston: Beacon, 1966, pp. 58ff.

13. Feuer, *Spinoza*, pp. 1-37.

14. *Ethics*, part 1, Prop. XVII, pp. 59-62.

15. *Ethics*, part 3, p. 129.

16. *Political Treatise* (with *Theologico-Political Tractatus*), p. 288.

17. *Ethics*, part 2, prop. XLIV, corollary II, p. 117.

18. *Ethics*, part 5, p. 246.

19. Cf. Feuer, *Spinoza*, pp. 38-57.

20. Cf. Jean Calvin, *Institutes of the Christian Religion*, J. McNeill (ed.), F. Battles (tsl.), Philadelphia: Westminster Press, 1960.

21. Cf. Stuart Hampshire, *Spinoza*, London: Penguin, 1952.

22. *Ethics*, part 1, Prop. XI, pp. 51ff.

23. *Ethics*, part 2, Prop. VII, p. 87.

24. *Ethics*, part 2, Prop. XIII, Note, pp. 92ff.

25. Cf. Frederick Pollack, *Spinoza, His Life and Philosophy*, London: C. Kegan Paul, 1880, pp. 390ff.

26. Friedrich Schleiermacher, *On Religion: Speeches to Its Cultured Despisers*, J. Oman (tsl.), New York: Harper and Row, 1958.

27. Cited in Ronald Cook, *Einstein: The Life and Times*, New York: World, 1971, p. 19.

28. Ch. 3, p. 74ff.

29. F. W. J. Schelling, *System des Transzendentalen Idealismus Schriften von 1799-1801*, Darmstadt: Wissenschaftliche Buchgesellschaft, 1982, p. 607.

30. Buber, *I and Thou*, p. 123.

Chapter 12. Gottfried Wilhelm Leibniz

1. *Lettre à Arnauld*, cited in R. Latta, *Leibniz: The Monadology and Other Philosophical Writings*, London: Oxford University Press, 1951, p. 47. (Henceforth references to Latta's own comments will be indicated by "Latta," followed by the page number; references to the works of Leibniz gathered in this volume will be indicated by "L," followed by the page number.) Unnamed references in this chapter are to Leibniz.

2. R. W. Meyer, *Leibniz and the Seventeenth-Century Revolution*, J. Stern (tsl.), Chicago: Regnery, 1952. Cf. also Leroy Loemker, *Struggle for Synthesis*, Cambridge: Harvard University Press, 1972.

3. Cf. *supra*, p. 128.

4. Latta, *Leibniz*, p. 319.

5. Leibniz, *Theodicy, Essays on the Goodness of God, The Freedom of Man and the Origins of Evil*, E. M. Huggard (tsl.), LaSalle, Ill.: Open Court, 1985, p. 172; *New System*, (1695), L, p. 304.

6. Michael Polanyi and H. Prosch, *Meaning*, Chicago: University of Chicago Press, 1975, pp. 24ff.

7. *Monadology*, #56 & 57, L, p. 248; *Principles of Nature and Grace*, #12, L, p. 418. The term "compossible" comes from the *Lettre à Bourquet*, cited in Latta, p. 64, n. 2. This is also connected with Leibniz's view of the whole as a *plenum: Mondadology* #60, L, p. 251.

8. *Monadology*, #1-3, L, pp. 217-18; *Principles of Nature and Grace*, 3, L, p. 409.

9. *Monadology*, #63, L, p. 253.

10. "De modo distinguendi phenomena realia ab imaginariis," cited in Latta, Introduction, pp. 99-101.

11. Cf. *supra*, p. 128.

12. *Principles of Nature and Grace*, #6, L, p. 414. Cf. the discussion in Latta, Introduction, pp. 74ff.

13. *Discourse on Metaphysics*, XVII-XVIII, in *The Rationalists*, G. Montgomery (tsl.), with revisions by A. Chandler, Garden City, N. Y.: Doubleday, 1974, pp. 428-31; *Specimen Dynamicum*, L, p. 353; cf. also the discussion in Latta, Introduction, pp. 89ff.

14. *Epistola ad R. C. Wagner*, in L, p. 96, n. 1.

15. *Monadology*, #9-13, L, pp. 222-23.

16. *Monadology*, #61 and 65, L, pp. 250-51 and 255; *New Essays on the Human Understanding*, in L, pp. 385-86.

17. Aristotle, *Physics*, 204ff.

18. *IVme Lettre à Clarke*, #4 & 6, cited in Latta, p. 37, n. 1.

19. Latta, pp. 78ff.

20. Cited in Frank Thilly and Ledger Wood, *A History of Philosophy*, New York: Holt, Rinehart and Winston, 1966, p. 516.

21. *Monadology*, #18, 22, and 79, L, pp. 229, 231, and 263; *New System*, #3, L, pp. 300-01.

22. *Principles of Nature and Grace*, #10, L, p. 417.

23. Friedrich Nietzsche, "On the Uses and Disadvantages of History for Life," in *Untimely Meditations*, R. J. Hollingdale (tsl.), Cambridge: Cambridge University Press, 1983, p. 63.

24. *Monadology*, #14, L, p. 224.

25. *New Essays on the Human Understanding*, L, pp. 370ff; *Mondaology* #21, L, p. 230.

26. *Principles of Nature and Grace*, #3, L, p. 409.

27. *Monadology* #28, L, p. 233.

28. *Discourse on Metaphysics*, XXXIV, in *The Rationalists*, p. 449; *Monadology*, #30, L, p. 234.

29. *Monadology*, #83, L, p. 266.

30. *Principles of Nature and Grace*, #18, L, p. 423.

31. Cf. Leroy Loemker, "Leibniz and Our Time," *The Philosophy of Leibniz and the Modern World*, Ivor LeClerc (ed.), Nashville: Vanderbilt University Press, 1973, p. 5.

32. *Monadology*, #31ff., L, pp. 235ff.

33. *Monadology*, #46, L, pp. 243.

34. *Monadology*, #45, L, pp. 242-43.

35. *Monadology*, #36-45, L, pp. 237-42; *Principles of Nature and Grace*, #7-8, L, pp. 414-15.

36. *Discourse on Metaphysics*, II, in *The Rationalists*, pp. 410-11.

37. Cf. *Discourse on Metaphysics*, XIX, in *The Rationalists*, p. 432: "If we think that God had made the world only for us, it is a great blunder." That debunks the Pangloss image of Leibniz's thought in Volatire's lampoon, *Candide*.

38. *Principles of Nature and Grace*, #10, L, p. 417.

39. *Theodicy*, pp. 123ff.

40. "On the Ultimate Origination of Things," L, pp. 347ff.

41. Ibid., p. 349.

42. Ibid., p. 347.

43. Job, 38: 4.

44. Loemker, "Leibniz and Our Time," p. 9.

45. Hans-Georg Gadamer, *Truth and Method*, G. Barden and J. Cumming (tsl.), New York: Crossroad, 1982, pp. 325ff, and *Reason in the Age of Science*, F. Lawrence (tsl.), Cambridge: MIT Press, 1983, esp. pp. 44-45; Jürgen Habermas, *Communication and the Evolution of Society*, T. McCarthy (tsl.), Boston: Beacon, 1979; Richard Rorty, *Philosophy and the Mirror of Nature*, Princeton: Princeton University Press, 1979, esp. pp. 389ff; cf. Richard Bernstein, *Beyond Objectivism and Relativism: Science, Hermeneutics and Praxis*, Philadelphia:University of Pennsylvania Press, 1983.

Chapter 13. Immanuel Kant

1. Kant, *CPR*. Unnamed references in this chapter are to Kant.

2. .*FMM*.

3. *CPrR*.

4. Friedrick Paulsen, *Immanuel Kant: His Life and Doctrine*, J. Creighton and A. Lefevre (tsl.), New York: Ungar, 1972, p. 53.

5. *CPrR*, Conclusion, p. 166.

6. *Critique of Judgment*, #23, J. H. Bernard (tsl.), New York: Harper, 1966, pp. 82ff. (Henceforth *CJ*.)

7. Rudolf Otto, *The Idea of the Holy*, J. Harvey (tsl.), New York:Oxford University Press, 1958, pp. 12-40.

8. *CPrR*, Bk. II, V, pp. 128-36.

9. Cf. *supra*, p. 190.

10. Cf. *supra*, pp. 56 and 95.

11. Sequence of the Roman Catholic Mass for the Feast of Corpus Christi.

12. *ST*, I, 84, 1.

13. *CJ*, #77, pp. 253ff; cf. also #88, pp. 307-08 and #90, pp. 315-17.

14. *CPR*, B 72, p. 90 and A 68 (B93), p. 105. Cf. M. Heidegger, *Kant and the Problem of Metaphysics*, J. Churchill (tsl.), Bloomington: Indiana University Press, 1965, #6, pp. 30-39.

15. *CPR*, Bxv, p. 22.

16. *Prolegomena to Any Future Metaphysics*, P. Carus (tsl.), revised by J. Ellingtion, Indianapolis: Hackett, 1977, first part, remark III, p. 34.

17. Heidegger, *BT*, pp. 78ff.

18. Cf. *supra*, pp. 68f.

19. Cf. *supra* ch. 9, pp. 163ff, and ch. 10, pp. 177ff.

20. "Transcendental Aesthetic," *CPR*, pp. 65-91.

21. "Transcendental Analytic," *CPR*, bk I, sec. 3, pp. 111-19.

22. "Transcendental Dialectic," *CPR*, bk I, pp. 308-26.

23. *CPR*, A 51 (B 75), p. 93.

24. *CPR*, B 38 (A 24)f, pp. 68-69.

25. *CPR*, A 33 (B 50), p. 77.

26. *CPR*, A 23, n. 3, pp. 68-69.

27. *CPR*, B viii, p. 17.

28. D. P. Dyer, *Kant's Solution for Verification in Metaphysics*, London: George Allen and Unwin, 1966, pp. 74ff.

29. *CPR*, A 70 (B 95), p. 107.

30. *CPR*, A 55 (B 79), pp. 95ff.

31. *CPR*, A 137 (B 176), pp. 180ff.

32. *CPR*, A 141, p. 183.

33. *CPR*, B 131, pp. 152ff.

34. Cf. *supra*, pp. 230ff.

35. *CPR*, A 304 (B 361), p. 304.

36. *CPR*, A 340 (B 398), p. 328.

37. Cf. *supra*, pp. 171ff.

38. Aristotle, *Physics*, VIII, 1, 251bff.

39. *CPR*, A 532 (B 560)-A 558 (B 586), pp. 464-79.

40. *CPR*, A 344, (B 402), pp. 331ff.

41. *CPR*, A 358, p. 339.

42. *CPR*, A 590 (B 618), pp. 499-500.

43. *CPR*, A 598 (B 626), pp. 504-05. On Aquinas, cf. *supra*, pp. 182ff.

44. *CPR*, A 603, (B 631), pp. 507ff.

45. David Hume, *Dialogues Concerning Natural Religion*, N. K. Smith (ed.), Indianapolis: Bobbs-Merrill, 1947; CPR, A 620 (B 648), pp. 518ff.

46. Arthur Schopenhauer, *The World as Will and Representation*, #28, pp. 153ff.

47. *CPR*, B viiiff, pp. 17ff.

48. *CPR*, A 11 (B 25), p. 59.

49. Besides the *Critique of Practical Reason* and the *Foundation of the Metaphysics of Morals*, there are *The Metaphysics of Morals*, with two parts: *The Metaphysical Elements of Justice*, J. Ladd (tsl.), Indianapolis: Bobbs-Merrill, 1965; and *The Metaphysical Principles of Virtue*, J. Ellington (tsl.), Indianapolis:Bobbs-Merrill, 1964; *Lectures on Ethics*, L. Infield (tsl.), Indianapolis: Hackett, 1963. *Religion within the Limits of Reason Alone*, T. Greene and H. Hudson (tsl.), New York: Harper, 1960, presents an ethical interpretation of religion.

50. *CPR*, B xxx, p. 29. On superstition and fanaticism, cf. *Religion within the Limits of Reason Alone*, pp. 48 and 162-63.

51. *CPR*, p. 29, pp. 107ff; *FMM*, pp. 64-67.

52. *FMM*, pp. 31ff.

53. *FMM*, p. 39.

54. *FMM*, p. 47.

55. *FMM*, pp. 29 and 51; *CPrR*, pp. 33-34.

56. *FMM*, pp. 49 and 55.

57. *FMM*, pp. 54-55.

58. *CPrR*. pp. 114 and 126ff.

59. *CPrR*, pp. 128ff; *CPR*, A 804 (B 832), pp. 635ff.

60. *CJ*, #86, pp. 292ff.

61. *CJ*, Introduction, v, p. 21.

62. *CJ*, #9, p. 52; #13, p. 59.

63. *CJ*, #2, p. 38.

64. *CJ*, #10 and 11, pp. 54ff.

65. *CJ*, #60, p. 202.

66. *CJ*, #23, pp. 82ff.

67. *CJ*, #28, p. 101.

68. *CJ*, #59, p. 200.

69. *CJ*, #46, p. 150.

70. *CJ*, #49, p. 157.

71. *CJ*, #61, p. 206.

72. *CJ*, #64-65, pp. 216ff.

73. *CJ*, #64, p. 217.

74. *CJ*, #63, pp. 212ff.

75. *CJ*, #82, pp. 274ff.

76. *CJ*, #83-84, pp. 279ff.

77. For an approach to the Kantian project based on the third critique, cf. my "Aesthetics within the Kantian Project," to appear in D. Dahlstrom (ed.), *Philosophy and Art*, Washington, D.C.: Catholic University of America Press, 1990.

78. Jaspers, *Reason and Existenz*, pp. 141ff.

79. Cf. *CJ*, #91, pp. 318ff.

80. H. J. Paton, *Kant's Metaphysic of Experience*, 2 vols., New York: Macmillan, 1951.

81. Paul Ricoeur, *Husserl: An Analysis of His Phenomenology*, E. Ballard and L. Embree (tsl.), Evanston: Northwestern University Press, 1967, p. 201.

82. Cf. Hegel, *Logic EPS*, I, p. 77.

83. *CPR*, B x1, p. 34n; Heidegger, *BT*, p. 249.

84. Buber, *I and Thou*, pp. 135-36.

Chapter 14. G. W. F. Hegel

1. Hegel, *LHP*, vol. 3, pp. 428-29. Unnamed references in this chapter are to Hegel.

2. *Logic ESP*, I, pp. 68ff.

3. *PS*, #20, p. 11.

4. On Absolute Knowing see *PS*, #788ff, pp. 479ff.

5. G. Lessing, *Die Erziehung des Menschengeschlechts*, #4, Stuttgart: Reclam, 1965, p. 8.

6. See Karl Rahner, *Foundations of Christian Faith*, W. Dych (tsl.), New York: Seabury, 1978, for a development of these ideas.

7. *PM, EPS*, III, #573, pp. 302-13.

8. *On Christianity: Early Theological Writings*, T. M. Knox (tsl.), New York: Harper, 1961, p. 312. The expression is repeated in the *Logic*, p. 74.

9. This has been central to our exposition in part 1. Cf. *supra*, pp. 00ff and p. 000.

10. Plato, *Symposium*, 200.

11. *Logic*, pp. 82ff.

12. *PS*, #90-165, pp. 58-103.

13. *PS*, #166-196, pp. 104-119.

14. Cf. ch. 1, p. 12.

15. *PS*, #199, p. 121.

16. *PS*, #202-205, pp. 123-26.

17. *PS*, #206-230, pp. 126-38.

18. Ludwig Feuerbach, *The Essence of Christianity*, G. Eliot (tsl.), New York: Harper, 1957, p. 13.

19. Arthur Schopenhauer, *The World as a Will and Representation*, IV, #54, pp. 189ff.

20. Friedrich Nietzsche, *Anti-Christ*, #18, published with *Twilight of the Idols*, p. 128; *Birth of Tragedy*, p. 11; *Geneaology of Morals*, p. 199.

21. *PS*, #231-437, pp. 139-262.

22. *PS*, #438-671, pp. 263-409.

23. *PS*, #672-787, pp. 410-78.

24. *PS*, #788-807, pp. 479-93.

25. *Logic*, pp. 82ff.

26. Nietzsche, *Twilight of the Idols*, p. 37.

27. *Logic*, p. 85.

28. *PS*, #808, p. 493; also *Logic*, pp. 734ff.

29. *Lectures on the Philosophy of Religion*, vol. 1, E. Speirs and J. Burdon Sunderson (tsl.), New York: Humanities Press, 1962, p. 10 (henceforth *LPR*).

30. *Logic*, p. 538. Cf. also *PM*, #389, *Zusatz*, pp. 30-34 and #573, pp. 307-10.

31. *PS*, Preface, #17ff.

32. Harris, *Nature, Mind and Modern Science*, pp. 228-55 and 439-52. Cf. the entire argument of Harris's *FSM*.

33. *Logic*, pp. 88-89.

34. *Logic*: on quality, pp. 81-184; on quantity, pp. 185-326; on measure, pp. 327-88.

35. *Logic*, pp. 389ff.

36. *Logic*, pp. 575ff.

37. *The Encyclopaedia of the Philosophical Sciences* traces this development in three large phases, from the Logic (God apart from the world), through Nature to Spirit.

38. *Hegel's Philosophy of Nature, EPS*, II, p. 15.

39. Ibid., pp. 299ff and 356.

40. Cf. *supra*, pp. 257ff; cf. *Logic, EPS* I, #205ff, pp. 267ff.

41. *PM*, #403, pp. 92ff.

42. *PM*, #381, p. 8; #410, *Zusatz*, p. 145.

43. *PM*, #474, p. 235; #482, p. 239, #483-552, pp. 241-91; *Hegel's Philosophy of Right*, T. M. Knox (tsl.), New York: Oxford, 1967.

44. *PS*, #788-808, pp. 479-93; *PM*, #553-577, pp. 292-315.

45. *PM*, #557, p. 293. Cf. the lengthy *Lectures on Fine Art* for a rich development of this region.

46. *Aesthetics: Lectures on Fine Art*, vol. 1, T. Knox (tsl.), Oxford: Clarendon Press, 1975 (henceforth *LFA*).

47. *LFA*, I, pp. 332ff.

48. *LFA*, I, pp. 427ff, especially pp. 431-36.

49. *LFA*, II, pp. 792-96.

50. *LFA*, I, pp. 85-89.

51. *LFA*, II, pp. 797ff.

52. *LFA*, II, pp. 888ff.

53. *LFA*, II, pp. 971ff.

54. *LPR*, I, pp. 20ff.

55. *LPR*, I, p. 4.

56. *LPR*, I, pp. 270ff.

57. *Philosophy of Nature, EPS*, II, #245-252, pp. 4-27.

58. *LPR*, II, pp. 170ff.

59. *LPR*, III, pp. 7ff.

60. *LPR*, III, p. 73.

61. *LPR*, III, pp. 97ff.

62. *LHP*, III, pp. 409-10, 545-54.

63. *LPR*, I, p. 4.

64. *LPR*, I, pp. 18ff.

65. *PS*, #527, pp. 321ff.

66. *LPR*, II, 327ff.

67. *LHP*, I, pp. 171ff.

68. *LHP*, I, pp. 249ff.

69. *LHP*, II, pp. 1ff.

70. *LHP*, II, pp. 117ff.

71. *PM*, #378, p. 3; #577, p. 315.

72. *LHP*, I, p. 19; *LHP*, III, pp. 545ff.

73. *LHP*, I, pp. 71ff.

74. *LHP*, III, pp. 217ff. See especially pp. 250-52.

75. *LHP*, III, pp. 252ff. See especially p. 288

76. *LHP*, III, pp. 325ff. See especially p. 348.

77. *LHP*, III, pp. 423ff. See especially p. 444.

78. *LHP*, III, pp. 409-10.

79. Cf. Harris, *Hypothesis and Perception*, pp. 372ff.

80. Herbert Marcuse, *Reason and Revolution: Hegel and the Rise of Social Theory*, Boston: Beacon, 1960, pp. 251ff.

81. Aristotle, *Politics*, VII, 10, 1329 b 24.

82. Cited in Ronald Clark, *Einstein*, p. 18.

83. Aquinas, *ST*, I-I, Qs. 1.

84. Hegel, *Philosophy of History*, J. Sibree (tsl.), New York: Dover, 1956, p. 456.

85. Karl Marx, *Capital*, vol. 3, E. Untermann (tsl.), Chicago:Charles Kerr, 1905, p. 954.

86. Karl Marx, *Theses on Feuerbach*, appendix to Frederick Engels, *Ludwig Feuerbach and the Outcome of Classical German Philosophy*, New York: International Publishers, 1967, p. 84.

87. Cf. Jaspers, *Reason and Existenz*, pp. 23ff.

88. Sören Kierkegaard, *CUP*, pp. 169ff.

Chapter 15. Alfred North Whitehead

1. Harris, *Nature, Mind and Modern Science*, p. 415.

2. Cf. Charles Harthshorne and William Reese, *Philosophers Speak of God*, Chicago: University of Chicago Press, 1969, pp. 273-85, for an explicit treatment of Whitehead. The index listings on Whitehead are longer than for any other thinker.

3. Whitehead, *PR*, p. 11. Unnamed references in this chapter are to Whitehead.

4. *PR*, part 2, ch. 4, sect. 4, pp. 147ff.

5. Whitehead, *SMW*, pp. 39-55, pp. 100ff.

6. *PR*, part 2, ch. 1, sect. 1, p. 63; *Adventures of Ideas*, New York: Free Press, 1967, p. 228 (henceforth *AI*).

7. *PR*, part II, ch. 1, sect. 1, p. 63.

8. *SMW*, p. 17; *PR*, part 1, ch. 2, sect. 3, pp. 100ff.

9. *SMW*, pp. 39-55.

10. A. N. Whitehead, *Modes of Thought*, New York: Capricorn, 1958, p. 211 (henceforth *MT*).

11. *MT*, pp. 208ff.

12. *SMW*, p. 65.

13. *PR*, part 1, ch. 2, sect. 2, pp. 34-35.

14. *MT*, p. 13.

15. *AI*, pp. 111-13.

16. *PR*, p. 68. Cf. also C. S. Peirce, "The Doctrine of Necessity Examined," *Philosophical Writings of Peirce*, J. Buchler (ed.), New York: Dover, 1955, pp. 334-35.

17. *MT*, p. 212.

18. *AI*, pp. 176ff.

19. *PR*, part 3, ch. 1, sect. 2, pp. 337ff; part 2, ch. 1, sect. 5, pp. 443ff.

20. John Ruskin, "The Pathetic Fallacy," *Selections and Essays*, F. Roe (ed.), New York: Scribners, 1918, pp. 114-30.

21. *SMW*, pp. 75-94.

22. *PR*, part 3, ch. 3, sect. 3, pp. 379ff; ch. 2, sect. 2, p. 366.

23. *PR*, part 2, ch. 6, sect. 3, p. 224.

24. *AI*, pp. 203ff.

25. *PR*, part 2, ch. 3, sect. 2, p. 138.

26. Locke, *An Essay Concerning Human Understanding*, bk. 2, ch. 22, 2.

27. Cf. *supra*, pp. 162ff.

28. *SMW*, p. 123.

29. Aristotle, *Physics*, II, 8; Empedocles, *PrP*, pp. 336ff.

30. *PR*, part 5, ch. 2, pp. 519ff.

31. *SMW*, pp. 173-79; *PR*, part 2, ch. 3, sect. 1, p. 135.

32. Sartre, *BN*, pp. 438ff.

33. *PR*, part 1, ch. 1, sect. 4, pp. 14ff.

34. *PR*, part 1, ch. 2, sect. 4, p. 44; *AI*, p. 237.

35. Cf. Charles Harthshorne, "The Standpoint of Panentheism," *Philosophers Speak of God*, pp. 1-25.

36. *PR*, part 1, ch. 1, sect. 1, p. 11.

37. *AI*, pp. 119ff; cf. *Sophist*, 249.

38. *AI*, pp. 147, 274ff, and 284.

39. Plato, *Timaeus*, 49f.

40. *AI*, p. 150.

41. *Timaeus*, 30c.

42. *PR*, p. v; *SMW*, p. 150.

43. *Symposium*, 207.

44. *AI*, pp. 11, 148.

45. *AI*, pp. 273ff.

46. *Timaeus*, 30 and 49f.

47. *AI*, pp. 69ff.

48. Cf. Errol Harris, *FMS* and *Nature, Mind and Modern Science*.

49. *ST*, I, 23, 1-8.

Chapter 16. Martin Heidegger

1. Heidegger, *QCT*, especially the essays entitled "The Age of the World Picture" and "Science and Reflection." Cf. also his *What Is a Thing?* F. Wieck and J. Glenn Gray (tsl.), Chicago: Regnery, 1967, esp. pp. 65ff. Unnamed references in this chapter are to Heidegger.

2. *BT*, p. 50.

3. See my "Phenomenology" scheduled to appear in G. McLean (ed.), *Reading the Philosophers*, New York: University Press of America, 1989.

4. Edmund Husserl, "Philosophy as a Strict Science," in *Phenomenology and the Crisis of Philosophy*, Q. Lauer (tsl.), New York: Harper and Row, 1965, pp. 71ff.

5. Max Scheler, *Formalism in Ethics*, pp. 295ff.

6. *WBG*, pp. 206-21.

7. *BT*, pp. 27 and 67ff.

8. Cf. Heidegger "Letter on Humanism," in *Basic Writings*, D. Krell (ed.), New York: Harper and Row, 1977, p. 214.

9. Heidegger, *Identity and Difference*, J. Staubaugh (tsl.), New York: Harper and Row, 1969, pp. 42-74; *WB, pp. 217f.*

10. Ibid.

11. *"On the Essence of Truth," Basic Writings*, pp. 117ff.

12. *BT*, pp. 78ff.

13. Kant, *CPR*, B x1, p. 34n.

14. *BT*, p. 249.

15. *BT*, p. 174.

16. Husserl, *Ideas*, pp. 119ff.

17. *BT*, p. 90.

18. Cf. *supra*, p. 210.

19. Heidegger, *Poetry, Language, Thought*, A. Hofstadter (tsl.), New York: Harper, 1971, pp. 106ff. (henceforth *PLT*); *BT*, pp. 401-2.

20. "On the Essence of Truth", *Basic Writings*, p. 132.

21. *OWA*, in *PLT*, p. 26; *BT*, p. 207.

22. *BT*, pp. 188ff.

23. *BT*, pp. 114ff.

24. *BT*, pp. 79ff.

25. *BT*, p. 47.

26. *BT*, pp. 279ff.

27. *BT*, p. 332.

28. *BT*, pp. 42-43.

29. Heidegger, *On Time and Being*, J. Stambaugh (tsl.), New York: Harper and Row, 1972, pp. 19ff; *OWL*, pp. 127ff.

30. "Poetically Man Dwells . . . " in *PLT*, pp. 213-29.

31. *What Is a Thing?*, pp. 85ff; *QCT*, p. 119.

32. *PLT*, pp. 149-51, 172-74, 199.

33. *PLT*, pp. 41-56.

34. *BT*, p. 205; *OWL*, pp. 98-101; *PLT*, p. 208; see my "Heidegger on the Way to Language," *Semiotics, 1985*, J. Deely (ed.), New York: University Press of America, 1987.

35. *QTC*, pp. 26-28.

36. *OWL*, p. 107.

37. *PLT*, p. 223.

38. "Hölderlin and the Essence of Poetry," in *Existence and Being*, W. Brock (ed.), Chicago: Regnery, 1959, pp. 270-91.

39. *PLT*, p. 174.

40. *PLT*, p. 203.

41. *IM*, p. 63.

42. *QCT*, pp. 17-20.

43. *OWA*, in *PLT*, pp. 48ff.

44. Heidegger, *WCT* pp. 138ff.

45. *QCT*, pp. 157ff.

46. Friedrich Nietzsche, *Thus Spake Zarathustra*, II, 12, in *The Portable Nietzsche*, W. Kaufmann (ed. and tsl.), New York: Viking, 1958, p. 225.

47. *Discourse on Thinking*, J. Anderson and E. H. Freund (tsl.), New York: Harper and Row, 1966, pp. 54-56.

48. *Kant and the Problem of Metaphysics*, pp. 131ff.

49. Cf. Heidegger, "Plato's Doctrine of Truth," in *Philosophy in the Twentieth Century*, vol. 3, W. Barrett and H. Aiken (eds.), New York: Random House, 1962, pp. 251-70.

50. Heidegger, *Early Greek Thinking*, D. Kreel and F. Capuzzi (tsl.), New York: Harper and Row, 1984, pp. 59-78; *IM*, pp. 127ff.

51. Cf. "Plato's Doctrine of Truth," pp. 251-70.

52. *What Is Philosophy?*, pp. 78-85.

53. In *QCT*, p. 85, Heidegger gives a thumbnail sketch of "the history of truth," which we have followed here.

54. *OWL*, pp. 90ff.

55. Buber, *I and Thou*, pp. 115-16.

56. Buber, *Between Man and Man*, R. G. Smith, tsl., Boston: Beacon, 1961, pp. 163-81.

57. Emmanuel Levinas, *Totality and Infinity*, A. Lingis (tsl.), Pittsburgh: Duquesne University Press, 1969, pp. 45, 298.

58. Edith Wyschograd, *Spirit in Ashes: Hegel, Heidegger and Man-Made Mass Death*, New Haven: Yale University Press, 1985, p. 203.

Epilogue

1. Paul Ricouer, *Freud and Philosophy*, D. Savage (tsl.), New Haven, Yale University Press, 1970, pp. 33 and 43ff; also by Ricoeur, *Conflict of Interpretations*, D. Ihde (tsl.), Evanston: Northwestern University Press, 1978, p. 17.

2. Cf. Lonergan, *Insight*, pp. 335ff.

.3 Cf. Aquinas, *ST*, I, 79, 4.

4. Paul Ricouer, "The History of Philosophy and the Unity of Truth," in *History and Truth*, C. Kelbley (tsl.), Evanston:Northwestern University Press, 1965, pp. 41-56.

5. Gadamer, *Truth and Method*, p. 273.

Bibliography

Abbott, Edwin. *Flatland.* New York: Barnes and Noble, 1963.

Anderson, J. *Introduction to the Metaphysics of St. Thomas Aquinas.* Chicago: Regnery, 1953.

Anselm. *Proslogion, Opera Ommia.* Vol. 1. F. Schmitt, ed.. Stuttgart: Friedrich Frommann, 1968.

Aquinas, Thomas. *Commentary on the Metaphysics of Aristotle.* 2 vols. J. Rowan, tsl. Chicago: Regnery, 1961.

————. *On Being and Essence,* A. Manrer, tsl. Toronto: Pontifical Institute of Medieval Studies, 1983.

————. *Expositio Super Librum Boethii De Trinitate (Commentary on Boethius's De Trinitate).* B. Decker, ed. Leiden: E. Brill, 1965.

————. *On the Power of God (De Potentia Dei).* 3 vols. L. Shapcote, ed. New York: Benzinger, 1932-4.

————. *Summa Contra Gentiles.* 4 vols. A. Pegis et. al., tsl. Notre Dame, Ind.: Notre Dame University Press, 1955.

————. *Summa Theologica.* 3 vols. Fathers of the English Dominican Province, tsl. New York: Benzinger, 1947.

————. *Truth (De Veritate).* 3 vols. R. Mulligan, tsl. Chicago: Regnery, 1952.

Aristotle. *Categories.* H. Cooke, tsl. Cambridge: Harvard University Press, 1962.

————. *Metaphysics.* 2 vols. H. Tredennick, tsl. Cambridge: Harvard University Press, 1967.

————. *Nicomachean Ethics.* H. Rackham, tsl. Cambridge: Harvard University Press, 1975.

————. *Physics.* 2 vols. P. Wicksteed and F. Cornford, tsl. Cambridge: Harvard University Press, 1980.

————. *The Politics of Aristotle.* E. Barker, tsl. Cambridge: Oxford University Press, 1970.

_____. *Posterior Analytics.* H. Tredennick, tsl. Cambridge: Oxford University Press, 1960.

_____. *On Sophistical Refutations* and *On Coming-to-Be and Passing Away,* E. S. Forster, tsl. Cambridge: Harvard University Press, 1955.

_____. *On the Soul.* W. Hett, tsl. Cambridge: Harvard University Press, 1975.

Augustine. *Confessions.* 2 vols. W. Watts, tsl. Cambridge: Harvard University Press, 1977.

Ayer, A. J. *Language, Truth and Logic.* New York: Dover, 1946.

Bacon, Francis. *Novum Organum.* F. Anderson (ed.). New York: Liberal Arts Press, 1960.

Barfield, Owen. *Saving the Appearance.* New York: Harcourt, Brace and World, n.d.

Beck, L. J. *The Metaphysics of Descartes.* Oxford: Clarendon, 1967.

Bergson, Henri. *Creative Evolution.* A. Mitchell, tsl. New York: Modern Library, 1944.

_____. *The Creative Mind.* M. Andison, tsl. New York: Philosophical Library, 1946.

_____. *Two Sources of Morality and Religion.* R. Andra, C. Brereton, and W. Carter, tsl. Garden City, N. Y.: Doubleday, 1935.

Berkeley, George. *Three Dialogues between Hylas and Philonous.* La Salle, Ill.: Open Court, 1945.

_____. *Philosophical Commentaries, The Works of George Berkeley.* Vol. 1. A. Luce and T. Jessop, eds. London: Nelson, 1948.

Berstein, Richard. *Beyond Objectivism and Relativism: Science, Hermeneutics and Praxis.* Philadelphia: University of Pennsylvania Press, 1983.

Blake, William. *The Complete Writings of William Blake.* G. Keyes, ed. London: Oxford University Press, 1966.

_____. *The Poetry and Prose of William Blake.* D. Erdman (ed.). Garden City, N.Y.: Doubleday, 1970.

Bloom, Allan. "Interpretive Essay." In *The Republic of Plato.* New York: Basic Books, 1968.

Bonaventure, *De Septem Donis Spiritus Sancti, Opera Omnia.* Vol. 7. A. C. Peltier, ed. Paris: Vives, 1866.

_____. *In Hexaemeron, Opera Omnia.* Vol. 5. Quarrachi: College of St. Bonaventure, 1891.

Brann, Eva. "The Music of the *Republic.*" *Agon* 1 (1966), pp. 1-117.

Broad, C. D. *Scientific Thought.* London: Routledge and Kegan Paul, 1923.

Buber, Martin. *Between Man and Man.* R. G. Smith, tsl. Boston: Beacon, 1961.

———. *Daniel: Dialogues on Realization.* M. Friedman, tsl. New York: McGraw-Hill, 1965.

———. *I and Thou.* W. Kaufmann, tsl. New York: Scribners, 1970.

———. *The Knowledge of Man.* M. Friedman and R. G. Smith, tsl. New York: Harper and Row, 1965.

Buchler, J., ed. *Philosophical Writings of Peirce.* New York: Dover, 1955.

Calvin, Jean. *Institutes of the Christian Religion.* J. McNeill, ed. F. Battles, tsl. Philadelphia: Westminster Press, 1960.

Camus, Albert. *The Myth of Sisyphus.* J. O'Brien, tsl. New York: Random House, 1955.

Cannon, William. *The Wisdom of the Body.* New York: Norton, 1963.

Cassirer, Ernst. *An Essay on Man.* New York: Doubleday, 1944.

———. *The Individual and the Cosmos in Renaissance Philosophy.* M. Domandi, tsl. New York: Harper, 1963.

———. *Kant's Life and Thought.* J. Haden, tsl. New Haven: Yale University Press, 1981.

Chenu, M. D. *Toward Understanding St. Thomas.* A Landry and D. Hughes, tsl. Chicago: Regnery, 1964.

Clark, Ronald. *Einstein: The Life and Times.* New York: World, 1971.

Comte, Auguste. *Cours de philosophie positive.* Vol. 1. Paris: Editions Anthropos, 1968.

Coreth, Emerich. *Metaphysics.* J. Donceel, tsl. New York: Herder and Herder, 1968.

Cornman, J. "Philosophical Analysis and the Future of Metaphysics." In R. Wood, ed. *The Future of Metaphysics.* Chicago: Quadrangle, 1970, pp. 32-49.

Cusanus, Nicholas. *Of Learned Ignorance.* J. Hopkins, ed. and tsl. Minneapolis: Arthur J. Banning Press, 1981.

de Chardin, Pierre Teilhard. *The Phenomenon of Man.* B. Wall, tsl. New York: Harper, 1959.

de Finance, Joseph. "Being and Subjectivity." In *A Modern Introduction to Metaphysics.* D. A. Drennan, ed. New York: Free Press of Glencoe, 1962, pp. 272-282.

Descartes, René. *Discourse on Method.* In *Philosophical Writings of Descartes.* Vol. 1. E. Haldane and G. Ross, eds. and tsl. New York: Dover, 1955.

_____. "Letter to Picot," *Principles of Philosophy.* Vol. 2. Haldane and Ross.

_____. *Meditations on the First Philosophy.* Vol. 1. Haldane and Ross.

_____. *Passions of the Soul.* Vol. 1. Haldane and Ross.

Dessauer, Philipp. *Natural Meditation.* New York: Kennedy, 1965.

DeWitt, Norman Wentworth. *Epicurus and His Philosophy.* Minneapolis: University of Minnesota Press, 1954.

Dilthey, Wilhelm. *Pattern and Meaning in History.* H. P. Rickman, ed. New York: Harper, 1962.

Dionysius the Areopagite. *The Divine Names.* C. Rolt, tsl. London: SPCK, 1983.

Dreyfuss, Hubert. *What Computers Can't Do.* New York: Harper and Row, 1979.

Dubos, René. *A God Within.* New York: Scribners, 1972.

Dyer, D. P. *Kant's Solution for Verification in Metaphysics.* London: George Allen and Unwin, 1966.

Ebert, H. "Man as the Way to God." R. Wood, tsl. In *Philosophy Today* 10, no. 2 (Summer 1966) 88-106.

Eckhart, Meister. *Meister Eckhart, a Modern Translation.* R. Blakney, tsl. New York: Harper and Row, 1941.

Einstein, Albert. *Ideas and Opinions.* S. Bargmann, tsl. New York: Bonanza, 1954.

Elias, Julius. *Plato's Defense of Poetry.* Albany: State University of New York Press, 1984.

Eliot, T. S. *Four Quartets.* London: Faber and Faber, 1945.

Engels, Frederick, *Ludwig Feuerbach and the Outcome of Classical German Philosophy.* New York: International Publishers, 1967.

Epicurus, "Principal Doctrines." In *The Stoic and Epicurean Philosophers.* W. J. Oates, ed. New York: Modern Library, 1940.

Feuer, L. *Spinoza and the Rise of Liberalism.* Boston: Beacon, 1966.

Feuerbach, Ludwig. *The Essence of Christianity.* G. Eliot, tsl. New York: Harper, 1957.

Feyerabend, Paul. *Against Method.* London: Verso, 1978.

Foster, K. *The Life of Saint Thomas Aquinas.* Baltimore: Helicon Press, 1959.

Freud, Sigmund. *Civilization and Its Discontents.* J. Strachey, tsl. New York: Norton, 1961.

————. *The Ego and the Id.* J. Riviere, tsl. New York: Norton, 1960.

Fromm, Eric. *Beyond the Chains of Illusion: My Encounters with Marx and Freud.* New York: Pocket Books, 1963.

Gadamer, Hans-Georg. *Reason in the Age of Science.* F. Lawrence, tsl. Cambridge: MIT Press, 1983.

————. *Truth and Method.* G. Barden and J. Cumming tsl. New York: Crossroad, 1982.

Garrett, W. Introduction to E. Abbott, *Flatland.* New York: Barnes and Noble, 1963.

Gilson, Etienne. *The Christian Philosophy of St. Thomas Aquinas.* L. Shook, tsl. New York: Random House, 1956.

————. *History of Christian Philosophy in the Middle Ages.* New York: Random House, 1955.

————. *The Unity of Philosophical Experience.* New York: Scribners, 1937.

Goudge, Thomas, "Evolutionism." In *Dictionary of the History of Ideas.* Philip Wiener, ed. New York: Scribners, 1973, pp. 174-189.

Gurwitsch, Aaron. *The Field of Consciousness.* Pittsburgh: Duquesne University Press, 1965.

Habermas, Jürgen. *Communication and the Evolution of Society.* T. McCarthy, tsl. Boston: Beacon, 1979.

Hampshire, Stuart. *Spinoza.* London: Penguin, 1952.

Hare, R. M. *Freedom and Reason.* Oxford: Clarendon, 1963.

Harris, Errol. *The Foundations of Metaphysics in Science.* New York: University Press of America, 1983.

————. *Hypothesis and Perception.* London: Routledge and Kegan Paul, 1972.

————. *Nature, Mind and Modern Science.* London: George Unwin, 1968.

Hart, Charles. *Thomistic Metaphysics.* Engelwood Cliffs, N. J.: Prentice-Hall, 1959.

Hartshorne, Charles and William Reese, eds. *Philosophers Speak of God.* Chicago: University of Chicago Press, 1969.

Hazard, Paul. *The European Mind, 1680-1715.* J. Lewis May, tsl. New York: Meridian, 1971.

Heer, Friedrich. *The Medieval World: Europe, 1000-1350.* J. Sondheimer, tsl. New York: Mentor, 1963.

Hegel, G. W. F. *Aesthetics: Lectures on Fine Art.* T. Knox, tsl. Oxford: Clarendon Press, 1975.

_____. *Hegel's Logic.* part 1 of *The Encyclopaedia of the Philosophical Sciences.* William Wallace, tsl. Oxford: Clarendon Press, 1975.

_____. *Hegel's Philosophy of Mind.* part 3 of *The Encyclopaedia of the Philosophical Sciences.* W. Wallace and A. V. Miller, tsl. Oxford: Clarendon Press, 1973.

_____. *Hegel's Philosophy of Nature.* part 2 of *The Encyclopaedia of the Philosophical Sciences.* William Wallace, tsl. Oxford: Clarendon Press, 1974.

_____. *Hegel's Philosophy of Right.* T. M. Knox, tsl. London: Oxford, 1967.

_____. *Hegel's Science of Logic.* A. V. Miller, tsl. London: George Allen and Unwin, 1959.

_____. *Lectures on the Philosophy of Religion.* E. Speirs and J. Burdon Sunderson, tsl. New York: Humanities Press, 1962.

_____. *On Christianity: Early Theological Writings.* T. M. Knox, tsl. New York: Harper, 1961.

_____. *Philosophy of History.* J. Sibree, tsl. New York: Dover, 1956.

_____. *The Phenomenology of Spirit.* A. Miller, tsl. London: Oxford University Press, 1977.

Heidegger, Martin. *Being and Time.* J. MacQuarrie and E. Robinson, tsl. New York: Harper and Row, 1962.

_____. *Discourse on Thinking.* J. Anderson and E. H. Freund, tsl. New York: Harper and Row, 1966.

_____. *Early Greek Thinking.* D. Kreel and F. Capuzzi, tsl. New York: Harper and Row, 1984.

_____. "Hölderlin and the Essence of Poetry." In *Existence and Being.* W. Brock, ed. Chicago: Regnery, 1959.

_____. *Identity and Difference.* J. Stambaugh, tsl. New York: Harper and Row, 1969.

————. *Introduction to Metaphysics.* R. Mannheim, tsl. New Haven: Yale University Press, 1959.

————. *Kant and the Problem of Metaphysics.* J. Churchill, tsl. Bloomington: Indiana University Press, 1965.

————. "Letter on Humanism." In *Basic Writings.* D. Krell, ed. New York: Harper and Row, 1977, pp. 205ff.

————. "Metaphysics as History of Being." In *The End of Philosophy.* J. Stambaugh, tsl. New York: Harper and Row, 1973.

————. "On the Essence of Truth." *Basic Writings,* D. Krell, ed. New York: Harper and Row, 1977.

————. *On the Way to Language.* P. Hertz, tsl. San Francisco: Harper and Row, 1971.

————. *On Time and Being.* J. Stambaugh, tsl. New York: Harper and Row, 1972.

————. "The Origin of the Work of Art." In *Poetry, Language and Thought.* A. Hofstadter, tsl. New York: Harper and Row, 1971.

————. "Plato's Doctrine of Truth." In *Philosophy in the Twentieth Century.* Vol. 3. W. Barrett and H. Aiken, eds. New York: Random House, 1962, pp. 251-270.

————. *Poetry, Language, Thought.* A. Hofstadter, tsl. New York: Harper, 1971.

————. *The Question Concerning Technology and Other Essays.* W. Lovitt, tsl. New York: Harper and Row, 1977.

————. "The Way Back into the Ground of Metaphysics." In W. Kaufmann, ed. *Existentialism from Dostoevsky to Sartre.* Cleveland: World Publishing, 1956.

————. *What Is a Thing?* F. Wieck and J. Glenn Gray, tsl. Chicago: Regnery, 1967.

————. *What Is Called Thinking?* J. Glenn Gray, tsl. New York: Harper and Row, 1968.

————. "What Is Metaphysics?" In *Basic Writings,* pp. 100-101.

————. *What Is Philosophy?* Wm. Klukbak and J. Wilde, tsl. New York: Twayne, 1958.

Heim, Karl. *Christian Faith and Natural Science.* New York: Harper and Row, 1957.

Hesse, Herman. *Siddhartha.* H. Rosner, tsl. New York: New Directions, 1951.

Hicks, J. and A. McGill, eds. *The Many-Faced Argument*. New York: Macmillan, 1967.

Hobbes, Thomas. *De Corpore*. In T. V. Smith and M. Grene, eds. *From Descartes to Kant*. Chicago: University of Chicago Press, 1950, pp. 168ff.

_____. *Leviathan*. M. Oakeshott, ed. New York: Collier, 1973.

Hume, David. *Dialogues Concerning Natural Religion*. N. K. Smith, ed. Indianapolis: Bobbs-Merrill, 1947.

_____. *An Enquiry Concerning Human Understanding*. Indianapolis: Hackett, 1977.

_____. *Treatise of Human Nature*. 2 vols. D. MacNabb, ed. Glasgow: William Collins, 1962.

Husserl, Edmund. *Cartesian Meditations*. D. Cairns, tsl. The Hague: Martinus Nijhoff, 1960.

_____. *The Crisis of European Sciences and Transcendental Phenomenology*. D. Carr, tsl. Evanston: Northwestern University Press, 1970.

_____. *Experience and Judgement*. J. Churchill and K. Americks, tsl. Evanston: Northwestern University Press, 1973.

_____. *Ideas: General Introduction to Pure Phenomenology*. W. Boyce Gibson, tsl. New York: Macmillan, 1958.

_____. "The Origin of Geometry." In *The Crisis of European Sciences and Transcendental Phenomenology*. David Carr, tsl. Evanston: Northwestern University Press, 1970.

_____. "Phenomenology." C. Solomon, tsl. In *Encyclopaedia Britannica*. Vol. 17. 14th ed., 1972, pp. 699-702.

_____. *Phenomenology of Internal Time-Consciousness*. J. Churchill, tsl. Bloomington: Indiana University Press, 1964.

_____. "Philosophy as A Strict Science." In *Phenomenology and the Crisis of Philosophy*. Q. Lauer, tsl. New York: Harper and Row, 1965, pp. 71ff.

Jaeger, G. Werner. *Paideia: The Ideals of Greek Culture*. 3 vols. G. Highet, tsl. New York: Oxford, 1945.

_____. *The Theology of the Early Greek Philosophers*. Oxford: Clarendon Press, 1960.

James, William. *Varieties of Religious Experience*. New York: Modern Library, 1902.

Jaspers, Karl. *Anselm and Nicholas of Cusa.* R. Mannheim, tsl. New York: Harcourt Brace Jovanovich, 1966.

―――. *Reason and Existenz.* W. Earle, tsl. New York: Noonday, 1959.

Jordan, Mark. "The Grammar of *Esse*: Re-reading Thomas on the Transcendentals." *The Thomist* (1977), pp. 1-26.

Jung, Carl, ed. *Man and His Symbols.* New York: Dell, 1964.

Kant, Immanuel. *Critique of Judgment.* J. H. Bernard, tsl. New York: Harper, 1966.

―――. *Critique of Practical Reason.* L. W. Beck, tsl. Indianapolis: Bobbs-Merrill, 1956.

―――. *Critique of Pure Reason.* N. K. Smith, tsl. New York: St. Martin's, 1929.

―――. *Foundations of the Metaphysics of Morals.* L. W. Beck, tsl. Indianapolis: Bobbs-Merrill, 1959.

―――. *Lectures on Ethics.* L. Infield, tsl. Indianapolis: Hackett, 1963.

―――. *The Metaphysical Elements of Justice.* J. Ladd, tsl. Indianapolis: Bobbs-Merrill, 1965.

―――. *The Metaphysical Principles of Virtue.* J. Ellington, tsl. Indianapolis: Bobbs-Merrill, 1964.

―――. *Prolegomena to Any Future Metaphysics.* P. Carus, tsl., revised by J. W. Ellington. Indianapolis: Hackett, 1977.

―――. *Religion within the Limits of Reason Alone.* T. Greene and H. Hudson, tsl. New York: Harper, 1960.

Keeling, S. V. *Descartes.* London: Oxford University Press, 1968.

Kennington, Richard. "René Descartes." In *History of Political Philosophy.* L. Strauss and J. Cropsey, eds. Chicago: Rand McNally (1963) pp. 379-96.

Kerferd, George Briscoe. "Sophists," In *Encyclopaedia Britannica, Macropaedia,* vol. 17, pp. 11a-14a.

Kierkegaard, Sören. *Concluding Unscientific Postscript to Philosophical Fragments.* D. F. Swenson, tsl. Princeton: Princeton University Press, 1941.

―――. *Fear and Trembling.* W. Lowrie, tsl. Garden City, N.Y.: Doubleday, 1954.

―――. *The Journals of Sören Kierkegaard.* A. Dru, ed. and tsl. London: Oxford University Press, 1959.

Kirk, G. S., and J. E. Raven, eds. *The Presocratic Philosophers.* London: Cambridge University Press, 1966.

Klages, Ludwig. *Der Geist als Widersacher der Seele.* 3 vols., Leipzig: J.A. Barth: 1929-1933.

Klein, Jacob. *A Commentary on Plato's "Meno."* Chapel Hill: University of North Carolina Press, 1965.

Klubertanz, George. *St. Thomas Aquinas on Analogy.* Chicago: Loyola University Press, 1960.

Köhler, Wolfgang. *The Mentality of Apes.* E. Winston, tsl. New York: Harcourt, 1924.

Kristeller, Paul O. *Renaissance Thought.* New York: Harper, 1961.

Kuhn, Thomas. *The Structure of Scientific Revolutions.* 2d ed. Chicago: Chicago University Press, 1970.

Latta, R. Introduction to *Leibniz: The Monadology and Other Philosophical Writings.* London: Oxford University Press, 1951.

_____. Lessing, G. *Die Erziehung des Menschengeschlechts.* Stuttgart: Reclam, 1965.

Leibniz, G. *Discourse on Metaphysics.* In *The Rationalists.* G. Montgomery, tsl. with revisions by A. Chandler. Garden City, N.Y.: Doubleday, 1974.

_____. *Leibniz: The Monadology and Other Philosophical Writings.* R. Latta, ed. London: Oxford University Press, 1951.

_____. *Theodicy: Essays on the Goodness of God, The Freedom of Man and The Origins of Evil.* E. M. Huggard, tsl. LaSalle, Ill.: Open Court, 1985.

Levinas, Emmanuel. *Totality and Infinity.* A. Lingis, tsl. Pittsburgh: Duquesne University Press, 1969.

Locke, John. *Essay Concerning Human Understanding.* 2 vols. A. Fraser, ed. New York: Dover, 1959.

_____. *Second Treatise of Government.* Indianapolis: Bobbs-Merrill, 1952.

Loemker, Leroy. "Leibniz and Our Time." In *The Philosophy of Leibniz and the Modern World.* Ivor LeClerc, ed. Nashville: Vanderbilt University Press, 1973, pp. 1-9.

_____. *Struggle for Synthesis.* Cambridge: Harvard University Press, 1972.

Lonergan, Bernard. *Insight.* London: Longman, Green, 1957.

Lotz, J. B. "Being and Existence in Scholasticism and in Existence Philosophy." R. Wood, tsl. In *Philosophy Today* no. 1 (Spring 1964), pp. 3-45.

―――. "Person and Ontology." *Philosophy Today*, no. 4 (Winter 1963), pp. 279-297.

Loyola, Ignatius. *The Spiritual Exercises of St. Ignatius.* L. J. Puhl, tsl. Westminster, Md.: Newman Press, 1959.

Marcel, Gabriel. *The Mystery of Being.* 2 vols. G. S. Fraser, tsl. Chicago: Regnery, 1960.

Marcuse, Herbert. *Reason and Revolution: Hegel and the Rise of Social Theory.* Boston: Beacon, 1960.

Maritain, Jacques. *Creative Intuition in Art and Poetry.* New York: Meridian, 1955.

―――. *The Degrees of Knowledge.* G. Phelan, tsl. New York: Scribners, 1959.

―――. *The Dream of Descartes.* M. Anderson tsl. New York: Philosophical Library, 1944.

―――. *A Preface to Metaphysics: Seven Lectures on Being.* New York: Mentor, 1962.

―――. *Three Reformers: Luther, Descartes, Rousseau.* London: Sheed Ward, 1950.

Marx, Karl. *Capital.* Volume 3. E. Untermann, tsl. Chicago: Charles Kerr, 1905.

―――. *Theses on Feuerbach.* Appendix to Frederick Engels, *Ludwig Feuerbach and the Outcome of Classical German Philosophy.* New York: International Publishers, 1967.

―――. *Writings of the Young Marx on Philosophy and Society.* L. Easton and K. Guddat, eds. and tsl. Garden City, N.Y.: Doubleday, 1967.

Matson, Floyd. *The Broken Image.* New York: Braziller, 1964.

Maurer, Armand. *Medieval Philosophy.* New York: Random House, 1965.

May, Rollo, ed. *Existence: A New Dimension in Psychotherapy.* New York: Basic Books, 1958.

McLuhan, Marshall. *The Gutenburg Galaxy.* Toronto: University of Toronto Press, 1962.

Merleau-Ponty, Maurice. *Phenomenology of Perception.* C. Smith, tsl. London: Routledge and Kegan Paul, 1962.

―――. *The Structure of Behavior.* A. Fisher, tsl. Boston: Beacon, 1963.

Merton, Thomas. *The Way of Chuang Tzu.* New York: New Directions, 1969.

Meyer, R. W. *Leibniz and the Seventeenth-Century Revolution.* J. Stern, tsl. Chicago: Regnery, 1952.

Mumford, Lewis. *The Myth of the Machine. Techniques and Human Development.* New York: Harcourt Brace Jovanovich, 1967.

Nass, Gisela. *Molecules of Life.* D. Jones, tsl. New York: McGraw-Hill, 1970.

Nietzsche, Friedrich. *The Birth of Tragedy* and *The Genealogy of Morals.* F. Golffing, tsl. Garden City, N.Y.: Doubleday, 1956.

_____. *The Gay Science.* W. Kaufmann, tsl. New York: Vintage, 1974.

_____. "On the Uses and Disadvantages of History for Life." In *Untimely Meditations.* R. J. Hollingdale, tsl. Cambridge: Cambridge University Press, 1983.

_____. *Thus Spake Zarathustra.* in *The Portable Nietzsche.* W. Kaufmann, ed. and tsl. New York: Viking, 1958.

_____. *Twilight of the Idols* and *The Anti-Christ.* R. Hollingdale, tsl. Baltimore: Penguin, 1968.

Otto, Rudolf. *The Idea of the Holy.* J. Harvey, tsl. New York: Oxford University Press, 1958.

Owens, Joseph. *An Elementary Christian Metaphysics.* Milwaukee: Bruce, 1963.

_____. *A History of Ancient Western Philosophy.* New York: Appleton-Century-Crofts, 1959.

_____. *An Interpretation of Existence.* Milwaukee: Bruce, 1968.

Pascal, Blaise. *Penseés.* W. Trotter, tsl. New York: Random House, 1941.

Paton, H. J. *Kant's Metaphysic of Experience.* 2 vols. New York: MacMillan, 1951.

Patterson, Francine. "Conversations with a Gorilla." *National Geographic* 154, no. 4 (October 1978), pp. 438-65.

Paulsen, F. *Immanuel Kant: His Life and Doctrine.* J. Creighton and A. Lefevre, tsl. New York: Ungar, 1972.

Peifer, J. *The Concept in Thomism.* New York: Record Press, 1952.

Peirce, C. S. *Philosophical Writings of Peirce.* J. Buchler, ed. New York: Dover, 1955.

Picard, Max. *The World of Silence.* Chicago:Regnery, 1956.

Pieper, Joseph. *Guide to Thomas Aquinas.* R Winston and C Winston, tsl. New York: Mentor-Omega, 1962.

———. *The Silence of St. Thomas.* J. Murray and D. O'Connor, tsl. New York: Pantheon, 1957.

Plato. *Euthyphro, Apology, Crito, Phaedo, Phaedrus.* H. Fowler tsl. Cambridge: Harvard University Press, 1977.

———. *Laches, Protagoras, Meno* and *Euthydemus.* W. Lamb, tsl. Cambridge: Harvard University Press, 1962.

———. *Lysis, Symposium,* and *Gorgias.* W. Lamb, tsl. Cambridge: Harvard University Press, 1975.

———. *Republic.* 2 vols. P. Shorey, tsl. Cambridge: Harvard University Press, 1969.

———. *Theatetus* and *Sophist.* H. Fowler, tsl. Cambridge: Harvard University Press, 1977.

———. *Timeaus.* R. Bury, tsl. Cambridge: Harvard University Press. 1977.

Plotinus. *The Enneads.* S. MacKenna, tsl. New York: Pantheon, n.d.

Polanyi, Michael. *Personal Knowledge.* New York: Harper and Row, 1964.

———. *The Study of Man.* Chicago: University of Chicago Press, 1958.

———. *The Tacit Dimension.* Garden City, N.Y.: Doubleday, 1966.

Polanyi, Michael and H. Prosch. *Meaning.* Chicago: University of Chicago Press, 1975.

Pollack, Frederick. *Spinoza, His Life and Philosophy.* London: C. Kegan Paul, 1880.

Porphyry. *Life of Plotinus.* In Plotinus, *The Enneads.* S. MacKenna, ed. New York: Pantheon, n.d.

Radhakrishnan, Sarvepalli, and Charles Moore. *A Sourcebook in Indian Philosophy.* Princeton: Princeton University Press, 1973.

Rahner, Karl. *Foundations of Christian Faith.* W. Dych, tsl. New York: Seabury, 1978.

———. *Spirit in the World.* W. Dyche, tsl. New York: Herder and Herder, 1968.

Ricoeur, Paul. *Conflict of Interpretations.* D. Ihde, tsl. Evanston: Northwestern University Press, 1966.

———. *Fallible Man.* C. Kelbley, tsl. Chicago: Regnery, 1965.

———. *Freedom and Nature: The Voluntary and the Involuntary.* E. Kohak, tsl. Evanston: Northwestern University Press, 1966.

_____. *Freud and Philosophy.* D. Savage, tsl. New Haven: Yale University Press, 1970.

_____. *History and Truth.* C. Kelbley, tsl. Evanston: Northwestern University Press, 1965.

_____. *Husserl: An Analysis of His Phenomenology.* E. Ballard and L. Embree, tsl. Evanston: Northwestern University Press, 1967.

_____. *Symbolism of Evil.* E. Buchanan, tsl. Boston: Beacon, 1967.

Rorty, Richard. *Philosophy and the Mirror of Nature.* Princeton: Princeton University Press, 1979.

Ruskin, John. "The Pathetic Fallacy." In *Selections and Essays.* F. Roe, Ed. New York: Scribners, 1918, pp. 114-130.

Russell, Bertrand. *Mysticism and Logic.* London: Longmans, Green, 1918.

Ryle, Gilbert. *The Concept of Mind.* New York: Barnes and Noble, 1949.

St. Francis Assisi. *The Little Flowers of St. Francis.* Translated by R. Brown. Garden City, New York: Doubleday, 1958.

Sallis, John. *Being and Logos.* Pittsburgh: Duquesne University Press, 1974.

Sartre, Jean-Paul. *Being and Nothingness.* H. Barnes, tsl. New York: Harper, 1965.

_____. "Existentialism Is a Humanism." W. Kaufman, tsl. In *Existentialism from Dostoevski to Sartre.* New York: Meridian, 1956, pp. 287ff.

_____. *The Transcendence of the Ego.* F. Williams and R. Kirkpatrick, tsl. New York: Noonday, 1957.

Scheler, Max. *Formalism in Ethics and Non-Formal Ethics of Values.* M. Frings and R. Funk, tsl. Evanston: Northwestern University Press, 1973.

Schelling, F. W. J. *System des Transzendentalen Idealismus, Schriften von 1799-1801.* Darmstadt: Wissenschaftliche Buchgesellschaft, 1982.

Schleiermacher, Friedrich, *On Religion: Speeches to Its Cultured Despisers.* J. Oman, tsl. New York: Harper and Row, 1958.

Schopenhauer, Arthur. *The World as Will and Representation.* 2 vols. E. Payne, tsl. New York: Dover, 1969.

Scotus, John Duns. *Philosophical Writings.* A. Wolter, tsl. Indianapolis: Bobbs-Merrill, 1962.

Sebeok, Thomas. "Talking with Animals: Zoosemiotics Explained." In *Frontiers in Semiotics.* J. Deely et al., eds. Bloomington: Indiana University Press, 1986, pp. 76-82.

Sellars, Wilfrid. *Science, Perception and Reality.* London: Routledge and Kegan Paul, 1963.

Shaffer, Jerome. *Philosophy of Mind.* Englewood Cliffs, N.J.: Prentice-Hall, 1968.

Smith, Gerard. *Natural Theology.* New York: Macmillan, 1951.

_____. Smith, Huston. *Forgotten Truth: The Primordial Tradition.* New York: Harper and Row, 1976.

_____. *The Religions of Man.* New York: Harper, 1958.

Smith, Preserved. *The Enlightenment, 1687-1776.* Vol. 2 of *A History of Modern Culture.* New York: Collier, 1962.

Smythies, J. R. "Aspects of Consciousness." In *Beyond Reductionism.* A. Koestler and J. R. Smythies, eds. Boston: Beacon, 1969, pp. 240ff.

Spiegelberg, H. *The Phenomenological Movement: A Historical Introduction.* Phenomenologica 6. The Hague: Martinus Nijhoff, 1960.

Spinoza, Baruch. *Ethics.* R. Elwes, tsl. New York: Dover, 1955.

_____. *On the Improvement of the Understanding.* R. Elwes, tsl. New York: Dover, 1955.

_____. *Theologico-Political Tractatus* and *Political Treatise.* R. Elwes, tsl. New York: Dover, 1951.

Stevenson, Charles. *Ethics and Language.* New Haven: Yale University Press, 1945.

Storer, William. *Man in the Web of Life.* New York: The New American Library, 1968.

Strasser, Stephan. *Phenomenology of Feeling: An Essay on the Phenomena of the Heart.* R. Wood, tsl. and introduction. New York: Humanities Press, 1977.

Suzuki, D. T. *Zen Buddhism.* W. Barrett, ed. Garden City, N.Y.: Doubleday, 1956.

Tanqueray, A. *The Spiritual Life.* H. Branderis, tsl. Tournai, Belgium: Desclee, 1930.

Thilly, Frank, and Ledger Wood. *A History of Philosophy.* New York: Holt, Rinehart and Winston, 1966.

Tillich, Paul. *The Courage to Be.* New Haven: Yale University Press, 1971.

_____. *Systematic Theology.* Vol. 1. Chicago: University of Chicago Press, 1951.

Toulmin, Stephen, and June Goodfield. *The Discovery of Time.* New York: Harper, 1965.

van Melsen, A. *From Atomos to Atom.* New York: Harper, 1960.

Veatch, Henry. *Realism and Nominalism Revisited.* Milwaukee: Marquette University Press, 1954.

Voegelin, Eric. *Plato and Aristotle.* Vol. 3 of *Order and History.* Baton Rouge: Louisiana State University Press, 1957.

Voltaire. *Candide* and *Zadig.* T. G. Smollett, tsl. New York: Washington Square, 1962.

Weiss, Peter. *Marat Sade.* New York: Pocket Books, 1965.

Weiss, Paul. *First Considerations.* Carbondale: Southern Illinois University Press, 1977.

Wheelwright, Philip. *The Presocratics.* New York: Odyssey, 1966.

Whitehead, A. N. *Adventures of Ideas.* New York: Free Press, 1967.

_____. *Modes of Thought.* New York: Capricorn, 1958.

_____. *Process and Reality: An Essay in Cosmology.* New York: Harper, 1960.

_____. *Science and the Modern World.* New York: Free Press, 1967.

Wittgenstein, Ludwig. *Tractatus Logico-Philosophicus.* D. Pears and B. McGuinness, tsl. London: Routledge and Kegan, 1961.

Wolfson, Harry. *The Philosophy of Spinoza.* Vol. 2 of 2 vols. Cambridge: Harvard University Press, 1962.

Wood, Robert E. "Aesthetics within the Kantian Project." In D. Dahlstrom, ed., *Philosophy and Art.* Washington, D.C.: Catholic University of America Press. Forthcoming.

_____. "Art and the Sacred," *Listening* (1984), pp. 30-45.

_____. "Buber's Notion of Philosophy," *Thought* 53 (1978), pp. 310-319.

_____. "Experience and the Totality." Delivered at the University of Dayton Symposium on Experience. *The University of Dayton Review* 8, no. 1 (Summer 1971).

_____. "Heidegger on the Way to Language." In *Semiotics, 1985,* J. Deely, ed. New York: University Press of America, 1987.

_____. Introduction to Stephan Strasser, *Phenomenology of Feeling,* pp. 3-39.

_____. *Martin Buber's Ontology.* Evanston: Northwestern University Press, 1969.

————. "Martin Buber's Philosophy of the Word." *Philosophy Today* (Winter 1986), pp. 317-324.

————. "Phenomenology." In G. McLean, ed. *Reading the Philosophers.* New York: Harper and Row, 1989.

————. "The Self and the Other: Toward a Reinterpretation of the Transcendentals." *Philosophy Today* (Spring 1966), pp. 48-63.

————. "Weiss on Adumbration." *Philosophy Today* (Winter 1984), pp. 339-48.

Wooldridge, Dean. *Mechanical Man: The Physical Basis of Intelligent Life.* New York: McGraw-Hill, 1968.

Wyschograd, Edith. *Spirit in Ashes: Hegel, Heidegger and Man-Made Mass Death.* New Haven: Yale University Press, 1985.

————. Zahner, Richard. *The Problem of Embodiment.* The Hague: Martinus Nijhoff, 1964.

INDEX OF SUBJECTS

INDEX OF NAMES